BETWEEN BEFORE
AND AFTER

*A true story about escape from
besieged Sarajevo*

EDITA MUJKIĆ

HAWKEYE
PUBLISHING

ISBN 9780645309959

 NATIONAL LIBRARY OF AUSTRALIA

A catalogue record of this book is available from the National Library of Australia.

www.hawkeyepublishing.com.au
www.hawkeyebooks.com.au

For Dario and Elena

SARAJEVO

DAY 1

Tuesday, May 19, 1992

I must have fallen asleep. The three of us squashed in a corner, two children asleep on top of me: my daughter in my lap, her sweetly perfumed baby hair tickling my face, my son sprawled over my legs. Crowded into one tiny bedroom with twenty to thirty other mothers and their children, most of them asleep on the floor, a few lucky ones on the only bed.

It took a while for the room to become quiet. Mums whispered comfort to their children, adults argued over space, someone laughed. Coughing, sneezing and all sorts of unidentifiable sounds came from everywhere. Tightly squeezed together and on top of each other, people could barely move. Even a minimal shift of someone's body caused discomfort for their neighbours. Every little while there was an 'ouch!' followed by muffled noise, until the body parts of several people fitted together like puzzle pieces pressed in by a young child— squashed at the corners and randomly placed.

Our corner was cold and uncomfortable. With as little movement as possible, I pushed my handbag behind my back to support my twisted body, and rested my head on the wall, all the while protecting my son's space on the floor. I listened to the sounds in the room, straining my ears to identify anything that could be coming from outside, worried about what might happen to us that night or the day after. Unpleasant scenarios played in my head. I pushed them away and visualised the three of us walking on the beach, my kids' hands in mine, waves hitting the shore, the warmth of the sunshine on our faces.

I listened to my daughter's calm breathing and synchronised my breath with hers. The trick that usually helped quiet down my thoughts seemed to work—I fell asleep.

A bang, the door crashed against a wall. I woke abruptly. A man dressed in black, a balaclava over his face and a machine gun in his hands, barged into the room. The lights from the hallway behind exaggerated his silhouette, huge in the doorway. Nausea surged from the stab of pain in my stomach, my accelerated pulse throbbed wildly in my ears.

This is it! This is the end. Frightening images flashed through my head—rapes, killings, children screaming, blood. In a few short seconds I imagined all the possible kinds of terror we were about to endure.

The lights in the room flashed on.

The man shifted the gun in his hands, as if preparing to fire. I kept my eyes semi-shut, pretending to be asleep, while he scanned the room. I clutched my children closer, waiting for more men to burst in, for machine guns to start firing. I didn't dare move, I barely breathed.

After a seemingly eternal silence the man barked, 'Move over.'

We all quietly shuffled to create space on the floor for another mother and her children.

No one said a word. Once the newcomers were settled, the lights turned off.

My children, Dario and Elena, didn't wake despite the noise and commotion. They moved their bodies a few times, stretching out, but kept sleeping peacefully. My heart pounded for a long time.

BEFORE

MY children and I had left Sarajevo earlier that day, in a convoy of cars filled with mothers and young children. Dario was eight, Elena a one-year-old baby. Our lives, so smooth and textbook-perfect, had changed almost overnight into a nightmare of barricades, grenades, snipers and food shortages.

From the end of World War II, until the death of the president Marshal Tito, the six multi-ethnic republics of Yugoslavia lived under the slogan of brotherhood and unity. I grew up in a country with a stable government, free health care and free education. The majority of people living in urban areas, at least us in Sarajevo, had similar uncomplicated lives: stable jobs with sufficient monthly income to pay utility bills, food, clothes and some entertainment. Extreme wealth was out of reach for almost anyone, regardless of education or family origins. Unemployment seemed relatively low; everyone around me who was qualified to work and wanted to work, had a job. Once employed, there was no fear of losing the job unless one broke the law by stealing or committing fraud. If you worked hard, you'd be promoted more quickly to a higher position and a better salary. If you didn't, you could stay in the same job, earning the same pay, your whole career. Of course, there were differences in salaries for different jobs and different levels of experience, but they weren't in ten-fold scales. The CEO of the company would have double the salary of the lowest paid professional employee, not ten, twenty or thirty times more. The hierarchy of positions and income were public and known to all employees. Men and women were paid equally when in the same position. Winter and summer holidays were spent in holiday houses— most families had one—in the mountains or at the seaside. Occasionally there would be a holiday abroad or a business trip to one of the European countries. Life was simple and stable.

After Tito's death in May 1980, while the majority of the nation wiped their tears from losing the big leader, the nationalists in all corners of Yugoslavia started raising their voices and their fists. Every state, other than Serbia, wanted independence from Yugoslavia.

After the states Slovenia, Croatia and Macedonia declared their independence in 1991, a referendum for the independence of Bosnia and Herzegovina was planned for February 29, 1992. The tension in Sarajevo grew from the moment the preparations for the referendum started. A significant percentage of Bosnian Serbs preferred that Bosnia stay within Yugoslavia, and boycotted the referendum.

In the early hours of the morning on March 1, I woke after an intense nightmare. I dreamed of watching gunfire from our kitchen window on the fourth floor of our building, the trajectories of fluorescent bullets sparkling between the bushes in the park below. Still dizzy from the bad dream, I heard the phone ringing. I checked the time. Five-thirty. I jumped up from the bed. *Who would call at this time?* My thoughts went to Goran who was on night shift at work—his software team was engaged in recording the referendum votes.

It was a close friend on the other side of the line. She spoke quietly, almost whispering.

'Hey. I must've scared you with the phone. Please don't be

worried. I know Goran is not there, I just wanted to tell you not to go to work today.'

'Why? What happened?' My thoughts fixed on Goran and his work engagement.

'They've raised barricades in the city overnight and some streets are blocked.'

'Barricades? Why? How do you know? What are they trying to do?'

'We just heard it on the radio. I don't know what they want. I guess it's something to do with the referendum.'

'What do you think will happen?'

'I'm not sure. Just stay at home. Hopefully Goran will be home soon.'

I hung up and paced in the dark, from one window to another. I pulled the curtains aside to peek outside. *Did hearing genuine gunshots while I was asleep provoke my nightmare?* The streets were quiet and empty. I turned on the lamp in the hallway and went to check the children. They were asleep, undisturbed by my conversation. Unable to calm my thoughts, I stayed in their room for a long time.

While I looked at Dario that morning, his hair still streaked with blonde highlights from the summer spent at the seaside, my heart swelled with love for my big boy, my companion and ally when his dad was not around. I bent over Elena's cot, adjusted the cover as she slept on her back, legs and arms spread in all directions, her lips occasionally stretching into a smile. Dreaming of something nice.

Images from the past raced through my head: my happy childhood, the impulsive selection of university course that had led to meeting and marrying Goran, the births of our children.

As the only child of loving parents, I experienced childhood and young adulthood without a hiccup. My mum and dad were the proudest parents, never missing an opportunity to mention my impeccable school reports. At the time to decide what to study I picked architecture; it seemed a fine balance between technical skills and creativity. A long silence filled the room when I told my parents about it. My mum looked at my dad, my dad looked down at the table in front of him.

After a while my dad raised his head and said, 'You know the field of architecture is a sealed professional circle and it's hard to break into it. Almost impossible. How do you think you'll find a job with architecture? We have no connections at all. How will you find work? Why don't you consider something more practical? Civil, mechanical or electrical engineering?'

I didn't want to study any of the courses my dad suggested. They seemed too dry, uncreative. At the same time I knew I wanted to work and would need to find a job after I finished my degree.

When I heard that the electrical engineering faculty was moving to a brand new building I went to see it. It was impressive: a huge central hall several floors high, an enormous modern amphitheatre with rows and rows of seats in light timber, numerous rooms for lectures, labs and study over four levels. They had just opened the Department for Informatics, a completely new degree that seemed exciting. Imagining my dad's happy face when I told him about it, I went straight to the admin office to collect the application forms. I had no idea the selection of that university course would lead me to the man of my life.

Years went by, I studied, made friends, studied, lost friends, went on university trips, danced a lot, and then, half-way through the course, I met a tall, slim young man dressed in denim, with blonde hair in gentle curls falling to his shoulders, and my heart skipped a beat.

Our days were spent preparing exams over espressos at the sophisticated *Bečka kafana*, Vienna Café, in the hundred-year-old Hotel Europe. We sat at our favourite window table for hours, bent over our university books, two espresso cups in front of us hardly touched. The waiters never asked us to leave, no matter how long we stayed. Occasionally, they would walk past and ask if we wanted anything else but didn't mind if we did or didn't order more. The café was never so crowded that we needed to leave our places for other guests. *Bečka kafana* was considered an expensive place to have a coffee in Sarajevo, not many people wanted to spend that much for a little cup of Italian espresso coffee. Most people preferred Turkish coffee. The quietness of the place was another thing that an average Sarajevan did not appreciate much. But to us, the absence of noise was essential for our visits so we kept paying an exorbitant price for a cup of coffee.

In the evenings we went to *Sloga*, the gathering place for an amateur artists' company. Goran was a member long before he met me, and an active participant in their performances, as either a support actor, or more often the guy in charge of lighting. The people I met at *Sloga* were actors, directors, journalists and musicians. Such a different crowd from my scientifically-minded university colleagues. Surrounded by the clouds of smoke, the clinking of glasses and loud conversations, I observed them with curiosity. Most of them didn't attend university or go to work. I stared at them in wonder and daydreamed about one day becoming an artist like them, a writer maybe. I imagined my days spent typing at a desk, with a thick woollen scarf over my shoulders to keep me warm, and a cup of tea at my reach. Nevertheless, I kept studying for my engineering degree, knowing that it would bring me a job and the financial independence I craved. While others stayed drinking and smoking until the early hours of the next morning, I returned home early to get enough sleep before attending university classes the following day. Around ten every night Goran and I walked to the nearest bus stop and took bus number twelve to the suburb of Grbavica, where I lived with my parents. Although Sarajevo was the safest place on earth to walk around at night, it was unimaginable that Goran would let me go home by myself. He never did. The fifteen minutes bus ride was another fifteen minutes to spend together.

Inevitably, every night, we had to say goodbye to each other. After three years of dating we wanted to be together all the time, to live together. In Sarajevo, a place with very strong traditional values, living with a partner assumed being married. Immediately after graduating we decided to get married.

Since both of us had only just started to work, we couldn't afford a big wedding, nor did we see any reason to make it big. It was just a legal formality to please our parents. As soon as we found an apartment to rent, we booked a time at the registry office.

On a beautiful and unusually sunny day in February the five of us met at my parents' place: my future husband and me, my friend from university and Goran's cousin as our witnesses, and the cousin's wife. My mum and dad, a little confused about how minimal we wanted everything to be, invited the guests in.

We sat on two couches upholstered in red fabric, matching cushions supporting our backs. I looked around the living room as if I had never seen it before, trying to absorb every detail of the beautiful furniture my dad had made. This room turned into my parents' bedroom at night—one of the couches unfolded and a thin mattress, pillows and covers would be pulled out from its stomach underneath and a comfortable bed would materialise in minutes.

In the belly of the other couch my mum kept her special treasures: dresses made from exotic fabrics, their style out of fashion, but the fabric too beautiful to part with; a couple of her old handbags for which I hadn't yet found a purpose and had left alone. In one of them, made from intricately embroidered beige leather, my mum kept the most important parts of our lives: our birth certificates and my parents' marriage certificate, hand-written documents, folded in four, the paper yellowish, ink faded, corners frayed, with a tiny hole in the centre when unfolded.

Her old pearl necklace that needed re-stringing was tucked in an inside pocket and a small number of black-and-white photographs stored in a faded blue envelope. My mum and dad's families, my grandmothers and uncles in their best Sunday clothes, arranged in striking poses by a photographer, smiled at me from the photographs while I imagined their lives, which I knew so little about. Most of them lived in Livno, a small town less than two hundred kilometres west of Sarajevo. Our yearly pilgrimage to the place where both my parents were born and lived until they got married and moved to Sarajevo, a day-long bus trip, was the highlight of my summer holidays.

My mum's family gatherings revealed some sketchy details of their lives together, the 'who's-who' in the family: the funny uncle, the cheeky uncle, the serious uncle, the smart uncle, and my mum, the eldest of five, who looked after them for many years, after their dad died and their mum became ill. Many hilarious childhood stories were retold year after year. 'Do you remember that summer when we skipped school and went swimming in the river? And how clumsily you slipped on the rock and broke your arm? There was no way we could avoid telling mum where we were when we got you home all wet and with your arm bandaged with my shirt!' While the adults roared in endless laughter, I sat there with hazy eyes, imagining their younger, mischievous versions running in the fields, hopping from rock to rock in the river, teasing each other.

The atmosphere in the miniscule musty house above a vast field of sunflowers, where my paternal grandmother lived, was not as cheerful, but her love for us, for me, filled the air with an energy that made me light and happy.

My mum's voice interrupted my musings, 'Please, help yourselves to cake.'

Cakes and drinks were served on the beautiful round dining table covered by my mum's hand-crocheted tablecloth. We barely touched them. A bite and a sip. Each one of us nervous for different reasons. Mum and dad a little sad; their only daughter was moving out. Goran and I excited, yet unsure of how the day would unfold.

It was a simple ceremony in the registry office, with only five of us. In an above the knee skirt in beige-brown pepito fabric, with folded pleats, matching shirt in beige silk, brown blazer, and Italian black boots, with the glossy shine of a mirror, I looked like I did every day on my way to work. No white dress, nothing new, nothing borrowed, nothing blue. My own light make-up and freshly washed hair. No make-up artists, no hairdressers. Goran, in his only suit, made from a light-brown fabric, unexpectedly colour-matched my outfit. Tall and slim, with his long, blonde curly hair and his trademark dark beard, he looked very handsome. We listened to the celebrant's short speech, signed our marriage certificates and that was it—we were married. Moving from our parents' places to our own place, we felt grown-up.

From our rental place in the heart of Sarajevo, in Vase Miskina Street, most days after work we walked to Baščaršija, the Sarajevo old-town, treating ourselves to *pita* or *ćevapi* for dinner. We still went to *Sloga*, and still enjoyed having an espresso on Sunday mornings at *Bečka Kafana.*

Then unexpectedly, Goran was called to the Yugoslav National Army. All Yugoslav men had to serve a year-long service before they turned twenty-seven, unless they were studying or had health issues. Having completed his university course, Goran had no valid excuse to postpone it further. He went to Kosovo, one of the two autonomous provinces within Serbia, to serve in the army, and I returned to my parents, who were delighted to have me back for a while.

While in the army, for the first time in his life, Goran was questioned about his nationality. Goran's mother was born in Serbia, her grandfather was an Orthodox priest. Goran's father was of Bosnian Muslim heritage, his mother wore *dimije,* traditional Bosnian Muslim attire and prayed every day. Neither of Goran's parents practised religion. With such origins Goran could not see himself as anything else but a Yugoslav. And then he married me, the daughter of a family with Croatian Catholic origins. In ethnically mixed Sarajevo, many marriages were like ours. We shared the same sentiment—we were Yugoslavs. For some reason, this idea of Yugoslavian nationality did not agree with his army superior. He gave Goran a tough time for declaring his nationality as Yugoslavian. 'You are supposed to be either Croat, Serb, Muslim, or any other nationality but not Yugoslav. A Yugoslav does not fit anywhere,' he was told.

We did not think much of it; we thought the army guy was a bit odd, that was it. How could he not accept the Yugoslavian nationality? After all, in the 1981 census five percent of people in Yugoslavia declared their nationality as Yugoslav. We had no idea that already in 1981 in many parts of Yugoslavia nationalism was becoming stronger and everyone would soon be expected to pick a side. After Goran completed his army service, we returned to our life together and rarely talked about this.

A few years later our son was born.

During Dario's early years, Goran often travelled for work. He worked for the team that built and implemented software for the Sarajevo Winter Olympics in 1984 and later travelled to places hosting similar events to install their timing and scoring software and run it during the events. It was difficult for me to work full-time with a baby at home, even though my mum looked after Dario while I was at work. Once Dario started going to crèche, every workday was the same perpetual rush: crèche-work-crèche-supermarket-home. There were days when it rained in the morning and I left the house with a raincoat and a big umbrella, only for it to warm up while I was at work. Returning home on these days I would walk up the stairs to our apartment on the fourth floor sweaty, skin sticking to the clothes underneath the raincoat, shopping bags hanging in both hands, handbag falling off my shoulder, the umbrella's handle hurting my forearm, its long spiky end racketing on the stairs. Little Dario behind me, tired from running around crèche all day, pulling at my raincoat belt repeating, from the first floor up, '*Mama*, how many more stairs? I'm tired, I can't walk anymore.'

Permanently exhausted and overwhelmed, I could not imagine another child trailing behind me. On Dario's fifth birthday, Goran's sister, already a mother of two, asked, 'When are you planning the second one? Dario is already five. You don't want him to grow up as an only child.' I shrugged my shoulders. 'What's wrong with being an only child? I'm an only child and I turned out fine, didn't I?' Goran kept quiet. Reluctant to raise it after the guests went home, assuming Goran would definitely want another child, I kept tossing the question of the second child in my thoughts, unable to convince myself either way.

One evening, while Dario was asleep and the two of us were relaxing with cups of tea, I blurted out, 'Do you think we should have another child?'

Unprepared for the question, but obviously having thought about it before, Goran reached for my hand. 'I am so often away from home, and I don't know what my work will look like in the years to come. Maybe I will continue to be on frequent business trips for a while longer. I know it's all on you. Dario, our home, and your work. That's how it is at the moment. I would like us to have another child, but it's more up to you to make that decision.'

As I went through the days I imagined what everything would look like if we had two children, one of them a baby, with full-time work. Resigning from work to be a stay-at-home mum was not an option. Partly because one income was not enough, but mainly because I wanted to work. I wanted to have a career, contribute to the family budget, keep my financial independence, be an equal partner in our marriage. I imagined myself carrying a baby in my arms while Dario tugged at my raincoat as we walked up the stairs. I imagined dirty nappies everywhere, a messy house, constant fatigue reducing my ability to focus at work. It seemed too hard.

Then one day the images unexpectedly shifted. A thought came to my mind that I could regret having only one child. Having another one, a sweet little product of our love, I could never regret. Elena was born a month before Dario turned seven. My year of paid maternity leave beautifully coincided with Dario's first year of primary school.

And yes, life got messier with another child: struggling to find a good nanny for Elena, then finding Elena alone at home in her cot while the nanny went out to fetch a book from a friend, sacking the nanny, taking leave from work while finding another one, chatting to Dario about school while bathing Elena, preparing meals while holding Elena on my hip. But these were all little issues of normal family life. Goran and I were in love with each other and in love with our children. Hugging our children and feeling their love and unconditional adoration instantly erased the fatigue caused by the mundane repetitiveness of household chores.

The sound of Elena stirring in her cot brought me back to the room. I waited for her to wake up, but she continued sleeping. It was

16

still very early, not even six o'clock. I left the room, turned off the light in the hallway and walked to the kitchen to make us herbal tea, a family custom we acquired from my in-laws while spending summer holidays with them in Orebić, a gorgeous little town on the Croatian seaside where they had a holiday house. I put the kettle on the gas stove and pulled the jars with herbal teas from the cupboard to fill the teapot, the fresh fragrance of herbs transporting me instantly to our summers in Orebić.

My in-laws grew chamomile and mint in their garden in Orebić and during the cooler months they went to the hills around Sarajevo to pick other herbs. They then dried them, spread on old newspapers covered with tissue paper, for the whole family to enjoy throughout the year. I adored picking fresh mint leaves for the morning tea in Orebić, the minty perfume following me from the garden, illuminated with early morning sun, to the kitchen where the scent would explode in steamy clouds after I poured hot water into the pot.

An unsettling thought went through my head about how little food we had in the house that morning. *What if the barricades this morning turn into something bigger?* We would not have enough food for more than a few days. I made a mental note to remind Goran to stock up on some non-perishable food, just in case.

Hearing giggles from the children's bedroom I went there. Dario was pulling a little teddy bear in and out through the bars of Elena's cot. She laughed, trying to catch it. They looked so happy, just woken up, still warm from their beds, their skin soft and fragrant with the smell of their bed sheets. A light tremor went through my body. *Is this all about to change? Are their lives in danger?*

To keep us busy, and to occupy my worried mind, I pulled out photos of Elena's first birthday celebration that I hadn't yet had time to arrange in a photo album. The three of us sat around the dining table and Dario and I sorted the photos, picking the best ones to go in the album.

Dario, my sweet and serious boy, swiftly switched from entertaining Elena to ordering the photos. He would show a photo to

Elena and tell her what was in it and then place it on the pile for me to glue into the album.

'Here are grandma and grandpa, and a big present for Lena.'

'Here is Lena tearing the wrapping paper. And here is a big teddy bear for Lena. Yay!'

'And here is Lena with her bottle, trying to stand up.'

Elena kept repeating, '*Mama*, look, Lena. Lena.'

'Here is the cake. Lena blowing the candle.'

'Cake.' Elena smiled, clapped her hands and blew an imaginary candle.

We laughed and cheered and sang her a happy birthday again, but the tight knot of anxiety in my chest would not loosen. I was worried about Goran, stuck on the other side of Sarajevo, separated from us by the barricades. *Will we continue to live this happy life of summer holidays, birthday celebrations, friends and family, this life full of love and joy?*

Hours later, Goran arrived, pale and breathless. He slammed and locked the door, then checked through the peephole.

'What happened?' I asked. 'Why do you look so frightened?'

'You just wouldn't believe this. I don't understand what's going on.'

'Why, what happened?'

'You know how we were working on counting and recording the votes last night?'

'Yes,' I nodded.

'We were working in the parliament building. We kept going with the data processing until around two in the morning when some armed people turned up.'

'Who were they?' I asked.

'I assume from the police, they didn't say who they were. They held guns in their hands and ordered us to save the data and pack up. They shoved us all in a van and drove us to Hotel Belgrade, where I think we were the only guests, and locked us in. We hardly slept. They let us go this morning and I went to the office to drop off the disks with the data. Kemo then drove me home. At one of the intersections

18

a guy on a motorbike overtook us, pulled a gun out and fired it in the air. We slowed down to let him go, and then turned off the main road to get here. What's going on? This is crazy.'

Neither of us could understand why everything had started to change. Barricades, gunshots in daylight, in the middle of the street. In Sarajevo—the safest place on earth.

Although the people of Sarajevo dismantled the barricades that same night, the unsettled feeling in the city remained. Back at work several days later I had a mini-radio turned on all the time, carefully following the news, worried that if barricades went up again I might not be able to get back to my children. The results of the referendum were published. The majority of the electorate had voted *Yes*, and the independence of the Republic of Bosnia and Herzegovina was declared a few days later.

In the weeks to come, life appeared to regain some kind of normalcy as we pushed the thoughts of barricades to the back of our minds. But the tension in the air crackled.

On April 5, a hundred thousand Sarajevans of all nationalities went to the city centre to attend a peace rally. The peaceful gathering ended bloodily—snipers fired from the nearby Holiday Inn hotel building, killing and wounding several people.

The following day, we woke up in a war.

WAR

SOME people believed that war could not happen to us. Some knew it would and had left on time. I didn't know whom to believe. Goran was certain this would not last. We would not need to leave town. The world would not allow this to continue; the UN and the US would soon stop it all. A situation like this in the heart of Europe would not be tolerated for much longer. It was Sarajevo we were talking about, after all. We were special. We were Bosnian Serbs, Croats, Muslims— but we were all Sarajevans. Who would touch us and why? How could they possibly divide us? Impossible!

It wasn't. They did touch us. They did divide us. Almost instantly. First into those who left, and those who stayed. Then into those who survived, and those who didn't.

A day before the war started, I went for an afternoon walk with a friend. On a pleasantly warm spring afternoon, with Elena asleep in the stroller, the two of us walked the streets of our neighbourhood, talking about the political tension across Yugoslavia. A few cars packed with young men in camouflage uniforms zoomed by, their machine guns protruding through the open windows. I asked Jelena if she thought there would be war in Sarajevo. 'Oh no,' she said. 'It's all just a little political tension, it will all be sorted through dialogues and meetings, not through a war.'

She was a close friend, our children played together; we had shared many meals, coffees and cakes. Our families spent time together in Sarajevo, at their holiday house in Pale, and during summer holidays in Orebić, on the Dalmatian coast. I so wanted to believe her.

The following day, when the town was obstructed by barricades installed overnight and all exit roads were blocked, I phoned Jelena. I wanted to hear what she thought about the sudden changes in our town. The phone was answered by her brother-in-law.

'How come you're answering the phone?' I asked him. 'Where are Jelena and the children?'

'They are at their holiday house, in Pale.'

'But, we were together yesterday afternoon; she didn't mention they were going away…'

'They decided very late last night and left straight away.'

Silent and unable to say a thing, I hung up the phone.

From the first moment of the aggression toward Sarajevo, Pale, a small place on one of the mountains surrounding Sarajevo, was the administrative and military hub of the army of Republika Srpska and related para-military forces, the home of the malevolent plans to destroy Sarajevo. Why were our friends there? What were they doing there? How much had they known but didn't want or couldn't share with us? I would never know. I never saw them again.

Our friends were disappearing from town. Every day a phone call to a friend would go unanswered—the family had fled Sarajevo since the last time we had spoken. No one had the time or energy to think about others, to let their friends know they were leaving. Everyone was hurriedly packing necessities and using any mode of transport they could find to escape the worst nightmare anyone could ever imagine. Flights ceased early on, trains a few days later, regular inter-town buses soon after that, and then only unannounced convoys of buses left the town from time to time.

The sound of grenades and mortars falling on the city became permanent background noise. At first it seemed to be coming from afar, it was the old town that they shelled first, but it crept closer day by day. We moved the single mattress from Dario's bed to the narrow hallway between the rooms; having the protection of two walls on each side seemed safer. I squeezed in there somehow, with both children next to me, the discomfort of a crowded mattress more tolerable than the possibility of being killed by a grenade exploding in the bedroom. Goran slept on the floor of the dining room; this north side of the apartment was less likely to be hit as the Bosnian Serb army positions were mainly on the southern hills of the Sarajevo valley.

On one warm and sunny April Monday, after Goran came back from work, we all sat down to eat. I made us lunch out of the last bag of green beans from the freezer and some spices. All windows were open, late afternoon low light reflecting from the cutlery into our eyes. Dario moved his spoon around the plate, mouthing, 'I don't like green beans.' Elena continuously repeated, 'I want cheese,' between spoonfuls of bread and green beans disappearing into her mouth and smearing her face.

'You'll have to eat this; there is nothing else. There is no cheese,' I whispered while looking at my plate, feeling guilty that I could not offer anything else.

While Goran cleaned up the table after lunch, I carried Elena over to our bed to change her nappy. Bent over her, I unfolded the nappy and started changing it, when we heard planes overhead. They were low, the noise deafening. Visibly worried, Goran said, 'Aeroplanes. We should go down to the basement.' Overcome with the fear of what might happen next, I finished changing the nappy, dressed Elena and calmly walked out of the flat and down the stairs. Goran was fascinated with my composure and complete lack of panic. But I was not calm, I was in a state of shock. My brain was so frozen with the possibility of an air attack that I could not even feel fear. I was a human machine with no brain.

We joined our neighbours from the other eleven apartments—all of us crammed in one small flat in the basement, some people in chairs, some on the sofa, some on the floor. Everyone was silent, several heads turned up waiting to hear the first bombs, for the thunder to start, others too scared to look up, their heads down. No bombs were dropped that day. They were just breaking the sound barrier, intentionally. Just a warning of what might happen.

When we returned to our apartment I called Goran to our bedroom, away from Dario and Elena. 'We must take the children out of here,' I whispered. My voice trembled. 'This is becoming far too dangerous. I can't bear the thought of something bad happening to them. We can't just wait here for this to stop and do nothing to save them.'

Goran was hesitant. 'I don't know how. We have no money at home except the fifty American dollars left in my wallet after the last trip abroad. And how could we get out? Are the buses still going anywhere?'

The worsening economy and high inflation of the previous couple of years had dramatically devaluated the local currency. Fearing the banks would block accounts to prevent sudden withdrawals, and aware of increasing burglaries, we had stashed all our savings in foreign currency at my parents' house, thinking it would be safer there with a couple of pensioners who didn't leave the house much. However, the safest place to keep money before the war had become unreachable; Bosnian Serb army forces had enclosed Grbavica, the suburb where my parents lived, and no one could go in or out.

With no money, what chance do we have to go anywhere? What will we live from? My thoughts went round and round.

'Maybe something will come up,' I said. 'Let's keep our eyes and ears open.'

Goran nodded.

Days went by. I agonised over the decision to leave. Not only to leave my hometown, but my friends, my parents and even my husband. After the preliminary chaos at the start of the war, during which many male Bosnians left Sarajevo with their families, the Bosnian government banned Sarajevan men from exiting. Goran had to stay in town, to go to work, or to fight.

What would be better for my children? Let them stay in familiar surroundings, with their father but with little or no food for who knows how long, facing death every day, or take them away from this danger at any price, without even knowing what that price might be?

No matter how hard I tried to focus on what the future might bring, I could not see it. Too scared to stay, too scared to leave.

'Do you think it will be a real war?' I asked others for their opinions, anyone and everyone who had the patience to listen.

The answers ranged from a straight 'No' to 'I think there will be *something*, but it can't go on for long.' To the question, 'Are you planning to leave?' no one ever replied, 'Yes'. Yet family by family, people were quietly leaving the city, each departure a new punch of agony in my stomach. No one ever called to say that there was an available option for leaving. They just disappeared. With every day, and every missed opportunity, there were fewer and fewer chances. Days passed while I was in a vacuum full of war, noise, fear, and unknown. What was happening to us, and why? I had never identified with an ethnicity, a nationality, or a race. I believed that the fact that I was born in this particular part of the world, to particular parents, didn't make me any different to anyone else who lived around me, or anyone else anywhere in the world. Unexpectedly, this had all changed. The reality of belonging to a religion, to a nationality, was becoming the reason for the killing of people and children, and I was unprepared for it.

I futilely consulted Yi Jing, a renowned Chinese prediction book, only to get answers resembling these words: *You will not see what's at the end of the road unless you start walking on it.* I could not foresee what the right choice might be.

The fresh food we had in the house at the start of the war dried up within a week. Elena ran through the rooms repeating, '*Mama*, I want cheese.' She was too young to understand that I was not playing a game and hiding her beloved cheese, that there simply wasn't any in the house. She could not understand why she had to stay away from the windows while the grenades fell and the bullets from the hills hissed past our apartment building. At night, I paced the bedroom behind the carefully closed blinds of our apartment and carried my daughter in my arms to help her fall asleep in the midst of the rackets and mortars from the hills, and machine guns echoing throughout the streets. The radio was turned on, the voices of journalists and newsreaders from the radio masking the noise of shelling. The constant stream of local news made me lightheaded and shaky. Mothers crying for help, their children wounded. Ambulances couldn't reach them as the Bosnian Serb army forces barricaded the town streets. For a minute or two of silence between rocketing I would forget where I was. Was this really happening or was it all a bad dream? Another stream of rapid machine gun fire or a grenade explosion nearby would remind me abruptly that it wasn't a nightmare.

The snipers positioned on the surrounding hills started killing the innocent on the streets of Sarajevo. Their view over the town in the valley, over its streets and pedestrians, was perfect. There were no rules; anyone could be killed, anyone could be lucky enough to escape. Every time Goran left the apartment to go to work or in search of food in town, I could not relax until he returned. I paced the rooms, from window to window, listening to the fear-provoking noise on the streets, waiting to hear the doorbell, the key in the lock. I tried to busy myself with household work—relentless physical activity is a great tool for preventing thoughts going wild—but that didn't help for long. It didn't make sense to clean the house while war raged outside. It was hard to play normal when nothing was normal.

I had almost completely stopped eating, my stomach in a constant knot. I had no desire to eat, not that there was much food anyway. I had always adored food. With a healthy appetite and a slow metabolism, most of my adult life I struggled not to put on weight. Suddenly, I rapidly lost weight without knowing it, without wanting it.

The fear of what the future might hold for my children froze my brain. *We have to leave. Where could we go? How? With what money?*

SOMETIMES though, life arranges things and gives us a little extra push to make the right decision.

My friend Goga frequently phoned from her hometown, Split, in Croatia, to see how we were coping, whether we had enough food, if we were safe. One day she said, 'Why don't you come and stay with us for a while, just until the "political issues" are sorted out?'

No one wanted to mention the word 'war'. It seemed a bit less frightening if we didn't say it. If we didn't call it a war, maybe it wasn't a war. As brilliant as Goga's offer sounded, I couldn't see a way of us getting to Split, a town on the Croatian coast, several hundred kilometres away.

'I don't know how we can get there,' I said. 'People are saying that there will be no more convoys or buses, that none can be organised. The bus drivers that have already left do not want to come back.'

Nevertheless, I mentioned Goga's invite to Goran.

'You know I can't go with you?'

'I know. Hopefully it will not be for long. Someone will have to do something about it. It's unimaginable for this to be taking place in the heart of Europe.'

'What if it goes for longer than a month or two? You can't stay with Goga for months. Where do you think you can go, on your own with two children and no money?'

'Maybe I could go to Orebić? There is so much food in the house, sugar, flour, oil—enough for a couple of months. The neighbours have gardens; maybe we'll get some vegetables from them. I don't know. I just need to take the children out of here.'

Unexpectedly, a few days later, the radio announced, 'A convoy with private cars will be organised to leave Sarajevo in the days to come.' Anyone who had a car and enough petrol could join.

Hope surged through my body, until I realised that our car was out of reach, parked in a garage that belonged to my in-laws, several kilometres away from our place. We had thought it safer to keep the car in their garage than in the open carpark near our apartment building. Yet again, what had once seemed a safe solution proved to be impractical when we needed the car. An attempt to reach my in-laws' place and get the car would have been an act of suicide. As the only driver in our family, to get there I would have needed to walk past the Yugoslavian Army barracks, occupied by the Bosnian Serb army, a constant source of gunfire and shooting at the passing cars and pedestrians. That was not an option. I had to live to get my children out. My brain searched for other options, but none existed. If I didn't have the car, we could not leave.

That same day, Kanita, a friend from work, rang from a small town on the Croatian coast. She had left Sarajevo a few weeks prior, while the buses were still leaving town. She was worried about us and asked about our plans to leave Sarajevo. I told her about the convoy with private cars, and how frustrated and sorrowful I was that our car, our last escape option, was out of reach.

'Take my car,' Kanita suggested. 'It's at my brother's. Call him and ask him to bring the car to you. I'll call him now to let him know. He can probably get you some petrol too.'

Petrol by then had become unavailable and only sold on the black market. I was beside myself with this new hope for an escape and I thanked her endlessly, to which she replied matter-of-factly, 'Honestly, you will be doing me a huge favour if you bring my car to Croatia. I'll sell it and get some cash for living.'

I smiled to myself at her kindness and phoned her brother straight away.

'Yes, I will bring the car, and provide petrol, on one condition.'

I stopped breathing.

'You have to take my wife Slavica with you, she can't drive.'

I started to breathe again. Of course I would. I was more than happy to take one more person out of there. And having another adult companion might make things easier for me as well.

I needed to pack. The knot of anxiety in my stomach expanded.

Does leaving mean that we will never come back? Should I pack our photographs and important documents? No, no. I didn't want to pack as if we would never come back. We would be back. It would only be a few months away, until all the hot heads cooled down. It couldn't go on like this. The world would not allow it. The UN would not allow a war in the heart of Europe to keep going for much longer. I packed just a few things for the summer: two bags with clothes, disposable nappies, and a few important documents. Dario's new denim jacket was arranged by the door, ready to be picked up on our way out. That was it. That's all we needed. Then we waited and listened to the radio for further announcements.

My thoughts strayed to regrets. A regret that I never learned how to make *yufka,* the thin pastry that sprinkled with filling, rolled into a tray and baked creates the Bosnian national dish *pita,* or *burek* as they call it in other parts of the former Yugoslavia. In Sarajevo though, the term *burek* is only ever used for *pita* with meat filling. Misusing the term *burek* for a pastry with spinach or cheese easily reveals that the person is not from Sarajevo.

Most mums and almost all grandmothers mastered the skill of making this thin flaky pastry. Semi-dry *yufka* is covered with a filling of choice, rolled into a sausage-like shape, stacked into a round or square baking tin, and baked in a hot oven. A more modern version is made by layering the pastry and the filling, most often spinach, eggs and cottage cheese, and then, when it is baked, cutting it into squares. Coming hot out of the oven, *pita* is irresistible, and I don't know anyone who doesn't like it; everyone has their favourite version. The choice of filling makes the flavour distinct from the other types. Meat lovers are always keen on the mince and onion mix filled *burek,* and for everyone else there is a wide selection of options: spinach, eggs and cottage cheese, or just eggs and cottage cheese, or chopped potatoes and onions, or chopped pumpkin and onions.

Some young women learned how to make *yufka* by watching their mums and grandmothers making it over the years. My mum's *yufka,* thinly spread over the white sheet on our kitchen table while drying, became translucent and crumbly when baked. While the majority of my female friends tried and some even succeeded at mastering the skill, I consciously decided not to learn how to make it; I promised myself that I would leave at least one traditional housewife's skill out of my repertoire.

The year I turned twenty, my mum became unwell and stopped making clothes for me, something I truly enjoyed as it gave me more options than the modest and uniform selection in the shops. Sarajevo was a relatively small city with a limited number of shops. The choice of affordable garments was narrow. The boutiques that sold more unique items were usually too expensive for an average family. Most of my friends went to Trieste in Italy once every year or two to stock up on affordable Italian clothes from Ponterosso, the well-known marketplace in Trieste. My parents didn't think that was necessary, as my mum could make unique and exquisite outfits. Unhappy to go back to buying clothes in the shops, after my mum became ill, I slowly started learning how to sew, knit, crochet and do everything I could to replace what my mum did while I was growing up.

While I enjoyed the creativity of the process and proudly wore unique pieces, it was extremely difficult to find the time for that while I was studying and later on when Goran and I started a family. More often than not I was annoyed and frustrated with myself and my unfinished undertakings. I would buy fabric, start making something, and it would inevitably come to the point where it dragged on for days, weeks and even months when university exams or, later on, family activities filled up my time. Fragments of projects spread around the house, the sewing machine taking up half of the dinner table, baskets with wool and knitting needles tucked away in the corners so the children didn't fall over them. I often thought that it would have been better to not know how to sew and knit. And for that reason I decided to buy ready-made filo pastry for *pita* instead of making my own.

Of course, the store-bought *yufka* was not as good as the home-made one, just as the store-bought clothes weren't as good as the handmade clothes. At the back of my mind I knew I could always learn how to make *yufka*. When I was about to leave Sarajevo and my mum, I realised I may never have the opportunity. The *yufka* seemed to symbolise having my mum near me, near her grandchildren, all of us together at my parents' little holiday house near Sarajevo. The pain of leaving my family behind was somehow reduced to the inability to learn how to make homemade *yufka*.

Days passed and there was no further news about the convoy. *What if they have already announced it on the radio but I haven't been listening to the right program?* Anxiety overwhelmed my body. We had missed yet another chance.

Breathless, I called Kanita's brother. 'Did you hear anything about the convoy? Do you know when it will be leaving?' He hadn't heard anything.

We waited.

BEGINNING

A short message on the radio in the morning—the convoy would be leaving at ten that morning. A strike of hope and panic. Only a couple of hours to prepare. I called Kanita's brother fearing that he might not be at home. They had heard the announcement, and were coming to meet us in front of our building. Visibly shaking I lifted Elena in my arms and told Dario to hurry. Goran carried our things and we descended the five flights of stairs of our apartment building.

Minutes later they arrived with the car. Kanita's brother showed me the petrol that he had managed to secure. Two one-litre coke bottles of petrol. Everything around me faded. Panic rose. I pictured the car stopping in the middle of nowhere—deplete of fuel —and the convoy continuing past us.

'How far do you think this will take us?' I asked him weakly.

'There is some in the car already and there will be plenty of petrol as soon as you leave town,' he assured me. 'You can refill at the first petrol station.' I had no choice but to believe him.

I said goodbye to my husband, gave him one last quick kiss. My lips lingered on his, suppressed tears stinging my eyes, chest tight. We looked into each other's eyes in a painful silence. No one dared promise anything. He hugged the children, helped them into the car and I drove away. We remained quiet in the car, the children confused with what had just happened, Slavica and I anxious about what was in front of us.

Travelling along a wide city road left us exposed to the hills, and the snipers. The fear of dying there and then and failing to take my children to a safe place outside Bosnia throbbed deep inside me. I pulled my head lower as I glanced to the hills. Not that I could judge what was happening up there, nor could I save myself if a sniper had me on target. It was a primal desire to protect my life so that I could protect my children.

There was a long wait at the announced meeting point, a big commotion amongst people, stories being passed about unsafe roads and the possibility that everything could be cancelled. Finally we moved. Very slowly, but moving. Relief. My foot on the clutch perpetually in a stop-start action as we inched forward. Fifteen minutes later, our car engine started releasing steam. Petrified that something was wrong with the car, and we would have to return home, I turned off the engine. I had no idea what that steam meant. The bus driver in the lane next to us got out of the bus, and asked me to open the bonnet. He inspected the engine as I waited nervously.

'Don't worry, it's nothing serious. It's Škoda. Driving so slowly and riding the clutch for a long time can cause this. Turn the engine off while waiting, and you should be fine.'

I nodded and thanked him. *We should be fine.*

We started moving again. Bit by bit.

A young man ran towards us, screaming, 'You can't continue, you can't continue! The Serbs at the checkpoint will not let you pass! You must turn right here and go back!' Confused and unsure of what to do, I turned the car to a side street on the right. In the rear mirror I saw several cars following, while some other cars continued on the main road. Was it all just a hoax? Maybe the man just wanted to prevent us from leaving town? If we went home that could have been the end of our chances to leave Sarajevo. Ever.

Very quickly I made the decision to drive a lap around the block, through the side streets. Minutes later we rejoined the main road and the convoy, a kilometre or two behind our earlier position, but still in it. We were still leaving Sarajevo. I grinned, pleased with myself for making such a quick and smart decision. The silly man who tried to trick us into staying in town did not succeed.

The convoy slowly progressed. Unexpectedly, we forked off the main road to a side road. Why was that, I wondered? *Maybe safer. Maybe there is an issue with the checkpoint on the main road and we are now taking a safer route.* A short drive and we stopped. I assumed that this was the checkpoint and wondered how long it would take us to get to Split if we continued like this, stopping at each checkpoint.

Men wearing balaclavas and carrying machine guns walked around the cars. The news passed from car to car that we had been stopped by the Bosnian Serb para-army, armed men from local villages. We hoped it was just a quick check to verify that there were no men in the cars, as they were not allowed to leave town, and that we would soon be on the road towards our destination. But time passed and nothing happened. Everyone obediently sat in their cars. Elena was in my lap, playing with the steering wheel, hungry, tired and restless.

It was slowly getting darker and colder. May in Sarajevo is usually sunny and warm, but nights can be very fresh and dark falls early. I looked for warmer children's clothes in the boot. Dario's jacket wasn't there. We had forgotten it at home, hanging in the hallway. A spark of frustration flashed through my head. How could I forget Dario's new jacket? It was so expensive and practical. I pulled one of my jumpers from the bag for him to put on.

The men in balaclavas were back, approaching the cars and talking to people. I tried to make sense from the words I could vaguely hear.

'Serb mothers with children go inside the houses for the night.'

Seeing that there weren't that many Serb mothers in this convoy heading towards Croatia, they further announced, 'Mothers with children under three can go find places to sleep in the neighbouring houses, others must stay in the cars.'

What did that mean for me? What was I supposed to do with one child under three and one over three? I stared through the windscreen to check if there were any older children walking towards the houses. I couldn't see clearly and didn't dare ask. Frightening thoughts passed through my head. *Who will be in more danger of rape and death, those who go inside the houses, or those who stay in the cars?* I forbade my brain to contemplate it any further. I told Slavica we should go inside, it would be too cold and too uncomfortable to spend the night in the car. We grabbed a few things and went towards the nearest house. I pulled Elena up in my left arm, and tightly held Dario's hand with the right one. Walking across the lawn, I watched the masked men around us, monitoring their every move. I was worried they could stop Dario and request that he go back to the car. As one of them turned towards us, I pulled Dario closer to me, using my arm to hide his face from the armed man. While we picked up the pace to move away from him, I almost heard him say, 'Hey, you, boy…' But nothing happened. A few more steps and we were in the house, then up the stairs and in one of the rooms.

My hesitation to leave the car had given everyone else enough time to get inside and allocate space for themselves. The room was packed with mothers and children who occupied every little space on the bed and on the floor. I moved towards the corner where there seemed to be a tiny bit of space available for us. The news quickly spread through the room—we had been taken hostages by the Bosnian Serb para-army. They announced the lights would be turned off quickly.

There was no food, no milk for Elena. I filled her bottle with cold water from the bathroom, placed her on my lap, with her tiny head on my shoulder, and told Dario to lie down over my legs. Slowly the noise in the room died down, everyone with their own thoughts, trying to settle the children in these difficult sleeping conditions.

My brain buzzed with thoughts of uncertainty, anxiety, fear. What was all this meant to mean? Why didn't they let us go? What would happen in the morning? What could happen during the night? The inability to do anything about where I was and what I could do was something I never had to deal with before. It was paralysing and petrifying. *At least both of my children are here with me*, I repeated in my head. *Maybe everything will be better tomorrow.* I must have fallen asleep warmed by Elena's body on my chest, her sweet baby smell comforting me.

DAY 2

MORNING came, and I looked around in the daylight. The previous evening everything had happened in a haze of panic. In the opposite corner of the room I noticed a young woman I had met at a friend's birthday party a few years prior. She was there with her sister. A bit younger than me, she had no children, she had only just got married the year before. She didn't seem upset. I asked her what she thought this was all about. 'We'll be fine, don't worry,' she said. 'This is just a little political game.' And I thought, *You're a Serb, if anything goes wrong, the rules for you might be different. What can I count on with my Croatian first name and our Bosnian Muslim surname?*

The news spread that there was a phone in one of the rooms. A compassionate Serb girl from the little village in which the convoy had stopped brought her home phone and connected it to the wall socket. I wanted to call my husband and let him know where we were. I asked Slavica to keep an eye on my children and waited in the line of women trying to get in touch with their families.

Goran already knew that we were being kept as hostages; the news was broadcast on television. He repeated the same story I had heard from the young woman, which she must've heard from her husband a few minutes prior. 'Don't worry, this is just a little political game.' The public version of the cruel situation that involved about five thousand women and children from approximately one thousand private cars, twenty buses and ten vans: it was just a game, it would all be sorted out soon, and they would let us go. He said with so many people kept there the Bosnian Serb army could not do anything reckless, as everyone was waiting for their next move. They would be crazy to harm the hostages while the world's eyes were on them.

Somehow, that didn't make me feel any better. I did not think that I could trust logic or reason anymore. *Isn't all this already totally unreasonable? The war, the escape, our captivity. Why would things now start following a logical order?* Unsure of what the following day may bring, I went back to the corner where my children waited.

Elena needed a nappy change. I washed her in the bathroom, under the icy cold water. She screamed and I continued despite her loud cries. Dario was near me all the time, not asking questions, just soundlessly observing the absurdity that surrounded us. I was worried about what he thought, whether he was scared, but I had no time nor space to talk to him about it. I had no words to explain to an eight-year-old boy why his world had been abruptly turned upside down. I just made sure he was near me all the time, hugged him, and kissed him any second I could.

Late morning, orders were passed from person to person. 'Clean up everything, pack your things and go back to your car.' *A sign that we will leave soon?* Hopefully the political games were finished. Everyone sat in their cars for hours, but nothing happened. The four of us had no food left. We had already eaten the handful of things I had packed: a few sandwiches, some dried biscuits, and a little juice. I could see other women going to the nearby houses and coming back with food. Afraid to leave the children in the car, I asked Slavica to go. She was fearful and reluctant, but went anyway. She brought back a few slices of bread and some milk for Elena. We divided the bread and quietly ate it. The wait continued. As evening approached we were once again asked to go back to the houses. We silently went to the same houses, the same rooms, the same corners in which we had spent the previous night.

It was harder to keep calm, harder to find food. We thought it could not continue like this for much longer.

But it did.

We spent three long days in these conditions, unsure about our futures. Every day our spirits lowered and even the most optimistic amongst us started shaking their heads in disbelief. In the late afternoon on the fourth day, when we had lost hope that anything would change for yet another day, news spread that we would soon leave, and we did.

The convoy started moving again. We hoped that we were not just moving to yet another side road, to wait for yet another game to be played out.

As I drove, a new fear replaced the old in my head—how much petrol did we have in the car? *Will we be left to the mercy of the Bosnian Serb para-army because we don't have enough petrol?* But we kept moving towards Travnik, the first bigger town on our way to Split, where we were expected to spend the night. No open petrol stations anywhere.

Night fell quickly, and a heavy rain came with it. It was hard to see the road; my eyes were glued to the lights of the car in front of us. We drove past cars on the side of the road, unlucky cars in the ditch, cars without petrol, cars that had broken down, cars whose sleepy drivers had lost their focus and missed the road. My foot was starting to tremble on the accelerator, my knuckles white from gripping the steering wheel. I tuned out Elena's crying in the back seat, Dario's whispering to her to keep her calm, and Slavica's attempts to change her nappies in the moving car. I focussed on the road in front and repeated in my head, *Please let it be okay, please let it be okay, please let us have enough petrol to reach Travnik.*

Through the dark curtain of rain lights appeared, shimmering in the distance. We made it!

The convoy slowed and cars stopped alongside the road. People from Travnik approached the cars, offering to put families up for the night. I watched from the car, wondering if I should go out and look for a host, hopeful that there would be enough accommodation for everyone.

'Mum, where will we sleep tonight?' my son asked.

Thinking about what to tell him I heard a knock on the car window. As I rolled the window down and turned my head to an elderly man standing there, big raindrops fell on my face and dripped down. His wife smiled at us from behind him. The man moved closer and checked the inside of the car.

'Just you two and the children?'

'Yes,' I nodded.

'That's perfect, we only have one spare room.'

I opened the boot and rummaged in the dark through our bag to find a change of clothes, but the man offered to bring it all with us. I picked up my daughter, stretched my hand to my son's and with Slavica behind us carrying her bag we followed the couple to a nearby apartment building. As we entered their place, a whiff of a familiar cooking aroma reminded me of the life we left behind. On the dining table two trays of freshly baked *pita*. Tears of relief and sadness prickled in my eyes.

They showed us our beds with clean white sheets. After two sleepless nights, a lack of food and the long, nervous drive, I was so exhausted that I was unable to communicate, unable to eat. My brain was foggy and I could not relax. I listened to their questions about the hold-up and Slavica calmly chatting to them, while the scenes from the last few days replayed in circles in my head. The fear about what could have happened, still fresh in my mind, drained my body. Impatient to withdraw to the silence of our bedroom and to stretch out in a real bed, I waited for the children to eat, had a few bites, then excused myself to get the children ready for bed. I lay awake for hours, worrying, afraid of the following day and the long drive to Split. *How will I manage to drive on dirt roads for hours, weak and faint after many sleepless nights?* I hoped for a miracle, for enough strength and energy to drive us to Split.

Just as I managed to calm down, inhaling my daughter's baby smell and listening to her rhythmic breathing, it was time to get up and get ready. A quick breakfast, a couple of sandwiches and water to take with us and we were on our way again.

DAY 4

THE petrol station first. At least we could resolve that problem. The price of petrol was exorbitant, war profiteers already taking advantage of the situation.

The day was crisp and sunny—blue sky, birds singing. *Maybe I will be capable of driving after all—it isn't that far to Split.* It would have been perhaps four hours drive before the war, but now they had made new dirt roads through the forests to enable safe transport for food and ammunition outside of the main roads. *How long will it take us on these dirt roads?*

My thoughts were interrupted by a young man, tall and skinny, neatly dressed. He whispered, 'Are you with the convoy for Split?' At my nod, he said, 'Would you mind if I joined you? If they stop us at the checkpoint you can say that I'm your husband or your brother. I can't leave on my own, the Croatian army would not let me, but if I'm taking my family maybe they would be okay with that.' His friend was asking the driver of the car next to us for the same favour. Their car was full; they couldn't take another person. Suspicious of the situation, trying to figure out if he was honest, I checked the young man up and down. He could've been anyone. Deciding that he wasn't going to kill us on the way to Split, I wondered what would happen if the Croatian army stopped us and found that we had tried to help war deserters. Slavica and I looked at each other, she gently nodded and I agreed. I was relieved when the young man offered to drive. I moved to the back seat with Slavica and my children, the young man and his friend sat in the front.

We drove slowly along the bumpy road, not stopping for a long, long time. I needed the toilet, but I didn't dare ask them to stop the car. My legs were numb from sitting cramped up, with Elena asleep in my lap. We made only one quick break for the two men to swap seats, to stretch our legs and to go to the toilet behind the bushes.

As we were getting closer to our destination, I started believing that we would make it. I was not letting myself think much further than just reaching Split. I didn't want to think about anything past the first day and night. I didn't want to think about, 'what then'. We would all have a nice warm shower tonight; we would sleep in real beds again. Things that all my life I had taken for granted, and to which I paid no attention, seemed all of a sudden special and precious.

Goga was waiting in Split at the place where Croatian radio had broadcast the convoy would arrive. She was smiling; happy to see us, but I could see the pain and fear in her eyes. We hugged each other. No words, no questions, no complaints, only tears in my eyes. She kissed the children, both of them pale and tired. Goga pointed to where she'd parked and I followed her car to our new home.

SPLIT

DAY 5

THE three of us were given Goga's youngest son's bedroom, and he moved to share a room with his older brother. Elena and I in a single bed, Dario on a mattress on the floor. Nice, clean sheets, hot showers, delicious food—like staying in a five-star hotel.

Most importantly my children were safe.

Everything had a more positive spin. It was almost summer; school holidays were about to commence. Maybe the situation at home would be over in a month or two, and we would be back home in September, just in time for the next school year. I fell asleep with happy thoughts of spending the summer at the Croatian seaside.

The following morning when I started unpacking our clothes, my eyes filled with tears. What a silly superstition to think that if I didn't pack everything we needed, we would come back home sooner. That had been dumb and so plainly impractical.

While I stared at the small pile of clothes on the bed, Dario walked into our bedroom and found me in tears. Too scared to ask why I was crying, motionless, he stared at me with his big blue eyes, waiting for me to tell him the bad news. I hugged him. 'Everything is fine, I'm just a bit angry at myself for not bringing us more clothes.' I could feel his little shoulders relax in my arms.

Since the start of the war, Goga and Joško, her husband, had plenty of extra people to feed. Their house was full of refugees. Sometimes I didn't even know how we all fitted in their three-bedroom home. Goga's auntie was there; she had left her place in Sarajevo to stay with her niece before continuing to France where her daughters lived. And there was always someone else staying for a night or two while waiting for their connection to the next place. A young couple, Goga and Joško's friends from Mostar, were also there, waiting to be included in a UNHCR convoy to go to a European country that was still accepting Bosnian refugees. For a Bosnian Muslim man married to a Serb woman it was unsafe to stay in Bosnia. He was a young and talented soccer player and with his networks in sports circles, who in turn had links within the Bosnian government, they organised his permission to leave—as a man he would've needed to stay and either work or fight. I childishly wished that Goran had been a soccer player.

It must have been difficult for our hosts to never have their own family time—privacy they had before. Despite the house being full of people, they never uttered a complaint. They were infinitely kind to us, friendly and patient. Still, I tried to make the three of us as unobtrusive as possible to lessen the burden of our presence. Not an easy task with a one-and-a-half-year-old.

Every afternoon, when Goga's husband was about to have his well-deserved afternoon nap after working till late the night before, Elena and I went to our bedroom. We quietly played. I sang to her, hopeful that she would fall asleep. For some mysterious reason, singing French children's songs always had a calming effect on Elena. Since she was a little baby, when nothing else had worked to calm her, I would pull out the French songs I remembered from school and sing to her. *Au clair de la lune*, *Il était un petit navire*, *A la claire fontaine*, and *Frère Jacques* never failed to quieten her down. Whether it was the inability to understand the words, the musical quality of the language, or the melody itself, singing in French was a reliable method to tame Elena's energy and change the crying child into a placid one. But, during these afternoon hours while everyone in the house was quiet, there was always an unexpected moment, a chair in the wrong place that Elena would hit while trying to reach for a toy fallen too far, or a sudden unstoppable desire to have a drink that could not be contained until I fetched it from the kitchen, that triggered her to cry—loudly. A few minutes later Joško would emerge from his bedroom, rolling his eyes and commenting, albeit with a smile, 'Is there anything in the world that can make your little screamer quiet for a little while?'

Goga behaved like everything was normal, and we were just their guests for the summer, as if saying, 'It will all be over soon, let's try to make this a nice holiday.'

We went out for afternoon walks with our children along the Riva, Split's main esplanade, and ate ice creams, surrounded by enormous palm trees and joyful people in summer clothes unaware of the refugee family near them. We took photos and I sent them to Sarajevo to my family, pretending that everything was normal, that we were fine.

But nothing was normal. We were not fine. I was enveloped by a deep despair. If even for a second I forgot reality while I focused on household chores and minding the children, it would come back to me in a wild wave—swallow me, surround me with darkness and leave me with an even stronger pain in my chest.

I was hopeful that my sister-in-law would change her mind and leave Sarajevo with her children and that we would all go to our family holiday house in Orebić. Sadly, she seemed firm in her decision not to leave her parents and her husband. Nothing I said changed her mind. We all do what we believe is best—best for us, best for those we care about most. But we don't all think the same, or feel the same. I made the decision to take my children out of Sarajevo, out of war, whatever the cost. Not even for a second had I thought that this was a brave decision—to leave Sarajevo with two young children, without my husband, without money and without any plans for the future, plans for finding a job, or any source of income. Forced to choose between life and death, I chose life. I did not think about the 'what after'. I only thought about how to escape the 'now', how to rescue my children from imminent danger. Even though throughout the years that followed I often felt sad and isolated as if I did not belong to the people and places around me, I never regretted that decision. The days rolled on as if in a bizarre dream while I waited to wake up to real life, to the life I knew before. But I never questioned my decision to leave.

DAY 9

A sudden glimpse of the television news that afternoon made me stop what I was doing. A horrific massacre in Sarajevo. I ran to turn the sound up and saw people lying on the street covered in blood, limbs missing. Other people could be seen frantically running and screaming. One of the faces seemed familiar, he looked like a man whose family also had a holiday house in Orebić, a few houses from ours, but the camera passed over him too fast, I couldn't be sure. I thought I saw his leg missing.

The news reported, 'The shells from the hills hit a bread queue in the city centre, killing many and injuring many more innocent civilians waiting to buy bread from the bakery in the Vase Miskina Street.'

I ran to the phone and dialled our home number in Sarajevo.

No answer.

I dialled every fifteen minutes until finally, long hours later, Goran answered.

'Where have you been the whole day? Are you all right?' I screamed down the phone.

'I'm fine, I'm fine. I was at work.'

'Did you hear about what happened in Vase Miskina Street?'

'It's constantly on the news here. It's awful. So many dead and injured. I think I saw our neighbour from Orebić amongst the injured. Maybe it was someone who just looked like him. I will try to check with his family.'

It turned out it was our neighbour from Orebić, a man we both knew, lying on the street among the injured. A man trying to buy bread to feed his family—he lost his leg in the massacre. No one was safe.

I begged Goran to leave, but he said that it was simply impossible.

'What do you mean it's impossible? Almost every day I hear about men coming out of Sarajevo. How come they can leave and you can't?'

He explained, 'War rules are in place, everything has its price: one hundred German marks for a Croat man to leave Sarajevo, two hundred for a Serb, three hundred for a Muslim. Since I'm none of these—it is only a shot in the head that I can get.'

I was left wordless and miserable.

Many months later I learned that soon after this conversation Goran did manage to negotiate a price for his safe exit. The plan fell through at the last minute when my dad called him to say that my mum had had a stroke.

My mum's health had not been the best even before the war. She had two strokes two winters apart when I was in my early twenties and still at university. Luckily she recovered from both with no permanent damage and continued to live her life on medication for high blood pressure and as stress-free as she could. There was not much to be stressed about anyway. They lived in their modest apartment in Grbavica, a residential quarter on the west bank of the river Miljacka, built in the early sixties. The apartment buildings of four to six floors in their neighbourhood had the typical uniform look, familiar to the inhabitants of Eastern Europe: rectangular in shape, façades in pale colours, most apartments with one or two bedrooms, a living room, kitchen, one bathroom, a small balcony. Inside though, my parents' place looked different to most other apartments. All the furniture was handmade by my dad who was a skilled furniture maker. Amongst these were a beautifully designed round dining table in dark timber with an intricate wood veneer inlay on the top and four chairs in matching timber, with curved tall backs, upholstered in red tapestry fabric. Two folding sofas were upholstered in matching fabric, one of them unfolded every night to become my parents' bed. The other room was furnished in light timber: a single bed, a big desk, one whole wall covered in bookshelves. This was my sanctuary while I lived with them.

In their tiny country house not far from town my parents grew vegetables and had a few chooks. From spring to autumn they stayed there a couple of nights every week. There was no electricity nor running water in the house, but it didn't bother them to go to sleep when night fell and to wake with the sunrise. They spent the days in the garden, and afterwards washed with a wet cloth and a bowl of water. They cooked one-pot meals to simplify washing up. Never aiming for big money or power, my mum and dad were happy with what they had: each other, a daughter they adored who was happily married, and two grandchildren who they cherished.

Now, my parents were imprisoned in their flat in Grbavica, with the armed Bosnian Serb forces going door to door, inflicting malice and brutalising people of other nationalities.

My mum's level of stress and anxiety caused her another stroke.

As their car was stolen in the first days of the war, my dad carried my ill mum on his back to the nearest point outside Grbavica where it was safe for them to meet Goran who lived in our flat in a residential quarter unoccupied by the Bosnian Serb army, three kilometres from Grbavica. They quickly transferred my mum to hospital and luckily she fully recovered.

From that day my parents stayed in our flat with Goran. Everything they owned was left behind in their flat in Grbavica—their superb hand-made furniture, my mum's treasures in the couch, all their family photographs. With the looting of empty apartments going on, it was all lost forever.

And Goran's plan to leave Sarajevo was lost on that day too.

DAY 32

AS the weather warmed, we started going to the beach. We took sandwiches, fruit and drinks and stayed for hours. With books in our hands, Goga and I alternatively kept our eyes on the big boys, screaming and splashing in the water, throwing and catching a big air-filled beach ball, and racing against each other. The little ones sat on beach towels near us, picking pebbles and digging sand with their little hands, while Goga and I made sure not much of either ended up in their mouths. On one such day, a sudden strong wind ripped out the sun umbrella next to the happy local family sunbaking nearby.

Goga screamed at them, 'Hey, watch out, your umbrella!'

I followed the umbrella with my eyes as it swirled in the air for a few seconds in slow motion and then fell with a whoosh; its sharp spike stabbed the sand right next to Elena. I reached to move Elena away, realising that I was late in my attempt to save her. The spike was already in the sand. Rattled, I started trembling.

Through the tightness in my throat I rasped to Goga, 'Why did I take them out of Sarajevo when something dangerous can happen to them anywhere?' Equally shaken, Goga just stared at the umbrella.

Bizarre thoughts went through my head for days afterwards—about destiny and fate, and what could truly be avoided or changed in life. *Maybe what I am doing to save my children will not change anything. Maybe they would be equally safe or unsafe in Sarajevo as anywhere else in the world.*

Despite our hosts' immense hospitality and generosity, my complete helplessness and dependence on others was overwhelming. I would have preferred to have a job, any job, to support the children and myself, but there was no chance of that. Unemployment in Croatia was very high. Goga, who was a qualified Information Technology professional, just as I was, couldn't find a job despite her wide circle of contacts. What could I expect then? I didn't even try.

Instead, I made myself useful around the house whenever I could—cooking, cleaning, doing the laundry and ironing. I tried to economise with food and cooked simple and cheap yet tasty dishes. Many meals were transformed to their more frugal versions. Bolognese pasta sauce was made with equal amounts of chopped onion, chopped carrots and meat, and it was not only much cheaper than the original recipe, but milder and sweeter, and the children liked it better that way. Traditional Bosnian *burek*, made from filo pastry with beef mince and chopped onion filling, was converted to a cheaper version, where grated potatoes replaced half of the minced beef. Its appetising aroma filled the house and it disappeared from the table equally as fast as the proper one would have. Cheap desserts were made regularly to make simple meals look more inviting. An apple strudel and a plain *patišpanja*, dough made with equal parts of eggs, flour and sugar, when poured over with sweet sugary syrup and cooled down in the fridge, were deliciously refreshing on hot summer days.

Everyone's favourite meal though was potato soup, followed by a mountain of sweet crêpes. The children ate the soup without complaints, knowing that they would have an infinite number of crêpes filled with jam or *Eurocrem* (a version of Nutella) to enjoy after it.

The cheapest and simplest meal, the soup was made from chopped onions, potato cubes, and sliced carrots fried in oil, then cooked in stock, and thickened with a spoon of flour mixed with tomato sauce for colour.

The crêpes were a different story. Though cheap to make, they required my endless standing next to the stove to make fifty to sixty paper-thin crêpes for all of us. Sometimes the batter would stick to the pan and several crêpes would tear when turned over. Then the pan needed to be cooled down, scraped of any burnt batter and washed, before the process could recommence. The kids snacked on the ripped pancakes as a prelude to what was coming for the main meal. Playing close to the kitchen they listened in for when I would start ranting that the batter and the sticky frying pan were annoying me, as that inevitably meant that some ruined pancakes would come their way shortly. Dario's blonde head would pop behind the wall assessing the damage. He would appear and swiftly disappear, and I could hear him telling the others, 'Yes! Another one for us!' and the little ones cheering, 'Woo-hoo!' This cheap meal pleased the children endlessly, and it made me contented that I could help with the family budget. Nevertheless I still felt very uncomfortable that Goga and Joško had to pay for absolutely everything for us.

One evening, when we went to town for a walk with the children, I noticed a long queue of people waiting in front of a church. I asked a woman, with a little boy in her arms, what the queue was for.

'We are waiting for the parcels of humanitarian aid from Caritas,' she said.

I had heard of Caritas before, a Catholic organisation for international aid and development, but never knew where exactly to look for their help. She said she had come previously but they had closed the distribution before she reached the front of the queue. She was also from Sarajevo, renting a room in Split with her two children while waiting for her husband to leave Sarajevo.

Despite my strong feeling of humiliation, I joined the queue. I wanted to get any help I could, no matter how little. I would have preferred to have a job and earn money for our needs, but that was not possible. The long queue moved very slowly and I was embarrassed to be standing there expecting charity, to be a refugee waiting for humanitarian aid, but I persisted and kept returning day after day.

On the days when I was lucky to reach the end of the queue I was given a box or two with long-life food: a few cans, flour, sugar and rice, maybe some washing detergents and soaps.

As there was no shortage of those items in Goga's household, we reorganised them into smaller boxes, added a few extra pieces of good quality dried or canned food. We addressed them to our family and friends behind the siege, brought the boxes back to a different queue to send them with the Caritas convoy to Sarajevo, in the hope that they would improve the lives of our loved ones living without the basic essentials.

DAY 60

EVERY day since the beginning of the war the phone lines with Sarajevo had been fading. It was harder and harder to get through, and then, one day, it wasn't possible anymore. The main post and telecom building was hit by grenades from the hills in early June, and ended up in flames. Phone connections from Sarajevo to the rest of the world disappeared.

The phone lines with Serbia were cut off very early on, then with Croatia a month or so after we arrived in Split. The connections to other European countries still worked, so the news from home often came via our friends in Rome, Ziza and Šefko. Goran would call Rome, let them know how everyone was in Sarajevo, then Ziza would call me in Split to pass on the news.

Every time the phone rang butterflies in my stomach danced. Every phone call could bring the news that Goran had left Sarajevo. Equally, every phone call could bring tragic and heartbreaking news. My thoughts constantly flicked to the terrible situation in which my husband and parents lived. More often than not though, the phone call was not for me at all, and it was unrelated to Sarajevo and my family. As much as I looked forward to every bit of news from home, I feared that one day the news might not be positive.

Unexpectedly, a fax arrived for me from our friend's office in Ohrid, Macedonia. Goran's handwriting. I scanned it in panic then re-read it slowly. The news from home was grim. Goran's letter was straightforward—short sentences, simple information exchange.

My dearest,

I have been trying for days to reach you by phone, but it seems impossible. I can't even get through to Italy as easily as before. It seems that I can send a fax, hopefully this will reach you via Macedonia.

Unfortunately, no good news here. Water and electricity shortages continue. It is harder and harder to find the time when both are available so we can heat the water and have a shower, wash clothes or cook.

One window on our flat was broken the other day when a grenade hit a flat nearby and exploded. Fortunately we weren't injured and nothing else was damaged except for the window. Your dad sticky-taped plastic bags on the window glass to keep it in one piece. To save other windows from being damaged, he separated the frames of our old-fashioned double glazed windows; we keep one frame on each window, and the other one inside the flat.

Our parents, both yours and mine, are running out of the medication for high blood pressure and heart conditions. I have added the list of medications at the back. If you can find them in Split, send them addressed to your dad c/o Caritas Sarajevo, that's more secure. He'll collect them from there. And please send some powdered milk for your mum.

For many years before the war, milk was my mum's main source of food. Having inexplicable headaches most of her adult life, the cause of which was never examined properly, she took painkillers daily. They only slightly reduced her headaches, but badly damaged her stomach, pancreas and liver. Since I was a small child, I would often find her in the kitchen, heating milk on the stove. If I asked her, 'What are you making?' she would say, 'I'm not making anything. My stomach hurts, I need a bit of warm milk to help with the pain.' Sometimes she dipped bread in it, and added a bit of sugar for taste. Nowadays I wonder if she maybe had a gluten, lactose or nut intolerance that was poisoning her body and causing her headaches all along. Unfortunately at that time headaches were complicated to examine, often just dismissed by the doctors as migraines, so hers stayed undiagnosed. She treated milk like medicine for her stomach.

Straightaway Goga and I hurried to a pharmacy, bought supplies of medicines for everyone, then to a supermarket for bags of powdered milk. I packed it all up with a few words scribbled on a piece of paper and a couple of photographs to let them know we were well and dropped it at Caritas for their next convoy to Sarajevo.

Leaving Caritas, I could not contain the tears.

How much longer like this?

DAY 101

BOTH the phone calls and faxes stopped. The phone lines with Sarajevo seemed to be permanently disconnected.

Letters became the only method of exchanging news between the people under siege and the rest of the world. Yet, sending a letter from Sarajevo was not that easy. Letters could not just be dropped off at the post office and replies found in the letterbox. With the aggressor's barricades blocking the town exits the regular mail service stopped working in the early days of the war. As time went by, sending a letter from Sarajevo became harder and harder. Goran practically always had a letter ready to be sent and asked anyone who was leaving Sarajevo to take it out and post it to Split.

I looked forward to the news so much, expecting a positive turn of events, but every letter brought more distressing news.

Every day I waited with anticipation for the postman to arrive around noon. If we were out in the morning, I was the first one to run up the stairs to Goga's apartment to see what he'd delivered. If we were at home, I rushed to the door, asking, 'Anything for me today?'

Most days, the postman shook his head, avoided my eyes and handed me the envelopes with bills for the household. Sometimes though, he grinned and pulled out a letter for me, like a magician pulling a rabbit from a hat.

In his letter from early August, that arrived in Split a couple of weeks later, Goran confirmed that all the phones in Sarajevo were fully disconnected. No more phone calls from Sarajevo could be made to anywhere in the world.

I examined the letter for any news about his prospects to leave, but there was no mention of it.

The electricity supply has been off for such a long time that I can't remember how long ago we had it. We've stopped counting the days. Twenty days, maybe longer. Please send us batteries in the next parcel, as many as you can.

The water supply is never on; we have to get water from the neighbours' flat in the basement, which is strangely on a different water supply from the floors above. Sometimes there is no water in the basement either.

There is no bread to buy, no electricity to bake it at home. So we make a war version of uštipci, by mixing whatever flour we have in the house with some water and salt and frying the dough lumps in oil. We try to save the gas still left in the gas bottles and don't use it often. Day after day we eat plain pasta or rice, cooked in a bit of weak stock water, improved by a combination of spices and herbs we still have in the house. Your dad occasionally brings a plum, an apple or a pear from the fresh food market. The people who have gardens grow vegetables and sell their produce at the market. Fresh food is so incredibly expensive. Prices are in German marks—we can't afford it. They take pity on your dad looking old and frail and give him a piece of fruit or two for free.

Although the Bosnian *dinar* was introduced in 1992 as a replacement for the Yugoslav *dinar*, its high inflation rate and restrictions to the areas under Bosnian control made its use impractical across borders with Croat controlled areas of Bosnia, where they used the Croatian *dinar* or *kuna*, and Serb controlled areas, where they used yet another version of the *dinar*. Subsequently, German marks, although not the official currency of Bosnia and Herzegovina, became the currency of choice for the exchange of goods and services used in all parts of Bosnia.

Goran still went to work every day despite the snipers and shelling from the hills. His monthly salary was worth only a kilo of fresh onions at the market, so they exchanged things they had in the house and didn't need, for something fresh to eat. A box of cocoa for some fresh peas, enough to make two dinners for the three of them. A bit of tobacco, that my dad occasionally received from his old work friends, for a fresh tomato.

Receiving my food parcels from Split, when they arrived, was a huge source of happiness for everyone: for Goran and my parents, his parents, and his sister's family. The parcels were often 'checked' on their way to Sarajevo and things stolen—cigarettes mainly as they were highly priced on the black market. Knowing how much food they could get in exchange for a box of cigarettes, I hid packs of cigarettes deep inside the parcel, wrapped in aluminium foil, then buried in a box of rice. I would always place a few boxes of cigarettes on the very top of the parcel, to be easily found and taken, hoping that the rest of the box would not be searched.

In his letter Goran included news and short notes about other families, to pass on to our friends all over the world. Knowing how difficult it was to get messages in and out of Sarajevo, he checked everyone's status and included the news in his next letter ready to go. Some of the names and the updates were unclear to me—it probably followed on from something he had sent in an earlier letter that I hadn't received—and I didn't know what to do with this confusing information.

Branko's leg is better; tell his wife he'll be out in a few weeks.

Burdened with my own worries, fatigue, sleepless nights and anxiety, I was somewhat annoyed with these additional responsibilities.

Which Branko? Who's his wife? How do I contact her?

But being in constant touch with people he knew was not only keeping Goran's mind busy, it also uncovered useful information about food sources, and escape options. Sending our friends' news to their families outside of Sarajevo gave him the sense of usefulness in life that we all need to feel human and stay positive. So I passed on the news to their families and friends when I could, continuing the chain of usefulness that also made me feel a bit better. The simple fact that there were other people and other husbands stuck in Sarajevo, struggling in inhumane conditions, and their families somewhere in the world feeling worried, lonely and aimless, made me feel less isolated in my own pain, albeit only very slightly.

From Goran's letter I found out that a friend from high school was staying with her sister's family two floors below our apartment. She worked as an interpreter for UNPROFOR, the United Nations Protection Forces, in Sarajevo. On Goran's suggestion, from then on I started using her UN post as a safe destination to send my letters. I frequently sent small parcels with cigarettes via her UN colleagues when they travelled from Split to Sarajevo. Sending cigarettes was better than sending parcels with food, even better than sending money, as they exchanged cigarettes for anything else they needed.

Goran's letter arrived when the new school year was about to start. When we first arrived in Split in May, Dario went to school with Goga's son; they were the same age.

Then one day, a few weeks later, Dario came home and said, 'Mum, my teacher told me today that I couldn't go to school anymore.'

'What do you mean?' I asked. 'Why not?'

'Not sure, I think because I'm not Croatian.'

Goga called school and they confirmed that Bosnian refugee children who weren't Croatian citizens could not continue to attend school.

With my parents being of Croatian descent, in theory, I had the right to apply for Croatian citizenship. But my birth certificate did not state that my parents were Croats by birth, hence I could not prove my right to Croatian citizenship. With the new school year approaching I didn't know what to do about Dario's enrolment.

Maybe we would be back home soon and a month or two of

missed school would not be a big deal. Dario was a bright boy. When he was a toddler, while my mum looked after him, too unwell to take him outside to play, she read him picture books, over and over again. Dario learned the alphabet when he was barely two years old, and embarrassingly for us, he read out loud the street names and signs while we walked on the streets of Sarajevo. This must've helped him excel at school. Elena was a demanding baby and I didn't have any time left for Dario and his schoolwork. In fact, I wasn't even aware that other parents in Sarajevo spent lots of time helping their primary school children do their homework. My parents never helped me with my homework; they never needed to. And as many of us do, I followed the same parenting pattern with my son. Surely missing a few months of school for such a child would not be an issue.

Convinced that the war in Sarajevo would not be ending very soon, Goran insisted on enrolling Dario into a primary school in Split. Aware that the schools in Croatia were not accepting Bosnian refugee children, Goran sent my baptismal certificate from the Church of St Joseph in Sarajevo, where I was baptised when I was a baby. It was bizarre that something so tenuous, my only contact with the Catholic Church since I was born, could become so important—the key to obtaining Croatian citizenship. Everything in life seems to have its importance even if sometimes it's not obvious at the time. One step leads to another and another and that's how our life stories unfold. I was grateful that my mum insisted on having me baptised despite my dad's resistance.

With a solemn prognosis for a long-lasting war, Goran transferred his mother's pension to Goga's address in Split, to help with our cost of living, and he paid his mum back from his salary in Sarajevo. The monthly amount was very modest and not enough for us to rent a place and live on our own, but it did provide for the purchase of some personal items, new clothes or shoes when the children grew out of their old ones, and for some little treats when we went out for a stroll on the Riva.

There was a short note from my dad included with Goran's letter.

With his beautiful old-fashioned handwriting, he told me how grateful he and my mum were to be staying with Goran, how well Goran looked after them, how everything was fine, how much they loved the photos of the children I sent with my letters, and how they were looking forward to the phones being re-connected so that we could at least hear each other's voices. Not a word of complaint about their difficult lives.

My dear dad was so strict when I was a teenager; he insisted on my return home by a certain time at night. I was often annoyed with him. 'Why do I always have to be the first one to leave the party? How come everyone else can stay longer?'

'I don't care what others can and can't do, you are my daughter and you have to come home while there are still people on the bus and in the streets.'

When I grew up and had my own children, I understood that my father only wanted to protect me from the unpleasant experiences to which I could be exposed if I was out late at night. As I was getting older, he kept protecting me. When the 'going out' was replaced by the 'studying' and 'having a job', every now and then I was upset by an unkind act that was aimed at me—disloyal friends, unfair practices, unjust methods. My dad always advised me, 'Don't take it to heart too much.' I did not quite understand what he meant by it until I was much older. What he was saying to me was a piece of eternal wisdom that we only fully grasp as we gather more life experience: 'This too shall pass, don't lose your valuable energy worrying about it. Work on what you can change, but don't stress about things that are outside of your control.'

Even with his letters from the war, he spared me from the painful details of their everyday life. By including only what he knew wouldn't deepen my sadness, he continued the mission of a good parent: to spare their child from unnecessary pain.

DAY 122

FINALLY some positive news. In the letter I received on September 17, Goran's birthday, he mentioned that his mum was trying to find a way to leave Sarajevo with his niece and nephew. Overjoyed with the prospect of the six of us together in our family house in Orebić, I imagined us all living as we had been during summers before the war. I quickly organised a few letters of support for them, some from Goga, and some from our neighbours in Orebić, asserting that my mother-in-law and the children travelling with her would not ask for refugee status, so that they would be allowed to enter Croatia.

Yet, their plans couldn't eventuate; they didn't manage to leave Sarajevo. Months of careful planning fell through because someone somewhere had not signed a document for their exit, even though it had been promised, and my family missed their place on a rare escape convoy from Sarajevo.

Despite living with Goga's family, in a nice flat, in a sunny and beautiful city by the Croatian seaside, most of the time I felt deeply unhappy—isolated, alone, deserted. I couldn't burden Goga with my constant worries and fears, as she was already giving us more than anyone could expect from a friend, even a family member. I needed to find somebody in a similar situation, who was a refugee, with no money, separated from their husband, someone with whom I could share my deepest thoughts and anxieties. I was seeking comfort in the fact that I was not the only one in the world with such issues. One day it clicked in my head that Željka, a good friend from my university times, had in-laws living on the nearby island of Korčula. Hoping that Željka had left Sarajevo and was now living with them, I checked the local phone book, found a family with her surname in the town of Vela Luka on Korčula, and called them.

Without too much introduction, I asked the female voice who picked up the phone, 'Hello, I was wondering if I could talk to Željka?'

'One second,' she said. A surge of blood went into my head. Željka was really there. It turned out that they had left Sarajevo in the same convoy as us, in one of the buses. Her sister-in-law was there too, and their four children. Their husbands were in Sarajevo too. It was comforting to realise that I was not the only one whose husband was trapped in Sarajevo and unable to leave.

Excited to hear that I was living so close, Željka promised to take the boat to Split as soon as she could. A few days later, neither one of us able to afford a coffee, we sat on the edge of the sea bank, talking endlessly, our shoeless legs dangling over the calm blue seawater that gently gurgled when hitting the jetty, making thousands of little sea bubbles.

We exchanged stories of how we left Sarajevo and how it was hard to live as a guest for such a long time. How we missed our husbands and parents, and how we feared for them. Željka was very keen to find an opportunity to leave Croatia.

'I can't imagine us staying with my in-laws for much longer. I feel uncomfortable disturbing them for this long.'

'But at least you're with your family. Imagine how hard it is to be a guest at a friend's house for this long.'

'Yes, we are staying with family, but they are old people, used to living by themselves. It's too much for them, four children slamming the doors, running and yelling throughout the house. I need to find a way to move us to somewhere in Europe. We should check if the UNHCR in Split has any plans for Bosnian refugees.'

Until then, it didn't occur to me to even think about leaving Split.

'Don't you think we will be going back home soon? Is that a possibility at all?'

Željka shook her head. 'Things in Sarajevo could easily get worse and it might take much longer than a few months for the war to be over. It might even spread to Croatia.'

'It has been almost six months already, it can't go on like this forever,' I said. 'They must lift the siege. People are starving. They must let food in and people out.'

Although Željka's predictions made me even more concerned about my family's future, I believed we were safe to stay in Split, at least for a little longer. I was not prepared to leave the comfort of Goga's company and her flat, and move further away from Sarajevo, further away from my husband, from my parents, from the life I knew before this absurdity started. It seemed to me that by moving further away, by searching for a better life for the children and myself I would be abandoning my family in Sarajevo, leaving them to struggle on their own, cutting the ties between us.

Željka left Split with the promise to enquire with the UNHCR headquarters about the possibility of being moved to any of the European countries still accepting Bosnian refugees.

She soon learned about a plan to help a dozen Bosnian families move to the UK very shortly. Without much delay Željka went to see the UNHCR person in charge of the list and he invited her to come with the convoy as an interpreter. She phoned me from a public phone before going back to the island.

'They need another interpreter. I said you would come to see them tomorrow morning at eleven. Hope that's an okay time for you.'

'Željka, that's nonsense. I can't be an interpreter for English. You know I did French at school and at university. My French is great, but my English is weak, it's based on computer manuals and American movies. I can't interpret English for other people.'

'No one else can speak any English. You are better than all of them. Besides, that's their only chance to have another interpreter. And I want you to come with me.'

I wasn't very enthusiastic about leaving Split. Thoughts about leaving or staying were constantly on replay in my head. We came to stay with Goga and her family only for a little while, until the war settled down and we could return to our homes, to our lives, to our loved ones, to everything we had left behind in Sarajevo. Our plan to return after only a few months seemed like a crazy distant thought now.

Our town of birth, already terribly injured and bleeding when we left it, was becoming the target of more destruction every day. The war was getting worse and worse: all exits from town were carefully monitored by the three armies involved, and the shortage of food, water and electricity paralysed the lives of those who had stayed in town, by choice or by having no option to leave.

There was no return to Sarajevo, not for a long time.

Unable to discuss the prospect of leaving Split with my husband, I asked Joško, Goga's husband, for his opinion.

'There is a chance that I can go to the UK with a UNHCR convoy. Željka, this friend of mine from university, is going with her sister-in-law and their four children. What do you think about it? Should we join them?'

Without hesitation he told me, 'I think it's better and safer for you to stay in Split, who knows what awaits you in the UK. What if you end up in a refugee camp? It all looks a bit unsafe to me.'

His honesty shook me and intensified my hesitation to take my children away, to possibly more challenging conditions.

He's right, I thought. *What if we do end up in a refugee camp? What will I do then?* I tried to imagine what that could be like and in my mind's eye I saw us behind barbed wire, my children dirty and hungry, crying.

While I pondered his words, Joško added, 'But, if you still decide to leave, if anything ever goes wrong in the UK, you should return to Split straight away; we will gladly have you back.'

I was grateful for his words. Knowing we had a place to go back to made me less anxious about swapping Split for a place about which I knew nothing.

The following day, Elena woke up unwell with a heavy cold. I saw that as a sign that we shouldn't leave, and decided not to go to the interview. Željka was nevertheless very determined in her decision for us to leave together; she made me another appointment for a few days later. I went, reluctantly, deeply tense about speaking in English, about embarrassing myself in front of the UNHCR officer. And then I astonished myself with how well my English worked even though I was stressed. Once we started talking and I relaxed, the words and phrases in English somehow came to me and what I said made sense. The UNHCR officer seemed pleased with the conversation and subsequently I was offered places on the bus.

Making this important decision all by myself, unable to run it past my husband, was difficult. Would he have thought that this was a good idea or an unnecessary risky move? There was no way of finding that out before the trip. Aware that our host family's incredible hospitality could not last forever I knew we had to look for an alternative. So I accepted to be part of the convoy to England. Our names were added to the list. We were the last family to be included and the list was faxed to England that day. We only had a couple of days to get ready.

This time at least I didn't have to decide what to pack and what to leave behind. We hardly had any belongings. If anything, I was scared of not having adequate clothes for the cold English climate. In Split, the cooler weather had only just started. Although it was already October, we were still mostly getting away with bare legs and lighter clothes. The evenings were becoming a bit fresher but the air still smelled of summer.

On the last day before the trip, I asked Goga, 'Could we please go to the department store? I need to buy a few things for the journey.'

We didn't really need anything. I just wanted to have one more drive through Split before we left. While standing on a hill outside the department store I breathed in the sea perfume floating through the city, thinking about how lucky we had been to have spent five months in a beautiful city on the Dalmatian coast, sharing our life with this generous and warm family. How with this painful experience of war, family separation and refugee life we had acquired knowledge and experiences we otherwise would not have. How weird and unexpected this life was. For me, someone who always craved change, living in Split for five months would have been the best treat I could have wished for, if only I knew that my family was safe and would stay safe. I wished I had enjoyed it more. But when a change is forced upon us, no matter how desired it had been before, the ability to enjoy the change is inversely proportioned to the force bringing it about. For a few seconds there I daydreamed of what life could have been if all four of us lived in Split, and if Goran and I had jobs and a little flat, like lucky families who permanently lived in a safe place. But that was not us. We were packing up once again, leaving once again.

Thoughtful and bighearted as she'd been to us for months on end, the night before the trip Goga showered me with her clothes, claiming that she didn't wear them anymore, although they looked perfectly fine and practically new. At the last minute she threw in her almost-new padded leather jacket, a denim shirt she knew I liked, and a bit of cash. I burst into tears.

DAY 149

IT was a fresh and misty October morning when we gathered at a city square in Split, a dozen or so families from Bosnia and Herzegovina. The lucky ones who had been chosen to leave Croatia and go to England.

On the way to the meeting point we stopped at a nearby hotel to say goodbye to an old friend from Sarajevo. As we stood there, she handed me a couple of hundred American dollars, 'For whatever you might need in the new place.'

I so wanted to say, 'No need, thank you,' but I knew I needed the money and couldn't make myself decline the gift. Confused and lost for words, I stood there, looking for the right thing to say. Elena broke the tension by asking for her potty, which I had dutifully packed into our luggage. Someone there took a photo of us, three adults standing, silent, with grim faces, two-year-old Elena in front of us, with a huge smile, on her blue potty—a juxtaposition that would stick in my memory forever.

A small convoy of coaches was in the city square, waiting for us to be driven far away from the war to live in a safer place. Only then did I fully understand that the buses were taking us all the way to England. It seemed too far from Split to travel by bus, but obviously flights would have been unaffordable. Very shortly afterwards we learned that everything was privately organised by a few families and volunteers from Penrith, a small town in Northern England. Derek Robinson, the owner of a bookstore in Penrith, initiated it all and contacted the UNHCR in Split to offer help to a small number of refugee families from Bosnia. In all of the turmoil around getting on the bus, saying goodbyes, finding seats, settling my two-year-old daughter, I did not absorb the full importance of what these people had done. They were using their free time and their own money to come to Split, to hire buses and drivers, to bring blankets and food, to save a few Bosnian families from the war and help them start a new life somewhere far away, somewhere safe.

I looked around at the other families, trying to imagine their stories. There were a few teenage girls, sixteen or seventeen years old, with no parents. I wondered if their parents knew that their precious daughters were going on this long trip and how I would've felt if they were my children. There were a few single men too. They said they had health conditions and needed medical attention in the UK. And the rest were mothers with children—from little babies to tall teenagers. We found our places on the bus, waved goodbye to our friends who had come to farewell us, and the long trip across Europe began.

It all blurred into a long sequence of countries, towns, days, nights, stops, trees and houses flying by on the side of the road. I fell asleep in one country and woke up in another, and would not know where I was. I lost track of what countries were behind us, which ones yet to go through.

My two-year-old was restless. When she was not asleep, she ran between the two rows of seats, screaming with joy, taking her clothes off all the time, nappies included. I ran after her, packed her back in her clothes, trying to calm her down a bit, only to go through the same process ten minutes later. Then she would fall asleep in my lap, exhausted, and I would go back to my thoughts, worrying about what awaited us in the new country, and how long we would need to be there. My nine-year-old son watched me silently, with the wisdom of a ninety-year-old, his blue eyes monitoring my every move, my every word, looking for clues in my behaviour about whether what we were doing was a good idea, or a huge mistake.

ENGLAND

DAY 151

Friday, October 16, 1992

FINALLY we were crossing La Manche, almost there. A quick stop in Dover: filling in customs documents, leaving fingerprints. Everyone was excited. We had made it—we were in England. We were told we would spend the night at the Red Cross, in London. I looked forward to sleeping in a bed again. As with our arrival in Split after the long journey from Sarajevo, I was reminded that such a little thing, taken for granted before, seemed like an enormous luxury after two days and two nights on the bus. I imagined a nice big bed, fluffy pillows and white sheets, wondering if we would share a room with another family.

When we stopped in front of the Red Cross building, as I looked for Željka to have someone familiar with whom to share a room, we walked into a huge hall with improvised sleeping arrangements organised on the floor, mattresses lined up next to each other. Forget the bed and the white sheets. All of us would sleep on the floor, in one single room. Joško's words came to my mind: 'You don't know what to expect there, what if it is a refugee camp?' I was fearful about what it

74

would be like for us at our final destination, but had no time to waste on my worries. We were given food, allocated brief bathroom time per family, and shortly after we were in our makeshift beds. Lights were turned off. More driving to be done tomorrow. Comfortably stretched out, even if not in white starched sheets, I fell asleep with my two children asleep next to me: fed, dry and safe. *Maybe it will all be alright in the end.*

They woke us up very early to quickly get dressed, eat and be ready to leave. The drive from London to Penrith was much longer than we expected. Of course, no one amongst us bothered to find out where Penrith actually was, how far from London. We stopped near Kendal, to spend a couple of nights in Augill Castle, a beautiful Victorian mansion that looked like a small turreted castle, and which seemed to have been converted into a hotel. The crew of volunteers that came to Croatia to help get us to England must've made a special arrangement for us to have a little break in the castle before we reached our final destination. Or maybe, our final destination was not as yet ready to welcome us. The weather outside was grey, gloomy and wet. As we walked from the bus to the castle I was glad to have Goga's leather jacket to keep me warm.

We sat in small groups, spread over a few lounge rooms, waiting for dinner to be served and sleeping arrangements to be prepared. I sat in a corner, tired and lost in thought, holding Elena asleep in my arms and keeping my eyes on Dario to make sure he didn't stray too far. I was not sure whether I could trust my environment; the castle seemed so big, full of corridors and rooms. I didn't want to risk losing sight of him even for a minute. As Elena woke up, smiling and holding my face with her little chubby hands, I kissed her warm face, and my mood lit up immediately. I smiled back at her. A woman, older than me, very slim, fair-skinned and with permed light brown hair, wearing a flowery apron over her simple dress—just as I imagined a typical middle-aged English woman to be—approached. With a gentle smile, she signalled to follow her.

I was hesitant at first, not sure what she wanted. I looked at Dario and told him to come with me. We walked through narrow corridors, the woman in front of me, Elena in my arms, Dario just behind. We came to a small room with shelves filled with soaps, toothbrushes, toothpastes, cotton balls, pads and all sorts of personal hygiene items.

'Take what you need,' she told me with a smile, stretching her arm towards the shelves.

I took as little as I thought was reasonable, and what the three of us needed—three toothbrushes, a couple of toothpastes and soaps, one small talcum powder, a pack of cotton balls. She patiently waited and then packed it all into a paper bag and we walked back to the room where the other families were resting, quietly chatting and waiting to be told where to go from there.

I was unsure if I should tell the others about it, or if they would all get a chance to pick their share of products later on. I was wondering why she had chosen only me and not anyone else. Something in my sad expression must have stirred compassion and empathy in her; she had wanted to comfort me. While I was sitting there with the brown bag next to me, one of the Bosnian women came to ask me where I had gone. I told her. And all of a sudden, everyone was angry and shouting, 'Why you, why not me? Where is the room? I need toiletries too!'

I was unsure what to do. I understood that they all needed the same things. They must've been going without everything, toiletries included, while escaping Bosnia and later in Croatia waiting for something to happen, for the war to stop or for an opportunity to continue towards Europe. Afraid of making a foolish mistake, torn between my desire to help them get a few items for themselves, and unsure if that was a smart thing to do, I looked around for the English woman, but she had left the room. Feeling pressured, I agreed to take a few of the women to the storage room, hoping that they would take just the bare minimum. I was afraid that it would not be easy for them to remain modest while taking free things after months and months of living in poverty, without the bare basics, without the essentials that before the war we had all taken for granted.

While we passed through the corridor and the women discussed loudly what items they needed, my eyes filled with tears of embarrassment and humiliation.

I was reminded of the horror of people stealing everything in the first days of the war in Sarajevo, after the windows of the supermarkets and shops were shattered, allowing anyone to walk in and take anything they wanted. From our apartment on the fourth floor I watched people carrying supplies from the nearby supermarket. They took everything they could get their hands on—knitting wool, slabs of canned tomatoes, bottles of oil, rice, candles, anything. Food I could understand, but why wool, and things that aren't food? Many months later my husband explained to me that anything that was not food could be exchanged for food. The surplus of any product in the house was as valuable as gold. While he traded the cosmetic items and clothes I had left behind for food, many traded things quickly taken from supermarkets while the two of us were still confused and unsure about what was ahead of us.

But we weren't in a war zone. With teary eyes and a trembling voice I pleaded with them, 'Can you please only take as much as you truly need? Not too much, please. There are other people who also need it.'

They instantly calmed down and understood that we might be misusing our hosts' incredible hospitality. They took a few items each, and we slowly and quietly walked back to the main room. I was still worried about what we had done, and what the housekeepers of the castle would think about the Bosnian women, and Bosnians in general, if they discovered that we took a few toiletry items without asking for permission—even though it wasn't much, and we truly needed them. I did not want the owners and caretakers of the castle to think us unscrupulous people who didn't know how to behave.

I was aware that most Europeans considered Yugoslavia to be a communist country, a bit behind the rest of the developed world, where people lived in fear and had to make do with very little in their lives. When the news about the Bosnian war reached the world, television extracts were mostly full of people from the countryside:

older women with scarves over their heads, in traditional clothes. This was a simplified and inaccurate picture of Bosnia, and an untruthful portrayal of the lives of the majority of Bosnians who lived in cities. In cities we lived in apartments; we had dishwashers, cars, seaside holidays, we wore clothes imported from Italy. We were university educated. We had jobs. We lived happily and comfortably. We did not wear traditional clothes and headscarves; we did not care about ethnicities and religion.

Or, so I thought.

But then the war started and everything I was, and believed in, was turned upside down. Including people's perceptions about what was right and wrong. I wondered if I was naïve and just imagining that we were all equally proud of the place in which we were born, of our multicultural origins, rich with history. That we wouldn't do anything to damage the respectable image we had as a nation about ourselves. Was I just imagining that we didn't care about religion and ethnicities, that we lived together peacefully, respecting everyone's beliefs, raising our children to love each other, to help each other, to respect education and hard work? To love whomever they liked regardless of their origins? I wasn't sure anymore of anything.

Luckily, no fuss was made about the visit to the toiletries room. We had a lovely night as we sat by the fireplace, waiting for dinner to be served. The atmosphere was jovial—we were not only safe, warm and comfortable, but cared for and served, a luxury most of us hadn't had for months.

Our accommodation seemed lavish: a room per family, four-poster beds, stained glass windows, wood crackling in the fireplaces, lovely food, even a glass of wine with dinner. Dreamlike. For one weekend it seemed like the war had never existed, like everything was back to how it should've been, like we were here on a holiday. A holiday like we used to have before.

Just after dinner, I approached a tall man carrying a couple of plates in his hands, assuming that he was one of the waiters in the castle. Handing out Elena's bottle I asked, 'Could I please have a little bit of warm milk for my baby daughter?'

'Certainly,' he replied. 'And would you like a cup of tea for yourself?'

I gratefully accepted. He not only washed the bottle and returned it with warm milk, he also gave Elena a little rubber toy that made her very happy. Astonished by such warmth and generosity from a member of the hotel staff who certainly had other things to do, unable to adequately express my gratitude, I just kept repeating endlessly, 'Thank you, thank you so much.'

A couple of months later I learned that the man who so kindly brought us the warm milk was in fact one of the owners of the castle. Unperturbed by serving a refugee, he let me believe that he was a waiter. Surprisingly, I discovered he was not a very tall man, as I remembered him to be. I must've been very tired and felt so small that evening that everything in the castle looked bigger than it truly was.

PENRITH

DAY 154

FINALLY, we arrived at our destination—Penrith, Cumbria. 'You are in the picturesque Lake District area,' we were told. 'With numerous lakes and high peaks it's the UK's largest and most popular national park.' None of this had any meaning to me. All I cared about was that my children were near me, and safe.

We stopped in front of the Quaker Meeting House. The two rectangular buildings in greyed stucco, with sloped roofs covered with dark grey concrete tiles, looked nothing like a church—from the outside or the inside. No architectural characteristics or decorations with which I was familiar from numerous Catholic and Orthodox churches, Muslim mosques and Jewish temples in Sarajevo. No similarity with any of the religious buildings I had seen before.

They fed us tea and sandwiches, which we inspected with curiosity. So different from the sandwiches at home: chunky slices of crusty bread, with butter, ham and cheese. These were made from white, silky soft, thinly sliced bread, with the most unusual of fillings: boiled eggs and mayonnaise, tuna and cucumbers. Nevertheless everything was very tasty and after the first few bites, we smiled and nodded approvingly. The biggest surprise came when they served us tea with milk. This was not a common custom in the former Yugoslavia, where tea was almost always herbal and therefore never served with milk. To me though, tea with milk was not a novelty so I accepted a hot cup of nicely perfumed Earl Grey with great pleasure. Goran and I had started enjoying black tea with milk after we had visited London as university students. We continued having it at home most nights after dinner, with a biscuit or two, just as it should be had, or with a slice of a cake, as there was almost always home-made cake in the fridge.

While enjoying the tea and sandwiches I kept an eye on Elena running around the big icy hall in a great mood, laughing loudly and slowly shedding her clothes in the process, despite the cold. Every little while I would put her clothes back on, and she would slowly take them off in the next thirty minutes. And so our little game continued.

An English woman walked across the hall and introduced herself to me as Monica. With a gentle smile on her face and a lot of sympathy in her voice she told me how she had been observing for a while our little game of putting on and taking off clothes and my constant running after Elena while all the other mothers were chit-chatting, calmly enjoying the food and drinks.

'My daughter used to be like that when she was little, full of energy, a curious and active child,' Monica told me. 'And then she turned into a lovely young woman, full of wisdom and grace.'

I listened to her in disbelief and asked, 'How old was your daughter when she started changing?'

'About nine,' she said.

Seven more years like this! My brain screamed. *Will I be able to continue like this for seven more years? And maybe on my own?* I shuddered. But there was no time to ponder these questions. I had to catch Elena again and put some clothes on her—it was freezing in the hall. There was no time to consider the future; I had to focus on the now.

During the day the families were allocated to houses. The plan was, we were told, to have us all in individual houses and apartments within a few months, but in the meantime we had to share with others. Some families were sent to nearby little towns: Kendal and Appleby. Željka and her children went to Appleby where she would share a house with her sister-in-law's family.

My children and I were allocated to a house in Penrith, which we would share with two other families: one from Mostar, a mother with three sons, two teenagers and a boy a little younger than Dario, and the other one from Sarajevo, a mother with a five-year-old son and a daughter slightly younger than Elena.

Željka and I were sad to be separated, even though we understood that organising accommodation for so many of us was not an easy task. Perhaps we weren't clear enough in stating that we were friends and wanted to stay close to each other. Trying to see this as a positive that we would both have a place in a neighbouring town to go to when we craved a little change, we said our goodbyes and promised to visit each other as often as we could.

Our house on Old London Road was in an unattractive semi-industrial area, but in a convenient location, not far from a supermarket and the town centre. The families with whom we were to share the house joined us in our new home and we quickly inspected the inside and decided who would have which bedroom. Out of four bedrooms upstairs, my children and I ended up in the smallest room with two single beds—one for me to share with Elena, the other for Dario. Our bedroom had probably been the bedroom of a young child before: a wide wallpaper border with pale blue and yellow prints of animals and trains decorated the light blue walls and colour-matched the pale-yellow curtain with scattered imprints of light-blue ribbon bows. Floral sheets adorned the two beds. A small white bedside chest with animal stickers, placed in front of the fireplace, somewhat blocked the cold air coming down the chimney. Underneath the window was a tiny desk with curved legs, a wobbly lamp atop with an old-fashioned velvet shade. The built-in-robe on one side was bigger than we could fill up with our clothes. Our new kingdom.

We shared a bathroom with the family with two young children. A big room, covered wall to wall in dusty pink fluffy carpet, with several framed archaic photographs of people, flowers and landscapes decorating the walls, looked very different from the clean lines of tiled bathrooms in my country of birth. Both the large bathtub, elevated on a dark timber platform, and sink, built into a dark timber cupboard, had separate taps for hot and cold water. Although I had seen separate taps in London hotels years before, I thought that was an eccentric decoration to make hotels look authentic and old-fashioned. Seeing it in a residential place at first surprised me, then annoyed me endlessly. The mixer taps that we had at home, in Sarajevo, and at Goga's place, allowed for quick and simple water temperature adjustment. Here, I either burnt myself with boiling water or froze from icy cold water. Eventually, we bought a rubber shower hose for bath taps, but I never mastered the skill of using the sink without screaming.

Downstairs was a big kitchen with a dining area and two living rooms, each one with an open fireplace. From the kitchen we walked into a small courtyard at the back of the house, where I immediately imagined Elena playing with her toys while I prepared meals and watched over her through the kitchen window. My picture-perfect scene was shattered when I realised that the north-facing courtyard was in permanent shade, cold and mossy, and the low fence and unlocked gate offered no protection from the busy street and its traffic.

Once the initial excitement of finding a place to live settled, isolation, loneliness and sadness struck. The house looked nice, warm and inviting and if only the circumstances were different, I would have been thrilled to live in the old-fashioned English house on Old London Road, but I could not stop asking myself if this was really happening to us. Our surroundings looked so unreal to me that I often had this bizarre feeling of watching myself from the outside, walking around the house, talking to people, minding the children. It felt as though I was just acting in a movie, which, with any luck, would be over soon, and hopefully with a happy ending.

With not many other activities to fill our days, we kept going to the Meeting House every day, to exchange news with other Bosnian families and to meet with the English.

That's where I met Anna.

She approached me one day and asked, with a beautiful BBC English accent, 'Do you know any Bosnian women here?' Approximately my age, dressed in faded loose jeans and an oversized colourful jumper, with blonde hair and big glasses in orangey-brown frames, she carried a tiny blonde girl in her arms.

'Are you looking for someone in particular?' I asked.

'No, no, I am just looking for a Bosnian woman.'

'*I* am a Bosnian woman,' I replied.

And that's how my friendship with Anna began. We instantly clicked. We talked about our daughters and discovered that her daughter Ellen was born on the same day in England as my Elena was born in Sarajevo. What a coincidence, such a similar name and the same date of birth. And then we realised that Anna and I were born only eight days apart. Her mum's name was Edith, which is the English version of my name. I immediately liked her. Sweet and gentle, Anna was endlessly patient with my broken English, which did not really allow me to have a proper conversation. I was limited to simple phrases and to listening, more than talking, but we nevertheless related to each other. Her two sons got along well with Dario: Tim Dario's age, Ben a couple of years younger. Elena and Ellen played like they had known each other since the day they were born. The mix of two languages didn't affect them; they simply interchanged words in both. As much as that helped the development of Elena's English, it confused Ellen's mum. Anna once asked me, struggling to pronounce it, 'Do you maybe know what *sapun* and *charapica* are? Ellen uses these words when talking to me and I don't understand what she wants.'

Of course I knew what those words were. 'They are Bosnian words for *soap* and *little sock*,' I replied.

We laughed at Ellen's mastery of the Bosnian language.

Anna shook her head in disbelief. 'Isn't it weird that to Ellen they are just names for things, that she has no idea they are not part of her mother tongue?'

I smiled and nodded, 'It's so much easier for the children. They have no barrier of the first language.'

Wouldn't it be lovely if I could learn English like that? I thought.

Anna and her family lived in a big, charming farmhouse—extended, renovated and modernised—on a little hill in the middle of green fields. The next-door neighbour's house was not even visible from their property. The three of us loved spending time at their beautiful home. Anna drove us there in her big Volvo, across beautiful green Cumbrian fields, over tiny bridges with sparkling little creeks, to a lovely house where we enjoyed the warmth of their fireplace and of their hearts. I relaxed there, pretending, at least for a short time, that all was well, that we were visiting our friends and that our lives were all fine and in order. We drank tea and talked. With my limited vocabulary I tried to describe our life before the war, how we all lived happily and *never* expected that anything like this war could ever happen to us.

Anna would then leave me for a while to prepare lunch for us or get other things organised. While Ellen and Elena were asleep, and the boys quietly played, I browsed magazines stacked on the coffee table, pretending to be part of this lovely fantasy life in which everything was fine. But I couldn't stop my thoughts. My fears and anxieties would return and I'd sit there on the couch, eyes filled with tears, unable to explain the inexplicable: why we were there, why it was all happening, why the war, *why us*?

DAY 163

THE locals admired my ability to speak English. They found my swift switching from my mother tongue to English and vice versa astonishing. I, on the other hand, thought my English inadequate, my accent too strong. Speaking English in most of my own daily communication, and constantly interpreting for others, not only for the two families with which we shared the house, but also for anyone else in our group when they needed help communicating, was exhausting.

Whenever English people announced a visit to our place I was asked to be there, to sit with the guests around the dining table and help with the conversations.

The conversation was simple, slow and polite.

'How are you all today?'

'We are well, thank you, how are you?'

'Are you feeling comfortable in the house?'

'Yes, it's a good house, we are very happy here.'

'Do you need anything?'

'No, thank you, it's all fine. We have everything we need.'

The rest of the household would sit around the table with their lips politely stretched into smiles, occasionally asking through their teeth, 'What are they saying?' Then I would quickly translate the conversation into Bosnian.

Sometimes someone would say, 'Ask them when we will move into our own places.' Or, 'Ask them if they could bring second-hand shoes for my son, I can't afford to buy them and the rain is getting into his shoes.' I often didn't know how to translate certain words, like second-hand, so I would say something like, 'They need old shoes from someone, but not too old, still okay to wear when it rains.' And the three-way, four-way conversation would go on for a while, overwhelming my brain. Mostly I could get the meaning across, but sometimes I struggled. I often improvised with whatever words and phrases I could retrieve from the depths of my brain, sometimes entangling my sentences so much that by the time I finished one bizarre construction I would forget what I was trying to say. The inability to accurately express my feelings and opinions was frustrating and made me feel dumb.

Without a dictionary I had no choice but to rely on the limited knowledge of the language that I possessed. My sentences were often far more complicated than was necessary. When I couldn't find an accurate word I included a whole phrase instead. Steve, a young Englishman who came on the buses to Split to help bring us to Cumbria, once commented with a smile, 'You know, sometimes when you talk, you remind me of a lawyer, with long and complicated sentences, difficult to follow.'

I did not find this to be a compliment and my face showed my discontent. He laughed it off, saying, 'Don't worry. You still convey the messages correctly. And that's all that matters. I wish I could speak another language as well as you speak English. You know that most Brits can't speak a word of another language?' And I thought, *Yes, lucky Brits! Why would they need to speak another language when everyone has to speak English anyway?*

Elena was usually sitting on my lap, sometimes tired, sometimes hungry, but often restless, as this long process of sitting and talking didn't suit her energy levels. She could perhaps sense my tension, frustration and fatigue, my desire to run away and hide somewhere quiet. And that was what sometimes happened: I would excuse myself from these loud conversations and use Elena's restlessness, her need to eat or sleep, to find refuge in the silence of our bedroom. My head buzzed with a cacophony of the two languages; I replayed the conversations in my head trying to work out if my interpretations were accurate enough.

Although there were English classes organised for us, I could not attend—I had no one to look after Elena during the lessons. Instead I used my own method. I tried memorising new words, new phrases and new verb tenses used by the English people with whom I spoke. Then I repeated the new words whenever I had a chance until they became familiar and their usage natural. But there were so many rules to learn, so many intricacies in this new language so different from my mother tongue. Apart from the confusing definite and indefinite article, the present perfect tense was exceptionally challenging—there is no similar tense in Bosnian, or Serbo-Croatian as it was called when I was at school. In Serbo-Croatian it's either present or perfect. When do I say, 'I heard' and when do I say, 'I've heard'? And what about 'I was reading', 'I read', 'I've read' and 'I've been reading'? In my head—chaos.

In a hurry to quickly say or interpret something I would forget the words and rules I had learned, leaving me feeling helpless, thinking I would never ever master this confusing language well enough to feel at ease when I spoke or read it. My head was often overloaded to the point that it made me physically sick, and unable to speak either of the two languages. The words and phrases floated haphazardly in my brain, all mixed up, and I would find myself thinking in English for five minutes and then in Bosnian for the next five minutes, and that would leave me unsure of what I was thinking in the first place. Sometimes I would find myself putting together the sentences in my head in English, and then translating them into my mother tongue when talking to one of my fellow Bosnians. Weird.

English was becoming my first language of communication, although I still sometimes couldn't work out how to say the simplest things. The many variations of verb phrases and phrasal verbs, the numerous meanings for 'get', 'go', 'take' depending on the adverb or preposition following it. In, at, on, to—it was overwhelming. How could the milk go off when becoming sour if my alarm clock also goes off when waking me up? Why is the alarm clock not simply 'ringing' as it does in Bosnian? Or at least, why doesn't it 'go on'? It makes more sense for it to be 'on' when generating the alarm sound, than 'off', which in my head meant 'inactive'. Why does a person go down with the flu and an important date also goes down in history? Where is the logic? For many years I filled in salad bowls and filled up application papers.

I was in such utter mental exhaustion most of the time. However, my English was progressing at a rapid rate, my vocabulary expanding daily. Clearly, the best way to learn a new language is to be immersed fully with no choice of relying on any other language. It's painful, but it works. Of course, not everyone wanted or liked that kind of mental workout. Most of the people in our group happily continued to rely on my interpretation when socialising with English people. It was hard for me to comprehend that after several months in England they did not know at least a few basic words and phrases. Obviously, people's brains work differently and new knowledge is acquired not only based on previous education and perhaps talent, but also on the desire to learn and allow the endless capacity of the brain to expand further and absorb new things. It is far easier to say, 'I wish I could speak English,' and give up, to do something easier, simpler. But when we accept the challenge, we enjoy the immense benefits that come with acquiring new knowledge.

DAY 169

DAYS slowly rolled by into November. The first thing I did every morning was to check the mail. A few moments of looking forward to a letter from home while walking down the stairs—the chance of feeling loved, of being with my family in my thoughts even if physically they were not with us.

Every morning though, the same disappointment: no news from home. Occasionally, a letter from Goga arrived, or from another friend outside of Sarajevo, but no news from home, no news about my husband and my parents. I forced myself to believe that everything was okay, it had to be, after all, the aggressor's army couldn't kill everyone. But then I would lose myself in the flashes of frightening pictures going through my head: the Bosnian Serb army forces marching through town, door to door, killing family by family. The fictional events expanded in my head, anxiety burned in my chest. Every wounded or dead man with a beard in the television news from Sarajevo looked like my husband. I could not bear it; I had to stop watching the news for a while. But then I became terrified that things could get worse and I wouldn't know about it, so I turned the television on again, changed the channels in a panic to see more news and stared at the moving pictures of the systematic destruction of Sarajevo and its urban symbols, of the wounded and killed civilians, targeted only because of where they lived.

One morning in early November, a few weeks after we had arrived in Penrith, I received a call from the Bluebell bookstore—they had received a fax for me. *A fax? Why would anyone send a fax unless there was something urgent to tell me?* Petrified that it could be bad news from home, I quickly dressed Elena and sat her in the stroller. With shaky legs I walked to the shop as fast as I could. I was glad Dario was at school so I had time to compose myself before sharing the news with him.

Upstairs in the Bluebell office I scanned the fax. It was in Goran's handwriting. The news was disturbing, but nothing tragic had happened. Just an ordinary letter that Goga had received, and knowing I had had no news since late September, wanted me to read as quickly as possible. She faxed it to the bookstore as soon as she received it. It was written on October 10, a week before we had left Split.

My dearest,

I don't know when this will reach you. I don't know how quickly (or better to say slowly) the letters from Sarajevo reach their destination, if ever.

My mum and dad have decided to leave Sarajevo with my sister's children. They registered with the Red Cross and are now waiting for a convoy. Can you please send us new letters of support from Goga or from our neighbours in Orebić? The letters need to have the most recent date on them. Please state that they will not ask for refugee status or any help from the Croatian government; they will live in their own house in Orebić.

Other than that, there is no news.

There is still no water, no electricity. I have not had a shower for twenty-two days. Your father walks several kilometres almost every day to get us water for drinking, cooking and washing dishes. Luckily we have the trolley so he doesn't have to carry it in his hands. There is hardly any food in the house other than rice, pasta and a few cans and stock cubes from the last parcel you sent us. There is scarcely any food to buy; we have no money to buy it anyway. Your dad managed to buy one litre of fresh milk a few days ago, for the first time since April. It was all we could afford. The big town bakery is now making bread again and I get a loaf of bread from work every day. We have no gas in the bottle anymore, we sometimes cook on a communal stove that some refugees from central Bosnia brought with them when they took refuge in an apartment left vacant by owners fleeing Sarajevo. We are allowed to cook while someone's bread is being baked in the oven. We eat pasta and rice day after day, stretching the food as far as we can. We are hungry most of the time.

I still go to work every day. The whole office now works in the company basement, it is safer there than upstairs. The salary I receive is just enough to pay the bills; ironically we still have to pay the bills despite irregular or non-existent supplies of even the minimum needed for a civilised life. Even the phone bill needs to be paid despite the phone not working.

If you can send us anything, please send more cigarettes, the cheapest brand you can find. Send them to D's work address at her UN post, that is the safest option to receive them. I can always trade them for other necessities.

I love you all very much,

Goran

He obviously had no idea that I wasn't in Split anymore. And there was no indication of any plans for him to leave Sarajevo.

Half a page from my dad was included with Goran's letter. He was thanking me for the food I had sent, astonished that I knew to send them exactly what they needed. I smiled to myself thinking, it wasn't hard, my dear dad. I knew that whatever I sent, it would be needed.

Then again, no letters arrived for several weeks. I imagined that Goran would have sent them regularly with people who left Sarajevo, or with the UNHCR. He would have sent them to Goga using any available mail options and I knew she would forward them to me without delay. But none reached Split. Tremendously distressed, I feared the worst. Images of injuries, hospitals and operations flashed through my head several times a day while I tried to persuade myself that no news was good news.

I talked to Željka about it. She was also very worried about her

94

husband and her parents as she had no news from them for a long time. Then Željka thought of a possibility for a communication option: her brother worked for the Radio TV in Sarajevo and they had radio equipment. Željka found a group of radio operators in Cumbria who were willing to host sessions for us to connect with the radio operators' service at Radio TV Sarajevo. At first elated with this new option to talk to my husband after so many months, on the very day of the first session I was overwhelmed with fear and irrational panic. My vivid imagination made me extremely anxious. I imagined Goran walking from our apartment to the RTV building, along the road I drove on when we fled Sarajevo. Unprotected by the buildings, the road was like an open field, exposed to the sniper fire from the hills. *How selfish of me to ask him to walk on this dangerous road to come to the RTV building. Why am I risking his life for a chat? Why can't I be content with just knowing that he is well?* The unease rose in my chest, blurring my brain.

We gathered in the radio amateurs' room at the agreed time. When the connection couldn't be immediately established, fearful thoughts flashed through my head. *Something terrible must have happened in Sarajevo, they must be dealing with a dreadful situation there if they can't work on the connection.* When the connection finally opened and it was my turn to talk, strangely I couldn't recognise Goran's voice through the hissing sound of radio waves. The panic that had risen in my body since the morning played weird games with my brain and logical thinking. Afraid that it was all staged, that they had brought someone else to talk to me to trick me into believing that my husband was still alive, I kept asking Goran if it was truly him, repeating senseless questions about the details from our life together to verify if it was really my husband on the other side of the line.

'Which cake did I usually bake for our birthdays?'

'The one with walnuts?'

'Many cakes are made with walnuts. Which exact one?'

'I can't remember the name now.'

'I'm not sure if you're really Goran.'

Goran was confused, and kept saying, 'Eda, it is me, it is me,' which made me even more suspicious.

I mechanically said words that we were okay, that Dario was at school, Elena was with me. Elena managed to say, 'Daddy…' and then the connection was gone before I managed to hear anything vital about him, or my parents. For days afterwards my absurd behavior—the lost opportunity to talk—upset me deeply. I worried that something could have happened to Goran on his way back home; all the happiness of hearing his voice destroyed by my anxiety. I was unsure if I would have the strength for another session if the chance was presented. Even though talking to my husband another time would be lovely—if I could remain calm and rational—I didn't know if I could again expose Goran to the great risk of travelling to the radio connection.

In his letter from December 1, written just after our radio operators' connection, Goran didn't mention my irrational behaviour.

Dear Eda,

It's Tuesday today. We have had no electricity since Thursday and I couldn't listen to the recording of our conversation until today. They taped it so we can re-listen whenever we want, or better to say whenever we have electricity. It meant so much to me that I was able to hear your voice.

Tonight the electricity was on and off about four times. I started writing this around six this evening, when the light was on, then when around seven it went off, I went to bed. An hour later it came on again so I got up and continued writing, then shortly after it went off again, so I lit a candle to finish the letter.

I don't have many people I can talk to these days. Very few of our friends are still in Sarajevo. And with those that are, I can't get in touch easily. I miss human contact and decent conversation. I spend most of the time reading books and thinking about you. I started writing a diary, to remind me of what to tell you in my letters, but most days I don't write anything down. Not much is happening really. Every day is almost the same as the one before. A lot going on in the sense of war and danger, but nothing really happening in the sense of change to my life and the lives of all of us trapped in Sarajevo. I am still going to work every day; there is still work to be done in the office. And I am still being paid, not much, but better than nothing.

My dad's not well, he's on medication and they decided not to go to Orebić after all, just after I received the letters of support you sent us. Luckily my mum is well. Most of the time she is out searching for food. Regardless, last time I saw them, they had no canned food at all, so I went back the following day and brought them six cans from our stock. I am very careful with cooking and I use our canned food frugally; I always water it down to make more from a single can. I have not told them about my intentions to leave Sarajevo as soon as I can. It is hard to talk about it. I gave all Dario's old clothes to my sister's children. After wearing the same old faded and thinned garments for months on end they were over the moon with the new collection of outfits.

Your parents are as well as they can be, your mum's health is probably better now than before the war. Or maybe she's just not complaining about it as much as before. They are trying to be useful around the house, to clean at least. I seem to be better at cooking and improvising with the ingredients we have. Sometimes their logic is not the best, for example saving on the electricity cost and not turning on the hot water heater when there is both water and electricity supply. Hence I sometimes don't shower for twenty or thirty days. But I understand that they do it with the best of intentions and can't really be angry with them. This is all too much for everyone.

Our car is still in one piece in my dad's garage. It's now worth one hundred fifty German marks. They say it's a good price. You remember we bought it just before the war for five thousand German marks? For a packet of cigarettes, worth twenty German marks, I can buy a second-hand television, or a kilo and a half of potatoes, or half a kilo of coffee beans.

We are preparing for the winter. Your father's workmate is making us a wood heater cum stove from an old hot water boiler. Someone else is providing the exhaust pipe for the stove. We bought a bag of coal and collected some loose wood and some parquetry flooring for burning.

I am constantly and endlessly exploring options to leave Sarajevo. There is a slight chance of having some assistance from our neighbour's sister. She works for the Red Cross and UNHCR and her English boyfriend could possibly help me with the necessary paperwork to leave Sarajevo. I don't have all the details yet. It is hard to talk about it very openly; people are scared of showing their cards and destroying their chances to leave. There is also another option with an evacuation of Italian citizens trapped in Sarajevo that is expected to happen any day. Can you try to organise a letter from Ziza and Šefko, to say there is a job waiting for me in Rome? That might help get a place on that convoy.

And another page added at the end, on paper torn out from a small diary, words lopsided as if written in a hurry.

Thursday, December 3

I picked up your parcel yesterday. We were all happy like little children. Surprisingly it seems no one has tampered with it. All the parcels that you sent to our friends in that delivery also arrived untouched. Everyone is now okay with food reserves.

Imagine, we have electricity this morning. I am having toasted bread and hot tea for breakfast before going to work. Bliss!

I am so happy that the three of you are safe and far from the war. Send me more photos when you can. We have decorated our walls with the photos of you and the children; it makes this hell a bit more bearable when we look at the three of you in the photographs.

Take good care of yourself and the children, everything will be fine.

Lots of love to all of you, Goran

DAY 197

THE conversations in our shared house seemed to me far too cheerful and jovial considering what had brought us there and what we had left behind in our country of birth.

While I could not stop worrying about the wellbeing of my husband and my parents, and the horrific conditions in which they lived, the two other mothers, also separated from their husbands just as I was, were bubbly and joyful all the time. They laughed until late at night in the kitchen downstairs while upstairs, in our tiny bedroom, with my children asleep next to me, I stared at English children's books forcing myself to read them, to improve my language, to fight off my worrying thoughts about what might've happened to my husband and my parents since I had last heard from them. I read and re-read Goran's letters, thinking about what the future might bring to our family.

Each day one of the other mothers would comment to my sad face, 'Don't worry, he's alright, most likely better than you think…' and they would look at each other, laughing loudly. Although I found their jokes cruel and their subdued gist about Goran enjoying his time without me in Sarajevo hurtful, I often questioned myself for being so anxious all the time. I wondered how they could keep their concerns under control while I couldn't. Why was I so sensitive about the separation from my husband and my parents and unable to enjoy life?

Not long after, someone in our group mentioned that the husbands of my co-habitants were both safe, one in Croatia, the other one in Norway, while their wives were working on their imminent family reunions in the UK. I was stunned.

It was so naïve of me to think that everyone in our group was in the same situation, that everyone's husband was trapped somewhere in Bosnia, unable to leave. It made me feel angry and betrayed that they played this game, telling me to be positive, to believe that everything was going to be fine. They joked and laughed and made fun of me and my anxieties. Their insensitive comments made me feel ridiculous about my worrying. Such frauds.

From then on, I distanced myself from them, limiting the conversations to polite smiles and small talk without showing any closeness and desire to be friends. I could not get over their dishonesty. I tried to spend as little time in the house as possible. I went on long aimless walks around town, pushing Elena's stroller, and impatiently waited to be allocated a little place for just the three of us, which had been promised when we moved to the shared house. It hurt to lose the friendships after I had already lost all the friends I had before. Quiet uncontrolled tears often rolled down my cheeks. I felt lonelier than ever before.

A couple of weeks before Christmas Dario brought home a beautiful poem he wrote at school, dedicated to Vedran Smailović, known as the 'Cellist of Sarajevo'.

At first the cellist had played classical music outside the Vase Miskina Street bakery, shortly after the bread queue was bombed and people were killed in the massacre. He then played every day in different places in the ruins of Sarajevo, protesting against the madness overtaking his city in the only way he knew.

I had never spoken to Dario about the cellist. I avoided any talk about Sarajevo, about the war. It seemed to me, wrongly or rightly, that I should spare him from speculating about if and when his father would come. Afraid that it might lead to questions I couldn't answer, I tried not to mention Sarajevo and anything related to Sarajevo at all. Nevertheless, he had most certainly caught a glimpse of the television news and they had talked about it at school. He showed me the poem and said his teacher wanted him to read it at the school Christmas celebration. A few small mistakes, expected from a child who had only been speaking English for a few months, did not lessen its beauty and important message.

The Cellist of Sarajevo

In Sarajevo,
A city of war,
Where grenades fall everyday,
Where a rain of bullets falls down,
There was a queue for bread.
A grenade hit the queue,
Twenty-two were dead,
Blood was all over the place!

Nobody has hope that this will finish,
Nobody but one!
Everyday, after that,
Everyday, at the same place,
Everyday, at the same time,
In his evening dress,
Vedran plays his cello.
Bullets and grenades all around him, He didn't care!
He wanted to play the music for everybody.
Perhaps because he believed that –
MUSIC CREATES ORDER OUT OF CHAOS.

My eyes filled with tears, my heart swelled with pride, my brain became confused. *How has this boy, only ten years old, grasped the complexity of what the cellist is trying to say with his music in a city where grenades and a rain of bullets fall every day?* Clearly my efforts to protect Dario by not talking about the war in front of him and by pretending we lived like we did by choice had not tricked him. I believed that he didn't ask questions because he didn't have any. In reality, he was much wiser than I thought, and in his childlike way respected my silence by never asking any questions.

One day in late December Željka came to see me in Penrith and brought along her American friend Liza who was visiting her in Appleby.

'This is Liza,' Željka introduced her friend. 'Remember I told you that Liza and I have known each other since high school? Liza spent a few months in Sarajevo on a school exchange and stayed with my family. We've been exchanging letters ever since.'

Around our dining table, with cups of coffee in our hands, we talked for hours about how our lives had changed, about whether we had seen any signs of what was going to happen before the war had started, about the options for our husbands to flee Sarajevo. Knowing where we came from, what sort of society we lived in before and how peaceful and enjoyable our lives were, Liza was extremely upset by everything that was happening in Bosnia and by everything Željka and I were going through since the war had broken out. She wanted to help in any way she could.

Liza lived in a little town on an island off the west coast of the US, in a small community, shaken by the news from Sarajevo.

'I have a friend on the island who would like to get in touch with one of the refugee families, to see if she could help them in any way,' Liza said to me. 'Knowing how much you and your friendship mean to Željka, I instantly thought of you.'

Liza pulled out two packages from her bag, and an envelope.

'Madelyn would have liked to come here with me, but she already had a trip planned for this time of the year. Here is her letter.' She handed me the envelope. 'And Christmas presents for you and the children.'

Confused with this unexpected kindness and interest in us from a complete stranger, I wrote down a few awkward words to thank Madelyn, and Liza took it back with her when she returned to the island.

We spent a few pleasant days in Appleby during the Christmas holidays at Željka and her sister-in-law's place. We were like one big family, three mothers and six children living in one place, making crêpes for breakfast, children playing and laughing, women talking, cooking and cleaning. It reminded me so much of the happy times in Sarajevo before the war, times spent with my dear friend Ziza, her sister, and their families. Our three families had regularly spent the whole Sunday together at one of our homes. While one mum looked after the children, the other one cleaned the place, and the third one cooked dinner. The men pretended to help but mainly just spent their time discussing sports and politics.

I watched my children play and wondered how much they understood, how much they sensed that our lives weren't what they seemed. Seemingly happy from the outside, reminded of our past, I struggled with the sadness inside me. Even while taking part in the chats and the activities with the children at Željka's place, I was unable to shake off the unnatural feeling that this was not the place we were meant to be.

DAY 239

IN the new year our days continued with the same routine.

First thing in the morning, after hearing the clack of the letterbox on the entrance door, I ran down the stairs to check if there was a letter for us. There weren't many people who knew where we were; in the beginning there were hardly any letters. I was slowly informing friends outside of Bosnia about our address and gradually letters from friends all over the world started arriving.

A few weeks after Liza's departure, Madelyn's first letter arrived. I stared for a second at the airmail envelope, with the unfamiliar pretty handwriting on it and unusual stamps. I took the letter upstairs to our bedroom, holding it gently like a precious gift. I sat on the bed and opened it with great care, making sure not to rip the envelope and damage the stamps. I pulled the letter and two notes of twenty American dollars flew out. I started crying. I could not believe her kindness. Madelyn didn't even know me, didn't know us at all. Such kindness from a complete stranger rebuilt my trust in humanity. The trust that had been shattered by the people with whom I went to school and university, with whom I worked, my neighbours, who then went to the hills around my hometown to kill innocent women and children, to fire grenades on our city. People who chose nationality and religion over friends and neighbours. *Maybe not everyone has gone mad. Maybe not everything in which I believe is lost.*

In the beginning it took me hours to understand the few pages of Madelyn's handwritten letters. Sometimes even a dictionary, which eventually arrived from a friend in Croatia, couldn't help. There were so many translation variations for every word. Often I was lost for a long time before the sentence would finally make sense to me. And sometimes it would not make sense no matter how hard I tried.

After I wrote to Madelyn about how difficult it was to look after Elena, how much attention she needed all the time, how sometimes I simply felt that I couldn't deal with that for one more day, she responded how she knew really well what two-year-old children were like. She explained in her letter how she had recently talked to a wealthy woman in Los Angeles who shared with Madelyn her secret of bringing up children, 'You get one live-in maid per child.'

I looked up the words 'live-in' and 'maid' in the dictionary but their explanation didn't make sense to me in that context. Maid: unmarried girl, chambermaid. I could not understand the word chambermaid, I didn't know what I was supposed to do with an unmarried girl, so I wrote back and asked what she meant. Madelyn patiently explained in simpler words how it confirmed that children were difficult to raise and how this rich woman thought we should have someone, a maid, a servant, to help us with every child we had. Mmm, yes, I agreed. Now the words *maid* and *chambermaid* made sense: chamber, like *chambre* in French, and an unmarried girl to tidy up the *chambre* and look after the kids.

Every two to three weeks a letter from Madelyn arrived, almost always with one or two twenty-dollar notes in it. That was a fortune to me. It equalled almost half of the weekly allowance given to us by UK welfare. Our weekly allowance was eighty-one British pounds, but 40 percent of that was paid to our volunteers for rent and the utility bills, leaving me with fifty pounds a week, approximately seventy-five American dollars for food and everything else, including the phone bill and food parcels to Sarajevo. When I thanked Madelyn for the money, saying that she shouldn't send that much, she just said, 'I saved it. Don't worry, it's fine.' How kind, generous and thoughtful. Of course, she saved it because she wanted to send it to us. It would have been so easy to spend it on something for herself or her family, but she sent it to us instead. And for that I was immensely grateful. I guarded the money, every dollar she sent, in an envelope hidden deep inside our wardrobe. And every time I added a new note I counted my treasure, knowing that one day this money would be very much needed for our trip to Australia.

We had applied for an Australian visa on the basis of independent points-based skilled migration in September 1991, many months before the war started. A couple of families we knew had already migrated to Australia by then, and another was preparing their paperwork. The economy in Yugoslavia had been weakening every day and even with two incomes we had not been able to afford much. Goran and I thought that it would be a smart idea to apply, and if successful, we could decide if we wanted to migrate or not depending on how the economy looked by then. Our incomes were so low compared to world prices that to pay for the visa application we had to take out a personal loan.

When six months later the war started, all our original documents, birth certificates, marriage certificate and university diplomas were stuck in the Australian Embassy in Belgrade, the capital of Serbia. In the first days of the conflict, while I was still in Sarajevo, and while the phone connections with Serbia still worked, apprehensive about leaving the documents in Belgrade, I phoned the Embassy and asked for our documents to be sent to Goga's address in Split, assuming that one day I would be able to get them from her. The Embassy informed me that we had successfully passed all the visa application steps and only needed to submit our medical certificates for the visa to be completed. However, they could not send the documents to an address. All they could do was either transfer them with our file to the Australian Embassy in Vienna or have the documents picked up from the embassy in Belgrade by someone who had our authorisation to do so. Uncomfortable about the possibility that, by some weird mishap, all the documents could disappear while in transfer to Vienna and how complicated it would be to reissue them in the war situation, we quickly faxed the authorisation to my friend Brankica in Belgrade, and she collected our documents from the Embassy.

Shortly after the children and I arrived in Split, I asked Brankica to mail the documents to Split. Alas, that wasn't possible anymore—all the mail connections between Serbia and Croatia had ceased. So Brankica sent them to Goran's cousin in Switzerland, and he then mailed them to Goga's address in Split.

After we came to Penrith, I immediately asked for our case to be transferred from Vienna to the Australian Consulate in Manchester, and stayed in regular touch with the officer in charge.

I firmly believed we would make our way to Australia one day, even though at that time we had no valid passports, hadn't completed our visa application process, needed to do the medical examinations, needed the money for the tickets, and most of all needed Goran to join us. All of that looked so challenging to achieve, but I believed in it nevertheless and saved the money for it.

In her first letter Madelyn asked if there was anything we needed that she could send us.

What does one need after losing everything and then re-establishing a life with the bare minimum of welfare money and second-hand goods donated by kind Cumbrians? Everything, and nothing. Every day I noticed something that we had before and did not have anymore, and every day I reminded myself that material possessions were unimportant as they could be taken away at any minute. What were truly important was family, and the memories and experiences that no one could take away from us.

To preserve the memories from our life in Cumbria and send the photos back home I had to ask our friends who had cameras to take photos of us. I imagined Goran looking at the photos and picturing our life in England and how much Dario and Elena had grown up and changed since he last saw them. So I asked Madelyn if she could perhaps send us a cheap camera. In less than two weeks, a Royal Mail parcel arrived with the camera in it. Our own camera, how very special! Despite the film and developing the photos being enormously expensive, I splurged on using up a film of twenty-four photos (not thirty-six, that was too expensive) on one of our excursions to the lakes, had the photographs developed and sent them to Goga in Split to be forwarded to Sarajevo by whatever reliable mail option she could find.

DAY 254

WHILE shopping for groceries at the supermarket, I inspected the different preserved foods and envisaged sending some to Sarajevo, thinking how much it would mean to them: all sorts of exotic dried fruits, many types of dried vegetables, egg replacement, all the things that couldn't be bought in Split.

But my only option to send food parcels to Sarajevo was still from Split. I had not yet found a way to send food directly from England. Sending by mail to Sarajevo was not possible, sending by post to Goga, to be forwarded to Sarajevo, was too expensive. I occasionally sent small parcels to Goga with dried eggs and dried vegetables. With six British pounds per kilo postage, that was all I could afford. Goga used some of the money from my mother-in-law's pensions to buy food and send parcels to Sarajevo, but the choice of preserved and dry food in Split was poor, mainly pasta, flour, rice, sugar, salt and canned meat and vegetables. After a while Goran said in his letter that they had plenty of dry and canned food at home and that he exchanged some of the cigarettes I sent for a little bit of fresh food. Since the start of the war he had traded all of the clothes and cosmetics I had left behind for fresh food that couldn't be sent in parcels. A couple of potatoes, or an onion could greatly improve the taste of the stock-cube-based soup that they ate day after day after day.

In his letters Goran included the meticulous details about how the food I sent was divided amongst the three families: Goran and my parents, his parents, and his sister's family. I imagined that there were maybe questions raised amongst them about the fair food distribution and who got what. Everyone was hungry and everyone needed more food than they had. I carefully examined his sentences trying to understand what it was that he was conveying to me: his distressed thoughts or just plain facts. But I was not there—I could not grasp the complexity of their situation no matter how hard I tried. Asking questions about it was pointless. Our mail exchange was haphazard and disjointed. Letters travelled weeks and months both ways. Often when I responded to something he had asked, he would receive my response months later, and in the meantime we had both received other letters, and sometimes the text in the letters didn't make sense.

But mostly Goran's letters were about their general state of despair, the hard situation in Sarajevo, and the lack of everything: lack of friends, communication, food. He wrote how he tried to maintain a decent quantity of dried and preserved food at home at all times. Continuously hoping that an escape option would finally work out, he wanted to make sure that there was enough food in the house for my parents to survive without his help. He took out our car battery and installed it in our flat as a source of electricity so they could listen to the radio and have a source of light during the night when there was no power.

I couldn't understand why his every escape option failed. Even the last one that Goran so enthusiastically wrote about in one of his previous letters, where he had hoped for escape assistance from the English boyfriend of our neighbour's sister.

Thankfully, a new plan was already on the go.

I think I can obtain Croatian citizenship based on your Croatian citizenship. Then I will simply leave Sarajevo as a Croatian citizen. I have a school friend who now works in the Bosnian Embassy in Zagreb. He will help me. I am absolutely certain this plan will work. I paid for one of the documents I needed with the car battery I installed in our flat a few months ago. No more radio news for us about what is happening in Sarajevo and in Bosnia and what the world is planning to do about it. That's a very small price for a fresh hope to leave Sarajevo and reunite with you and the children. I sent a letter of authorisation to Goga, to work on my citizenship certificate.

We desperately hoped the plan would work out.

A letter that arrived in late January was full of gloomy news.

My dear Eda,

The winter is hard. The extremely cold weather froze the river and the children now play on the ice. We have had no electricity for twenty-nine days, and no water for approximately that long either.

Our little furnace is saving our lives, it's on all the time. We still have some coal, I sometimes bring some firewood from work and your father goes out every night in search for wood. All the trees in the city are cut down for firewood; there is not a single tree in front of our apartment building. We are pleased that we can now cook at home and heat the place at the same time, instead of cooking on the shared stove installed in the communal space between the apartments. We can finally cook some of the dried beans we have.

At night, despite the sub-zero temperatures, we have to extinguish the fire to save wood. We sleep wearing multiple layers of clothing, hats and woollen scarves, covered with all the blankets we have. It becomes so cold overnight that when a hand accidentally ends up outside of the covers during the night, we wake up with our fingers red with frostbite appearing.

After so many months of living in very difficult conditions our neighbours that used to be friendly have become selfish, intolerant, angry. It seems that the constant extreme circumstances that the town and its people are going through have started breaking the soul of Sarajevo. Some neighbours are openly showing their envy that I still have a job and that my family is safe in England, far from the war that is

111

becoming uglier every day. Just as the monsters on the hills and their leaders planned, differences in ethnic origins have become important to many. With my mixed ethnic background I often feel out of place and uncomfortable for refusing to identify with any of the three main ethnic groups. I simply can't, I don't feel like I belong to any.

Still, many people are true to the Sarajevan spirit, where name and ethnic origins don't mean anything. All that counts is how good a person is. So while some people at my work and in our apartment block have become unapproachable and openly unfriendly, others are still kind and help with whatever they can.

All in all, we are fine, considering the situation. The war will end soon. Many battles with the Serbian army have been won, and although there are many more yet to be won, the end is near. I am missing you terribly and I am still frantically looking for options to join you. Please don't worry about me, look after the children and yourself as best you can. And please send me more photos; they remind me that there is something I need to live for.

Many kisses from your Goran

Once again, no mention of progress with his escape plan.

By then I knew that officially he could not obtain Croatian citizenship based on his marriage to a Croatian citizen. The rules were much stricter. And anyhow, having a Croatian passport was not enough to leave. It was not like he could take out a Croatian passport, buy a ticket, go to the airport, board a plane and depart for Croatia, or anywhere else in the world. Nevertheless, I was hoping it would all work out somehow.

DAY 289

ONE cold morning in early February 1993, Jan came to visit our shared household and after a cup of tea and a chat she said, 'The landlord wants to sell the house, we'll have to move you out within a month.'

Move us out to where? If no suitable rental properties are available in this small town, where could we go? Perhaps we would need to squeeze in with other Bosnian families?

I wasn't looking forward to adjusting my life all over again to someone else's habits and lifestyle. Once again I would need to explain my unusual parenting style, where no yelling or screaming was ever used no matter the situation, and every tantrum was resolved by cuddles and a quiet chat. Not that I was trained in this parenting style. I just don't like yelling. It is simply natural to me that everything could be and should be resolved by a peaceful discussion and I could see no reason to yell at anyone, let alone at my own children.

The time to move out drew closer but there was no information about where we would go. Then miraculously, only a few days before we needed to vacate the house, Jan came with good news. 'A few rental properties became available last week and you will be all allocated separate accommodation.'

In the first week of March my children and I moved to a small two-bedroom flat in Wordsworth Street, a nicer looking area than our old neighbourhood, with the same walking distance to Dario's Beaconside Primary School.

The flat was on the first floor of a semi-modern building with a dusty pink façade, and already furnished with simple furniture: beds, wardrobes, kitchen items, and all the basics needed for day-to-day life. I shared the bigger bedroom and a double bed with Elena, and the other smaller bedroom with a single bed was for Dario. We had our own white-tiled bathroom and our own open-plan lounge with a dining area and kitchen, with French doors opening to a Juliette balcony, overlooking a small lawn area with a few trees. I felt like screaming with joy from the balcony to let everyone in the neighbourhood know how divine the feeling of freedom is when living in one's own place. A small television I hired through a rental company completed it—the first real home on our own, after ten months of sharing, crammed into one bedroom.

The intense anxiety and tension I constantly had in my chest relaxed a bit. The mental fatigue from interpreting and translating everything for everyone slowly dissolved. Not that the new place made our lives perfect, but at least we had our own space and I didn't have to constantly make sure my children were not in anyone's way. I could freely talk to them about anything I wanted, ask Dario about what he did at school and what he had for homework.

I was finally able to plan our days and our meals without checking with everyone else in the household whether I was imposing on their plans. I could economise better with the little money we had, without justifying to anyone what I cooked for my children and whether I should make do with cheaper meals. If I wanted to treat my children with an occasional nice piece of meat, I could do that without worrying that other children from the household would either snatch a piece and leave my children without it, or that they would look at our meal enviously while their mums cooked something less appetising with the reasoning that it was an unnecessary luxury for the children to eat good cuts of meat.

One day, after coming home from school, and seeing his favourite crumbed chicken schnitzel on the dining table, Dario said, 'Mum, I think you cook much better now than in the old house.' I smiled and replied, 'That's because I am now fully in charge of what we eat.'

'And you weren't before? Who was in charge of cooking in the old house?'

'It's not that I wasn't in charge; it's just that I couldn't cook what and when I wanted as we shared the kitchen with others. It felt unfair to fry three chicken schnitzels for the three of us, and not offer it to others, but then I couldn't really afford to make enough for everyone, so I cooked what was easier to share.'

He nodded with understanding. 'I'm glad you can now cook what I like.'

I still had to budget carefully though.

We mainly ate vegetarian food, occasionally cheap cuts of meat, mostly mince beef, and inexpensive cheese and salami for sandwiches. Every penny was carefully counted. Fruit yogurts were a luxury and I only occasionally bought one or two small ones which Elena and Dario shared with gusto, and I scraped a few licks from the inside of the empty plastic tub. Almost every day I stopped in the supermarket aisle with chocolates and compared their prices, putting a bar in the basket, then taking it out, fantasising about having enough money one day to buy some of the most expensive and finest. Rarely buying any, only once in a while did I dare spend the money on the cheapest and most economical block for us to carefully enjoy in very small quantities over many days. Nevertheless, we had enough to eat, and all the meals were homemade and healthy, simple and tasty.

I made cheap cakes almost every week; I wanted to always have something special in the house to offer with coffee and tea when our new friends visited. It was cheaper to bake than to buy biscuits. A few eggs, a bit of flour and a bit of sugar, mixed with cocoa, sometimes with fruit, or some nuts. The house smelled so homely when cakes were in the oven. Like a real home. A happy home. Most of the time I improvised, based on my memory of the cakes I baked in Sarajevo, or even more so of the cakes my mum made, which were always of the cheaper kind. Naturally, I did not bring any recipes with me when we fled Sarajevo, nor did I remember to take any of Goga's when we were leaving Split. Who could think about baking cakes when running away from danger, or leaving the comfort of a dear friend's place? The first time I wanted to bake a cake, I could not remember how to make any of the desserts I used to make regularly in Sarajevo and for which I knew the recipes by heart. I was lost without my recipe book. I started asking friends who were writing to me to include a recipe or two in their letters and collected the recipes from other Bosnian women in our Cumbrian group. I bought a cheap little spiral notebook with a light blue cover and teddy bears on it and my collection of recipes in it slowly grew.

Then one day I noticed a Greek recipe magazine on the shelves of the local newsagency. The food style, especially the desserts, was very similar to what we cooked and baked in Sarajevo. Even those that looked different were more similar to Bosnian desserts than anything I had tried in England. I really wanted to buy the magazine, yet I had to be very careful with money, so I pondered for ages if it was really necessary to spend the money on it. I must've looked suspicious to the shopkeeper, standing there, picking up the magazine, leafing through the pages, putting it back on the shelf, picking it up again. In the end I bought it. I came home and looked at the pictures and inspected the recipes from cover to cover many times. By then I knew that I could buy pastry sheets in the supermarket, the same type we used to make *pita* in Sarajevo. I eagerly awaited a special occasion to use the pastry sheets to make the baklava cigars from the cookbook. They were so easy to make, light and tasty, an instant hit with all our visitors. I kept making them every time I could afford to buy the ingredients, when we had special visitors or when I wanted to take a plate to a lunch or dinner. To this day they never fail to attract compliments.

While baking, I could forget the pain. On some days, for an hour or two, for half a day, life almost seemed normal, as if we weren't war escapees, struggling emotionally and financially, unsure of our future. Occasionally on a nice sunny afternoon, with the warm rays of sunlight and fresh air coming through the open balcony doors, the birds chirping on the trees outside, if we had had relatively recent news from home that everyone was fine, and if I managed to push aside my anxieties about the future, I would start feeling happy, listening to the music from the radio, humming a song to myself while baking cakes or preparing dinner. And then, something unexpected, the word 'Bosnia' or 'Sarajevo' coming from the radio, a sudden loud bang from outside, would bring back a quick flash of a moment from our recent past. I would remember everything. And the sharp pain in my chest would return. Then I felt guilty that I had been happy and had forgotten even for a moment who we were and why we were there. It seemed to me that if I were happy, life would hurt me more with bad news from home. By not letting myself be happy I was protecting myself from any future disappointments.

DAY 302

MOST mornings after we had had our breakfast, and Dario had left for school, I strapped Elena in her stroller and went out to buy groceries. From the outside we looked normal, as though we were an ordinary family from Penrith, the dad away, maybe at work or on a business trip, the mum looking after the children, buying groceries, cooking dinner, cleaning the house. Busy with the daily rhythm.

If the weather was nice, before stopping at the supermarket, Elena and I sometimes walked around for a bit longer, Elena waving her little hands in the stroller in front of me or mumbling along while pretending to read a picture book. Occasionally, on a sunny day, I treated us with a cheap takeaway sandwich from one of the cafés, tuna and cucumber, or egg and mayonnaise, and we sat in the park next to St. Andrews church, basking in the sunshine, sharing the sandwich and watching children play while their mums chatted on the benches. Elena often fell asleep after the snack and I sat there on the bench, surrounded by the green grass, sunshine, crisp and clear air, and the birds singing. Instead of breathing in the fresh air with a big smile, happy to be alive and able to enjoy the beauty around me, I often sank under the weight of responsibility, loneliness, isolation, anxiety and fear of what might happen to us next. Some days quiet tears rolled uncontrollably down my face. I felt lost and helpless. Unable to do anything about the complicated situation in which we found ourselves. My sorrows were usually interrupted by Elena waking up, asking to have a drink, to step out of the stroller and run around the park for a bit. I was so grateful for her company and her demands, as without them I would have sunk into a deeper despair.

The two of us would then do the daily grocery shopping. The supermarket aisles with food, fridge lights and people's chatter appeared surreal to me, as if I was an external observer of my life, not a participant.

In this life within life, things did not make sense.

Making the decision about what to cook for dinner seemed insignificant, and I aimlessly walked the aisles, my brain fuzzy, unable to remember what I needed to buy and what I had planned to cook. I wanted to scream to the other shoppers, 'Do you know that there is a bloody war going on not far from here? Do you know that my husband is trapped there and can't leave? How can you just buy your groceries like that, as if everything is fine? It is not!'

Sometimes my legs and hands shook in the middle of the supermarket and I felt nauseated and weak as if I were about to faint. But then I remembered that I couldn't afford to feel unwell, that I couldn't afford to faint there in the supermarket, it would scare Elena. Plus, I had to be home before Dario returned from school, otherwise my absence would scare him too. I had to cook something for my children to eat. This stupid war was not their fault. They didn't have to suffer more than they already had by losing the comfort of their home, living without their dad, without their grandparents and cousins, without their friends. I would then lean with my back against a cold supermarket wall, take slow deep breaths and gather all my strength to regain my focus. I would make a quick decision about what to cook with the cheap ingredients available to buy and the two of us would slowly make our way home, up the hill. After such flashes of extreme physical weakness I was emotionally drained, sad and lost, but I had a task in front of me, I had to prepare a meal for Dario and Elena and that gave me enough energy to push the stroller up the hill and get on with my day.

Days passed. Nothing changed. I often didn't feel like getting up or seeing people. I had no desire to talk. There was nothing to discuss—no plans, no change for us. It was still the same despair as the day before, the week before, month before. Our English friends nevertheless came to visit us almost daily, to fill our days with chats and activities, to make us feel welcomed, to make our wait for Goran less traumatising and our daily lives easier. Anna, Jan, Charlotte, Steve, Monica, Jacqui—they instinctively knew they had to come and interrupt my loneliness. They made conversation with me. They smiled warmly and complimented my children. How Elena was cute, and how she had such a lovely bubbly personality. How Dario was sweet and smart, how his English already sounded so Cumbrian. Jan, whose daughter Hannah went to the same school as Dario, told me one day in wonder, 'I was at the school last night and I heard my daughter Hannah talking behind me, I turned around and it was in fact Dario. Can you believe that he sounds so Cumbrian already?'

Even though I knew that everyone was sincere in their care, I was incessantly aware of the main reason these friendships existed—we came as refugees from a war-torn country and these people wanted to help us. Nevertheless, I was very grateful for the time they spent with us. With people around us life almost seemed normal, as if we weren't refugees.

Jan, with her eternal smile, was like our fairy godmother. Anything we needed, she materialised for us. Anything I mentioned in our conversations, if Jan guessed I could not afford to buy it, would appear a day or two after: a warmer blanket, another set of sheets. A couple of days after seeing Dario do his homework on the dining table while I prepared a cake mixture next to him and some of the flour sprinkled on his textbook, Jan appeared with a little desk for his bedroom.

Jacqui, always with her happy laugh, often invited us to her place. She lived on a farm, in a huge converted barn where in the numerous rooms and corridors I literally lost my way many times. Dario and Elena loved playing with her children, Mac and Freya: riding their horses, freely running after the cows in fields, collecting eggs for breakfast. We ate beautiful food, Jacqui played piano for us, the children laughed, and for a few hours, at least on the surface, life seemed normal and happy.

Charlotte and Adam cooked us delicious meals and hosted warm dinners in their lovely home only a few houses down from our little apartment. They admired my courage and my ability to speak English, neither of which truly deserved their admiration. I was not brave; I was only doing what I had to in order to save my children's lives. My broken English was a tool I had no choice but to use as there was no other way of communicating. I struggled to describe our complicated story and sometimes used words that I didn't know even existed. They were such a nice family. They talked about their uncomplicated lives, their plans for the future, and were amazed with what had happened to us. That I managed to look after my children by myself, and that we appeared so normal despite everything we were going through. Shortly after we met, Charlotte organised a place for Elena in the nearby crèche where their daughter Amy went and where I could leave Elena to play with other children for a few hours a couple of mornings a week without even paying for it. I used the time to look for any information about the escape options for Goran. I called people who had recently left Sarajevo and asked how they had managed to leave, but there was not really much useful information.

Monica, whose heart-to-heart about a bossy little girl turning into a graceful young lady I remembered every time I saw her, lived relatively far away. Although she had her own three children, she generously agreed to board one of the three teenage girls I noticed on the day of our departure from Split. She only visited once every couple of weeks, but she often phoned to check if we were well and if we needed anything.

One day when Monica phoned she found me in a low mood. Elena and I had just arrived home. Despite the miserable, cold and rainy weather I had to go out and buy ingredients for dinner—our fridge and pantry were empty. With no one available to look after Elena, I took her with me. I waited until the rain eased and we quickly ventured to the supermarket. By the time we finished the shopping, the rain started pouring again. We had no choice but to walk back home in the cold wind while icy rain fell directly on Elena's little face, soaking her jacket. I had nothing to protect her. I tried to hold the umbrella in front of her face but could not walk and push the stroller like that for very long. So I gave up on that idea and tried to push faster, to get home quicker. Elena was cold and crying and I could do nothing to help her. I cried with her as I pushed the stroller and the groceries up the hill to our apartment, my tears mixing with the icy drops of rain. I couldn't protect my own child from the cold, and I had no one to look after her for a couple of hours while I did the grocery shopping.

As we walked into the apartment the phone rang. Still very shaken and deeply frustrated and angry that I had lost everything we had, not only our apartment, my job and income, but with it my ability to protect our children, I could not sustain my emotions and started crying while talking on the phone to Monica.

Fearful of bad news from home, Monica gently asked, 'Is everything alright? Why are you crying?'

I told her that I couldn't offer my baby girl the minimum of comfort because I couldn't afford to buy a plastic rain protector for the stroller no matter how hard I tried to economise. And yes, I knew that I did not often need to go out with Elena in her stroller in rainy weather, but doing it even once hurt to my core. I slowly calmed down and we chatted about the news from home, or rather the lack of news from home, and she said she would try to come see us the following day.

When Monica arrived the following morning she brought with her a plastic rain protector that perfectly fitted Elena's stroller. I was so very pleased and I exclaimed in amazement, 'Oh, where did you find it?', thinking that perhaps Monica knew a family that didn't need it any more for their children, or perhaps she was lucky enough to find it in an op-shop on her way to see us. She just said, 'I bought it,' with her gentle smile. And I started crying again. I was grateful, of course, but my emotions were confused by the distress of the day before still fresh in my mind, by such simple generosity from a relative stranger, someone who had only known us for a few months. I was also a little envious that anyone could so easily go and buy things for other people's children and I couldn't do it for my own child. It seemed so unfair. I realised that my crying on the phone the day before had prompted Monica to buy this for us, and this thought made me uncomfortable. Ever since we left Sarajevo, the feeling of dependence on others sat heavily on my chest. It often spoilt the purity of gratitude for their wholehearted generosity and brought confusion to my thoughts. In the past, I had always been happy to be generous and to receive others' generosity. Suddenly, generosity had turned to help, which was much heavier to receive.

I said, 'Oh, you shouldn't have really. I'm sure we will not need to go out in the rain much more, and maybe if I had looked harder I could have found a second-hand one somewhere...'

To which she just said, 'Don't worry about it; it wasn't really expensive, I was glad I could help.' And that was it.

Generosity in its simplest and humblest form was something that we experienced numerous times while we lived in Split and Cumbria. I often felt almost humiliated that I couldn't provide for my children everything that they needed. Yet, I was very grateful that people were so compassionate and gave when and what they could. Without their kindness our lives would have been much harder.

After that day Elena and I braved the cold, rainy days with ease. I had my beautiful warm leather jacket from Goga, and with layers of jumpers underneath I was fine in the coldest weather. Elena now had the rain protector, a warm little padded jacket inherited from one of Penrith's children, and a cute woollen knitted beanie in baby pink, embroidered with colourful flowers, brought from Sarajevo. The little beanie initially belonged to Asja, my dear friend Ziza's daughter. After their family went on an extended holiday to Rome six months before the war started, not knowing that they would not be coming back to Sarajevo, I kept Asja's little knitted beanie for Elena. It was a keepsake from our happy life before the war, a little piece of our special friendship. It travelled the world with us and people always commented on how adorable it looked on Elena. And although Elena and the beanie were truly very cute, I always thought that people reacted because they could sense the years of love and friendship entwined in that little beanie.

Steve, with plenty of free time in his days between finishing university and starting his first job, visited us almost daily. He told jokes and made us laugh. He tickled Elena while she giggled and playfully wrestled with her on the floor. He played cricket with Dario and praised his cricket skills and his intelligence, telling me that Dario would for sure end up studying at Oxford or Cambridge if we decided to stay in England. Steve often took us on excursions to see the beautiful lakes of the Lakes District. Once, while returning home by car at night, Steve driving and Dario next to him, Elena and I in the back seat, as we turned down a curved road, the lights of Penrith appeared sparkling in the distance. The beautiful warmth of absolute happiness came over me for a split second. My brain had mistaken this scene with one from my past, when, coming home from a day trip to the picturesque green mountains around Sarajevo, I spotted the city lights in the distance. The happy feeling of how wonderful life was and how uniquely magical it was to return home after a magnificent day spent in the countryside. Except this time we were not going back to our true home. We were going back to our temporary life, while waiting for our old life to be returned to us.

DAY 305

ANNA was like my shadow, like the sister I never had. Gentle and compassionate, constantly asking about our family and whether there was anything she could do to help. She took us out almost every day in her big Volvo. She sometimes looked after Elena to give me a bit of breathing space, even though I generally didn't know what to do with the free time. Without the focus on my children and their needs, I felt lost and lightheaded, unable to relax, unable to rest. Sometimes the girls came back from their time together wearing matching new clothes.

One warm day we all went out to town and Anna took the girls for a walk so I could have a bit of quiet time to myself. We agreed to meet around the main town square. After aimlessly going through a few shops with no money to spend, I arrived there early, sat on the stone steps of the clock tower in Market Square with my face turned to the sun and waited for them. Then I saw them: two little girls in identical Benetton summer dresses, sleeveless, yellow with miniscule multi-coloured flowers, with tiny frills around the neck and at the bottom. They looked adorable—Ellen so tiny, Elena half a head taller.

When Anna needed to finish errands in town she left Ellen with us for a few hours. While Ellen and Elena invented games with the small number of toys we had and played dress-ups in my bedroom, I had a bit of time to think and plan. After a while the quiet time turned into a wild chase through our barely furnished flat. I kept moving pieces of furniture with sharp corners out of their way and bribing them into reading a picture book, but they screamed with joy and played around me as if I was a big toy placed there to make their chase more interesting. Once their energy levels went up, nothing else could calm them down but their own body fatigue. Exhausted, they eventually collapsed on the floor and fell asleep, their little legs and arms spread in odd positions. I dragged blankets from the bedroom to cover them so they wouldn't catch a chill, and enjoyed the return of the silence for a while. But the silence never lasted long. The excitement of having company made their sleep light and even though I tiptoed around to prolong their sleep, any little sound easily woke them.

Once I was preparing chicken soup for lunch while they slept. I moved the pans and lids slowly making sure I didn't clink them, adding previously prepared chicken and chopped vegetables. While everything in the pan slowly brewed on the stove, I finished writing a few letters and then stood up to add vermicelli noodles to the soup. As I opened the packet, the plastic bag rustled and Elena jumped, exclaiming, 'I want some chips too!' imagining the rustle was from a chip packet. The idyllic silence was over.

On my birthday the four of us went to the town library together. One of my most loved surroundings ever since I was very young, the quiet and peace of a library, bursting with mysterious stories, real and fictional, never ceased to fill me with amazement, curiosity and a desire to read each and every book on the shelves. The library in Penrith was better and bigger than any of the libraries I had seen before, with books, magazines, a reading area and an area where children could quietly play or read. We stayed there for hours in the warmth and silence. Anna and I looked through books and magazines. I tried to enhance my vocabulary with new words and phrases every day. Elena and Ellen played with the toys or looked through picture books. Even Elena's energetic personality surrendered to the overwhelming tranquillity of the place. I enjoyed not only the quietness of the library but also the closeness of a dear friend, a person who truly cared for us. The absence of conversation enforced the strong bond that connected the four of us.

On the way back to our place, we stopped in town. Anna bought us lunch from Marks & Spencer: tasty sandwiches, fruit yogurts, the best chocolates and juices, and in a nearby park we had a picnic on a blanket from Anna's car. The food tasted so extraordinarily delicious to me; we could not afford anything like this. Elena and Ellen played and laughed and communicated using their own unique language. Elena a bit chubby and bossy, Ellen much smaller, quiet and shy, with the light blonde feathery hair of a little doll. They endlessly enjoyed each other's company. Anna and I watched our little girls with happy smiles stretched on our faces. From time to time Anna would ask, 'What did she say?' when Ellen, unaware of any difference, used a Bosnian word. It felt warm and comfortable to be with them.

We collected the empty food packaging, folded the blanket and placed it all in the car. Picking up sleepy Ellen in her arms, Anna said, 'Let's walk this way.'

'I think the girls are tired, maybe it's better to go back to my place,' I suggested.

'It won't take long,' she replied.

I followed her with Elena's hand in mine, patiently waiting for Elena to start pleading with me to pick her up. We turned a corner and stopped in front of a shop. Laura Ashley. I had never seen it before; it was not on my route from home to the supermarket. Even if I did see it, I would not have walked in—it looked too elegant and exquisite. I waited at the entrance, while Anna walked straight in. She turned towards me and said, 'Come in, come in.'

So I did. I picked Elena up so that she wouldn't touch any of the pretty clothes. Anna made a couple of rounds through the shop, then came to me and said, 'Pick anything you like as a present from me for your birthday.'

I hesitated, but she insisted. 'Please.'

She lowered Ellen to the floor and took Elena from my arms. 'Find something you like.'

I turned towards the racks with clothes, one thing more beautiful than the next. I saw a nice long cotton cardigan in beige with two navy stripes around the neck and the cuffs. I checked the price tag. My vision blurred from the shock. *No way! Incredibly expensive.*

I checked the tag on a shirt next to it, and then the next one. Not much cheaper. I turned to Anna and shook my head. 'I'm sorry, I can't. It's far too expensive.'

I took Elena from her arms and slowly walked out of the shop. My eyes prickled with tears—from my inability to afford nice clothes, from Anna's generosity. A few minutes later Anna came out from the shop with a shopping bag in her hand. A little wave of envy went through my chest. I wished I could afford some of those lovely clothes.

In front of our apartment building Anna said she would love a cup of coffee before driving back to her place. We walked in; I turned the kettle on and looked through the cupboards for a few biscuits. I made the coffee and brought it to the table. There, on the sofa, a parcel wrapped in Laura Ashley soft tissue. I looked at it, wondering what she bought, assuming she wanted to show it to me. She handed me the parcel and said, 'Happy Birthday!'

I stood there for a minute, unsure what to say. 'But…' I started.

'I think the size is right, please open it,' she said.

Inside was the beige cardigan. I tried it on and the size was perfect. With tears now freely falling from my eyes, I hugged her. 'It's beautiful. Thank you so much.'

Enriched with love and friendship I continued on throughout the day with less anxiety and worry. The feeling of subtle happiness lasted until the next time I watched the news on television.

DAY 328

THE reports from Bosnia were always top news.

Five days after the first anniversary of the siege, an Easter Service was held in the Sarajevo Cathedral, the largest cathedral in Bosnia and Herzegovina. The city was trying hard to preserve its spirit of multi-ethnicity despite the war not slowing down.

Ceasefires were negotiated daily, only to be broken the same or following day.

The number of people injured and killed could not even be properly estimated. In footage from the concentration camps in Bosnia, run by Bosnian Serb forces, the Bosnian men looked like those in World War II documentaries. Skeleton-like with bony faces, eyes that had lost their sparkle, ribs protruding over non-existent stomachs. The news reports spoke of mass killings and mass graves. About Bosnian women being raped.

Such terrible atrocities made me doubt myself, my childhood memories, my origins, and everything I ever thought about my country, my friends, neighbours, school friends, everyone I had ever met in Bosnia. *Was it all just an illusion? Is it possible that I grew up amongst people who decided to destroy a whole town, its icons, and its people in the name of a nation and religion?*

I could not see the end of the war. *How long will this last? Weren't there cases of hostilities that went on for decades, like the Israeli-Palestinian conflict? Will this one be like that, a never-ending war amongst three nations that once, not so long ago, lived happily together?*

Once the winter was over and the warmer weather made moving around a bit easier almost everyone tried to flee Sarajevo. Even the most optimistic people had lost hope that the war would be over soon. But it was harder and harder to find a way to escape. All the options with fake journalist papers had already been tried and did not work anymore.

Željka worked intensely on arranging permission for her husband to leave town based on their Canadian visa, and therefore Canadian citizenship, being granted since she left Sarajevo. She suggested I should try to do the same.

I called the Australian Consulate in Manchester and asked if they could provide Australian citizenship documents for Goran, based on our visa application.

Although infinitely friendly and kind to me over the phone, and exceptionally patient with our extremely slow application process, the Consulate showed no interest in providing me with proof of Goran's Australian citizenship. Our visa was still incomplete; the medical certificates were not yet submitted. Eventually I received a letter from them confirming that we had applied for a visa, but such a letter could not be used to organise an escape for Goran as a foreign citizen. Without his medical certificate we couldn't finalise the visa process. What irony: to finalise the visa and use it to help Goran leave Sarajevo, he needed to be outside of Sarajevo to complete his medical certificate. There was not much chance that he could complete a full medical examination in Sarajevo. In a city where the number of medical interventions was far higher than the number of doctors, nurses and other medical staff, in a place where there was hardly any water and electricity supply, where people were dying and losing their limbs, for

Goran to ask to have a test necessary for a medical certificate sounded like a cruel joke.

I didn't hear much from Željka about how her plan was unfolding. I had no idea how well it was advancing. Knowing our situation, she perhaps didn't want to upset me with constant updates on her progress. One day in April she phoned and very quietly, almost whispering, with a trace of discomfort in her voice, told me, 'I know you will be upset by this. I have to tell you regardless.'

My body tensed. Blood went to my head. My feet couldn't feel the floor anymore. *Did she hear that Goran was injured? Or killed?*

'What happened?' I stuttered.

'My husband and my brother arrived in Appleby yesterday.'

For a long few seconds I was in shock and unable to say anything.

'What about Goran?' I asked.

'I am so sorry that Goran did not come with them.'

The whole world spun. As much as I was genuinely happy for Željka, for their families to be reunited, my heart sank with pain. All I could think about was how Goran must've felt. Željka's husband and her brother had spent much time with him, planning their escapes, and now he was left behind with no one to talk to. I found no comfort in knowing and understanding that the final details of leaving Sarajevo could not be and must not be shared. Not with friends, not even with relatives. Anyone who knew too much could potentially impact the plan, knowingly or unknowingly. Plans were kept secret and the news about an escape would only become public a few days after someone had left town and people speculated about how and what they could have done to escape.

Mute from the panic and anxiety running through my body I didn't ask a single question about how her husband and brother were, how they made it to Appleby. I didn't even ask about Goran. Eventually, after a seemingly long pause Željka said, 'They say Goran is as well as he can be, and he sends his love to you and the children. I will come see you as soon as they recover from the trip.'

When I saw her in the days that followed, Željka gave me a long letter from Goran.

Saturday, April 3, 1993

My dearest,

I included some of our old photos with this letter, at least a few for you to have. I want to preserve a few moments of our lives to remember how we once lived. I am hoping that I would be able to send out more of them before I leave. My situation is still undefined. It appears that everything is almost ready for me to leave; yet, at the same time, some main steps aren't prepared. Hopefully not for much longer. Patience, patience.

There is nothing new to say about Sarajevo. The shelling seems lighter, however every day at least three people are killed. It is still very dangerous to walk through the street. I don't often go to see my parents, it's too risky. Their phone line started recently working, I call them when we have electricity and the phones are working.

The situation with food is the same. Mainly beans, pasta and rice, day after day. Occasionally we open a tin of fish and I make us a fish broth. Sometimes I even add mashed potato from the packets you sent. Your mum is mainly taking care of having a meal ready by the time I come back from work, but anything to do with the food you send us I need to prepare. I have written down a few English words for them to help them understand what's in the packages and tins, but when instructions are involved, it's easier if I make it than if I explain the steps.

We still have plenty of tea in the cupboard. As much as I was annoyed with your obsession to bring us back a box of tea from everywhere you went, I am now grateful that we can at least have a decent cup of tea from time to time.

When the power is on, we watch television from two TV sets—one has picture and the other has sound. If it weren't so sad and depressing all around us, this would almost be funny.

I feel that I don't belong to this place anymore. I cannot identify myself with any of the three sides. When our Croat neighbours wish me all the best for Eid, I have this urge to explain that I have never celebrated it and I still don't. And that somehow sounds wrong, like I'm pretending, but I'm not. You know I'm not. We have never celebrated any of the religious holidays, not with my parents, not with you. Now, however, everyone must choose a religion and celebrate its festivals. I feel lost.

A few days later, when I calmed down a bit, Željka told me that no one else could help Goran leave Sarajevo but me. That nothing could be done from the inside, that the help must be organised from the outside.

But what can I do to help him? I had no connections. I knew no one of any importance who could do anything for us, maybe organise papers that would enable Goran to leave Sarajevo. I had already tried the Australian visa option and that hadn't worked out. *What else could I possibly do?* The sense of powerlessness consumed me.

Day and night I thought about what I could do to arrange my husband's escape. I was obsessed with it. I kept searching, but the search was not bringing me closer to an escape plan. I phoned anyone that I heard had left Sarajevo recently. I questioned them, looking for clues and ideas, but was offered only vague stories about what they did, without facts, without names. Everyone was scared to share the details of their escape and the names of their connections. They were afraid that publicising the names could cause harm to the people who had helped them.

After a while I realised that only some kind of exceptional magic could help us.

I just didn't know what to do to make that magic happen.

DAY 344

THE local paper, *Evening News and Star*, called to ask for an interview. I accepted, fantasising that an article would attract the attention of someone with authority and they would find a way to save the father of my children and reunite him with his family. Two days later the article, 'War of Shame', was published. Half a page, citing my sharp and factual words about the misery and senselessness of the war, and the pain it was causing our family. And to my disbelief, a happy looking photo of me in one corner, my head tilted to one side, without a trace of the pain I was going through. Alas, there was no follow up from anyone that could help us.

The relentless search for an escape plan continued, but I could not come up with any clever new ideas.

Eager to remove any obstacle to our future happiness, no matter how miniscule, I decided to sell my precious gold ring with blue sapphires to a gold merchant in Penrith. A few times in the past people had commented that blue sapphire brought bad luck to people wearing it. I left my beloved ring in the jewellery shop in exchange for a few pounds. For days afterwards I walked past the shop window and glanced at my ring, sad after parting with it, remembering how Goran and I bought it on our honeymoon from a well-known jeweller in Korčula, the pretty little Croatian island town.

Madelyn offered her help, but like me, she could not come up with any ideas for how to help, or where to start.

One night, sleepless in bed, I thought of something. Impatient to wait for the morning, I got up and scribbled a letter to Madelyn. In a few clumsy sentences, without much introduction, I tried to explain that a lawful request from a US media outlet for Goran's assistance could help him leave Sarajevo as a journalist on the job.

Dear Madelyn,

What I know is that some important person (president, or vice-president, or manager) from TV network or newspaper should send fax to UN in Sarajevo and explain that they need someone for doing some kind of jobs for them.

I am sure that you can find all information if you ring this phone number (in Sarajevo).

I hope you can find something. Please try to check if NATO is doing evacuation now.

Love, Edita

In the morning I added the UN phone numbers in Sarajevo and Goran's date of birth, passport number and address. As soon as Dario left for school I hurried to the Bluebell Bookshop, pushing Elena in her stroller, and faxed it to Madelyn.

In a hurry to send it, I didn't explain my plan well enough. I didn't mention that having Goran engaged on a job for US media would make him look like their correspondent or reporter and on that pretence he could request a journalist pass from the UN, and with that pass he could potentially leave Sarajevo.

When Madelyn received the fax, she was confused by my fragmented description of the plan. Sensing the urgency she immediately phoned to ask for a better explanation. Using simple and brisk phrases and frustrated that my English was not yet adept at explaining complex scenarios, I sounded angry. She asked, 'Are you angry because I can't understand what you want me to do?'

Of course I was not angry with her. I was angry with myself and my inability to clearly explain my ideas. The inadequacy of my English. The inability to run my life without other people's help. And more than anything, I was tired beyond anyone's comprehension. It was a year since we had left Sarajevo, and I was on my own with two children, my head full of worries and not enough money in my pockets. Every day I felt more and more tired. At night I was too exhausted to relax. I spent sleepless nights worrying about Goran and my parents in Sarajevo. Sometimes anxious about our future. Sometimes considering new escape possibilities. Still I had to get up early in the morning to help Dario get ready for school, then clean and cook and entertain Elena. After only a few words Madelyn understood how drained I felt and how the plain effort to explain what I wanted was making my voice sound tense and angry.

Madelyn phoned everywhere asking for help. She asked for financial help from her friends and acquaintances and sent money to me. Many years later, amongst my letters that she had kept for decades and returned to me when I was ready to document our story, I found the traces of her numerous notes and the phone numbers she called.

She mailed me a copy of an announcement she received from the International Rescue Committee from Seattle. It was about US plans to expand the Bosnian Refugee Admission Program, with details of who was eligible and where the refugee processing agencies were in Europe. She said she would be very happy to offer their home to us and that we should consider migrating to the US. Of course, the refugee agencies nearest to Sarajevo were in Zagreb and Belgrade, and for us to appear there Goran needed to be out of Sarajevo. That plan was out of the question for us.

After she had heard from US immigration that there was a Swedish Embassy in Sarajevo, Madelyn contacted the Swedish Embassy in Seattle, hopeful for their help to organise an escape. The person to whom she talked didn't even know where Sarajevo was and told her that if Goran could make his way out of Sarajevo, they might be able to help him. If only he could make his way out of there!

She talked to the director of the American Israel Public Affairs Committee who sounded very positive and asked numerous questions about us, and our situation. I faxed her a long letter with the details of our story. Madelyn was optimistic about their help, but in the end every single plan required Goran to go see someone somewhere outside of Sarajevo. For all the refugee assistance programs it was crucial that Goran was a refugee, that he was already outside of his country of birth, and that was the impossible step.

Even though many people sent her money for us, and many ideas were thrown around, no one could truly help us get Goran out of Sarajevo.

For a little while, Madelyn and I considered if I should apply for Canadian citizenship. Perhaps the Canadian Embassy in London would be more supportive in helping us. I requested the visa application papers from the Embassy and asked Madelyn to look for sponsors for us. But very shortly afterwards I abandoned that plan. A new visa process would take months to complete and I had no energy, time nor money for it.

DAY 382

ONE morning in early June, like many times before, Elena and I were with Anna and Ellen in their beautiful house. Anna and I were unusually silent, lost in our thoughts. Anna glanced towards me several times while preparing lunch and cleaning up the food scraps and crumbs from the bench, as if checking that I was still there. I had no strength left in me to pretend that I was fine, that I was positive, that everything would work out in our favour. I just sat there, silent, staring at the floor, thinking, *How much longer must we live like this? How much longer on hold, waiting to re-start our lives?* Anna looked worried but didn't ask questions, didn't try to initiate conversation. After lunch she suggested, 'Would it be okay if we go visit my friends, Máire and Guy? They live in a nearby village.'

I raised my head. I looked at Anna and shrugged my shoulders with a sigh. 'I'm feeling so tired and miserable today, I don't think I will be good company.'

'Guy could maybe help with a press card for Goran.' Anna kept her gaze on me, waiting for me to agree.

Feeling vulnerable and gloomy, I was not keen on repeating our story once again. It always brought me to the very edge of crying and I didn't want to cry in front of people I didn't even know. I was doubtful that much could be done about the press card anyway. I had just recently made another attempt. I obtained a fake press card, sent it to Goran and regretted it straight away. A huge mistake. A false press card could actually bring trouble rather than help with an escape. After all, even genuine foreign journalists were not safe in Sarajevo. Only a few days earlier there had been news on the television about a French journalist who had been picked up on the streets of Sarajevo, sent to dig trenches in the hills and never came back.

But I didn't want to be ungrateful to Anna who wanted to help. So I nodded. And we went.

When we arrived, Máire opened the door. Petite and pretty, with dark hair and kind eyes, she had a big welcoming smile. She was just about to prepare lunch for Guy who was working in his studio. She said, 'I'll quickly make scrambled eggs for Guy and then we can all have a cup of tea and talk.' *Scrambled eggs,* I thought while we followed Máire towards the kitchen, *what is that?* I had never heard of scrambled eggs before. An omelette, fried egg, boiled egg, soft-boiled egg, even a poached egg, I knew what they were. I was curious to see what scrambled eggs were. Anna and I stood by Máire's big stove while she scraped the eggs in the pan, and I thought, *Right, so scrambled eggs are a messed-up omelette. I can do that.*

Máire and Guy were gentle and compassionate. They treated me as an old friend, softly asking about the war, my husband, the situation in Sarajevo, about the escape options. I answered their questions while struggling with a ball of pain in my chest, tight throat, and eyes burning from suppressed tears. We talked for a bit, then, as always, Anna drove Elena and me back home, just in time for Dario's return from school.

The sharp pain in my chest slowly dissolved as the day passed and while preparing the meal and cleaning up I pushed to the back of my mind the thoughts about the exchange with Guy and Máire. My emotional state was ambivalent. I wanted a miracle, but at the same I was afraid of yet another disappointment.

Desperate to try everything I could think of, I even sent a letter to Diana, Princess of Wales, hoping that our story would touch her kind heart and that perhaps she could do something extraordinary to rescue my husband. I saw things like that in movies. I heard about miraculous events in people's lives and hoped that it was just a matter of somehow triggering such an event. Trying to make it more personal, I included a photo of the children and myself, dressed in our best clothes, sitting on someone's old-fashioned sofa upholstered in floral fabric. We looked like the most normal and healthy family. How could anyone resist helping us?

For days afterwards I dreamed about receiving a letter from Her Royal Highness asking for more details about this poor man who'd been separated from his family for over a year, about a rescue mission that would fly Goran back to safety and to us, about us holding hands and dancing.

A few days later, Dario, Elena and I went to Edinburgh with the other Bosnian families to personally deliver food parcels that would be transported to Sarajevo. I packed three big parcels for our three families (Goran and my parents, Goran's parents, and his sister's family), and many smaller ones for our numerous friends in Sarajevo. In Goran's parcel I packed some of the coffee Madelyn sent me hoping that it would bring good luck and enable the parcels to be delivered to Sarajevo.

The previous time, in February, my parcels sent with the same aid organisation were not delivered. When the trucks with the parcels left, Steve went with them. He wanted to go to Sarajevo—he was adamant he could help with my husband's escape. I was terribly scared for the young man. What he was doing was risky and dangerous. He didn't fully understand the complexity of the situation in Bosnia, but he was young and he wanted to help, so he went. They didn't reach Sarajevo. They were stopped by the Croatian Defence Army in Kiseljak—a small town near Sarajevo—interrogated and threatened, their personal belongings looted, many personal letters and food parcels taken, and the trucks sent to a nearby town to unload humanitarian aid and the remaining parcels. Luckily no harm was done to any of the truck drivers and their crew.

I naïvely chose to believe that Madelyn's love would make a difference this time and didn't want to miss out on any magic that could help deliver the parcels.

DAY 386

THE letters from Sarajevo stopped arriving again, but I found out through friends that some phone lines were reconnected.

I so much wanted to hear my husband's voice.

I started dialling our home number, endlessly, night after night, with no success. And then one night it went through. It was incredible to talk to each other again, after six months of not hearing each other's voices.

Once we started talking, it was hard to stop.

I told him how Dario had learned to ride a bicycle, how he was already able to read books in English, how much Elena had changed. Although grateful that everything was well and the children were happy and healthy, Goran's voice sounded sad. His children were growing up and he was missing out on all of it.

In Sarajevo everything was still the same. The shelling continued. The siege continued. Goran and my parents were constantly on the verge of not having food and had not received any of my food parcels for many months. I knew from other Bosnian families that our first parcels sent from the UK in February did reach their families in Sarajevo, but mine didn't. There were so many hungry bodies handling the parcels, anyone in the delivery chain could have decided not to pass it onto the next step. It was an unpredictable gamble where I mainly lost, but I kept playing even for the most minimal chance of winning.

Goran told me about his attempt to organise permission papers to leave, but it was not going well. He had asked his manager at work to help him arrange the paperwork to go and visit his family in England, and that instantly changed Goran's work situation. Not only did he not receive his boss's help, he was shortly after dismissed from work. No more pay, however little money that was, and no more of the aid occasionally supplied from his work. Without his work duties, Goran immediately became eligible for army service. Fighting was not something my husband was cut out to do. With his tall and slender body, most certainly he would've been killed the first day he went to battle. I felt it deep in my bones and I feared for him even more.

Our conversation went on for over an hour. At first elated to hear my husband's voice, to know they were all well, afterwards I was anxious and distressed and couldn't sleep the whole night. Not only was I worried about my husband and my parents, knowing how difficult their life circumstances were, how hungry and scared they were, I was also worried about how much money the phone call would cost. It was incredibly hard to stretch out the little amount of welfare money we received on everything the three of us needed, the numerous parcels sent to Sarajevo and the astronomical phone bills. Every time I received a phone bill I was in shock and determined to take more care about how much time I spent on the phone, but the phone was the source of vital information and I couldn't use it any less than I did. A regular chat with the consulate in Manchester to make sure our case was still open, daily calls to anyone who had fresh news from Sarajevo, an occasional chat with Goga to discuss parcels and the conditions in Sarajevo. Bit by bit each phone bill became exorbitant.

Goran's letter subsequent to our phone call was a tiny bit more positive. They received the parcel I sent in June and they were absolutely ecstatic about everything in it. Hoping the parcels would reach Sarajevo without too much delay I took a risk and included some semi-fresh food, cheese, salami, onions and garlic, which brought huge joy to them.

They had the same problems as before. No electricity, no water, no job for Goran, and still no paperwork to leave. I could see from his writing style that he was trying to sound positive but his short abrupt sentences told me more than just their content—he couldn't bear the situation any more. It was now longer than a year since we had left. A year without his family, in a besieged city, at war, with no end in sight and with very little hope of leaving. We were desperate. Both of us. I was beside myself with the worries and stress of not being able to do anything to help him.

I patiently dialled Sarajevo night after night, from late evening until two or three in the morning, when the lines were hypothetically less busy. I could not get through for days and then weeks. But I kept doing it, for the small chance of exchanging a word or two with my husband. And on the nights when it did happen my energy levels would recharge a bit and for a while I would sleep better. Other times, when the television news from Sarajevo was extremely horrific, my inability to check if Goran was still alive drained all the energy from me. I dialled our home number with shaky hands for hours and hours just to hear the busy line, or the phone ringing and no one answering it, or the phone ringing and someone else answering as the lines crossed. Too tired to keep my eyes open I sometimes misdialled a number. A sudden joyful moment of hearing the connection click was followed by the disappointment of wasting money on a wrong number.

With the phone connections unreliable and Željka's brother, who was now in Cumbria, out of Sarajevo and unable to help with the radio amateurs' link any more, Željka searched for other options to hear from her elderly parents. Her American friend, Liza, sent Željka a phone card to connect to Sarajevo via satellite. Željka suggested I ask Madelyn to send me a card like that. I did it reluctantly as I knew the charges would be exorbitant, about seven pounds or twelve American dollars per minute, but the option of getting through quickly was invaluable. I promised myself that I would only use it in an emergency and would keep careful track of the time spent talking.

In the middle of June, the phone card arrived. Excited with the possibility that I could simply dial the number and speak to my husband, I had to check if it really worked as promised.

I dialled the number.

I was connected to a phone exchange from where they dialled the number in Sarajevo I had given them and I was connected at the first try.

Ah, the joy.

I so much wished I could afford to use it more often.

DAY 389

ONE week after our first visit we went back to Guy and Máire's place. Guy, a music producer and engineer, was working on a project with Clem, his colleague. Just like everyone else I met in Cumbria, Clem was interested in hearing our story about the war in Bosnia. He asked me the same question everyone asked, 'Why was Goran not allowed to leave Sarajevo with you and the children?'

'As a man, he needed to stay, to either work or fight with the Bosnian army,' I explained like many times before.

Without too many questions, Clem let me say as much as I wanted to say. And I talked, calmly, as if I were telling someone else's story. Most of the time I could not control my emotions when talking about what had happened to us. To prevent me from crying I usually kept the story sterile, with minimum details. 'No, we didn't expect the war. Yes, it is hard to live so far away from my husband and my parents. It is upsetting to think about what they might be going through. But Goran is glad we are safe and what keeps him alive is the hope to see us soon.' Occasionally though, like this time, stunned by the absurdity of our situation, I detached my emotional self from the narrative as if I was talking about a movie I had seen that had nothing to do with me. When I wasn't emotional I was able to include more distressing details, to present our story more intensely and accurately.

Clem listened intently, with narrowed eyes; he seemed to be absorbing my every word.

Yet again, I didn't expect anything from this conversation. I had met so many people who had asked about our lives, all of them shocked that something like this was happening in the twentieth century and not far from England, all of them wished they could help. But so far no one could.

A couple of weeks went by and then one day Anna showed me two letters with Anglia Television Limited in Norwich letterhead, signed by their News Organiser. The first one for UNPROFOR in Sarajevo, to introduce Goran as an Anglia TV producer, and the second one to certify that the bearer of the letter, Goran Mujkic, was a journalist employed by Anglia TV, England.

Although impressed with the letters and their sincerity, and delighted that someone I had never met would sign them, I had to disappoint Anna.

'The letters alone will not be enough to obtain help from UNPROFOR in Sarajevo,' I explained. 'We will at least need a good quality local press card to go with the letters.'

A few days later Anna walked into our place with an unusual urgency on her face and asked, 'Do you have a photo of Goran, something of passport quality?'

She didn't explain why she needed it except that Guy had asked for it. Hopeful, although skeptical at the same time, I retrieved the only photo of my husband I had: a black and white one from before the war, passport size. I had not deliberately brought it with me when we fled Sarajevo. I found it months later in the only handbag I had taken, stuck in a little pocket, waiting to one day become very valuable. We quickly went into town to make a copy of it. Anna took it back to Guy the same day.

147

I didn't dare hope too much. What could they possibly do? Provide a fake press card that would be of no real use? That was already an old trick in Sarajevo. Or a British passport?

All the possibilities seemed equally surreal and alarming: they could either work or cause damage, depending on the circumstances.

DAY 412

FINALLY, a response from St. James's Palace in London. Signed by the Lady-in-Waiting to Her Royal Highness, the letter stated that regretfully it was not possible for Her Royal Highness to help me personally, but that she sent us her best wishes for the future and hoped that we would soon be reunited. Grateful to receive their response, I was disappointed that yet another hopeful idea had been fruitless.

A letter from the British Immigration office arrived on that same day to our previous address at Old London Road, and then another one, five days later, to our new address in Wordsworth Street. Both of them with the same text, distressing and hard to understand with my limited English: 'You are a person who is liable to be detained.'

I sat on the couch for a long time trying to read into it, but I could not understand it.

What's 'liable' and what's 'detained'? I looked them up in the dictionary. Liable seemed to be like responsible, and detained seemed like arrested, imprisoned. *What am I responsible for? Is this letter saying that I will be arrested?*

Further on: 'You must report to an Immigration Officer at Dover East, at a date and time to be notified.'

What have I done wrong? I could not remember doing anything that could be illegal in any way, but then, I thought, *Who knows what can be brought up against a person who is connected to a country at war?* Was there something in the parcels that I wasn't allowed to send from England?

My brain churned the painful options of what would happen to Dario and Elena if I got imprisoned or deported. Would I be able to leave them with someone in Penrith? The agony continued until Steve came later on that day and explained that it was just a routine letter sent from the Immigration Office as a result of the application for political asylum submitted on our behalf when we entered the UK.

Focused on the daily chores and the battle to get Goran out of Sarajevo, I had not yet put two and two together to realise that our welfare payments and accommodation support were the result of the application for political asylum submitted on our behalf. In the past, these two words had held a harsh meaning to me; they had seemed related to political dissidents, people who, rightly or wrongly, rebelled against the political system in the country of their residence. And now, while my country of birth was at war, defending itself against the forceful attempts to deny its rights to self-government, our life away from the bloodshed had made us asylum seekers. Unexpectedly, political asylum became our pathway towards receiving help.

And we needed help. Most importantly I needed help in persuading UNPROFOR in Sarajevo that Goran was a journalist who therefore should be allowed to leave Sarajevo.

Anna and I asked Guy to send a fax to a UN official in Sarajevo, whose name Goran gave me earlier, who was sympathetic towards Sarajevans and would not cause trouble if everything looked legal. The fax carried the letterhead of Prometheus Productions, a film and television production house from Penrith.

12th July 1993

Dear Carlos,

I would like to request an airlift for GORAN MUJKIC a journalist who is working on a documentary our company is making for Channel Four Television in London.

He has an International Press Pass (details to follow as required).

We would be grateful if our colleague could be given transportation to the airport in Sarajevo to board the plane to Split.

Thank you for your help.

Yours sincerely,

Clem Shaw, Producer

I still thought this was not enough. We needed strong evidence that Goran was a journalist.

What could that be?

An article published under his name, in a newspaper? How could we organise that? Who would be so sympathetic to our story as to publish an article under Goran's name? It was not conceivable that any of the big British papers would do that. Maybe a local paper in Cumbria would do it, but would that be a bit too obvious? An article published in a newspaper from the area where his wife lived? I phoned Madelyn. She lived in a small community on Friday Island, in the US, where she and her husband ran a bakery and café. I assumed that she might have all sorts of local acquaintances and connections. I asked if she could use her contacts to publish an article in a newspaper on the island where she lived.

Madelyn enquired around. *The Journal of the San Juan Islands* was willing to do that for us. I translated parts of Goran's letters, faxed them to Madelyn together with a copy of Goran's photograph, and less than a week later I received several copies of *The Journal of the San Juan Islands* from July 14, 1993, with the headline 'Sarajevo journalist's letter to family is full of despair', signed by Goran's full name and with his photograph.

Sarajevo journalist's letter to family is full of despair: No water, no food, little hope

By Goran Mujkic

My only loving one,

I was not able to continue writing last time (May 4), I was in a very bad mood. I am a little better now—your parcel has arrived. We were almost without any food, so it came at the very last moment. At last something better happened to us. But what a long walk I had to do to get the parcel: behind the buildings on the other side of the river to the railway station (I was so lucky, I could hear the sound of sniper bullets but they missed me), then up to the Kosevsko Hill, then down to Krajiska Street, then Tepebasina Street, Gorica, Lupanjaska, then near the grammar school to the hospital. It's about four to five miles I think. And, of course the same way for coming back home...

But it was worth it. Everything in the parcel was wonderful, everything. You would not believe what we had before the parcel arrived: just a little bit of flour and a little bit of oil—only because we don't use cooking oil for light (as other people do), but only for the food. We don't have electricity again (it looks like it will be for a longer time again). We usually go to bed as soon as the night comes, and that's about eight o'clock. That is a way to save candles and matches, if there are any.

Should I say that we don't have water as well?

Oh, I feel so sick when I think too much about this war and what we can expect in the next few months. All my hope has been disappearing. This town and these people are forgotten by the whole world. Nobody is able to get out of the city. How long can we survive all these terrible things? I am so afraid it is going to be worse, not better.

The only thing that keeps me alive is the hope I'll be with you again. These fifteen months of separation look like fifteen years. It is so hard, so hard. You cannot imagine the living here.

I know how hard it must be for you, alone with two children, but we just don't have any choice. The thought that you and the children are safe gives me a tiny feeling of comfort. I love you so much, don't ever forget it. Take care of our children; give them kisses and hugs on my behalf.

I love you all very, very much.
Your Goran

The article had a street name I couldn't recognise until I realised it was misspelled, and a few grammatical errors. Some phrases sounded more like word-by-word translation than a text in English, but I assumed they left it all there for authenticity.

I immediately sent a couple of letters to Goran with the newspaper cuttings, using different mail options. One letter was sent to Split, leaving it to Goga to find a safe way to forward it to Sarajevo. Another letter was sent using ADRA UK, the Adventist Development and Relief Agency. I often sent letters and parcels with ADRA, but it was never guaranteed that they would be delivered. The trucks to Sarajevo were often randomly stopped and the parcels and letters, even the trucks, were confiscated by whatever para-army was in charge that decided Sarajevans should not be helped. More often than not the supplies of food, and such important letters of hope and love, were not delivered. The food ended up on the black market, but what happened to the letters and photographs?

I hated to think that some nasty, drunk soldiers laughed at the photographs of my children and me, and made fun of our caring messages.

DAY 423

WE were in the middle of summer and school holidays. I could not afford to introduce any small change to our daily routines as everything was costing money. Day after day Dario played outside with the Bosnian-English mix of kids. Sometimes he went to Anna's for a day, and that was it. Elena was mainly with me, demanding my time and attention to entertain her. Bored with the same scenery around her, she played dress-ups by herself, putting on anything and everything she could find in the drawers, messing up our bedroom, but giving me some spare time to think.

We were all tired of the repetitiveness of our days, when Jacqui phoned.

'Hello, how are you all?' she said in her chirpy voice. 'I was wondering if you'd like to spend a few days at our farm? It would be a nice change for you, and the children will love it—I could pick you up this afternoon.'

Satisfied with the progress of my plan, Goran's article published and sent to Sarajevo, and the fax sent to UNPROFOR, I gladly accepted Jacqui's invitation. I needed a break from thinking, planning, phoning, and the children needed a change from being in our flat and around the apartment building all the time.

'Thank you so much, we'd love that,' I replied. 'We need a couple of hours to pack a few things, so maybe after four this afternoon?'

'See you around four then.'

Excited with the idea, we packed for the short trip. Elena just pulled everything out from the drawers, Dario asked me questions about what to take, while I thought about what I could bake for our hosts to thank them for their generosity. After checking the kitchen cupboards for the ingredients I decided to make *hurmašice*, a simple and cheap dessert, and a distinctive example of Bosnian cuisine. I mixed the ingredients and baked this shortbread-like cake while heating the syrup on the stove, made from sugar, water and lemon slices.

The flat was full of energy and loud conversation, the aroma of cakes from the oven spreading in the air, when the phone rang.

It was the local newspaper, *Evening News and Star.* They asked if I could do an interview the following day. Not wanting to waste the opportunity to have our story in the paper again, but also not wanting to disappoint the children and cancel or postpone the visit to Jacqui's place, I suggested they come to the farm in Culgaith to do the interview. I expected them to decline, although Culgaith was not far from Penrith, but they agreed.

I was so thankful to be in Jacqui's cheerful company, to share the beautiful country charm of their home, the big space and the activities the farm offered the children. They collected eggs for breakfast every morning and we ate them fried or in omelettes with grilled sausages from the local butcher. Lunch was light, a slice of bread and cheese, but dinner was a big family affair around their enormous dining table, the four of them and the three of us, the table covered with plates filled with delicious food: roast meat, baked potatoes and all kinds of vegetables. Everyone loved the *hurmašice*. The children enjoyed the change of menu and I did too. Not only did I like what we ate, I appreciated that I didn't have to prepare it. I did help out here and there, peeling potatoes, chopping vegetables, and cleaning up after meals, but it was mainly Jacqui who prepared meals for us. She was abundant with energy, full of happiness and joy.

The positive energy in their home made me happier. Distracted from my endless worries and anxieties, I tried to be as happy as I could. We talked around the dinner table, the four little children teased each other and giggled, and Jacqui played piano for us after dinner. It felt as if we had all known one another for a long time, like we were close friends or even relatives who had come to visit. The marvellous, almost forgotten feeling of being close to someone, of being loved.

We talked about religion. Jacqui was a practising Christian; she went to church every Sunday morning and was active in the church community. Very carefully, inspecting my face for a reaction, one evening she suggested, 'Going to church might be beneficial to you. It's calming. Why don't you try it? You don't have to belong to a church, it doesn't matter which one you go to.'

Raised in a non-religious society, in a secular country, I had trouble accepting the idea of God. I did believe, and still do, that something bigger than the life we see and experience exists, a universal energy maybe, but I could not refer to it as God. I respect everyone's beliefs but I cannot relate to a religion—Christianity, Islam, Judaism, or any other. I do like how I feel in a church though. The thick silence that can almost be touched, the freshness of the air, the echo of sound. I never miss the opportunity to light a candle when I am in a church, for the health of the living, and the peace of the dead. And I don't care which church it is. If there were only one religion in the world and its practice could be selected based on what parts of it we liked, I would perhaps accept it. But knowing that religions separate the world, cause wars, and immensely intensified the war that I ran away from, I was not ready to open up to it. Still, reluctant to throw away the possibility of getting closer to any real or imaginary source of help, I agreed to go to the local church in Penrith.

Jacqui organised for her friends to meet us there so that we wouldn't feel isolated, and on Sunday morning the three of us, dressed up in our best clothes, went to the Penrith Methodist Church at the end of our street. We were seated in the first row, on the slightly elevated podium on the right-hand side of the altar.

I felt tense and observed. I could read a question in their eyes, 'Who is this young woman that we've never seen before?' Could they work out that I didn't know what I was doing there? Unaccustomed to the formality of the situation, the children were fidgety. Dario looked in all directions, inspecting the construction details; Elena swung her legs in their white stockings, too short to touch the ground. Occasionally she managed to hit the timber screen in front of us, and a soft thump echoed throughout the church. I would then put my hand on her knee and hold it—she would stop swinging her legs, but as soon as I moved my hand away she started again. I tried to focus on the service, but mainly just kept an eye on the children, afraid that they would talk too loudly and everyone would turn to look at us. Dario softly whispered, 'How much longer?' Elena said a bit louder, 'I want to go home…' I held their hands, gently smiling. 'Just a bit longer, please don't talk.' We managed to last until the end of the service without an incident. I politely excused myself from staying for the coffee and biscuits, explaining that the children were restless. And that was the end of our religious education.

A few days later, the interview with *Evening News and Star* was published on the centrefold, 'Never forget, I love you', with several photographs of the children and me, taken around Jacqui's farm and in their beautifully decorated living room, sitting on their sofa upholstered with striking multi-coloured fabric that matched the curtains behind me. We looked so normal and almost happy except for the deep sadness in our eyes. Even Elena, who was unaware of our situation and perfectly happy with her life, who was usually bright and bubbly and laughing loudly, had somehow ended up sad and melancholic in the main close-up photo. The long article described our idyllic life before the war, our love, our mixed ethnic origins and their insignificance until the nightmare started in April 1992.

Life was sweet for Edita and her husband Goran in pre-war Sarajevo. Not surprisingly, they took it all for granted.

Edita will never take anything for granted again. If happiness comes her way again, it will be savoured hungrily.

Because Edita now knows what it is like to live in hell. As long as her husband Goran is trapped in the misery of Sarajevo, Edita will be in torment.

A few of Goran's letters were published, some parts of the letter published in the San Juan Islands' newspaper and a part from an earlier letter that unexpectedly arrived a few days prior to our stay at the farm, which I quickly translated into English for the newspaper.

Sarajevo, May 4, 1993 (Tuesday)

My only loving one,

You can't imagine how I miss you, how I need you. I miss you so much that it hurts. It really hurts. You and our lovely children are everything I have and I can't be with you.

I have been watching very often that little two-year-old girl in our neighbourhood, the way she speaks, the way she walks and runs... She is the same age as our Elena! I can't write about it, it upsets me too much.

The only thing that keeps me alive is the hope I'll be with you again.

Reading the article that quoted my words and Goran's letters made me brutally aware of the hurtful and hard journey we were going through.

DAY 428

ON Monday, Anna appeared, beaming with happiness. Standing in the doorway, as if she didn't want to waste any time walking in, she handed me a passport-like document. As Ellen's blonde head appeared behind her mum, Elena jumped from the floor where she played with her toys and they went straight to my bedroom to start their dress-up game.

'What is it?' I asked Anna with a trace of hesitation. With its red cover it looked like a passport. The fear of the consequences of bearing a forged passport and the hope that it might get Goran out of Sarajevo made my legs shake.

'Have a look at it,' said Anna, unable to wipe the smile from her face.

What I held in my hands was an International Press Card with Goran's name on it. I could not believe my eyes. It looked so authentic, with Goran's photo, his true date of birth, and his true place of birth—Sarajevo. It stated his nationality as Bosnian, and his legal domicile as England.

I looked at Anna with disbelief in my eyes. 'How did you manage to get this?'

'Guy organised it.'

I turned it around, looked at it from all angles, searching for a sign of forgery. But the press card was legitimate, signed by the General Secretary of the National Union of Journalists. It certified that Goran was a professional journalist and requested from all authorities and affiliated organisations of journalists to extend their assistance to the bearer of this card in his mission.

'It's real,' said Anna. 'It's a lawful document.'

'But, how did he do it?'

I could not imagine what could have been involved in producing this. Even Anna didn't know all the details. She showed me the document that Guy had to provide to the issuer as a promise that the press card would only be used to help Goran escape Sarajevo and that it would be promptly returned to the issuer as soon as Mr Mujkic returned with it to the UK. Later on I learned that many people from Anglia TV and Channel Four had made it happen. Most of them, or maybe all of them, knew that Goran was not a journalist, but they wanted to help him escape the war and reunite with his wife and children.

That week Anna and I took a train to London to take the precious card directly to John B, an Englishman who we knew was about to go to Sarajevo. Determined to help Bosnian people, but not wanting to take actual part in the conflict, John had been regularly travelling to Sarajevo, carrying letters, money and small parcels from Sarajevans outside the siege to their families and friends in Sarajevo.

Anna and I didn't want to risk sending the press card to John by mail. Moreover, we wanted him to know what he was taking with him and why.

Upon seeing the press card John inspected it carefully from each side and asked me questions that made me really nervous about the whole plan.

'Why have you decided to have his nationality declared as Bosnian?'

I didn't know. I was not even asked what my husband's nationality was. And if I was, I wouldn't think that he could be anything else but Bosnian. *How could that be the wrong choice?*

'Why are you asking?' I stuttered.

He looked at me but didn't respond. Afraid of what he might say I left my question unanswered. It was too late to change it now anyway. John was meant to leave London in a few days, first to fly to Split, and from there find any transport he could to Sarajevo.

Afraid that a letter included with the document could make it too obvious that the press card was not for a real journalist, I did not want to send my letter to Goran with the press card. I needed to find a different way of communicating to Goran what I had sent him with John. A month or so earlier, I had organised a fake press card to be sent to Goran and immediately afterwards realised that I had made a terrible mistake, that he could be arrested for having it. So I sent him a message not to use it. And now I had to send him a message that this new press card was valid and that he should use it. If I just said, 'Use this new *parcel*, not the old one,' and the messages or press cards were delivered in the wrong order, that could cause a disastrous mistake. Fearful to send a very obvious message using the words 'press card', and describing each one, I decided to refer to the press cards as medications, and said in my message to Goran: 'The medications in the clear plastic bag that I sent you earlier were out of date, they could be harmful and you must not use them. I am now sending new *international medicines in red packaging* and they are safe to be used.'

The clear plastic bag referred to the small plastic sleeve in which the fake card was delivered, and the red packaging referred to the red cover of the lawful press card.

I dictated it to Goga over the phone and she forwarded it to Sarajevo. My message reached Goran before John came to Sarajevo and thoroughly confused him. What medications? He didn't ask for any medications to be sent, what was I talking about? It made him a little worried about the state of my mind.

Not knowing what had been prepared in England and was on its way to him, Goran continued searching for ways to flee. Several options were on stand-by: leaving with the next Jewish convoy if he could organise a place there, a few close friends with connections in the Croatian embassy and Croatian government were trying to help him obtain a Croatian passport. Some people promised to help if he could provide a couple of thousand German marks.

None of these plans progressed past the initial steps. All the scenarios to obtain the permit looked promising until someone in the chain of favours would change their mind or the escape could not be executed anymore or the important link could not be reached. Goran's descriptions of his numerous plans and the people involved confused me rather than encouraged me that our reunion was close. His short sentences jumped from one topic to another as if he was always writing in a hurry. Sometimes Goran's letters were indeed scribbled in a hurry, after he heard that someone was about to leave town and could take a few letters, but they were mainly written in the form of a diary. His thoughts became unclear after mulling over so many things that troubled him. It often seemed to me as though he was primarily trying to convince himself that this or that plan would work, that everything was okay, that he was positive about our future together.

His and my parents' lives revolved around receiving my parcels with food, and trying to prepare meals that weren't completely awful to eat, which, without a regular supply of electricity and water, was often impossible. The weather in July was hot, so using wood to cook was impractical, and whenever they had power for a short time and could cook, they could only prepare one meal at a time as without electricity the fridge could not be used to keep the cooked food fresh for long.

The only genuinely positive thing, apart from just being alive, was the promise of Goran completing his medicals for the Australian visa application.

A small step forward to achieving our final goal.

DAY 431

FOR a very long two weeks after Guy sent the fax to UNPROFOR in Sarajevo we received no reply. Nothing. I started doubting our plan. *Is everything we are doing pointless? We can't trick UNPROFOR.*

In a letter, Goran explicitly confirmed that the escape could only be organised from the outside. There was nothing he could do from Sarajevo. Allegedly it was possible to pay for a pass in Ancona, Italy, almost like buying a ticket for a Sarajevo–Ancona flight. Politicians and journalists used the flights regularly to go in and out of Sarajevo. Some people Goran knew were working on it for themselves. It was just that he had no exact information about who, where and how. He was trying to find himself a new job, to have a small source of income, and to keep himself busy and safe from being recruited for the army. The letter was, just as all those before, a mix of despair and hope. Plans and wishes for all of us to be together for Dario's birthday at the end of September mixed with descriptions of the complexities and unknowns about the possibility of his leaving. At least they received four of the five food parcels I sent. A little improvement to their daily menus:

dried vegetables, vitamins, dried fruit and nuts, even a small bottle of whisky that surprisingly wasn't stolen from the parcels.

I worried that sending Goran's press card with John might not help. Having a press card did not mean that he could go to a travel agency and buy a ticket out of Sarajevo. He needed to be airlifted with the help of the UN Protection Forces. That was the only legal way of leaving town. UNPROFOR needed to be persuaded that Goran was a true journalist, unlike other Sarajevans who tried to escape using fake press cards. We had to continue on with convincing the UN in Sarajevo to airlift him as soon as possible. We wanted to leave no doubt in presenting everything we could to make him look like a journalist so he could escape the war.

While Elena was asleep in the bedroom for her morning nap, and the television was on at a low volume, I tried to get some rest in my favourite armchair, drifting in and out of sleep in between thoughts about what more could be done to help Goran flee Sarajevo.

The sound of grenades from the television made me open my eyes. I sat up in the chair and moved forward to hear the newsreader.

'Yesterday was the worst day for Sarajevans since the commencement of the siege. The incredible number of 3,777 grenades fired at Sarajevo from several hundreds of mortars and tanks on the surrounding hills caused great damage. Many civilians were killed, many buildings demolished, including hospitals.'

My heartbeat increased. 3,777 grenades in twenty-four hours, that's two to three every minute.

A scene from Sarajevo was thumping with boom-boom-boom in the newsreader's background.

With every thump, those few people on the streets hunched their shoulders lower and ran faster through a fog of dust to find refuge.

But where could one hide when grenades fell every twenty to thirty seconds?

Long after the news switched to a different topic I stared at the screen. Where was my husband yesterday? What would happen to Sarajevo and everyone who was still left there? Where is this hatred coming from? It seemed that the torture of Sarajevans with hunger was not enough, that the aim of the Army of Republika Srpska was to destroy Sarajevo fully, and forever.

On this rare occasion, I dared to use Madelyn's Sprint card to make a costly one-minute call to check up on Goran and my parents. They were fine. I didn't ask how it felt to live through that many grenades in one day. I didn't mention the press card to Goran, partly because I was afraid of the phone lines being monitored, partly because I didn't want to give him false hope in case the card never arrived.

The sound of fallen grenades echoed in my head for hours after. While I dressed Elena, while we walked to the supermarket, while I chopped vegetables, while I folded the washing. Boom-boom-boom.

Anna called that evening.

'Guy had a phone call from UNPROFOR,' she said.

'What did they say?' I asked.

'It was an official from UNPROFOR in Sarajevo. Guy said her name was Yarmila, he couldn't pick up her surname.'

Keen to hear every little detail, hopeful for good news, I listened attentively without interrupting Anna with additional questions.

'She explained that Carlos had been on leave for five weeks, hence their delayed response, and that they wanted to help Goran leave Sarajevo.'

Anna waited for me to say something.

'That's good news, but surely someone else could have helped too.'

'Yes, I agree,' Anna said. 'But they need proof that Goran works for Channel Four; they need a letter from Channel Four stating it.'

'That would be hard to organise I imagine…' My voice trembled. There was always something impossible to produce and every plan fell short of completion.

'Well, the thing is, it doesn't work like that with Channel 4. Guy explained to Yarmila that Channel 4 did not explicitly employ people; they only paid for the programs created by independent producers. But he promised to fax a letter explaining Goran's engagement with Channel 4.'

I relaxed. There was still a hope this plan could work.

The fax was sent from Prometheus Productions to Carlos at UNPROFOR Civil Affairs, on July 23, signed by Clem, testifying that Goran worked with them for Channel 4 Television.

By then I had also found out, from talking to the men who had left Sarajevo, that Goran's international press card was not enough, that in order to obtain transportation he needed a UN pass. In the fax to UNPROFOR, Guy asked for the UN pass to be issued.

DAY 449

EVEN though John had not yet arrived in Sarajevo with Goran's press card, Anna, Guy and I were hopeful that he would be there very soon. It concerned us that we had no further news from UNPROFOR since Yarmila called and Guy sent back the fax confirming that Goran worked for Prometheus Productions on assignment for Channel 4. I asked Guy to send another fax to Sarajevo, this time to Miss Boyd, UNPROFOR's spokesperson, and to reference the phone call with Yarmila, who worked at the Press and Spokesman's Office.

In his one-page letter faxed to Miss Boyd on August 6, Guy included a detailed description of Goran's role in their production for Channel 4 Television.

I feel I must explain to you that Mr Mujkic has been engaged in research for film being made by ourselves for Channel 4 TV in the U.K., and will probably be seen all over the world. The film deals with the environmental and social impact on the region, as well as expressing the feelings of the people, following the events that have overtaken them in Sarajevo.

Goran Mujkic has been working with us for over a year now; he and his family are U.K. residents, and live in Penrith, a northern town in England. Because Goran has needed to be in Sarajevo, his nationality has made it difficult for him to move around freely, and more recently, has found himself to be virtually trapped. Under normal circumstances, his international press card, issued by NUJ in London, suffices to obtain access in and out of locations, naturally pursued by journalists on a day-to-day basis.

However, this understandably has changed. If not only for the film company, where he is key to the project, his family and Prometheus are extremely anxious that a U. N. pass be allocated to Goran, in order to secure his transportation to Split. This is the only way that he can return to the U.K.

Furthermore, Guy underlined how Yarmila, when they spoke, had fully understood the situation, for which Guy expressed his gratitude, and suggested that if they were in agreement, he would like to include both Miss Boyd and Yarmila in the film they were making. He asked Miss Boyd for help to issue a UN press card for Goran, which would allow him to get transportation to Split, from where he would find his way to the UK.

Understanding that issuing the press card and transportation was costly, Guy offered to help with the cost of transport and proposed to meet with Miss Boyd in Zagreb, if needed, to finalise the details. A copy of Goran's International Press card was faxed through, along with the details of his address in England.

While reading Guy's letter, I almost started to believe that Goran was truly working on a film for Channel 4. I was astonished with the accuracy and simultaneous impreciseness of the letter. It sounded so believable. Why weren't UNPROFOR doing everything they could to help this man who was trapped in Sarajevo by pure coincidence and whose business partners and family in England were worried about him?

One more fax was sent from Channel 4 Television to UNPROFOR in Sarajevo confirming that Prometheus Productions was making a documentary for Channel 4 in its Sunday night environmental slot, asking 'Could you please extend any such facility you are able to the above company and its associates in the making of this program?'

At the time these faxes were sent, Goran finally met John in Sarajevo. I received the news from my dad when, impatient to hear from them, I phoned home for a thirty-second update. He didn't explicitly tell me the names or the details, he just said that Goran was staying with a friend in town and that there was an English journalist in Sarajevo who had sent a message to Goran to meet him. I knew what it meant.

I contacted John's wife in London and she confirmed John had indeed reached Sarajevo. I was restless to know if Goran had received the press card and what he thought about it.

A few days later I decided to use Madelyn's Sprint card to phone home again, thinking it would only be a minute or so to ask if he'd met John yet. We ended up talking for twenty-two expensive minutes. With this astoundingly great news, we were too excited to think about time.

Goran mentioned that lately he had been looking into a new possibility to leave through the eight hundred metres long, low and narrow, Tunnel of Hope, dug out from the sieged residential area outside of Sarajevo airport, underneath the airport runway, to the outside of the sieged town. The tunnel was built to avoid crossing the runway, which, although controlled by the UN, was exposed to snipers and unsafe to use. It allowed for humanitarian aid and war supplies to be brought to town and for people to get in and out. However, to access the tunnel and leave Sarajevo a permit was required from the Bosnian government and it could not be obtained unless there was a genuine reason to leave. With the international press card in his hand, he was no longer annoyed that according to the Bosnian government, being separated from his wife and two children for longer than a year was not a legitimate enough reason to obtain such permission.

'Now I finally understand what you wanted to tell me.'

We laughed about my confusing message related to different medications. 'I was really worried about you; your message didn't make any sense at all. I'm relieved to know that you're well. I can't wait to be with you. This thing I have in my hand will get me out. I know it.'

DAY 457

GORAN had sent about fifty of our family photos with John. He carefully selected the most special ones from our albums. The events from our twelve years together and the births and lives of our two children compressed into fifty photographs. With them he included a miniscule plastic box with Dario's first baby tooth. Our most precious possessions.

When I called London to check if John had arrived, his wife said, 'No, he hasn't arrived yet. Unfortunately, he was robbed on his trip back through Bosnia and his valuable camera and other possessions were taken.'

'I'm so sorry,' I said. 'The most important thing is that John's not harmed.'

I assumed that our photographs and the precious little tooth were stolen too. But they weren't. John mailed it all as soon as he returned to London. It symbolically arrived on the day of Elena's third birthday. In Goran's letter included with the photographs, dated August 10, he wrote how so beside himself with happiness he was with fresh hope of escape, that he almost could not believe what John had given him.

When I phoned John to thank him for what he'd done for us, and for the letter and the photos that he had brought back, he told me that Goran was in good shape, positive and in a good mood. A little boost of energy for me to get through the birthday celebration.

Despite the complexity of the situation that we were going through, and my enormous fatigue, I decided to throw a small party for Elena. She was too little to miss her birthday celebration. I baked a fancy looking cake in the shape of a daisy, bought some nuts, potato crisps, ice-cream and cordial, and prepared a little party bag and a balloon for each child to take home. Modest, but festive.

While I prepared for the party, I was reminded of Elena's first birthday in Sarajevo, the whole family together, birthday cake, singing, presents, Goran taking a video of her first steps. All of us with big smiles in the video. No one could imagine, not in our most incredible dreams, that nine months later we would be separated by war and would celebrate Elena's next two birthdays without Goran, one in Split, the next one in England. I wished with all my heart to celebrate Elena's fourth birthday in Melbourne, with her father.

The birthday invitations stated that the party was from five to seven in the evening, but those who couldn't make it in the evening popped in during the day. In between the visits I hurried to clean the flat, stick balloons on the walls, organise the table and party bags, do the last finishing touches on the cake. At ten to five, sweaty from rushing around, I had just enough time to have a shower and change when the doorbell rang. Jacqui and her children arrived, all three grinning, hands full of presents, ready to have fun. I didn't expect anyone to turn up before five-fifteen! In Bosnia it was customary to be around fifteen minutes late to all parties, to give the hosts a little more time in case they were running late. Of course I hadn't thought about checking what's expected in England. I must've looked shocked. Jacqui had one quick look at me and asked, 'Is everything alright?' I quickly changed my facial expression, smiled, let them in and excused myself for five minutes to refresh and change my clothes.

That night, after so many sleepless nights in anticipation of John's safe arrival to Sarajevo, after seeing the photos that recollected our life together in Sarajevo and celebrating Elena's birthday, I was literally on the edge of fainting. I felt as if I would collapse and never wake up. The physical and emotional exhaustion were massive.

But the battle wasn't over.

I hoped that, on his next trip to Sarajevo, John would be able to help Goran leave with him. And for that, we needed to have all Goran's papers in check, the UN pass being the most important one. We needed to continue convincing UNPROFOR that Goran was a true journalist who was needed in England.

I tried to mobilise and include anyone and everyone who could bring additional help and attention to what we were trying to achieve. I never missed the chance to be interviewed by the local paper. More articles were published in the *Evening News and Star* with our pictures, painful details of our separation and the difficult life in Sarajevo. Although embarrassed with the sensational tone of the articles, I was pleased to see our story published, always hopeful that it would serve its purpose and attract attention.

Optimistic that our hard work to get Goran out of Sarajevo would soon bring results, I started planning to bring the rest of our family to a safe place. I secured a letter of financial support for my parents from Anna and her husband, and organised a letter from a solicitor to the British Ambassador in Zagreb requesting help in re-uniting us. Then I prepared letters of support for my parents-in-law, and for my sister-in-law and her family. Copies of these letters were sent to Sarajevo, with the great hope that they would help them arrange their own escapes.

DAY 463

EVERY atom of my body was stretched beyond its limits. Yet I hoped we were only a tiny thread away from success and knew we had to continue the momentum. Every couple of days I rang UNPROFOR and pleaded with Guy to call them too, to keep asking for help, to beg for help.

In the last week of August, Guy was informed that UNPROFOR had prepared a UN press card for Goran. Finally, a step forward.

By then, the phone lines between Switzerland and Sarajevo had re-opened. I was relieved to stop using Madelyn's phone card for the expensive satellite connection.

I called an ex-colleague from work in Sarajevo, who now lived in Switzerland. She called Goran from a different phone line and held the phones together with microphones and speakers in a head-to-toe position. The double connection was difficult, the conversation hard to understand. While we struggled to work out what the other person was saying, the extremely high cost of the two international connections that I had to pay for loomed in my head.

I explained to Goran the details of where the press pass could be collected and we agreed that I would call back in five days, allowing him enough time to safely go from our place to the General Post Office building in the centre of Sarajevo to get it.

Five days later the two-legged call to Sarajevo could not connect. We tried several times during the day, but the phone on the other side, in Sarajevo, rang and no one picked up. The level of anxiety in my body interfered with my breathing. I walked endlessly from one side of the living room to another, then to the window, then checked the time to assess how much longer before I could try calling Sarajevo again.

Why was no one picking up? My parents must be there; my mum never left the flat, not even to go down to the basement when the shelling was so heavy that it was dangerous to stay in the flat. Her health would not allow her to go down and up five levels of stairs in a hurry. It was equally as risky for her to walk the stairs as it was to stay in the flat and wait for the imminent danger and fear of death to be over. If no one was picking up the phone, what did that mean? *Are they all dead? Has something happened to one of them and the others don't want to talk to me, so as not to upset me? Has my mum had another stroke, a fatal one this time? Has something happened to my dad while going to get water? Has Goran been injured or killed on his way to retrieve the UN pass? Why did I ever insist on getting him the pass when moving around town was so dangerous? Why could I not wait a bit longer? Surely the war will end soon and we will be reunited without this extra risk?*

Hundreds of terrifying thoughts ran in circles through my head. I was unable to do anything else; I sat on the couch, letting Elena run around the house. Every couple of hours I rang Switzerland and we tried to connect to our flat in Sarajevo, but there was still no answer. Fear ran through my body. I hardly slept that night. *Something terrible must've happened.*

The following day Goran picked up at our first attempt to connect. I felt lightheaded from the relief of hearing his voice.

'I called yesterday and the phone kept ringing, no one picked up. Where were you? Why was no one at home? Are you all okay?'

'We are fine, we are okay. We didn't have electricity yesterday, the phone didn't ring.'

Relief. No one had been injured; no one had had a stroke.

'Did you get the UN pass?'

'Yes, I picked up the UN pass two days ago. It's not the right one. It's a local press card. I can use it to move more or less freely in Sarajevo, but it's inadequate to get a place on a UN flight.'

How was he issued the wrong pass? And why? UNPROFOR knew that the press card was to be used to leave Sarajevo. How could they make such a banal mistake?

There was no point in analysing it. Whether it was a genuine oversight caused by miscommunication somewhere along the line of the many handovers of information, or someone's intentional attempt to prevent Goran's escape, the press card was worthless.

Once again, it looked as if we were trying to achieve the impossible.

The people in the UNPROFOR office weren't helpful. It was irrelevant whether they didn't believe our story, didn't have enough time or didn't care to produce what Goran needed. In any case we weren't moving forward. In the two weeks since John had brought the press card to Sarajevo no progress had been made. Guy must've been getting tired of my continuous calls to check if UNPROFOR had contacted him and my pleading to send them yet another fax, make yet another call. All this was costing him a huge amount of money and it seemed fruitless.

My own phone bills were excruciatingly high, in excess of one hundred pounds every month. Two hardship grants from social security, several hundred pounds intended for household items, were spent on phone bills instead. Basic items and clothes were less important than finding out how my husband and my parents were. Certainly less important than letting my husband know about a vital next step in our plan for his escape. Two pairs of jeans, one pair of runners, a couple of t-shirts and one jumper were enough for me. The only other clothing I had was a pair of fashionable beige leggings with a long matching woollen jumper that arrived in a parcel from Rome from my friend Ziza. Dario and Elena's clothes were either hand-me-downs from Cumbrian families or from second-hand shops. Any household items we had were provided by our English friends and their friends and relatives. I didn't care if my plates were nice and matching, if we had enough cutlery, or enough sheets. We managed with what we had. We weren't hungry; we weren't cold. All we wanted was to be re-united with Goran.

DAY 485

UNSURE if Guy would want to continue with the story and if persisting with it would bring the solution, I had to think of other plans.

Desperate to find a new thread of hope, I asked Madelyn if Dennis, her newspaper contact in *The Journal of the San Juan Islands,* could produce a letter for an assignment for Goran, as a journalist, to go to Pale, the small town on the hills above Sarajevo that was now in the heart of Bosnian Serb Headquarters territory, to interview someone of high importance from the Government of Republika Srpska, a territory in Bosnia under the control of the Bosnian Serb army. My idea was for such a letter to take Goran out of town so that after the interview he might be free to travel to Serbia, instead of returning to Sarajevo. The plan was quite naïve. There was more chance of Goran being arrested and tortured by the Bosnian Serb army in Pale than that they would welcome him to conduct a political interview and allow him to continue on his journey out of the sieged city.

Within a week I received a fax with a letter from *The Journal of the San Juan Islands*.

This is a request for assistance involving Goran Mujkic, who is serving as a correspondent for my newspaper, The Journal of the San Huan Islands, in Washington State, United States of America.

Mr Mujkic has been engaged to travel to Pale, near Sarajevo, Bosnia and Herzegovina, where he will seek an interview with either the Minister of Health or the Minister of Social Security at the Serbian Political Headquarters.

If the reader of this correspondence could help him gain safe passage in order to achieve his goal and mission, it would be greatly appreciated.

Another letter, addressed to Goran Mujkic, Reporter, explained his task directly to him: to get an interview with the Minister of Health or the Minister of Social Security at the Serb Political Headquarters in Pale.

Unfortunately, once again I didn't explain well enough what I had wanted, I left it to Dennis to put the letter together. With the complicated relationships amongst Bosnian Muslims, Croats and Serbs, hard to comprehend for anyone who wasn't from the former Yugoslavia, Dennis had mixed up who was who. The letter said that Goran's interview with the Serb Minister in Pale was to provide detailed information about the status of the health and welfare of the residents of Sarajevo, something the Bosnian Serb Political Headquarters in Pale were absolutely not interested in. Quite the opposite, they did everything they could so that the health and welfare of Sarajevans was the worst it could be. The letter mentioned a large Serbian, Croatian and Bosnian population in the area of San Juan Islands who held much interest in what was occurring in Goran's country. In reality, two thirds of such a population anywhere in the world and equally in San Juan Islands could not care less what the Bosnian Serb Political Headquarters in Pale thought. But I had no choice—there was no time to ask for corrections. I sent both letters to John B, who was about to go back to Sarajevo. I was hopeful that maybe John could find a way to use the letters to help Goran leave town.

As the days went by I became more and more depressed with the situation. Why weren't the UN helping Goran get on a flight? He had an international press card. He had an article published in a US newspaper. They had numerous faxes from Guy describing Goran's important role in the documentary they were making. What else did they need to believe the story?

During another visit to Jacqui's farm, while listening to the complex details of our situation and my fears that we were heading nowhere with all our attempts, Jacqui mentioned Jim, a local Church Army officer. Knowing my attitude towards religion, Jacqui was cautious with her description of Jim and his apparent special connection with God, a special power to talk to Him directly. She asked if I would agree to meet Jim and pray with him.

It made me uncomfortable to imagine myself praying. It seemed a double betrayal: on one side a betrayal of my own views on religion, and on the other a betrayal of a true believer by giving him the impression that I believed too. But I accepted it without hesitation. Nothing was worthless and anything that could increase our chances to reunite should be performed. If I needed to pray, I would pray.

On the agreed day that Jim was free to see me, Jacqui drove us to her farm. I brought a little photo of Goran as Jim requested. I was nervous and apprehensive. Other than a few scenes from movies, and seeing both my grandmothers, when I was a young child, moving rosaries in their hands and whispering something, I had never seen anyone pray in real life. I didn't know what to expect, what to do, what to say.

Jim came on time. In ordinary clothes, corduroy trousers and a warm jacquard jumper, he looked like any other man his age. That surprised me a bit. I expected him to look different, to wear special clothes, a black cloak maybe. *Can someone who looks so ordinary really have a special connection with God?*

We sat at the table and Jim started praying, while I looked at the pattern of the tablecloth in front of me. Jim talked to God about our story, about my longing to rescue my husband from the war and reunite us, using clear and common words. The Latin I had heard in the movies was absent; there were no incomprehensible Ave Marias and similar prayers to help and save us.

Jim talked to God as he would talk to a close friend.

DAY 494

OUR phone contacts using the 'Swiss connection' were now regular, albeit short. Every morning we were filled with a fresh hope that that day everything would be ready for Goran to leave. By the time evening arrived and no news had come that he was out of Sarajevo, I knew I would hear the same words.

'I went to the UNPROFOR building this morning again, with just my Samsonite briefcase. Not much can fit in it, but I looked like I was going to work. I didn't want to attract anyone's attention.'

I listened carefully, hoping for a positive turn in the events.

'I waited at the UNPROFOR office for several hours, asked around if my paperwork was ready, and then in the afternoon I went back home.'

Goran was disappointed and unsure why he was not allocated to a flight leaving Sarajevo. I had nothing to say. I didn't understand either. It seemed that we had ticked all the boxes. He must've looked like a real journalist in the eyes of the UNPROFOR officials.

What was missing then?

One Friday morning in late September, after we had discussed the stagnant situation again and again, Anna picked up the phone and called *The Guardian*.

After being put through to someone who was a war correspondent or worked with them, Anna asked, 'What does a journalist need to look like a real journalist if they are reporting from a war zone, like in Sarajevo?'

She listened, nodded, looked at me, hung up and repeated what they told her.

'A flak jacket, they said. Every genuine journalist has a flak jacket. Without it, no one would believe they were a true journalist.'

A flak jacket? Where and how could Goran find a bulletproof jacket? I certainly couldn't find one, or buy one. Anna rang a few numbers and was told they cost around six hundred pounds, maybe more. Even if we could somehow buy one, how could we send it to Sarajevo? Not in a letter, not in a food parcel. I kept shaking my head in disbelief. Of course that was the missing puzzle piece. We were so blind in making our plans, we missed the obvious. All the effort was pointless without the flak jacket. I didn't know whether to tell Goran about it. I was afraid that this would shatter his hope for escape.

As soon as I got home I rang John in London to ask what he thought about it. He agreed. 'Yes, the flak jacket is the most important part of the picture of a real journalist.' He had no suggestions about where and how to get one, but promised to take it with him if we could arrange one before he returned back to Sarajevo on Monday or Tuesday the following week. It was Friday already. Not much time left. My brain was foggy, in a panic from this latest news.

Late that afternoon Steve came to see us. As I told him about the flak jacket it became clear to me that our hope for Goran's escape as a journalist was unreasonable. I was on the verge of crying when recounting it all to Steve. Guy, Clem and Anna had been working so hard on arranging the press card, spending so much money on the calls and faxes, ultimately for nothing, as we could not provide the last missing bit—the flak jacket. Of course everything is possible, but not when one has two children to look after and no money. If I had been in a movie I would have just gone and bought a flak jacket in a shop, got on a train to London and taken it to John. He would have taken it to Goran, and Goran would have gone to UNPROFOR and, having this last bit complete, they would have put him on a flight straight away. He would have come to his family and we would all have lived happily ever after. But I was not in a movie. I had no money for a flak jacket. Even if I did have the money, I didn't know where and how to buy it. And if I could somehow obtain it from somewhere, I had no one to look after my children on such short notice while I went to London to take it to John before he left for Sarajevo.

It was all impossible. My helplessness choked me.

Steve listened and seemed lost in thought, staring at the floor, with his eyes narrowed as if searching for the solution in the pale grey dots of the carpet. I assumed that this had shocked him too and he didn't know what to say, how to comfort me. Suppressing my tears, I observed the small dust particles flying around the room, visible under the late-afternoon sun rays, thinking how we all looked so normal in this living room in the north of England: Steve and I drinking tea, Dario on the couch reading a book, Elena sitting on the carpet quietly dressing and undressing her dolls. But nothing was normal. We were just fragments of lives randomly scattered without a frame to give us meaning. My throat tight, I struggled to keep the tears in. I didn't want to upset the children and couldn't keep talking.

The silence in the room was dense and unbearable. I was hoping Steve would say something cheerful to the children and break the stillness.

Steve slowly lifted his head and said, 'You know, my uncle works for the British Police Force, maybe he can hire a flak jacket from his work.'

I looked at him in disbelief. 'Hire a flak jacket? But you know that it may never come back? It could be stolen on the way there, or...' I didn't want to finish the sentence.

'We'll worry about that later,' he said, and left.

The following morning the doorbell interrupted our breakfast. *Who could it be so early?* I thought while walking to the door. Steve leant against the doorframe with a big cheeky smile on his face, proudly holding a flak jacket high up in his raised hand. 'I told you I would get it!'

I stared at him and the jacket, not understanding. It looked real. Dark blue, thick fabric, heavy. Thinking he must've bought it somewhere, I asked, 'Where did you get it from?'

'From my uncle,' he said. 'I told you he could hire one.'

I shook my head in disbelief. A man who had never met me hired a flak jacket from the British Police, to send it to Sarajevo in an attempt to rescue a man from the siege and reunite him with his family. Not far from a miracle.

But what now? How could I have it delivered to John in London by Monday morning, in less than forty-eight hours? It was impossible. It would have to wait until John's next trip, whenever that might be. Hopefully soon. And who knows, maybe another miracle would happen in Sarajevo in the meantime and Goran would be free to leave and join us. After all, it seemed that occasionally miracles do happen, even to us. The press card, the flak jacket, weren't they all miracles?

Jan popped in later on that evening to see how we were, and I told her about the ups and downs of the incredible flak jacket story.

'It's weird that I am a little upset now that I have the jacket, because I can't get it to John before his next trip to Sarajevo. And yesterday I couldn't even dream about ever having a flak jacket. Hopefully it will not be long before John goes to Sarajevo again. It seems that we are, after all, getting closer and closer to our family reunion.' I even managed to smile.

'Well, maybe we can do something about it,' Jan said.

She told me that the husband of a local woman we both knew worked in London. He usually came home to Cumbria every Friday night and went back to London every Sunday afternoon.

I phoned them immediately, and yes, the husband was at home, and was travelling to London on Sunday! They promised to pick up the jacket on Sunday before he left for London. I was restless to see him and hand over the jacket.

On Monday I called John to ensure he wouldn't leave London without it. The jacket was delivered safely to his door that night.

On the same day, Guy sent another long fax from Prometheus Productions to the UNPROFOR Press Office in Sarajevo, describing the mistake made with the UN press card, explaining the financial loss that Goran's absence was causing to their program and requesting urgent authorisation for Goran's travel to Split. Once again Guy faxed copies of all previously sent documents.

His letter was so strong and explicit as if Guy himself had started believing in what he was telling UNPROFOR, that Goran's prolonged absence from work on the film was costing them money.

In reality, the amount of phone calls and faxes sent to Sarajevo did cost Guy and Máire a fortune. I felt uncomfortable about it, but could not offer to give them money as I didn't have any. The small amount of social support that we received from the British government, supplemented with the money I received from time to time from Goran's mum's pension payments from Split, was not nearly enough for us to live on, for the food parcels being sent to Sarajevo, for my huge phone bills and for the money sent to Switzerland to pay for the phone connections to Sarajevo.

I economised carefully but nothing was ever saved.

I was ashamed that I couldn't offer them money for the calls and faxes. It was too awkward to mention it to Anna, although she must've been aware of it and I assumed she was helping them with the costs without ever mentioning it to me.

DAY 500

THE relentless wait continued.

My children gave me strength and energy when I thought I didn't have any left. Elena kept my thoughts occupied with her needs and saved me from over-analysing every little detail, from over-worrying about everything all the time. Even when I was annoyed by her constant demands for this and that, by her uncontrollable abundance of energy that caused many falls, injuries and tears, I was grateful for her infinite liveliness, broad smiles, and endless kisses and hugs. Holding her little healthy and strong body in my arms, her arms tight around my neck and her cheek next to my cheek, gave sense to my struggle. Dario, quiet and even-tempered, did not need much attention. He went through the days without making a fuss about anything.

Other than having additional English lessons with the other Bosnian children, Dario went to classes with the children who were native English speakers. He went to school, did his homework, and brought home good marks and exceptionally positive comments from his teachers without ever asking me for any kind of help. In turn, I never asked him to help around the house, or to look after his little sister, except when I needed to see the GP or dentist. On those occasions I would find them both in the same positions as I had left them: lying on the floor, Dario bored to death with an open book in front of him, waiting impatiently for my return and closely watching his little sister; Elena lost in her little games with a few dolls, books and other toys she had and a few lolly wrappers around her. She was too young to understand what was going on with our lives. She was easily pleased. Having a sweet here and there, some toys, and her mum near her all the time was enough to keep this three-year-old happy.

I wondered sometimes if I was shielding Dario from life's demands too much. In all other families older children looked after their younger siblings almost all of the time, but as I was an only child, I had no personal experience with that and didn't want to burden Dario with dragging his little sister around. I was delighted that school was going well for him, and that he wasn't getting into fights and arguments with other children—that was enough for me. It was not his fault that our lives had been hijacked and sent in a different direction. I did not want him to feel more distressed than he already did by not having his dad with him, nor his grandparents and cousins—the warmth that only a family can provide.

I worried though, that with my focus on Goran's escape and Elena's needs, Dario was somewhat left to cope by himself. I wondered if he was overwhelmed with everything new around him: new country, new school, new language. When I asked him how he was, he shrugged his shoulders and said everything was fine. Both of us avoided talking about our situation, afraid of discussing the painful truth, hoping to make it look smaller if it wasn't given the attention.

I tried to conceal my constant worries and anxieties as much as I could. To be discreet with my fears. But I couldn't pretend. I could not create the false impression that everything was fine, when it truly wasn't.

I never cried when the children were awake and near me. I saved it for when they were asleep.

And maybe I managed to trick Elena into believing that everything was well, but certainly not Dario. He hardly asked about his dad and his grandparents and I didn't question his silence. I knew that he hadn't forgotten them. It just hurt too much to bring up the subject and talk about it openly. I felt his gaze on me when he thought that I wasn't aware of it, analysing me, surely thinking that if I wasn't crying things at least weren't worse than before. He listened to my phone calls, while pretending that he was reading or watching television, and drew conclusions from what I told other people. I wondered if I should have been more positive and light-hearted with everything from the beginning. If I should have maintained a false sense of normalcy, never talked about killings and the difficult life in Sarajevo and pretended that it would be all resolved soon, that his dad was about to turn up at our door any minute. Maybe that would have given him a desire to write to his father, who was constantly asking about him. Instead, it was a sentence or two when I insisted on it.

At the start of his second school year in Penrith, Dario came home one day and pulled out a brochure from his school bag, handing it to me with a smile, without saying a word.

It was his photo on the front page of the pamphlet: light brown hair, olive skin, blue eyes, wearing the school uniform jumper, a plastic plate with a school lunch in front of him.

'What is it?' I asked flipping through it and turning it around.

It seemed to be a brochure advertising the school canteen and the good quality of the food served to the children.

'How did your photo end up on it?'

He shrugged his shoulders. 'They took photos of me and some other children last week and they gave me this today to show it to you.'

Out of all the children at Beaconside Junior it was Dario and an English girl they had picked for the Cumbria Catering Services brochure. He clearly looked so well and healthy that he could represent a typical British primary school child to the rest of the population.

This gave me a big boost of positive energy in my somewhat melancholic days. I carried the pamphlet with me and proudly showed it to everyone. I asked for more copies from school and sent a couple of them to Goran, in two letters using two different mail options. When he received the brochure, Goran was beside himself with happiness. Not only did he have a great big new photo of his son, but his son was representing all the children from his school for the catering services. A very special moment for Goran. It gave him additional strength to keep fighting in the murky circumstances of his daily life.

My big boy was now about to turn ten. His second birthday without his dad. Nothing could replace his dad's presence, but a birthday party could make us all forget for a little while why Goran was not with us. We invited ten boys, some from his school and several Bosnian boys. They played Monopoly, snacked on sandwiches, crisps and cordial, teased each other and laughed a lot. Elena mingled with them, while they gently ignored her. Dario was thrilled to see the familiar birthday cake, one that I always baked for his birthdays in Sarajevo.

'Grandma's Cake!' he exclaimed when I brought it out. 'Wow! Thanks Mum!'

The sweet, walnut-rich cake, based on Goran's mum's recipe, in three layers with a creamy filling, brought back memories of happy times when birthdays were celebrated with his dad, his grandparents, his aunty and her family and many of our Sarajevan friends.

As Dario blew out the candles on the cake and the children sang happy birthday, I wondered what birthday wish he was making.

DAY 508

THE wait to hear that John and the jacket had made it safely to Sarajevo was nerve-wracking. This time he managed to avoid the armed gangs and robbers, which was not easy in war-torn Bosnia. Different ethnic groups ruled in different areas and most of them had one thing in common: they considered all foreigners suspicious spies and robbed them of everything they carried.

Goran could not believe his eyes when John presented him with the jacket. I didn't want to tell Goran about it over the phone in case it never arrived. The highs and lows of hope and disappointment were with him every day and I didn't want to raise his hopes further for fear of making it all harder if it didn't come true. But we were lucky. John's trip to Sarajevo was smooth and the flak jacket made it to Sarajevo, and to Goran.

The next day, when Goran turned up at UNPROFOR, with his flak jacket on, they told him that his transport would be arranged soon. Worried that someone or something would affect the plan, he did not tell anyone that his departure was imminent. Not my parents, nor his parents, or his sister. No one. When on Friday, October 8, he didn't come home after he went out in the morning, unaware of Goran's plans, my parents were nervous about what might have happened to him. They decided not to phone his parents to check if he was there for the fear of causing panic. Late that night when they received a call from Switzerland, the mystery of Goran's disappearance was resolved.

In the letter my parents sent the day after, they wrote how, overjoyed with happiness, they hadn't been able to sleep the whole night. Of course they expected that Goran would go directly to England and would be reunited with his family in the shortest possible time. But it was not so simple.

The morning of Goran's departure, he was transported to the airport in a big white UNPROFOR vehicle. He went through another verification of his papers. The UN border officer was utterly confused with the odd mix of Goran's documents, the International Press Card issued in London and the red passport from the Socialist Federal Republic of Yugoslavia. Goran's fairly poor English certainly didn't make it look any more convincing. When the soldier asked him 'Do you have any foreign currency?' Goran took out a bunch of notes from his wallet, the first layer British pounds, then American dollars and German marks.

It was relatively unusual to have British pounds in Sarajevo, people mainly kept their savings in German marks. This odd detail may have convinced the man at the border that Goran did have some connections with the UK where his International Press Card had been issued. They let him board the light aeroplane set to leave for Ancona in Italy.

Inside the aeroplane there were no seats. Just netting on the sides and metal poles to hold on to. When everyone was on board and they finally took off, Goran screamed with happiness inside, but tried to look indifferent, as if this was something he did on a regular basis. There were eight passengers, one young man with a Bosnian passport, six foreigners, potentially journalists, and Goran. He wondered if the journalists could work out that he wasn't one of them, as they all mainly stayed in the Holiday Inn hotel in the city centre, and probably knew each other, if not personally then from the hotel corridors. He kept quiet during the flight.

When they landed in Ancona, one of the journalists invited Goran to share a taxi to town. Goran offered the money for the taxi but the man shook his head. He may have worked out from Goran's incredibly thin frame that he was a Sarajevan on an escape mission and did what he could to help a little bit. He dropped Goran off at the main train station.

In need of shelter for a few days, Goran bought a ticket for the next train to Rome where our friends Ziza and Šefko lived. No one as yet knew that he was in Italy. He sat on the train still not believing that he was out of the war and on the way to see his family. Seeing the waiter selling food and drinks on the train he felt confused and shocked that food could be bought so freely. He bought a sandwich with prosciutto, and a beer, but struggled to finish them in the three and a half hours from Ancona to Rome. After a year and a half of getting through the days mostly hungry, his stomach could not stretch enough for one sandwich and one beer.

He looked around in amazement at the lucky people who freely travelled from place to place. A young man in a suit going to a business meeting or a job interview. Two young women quietly but energetically chatting about something, waving their hands and exploding in laughter every few minutes. Maybe talking about the previous evening's outing with friends, or about their boyfriends, their parents, about something in their free and happy lives. A youngish couple with two pre-school-aged children, a boy and a girl, maybe going to visit their family, or returning home after staying with family, in or near Ancona. Semi-eaten sandwiches and half-empty bottles of juice and water on the train table in front of them. Goran imagined their big family in a country house on the outskirts of a village, kids laughing and running around in and out of the house, mum and grandma cooking in the kitchen, pots steaming with pasta and sauces, the beautiful smell of lemon-fragranced cookies coming from the oven. Dad helping grandpa repair the wobbly table outside, chooks walking around them, picking worms from the soil, the smell of basil and rosemary in the air as they brushed past the flowerpots. An idyllic portrait of a happy family that looked just like us less than two years prior.

All of the passengers were unaware of how lucky they were to be free: free to talk, laugh, eat, drink, travel. Blissfully unaware that only a short flight from there, in Sarajevo, the capital city of a European country, people lived in dreadful conditions. Under siege for eighteen months, surrounded by destroyed buildings, enveloped in the sounds of constant shelling from the hills, facing death every minute of their lives. Limited amounts and a miserable selection of food, not enough water even to drink. Unable to shower for weeks, unable to freely walk, not only throughout the city for fear of snipers and shelling, but also unable to leave town and see their family outside of the sieged city.

How could it be possible that the awful war and the unbearable conditions in Sarajevo had been going on for so long? Why was no one in the world interested in doing something to stop the Bosnian Serb forces from shelling the town from the hills, the snipers from firing on innocent civilians, not sparing anyone, not even women and children? Why didn't the UN do something? They had so many troops and vehicles in Bosnia, surely they could do more than what they were doing. In whose interest was it to keep this war going? What plans did the world have for the small European country that had just come out of socialism, and wasn't rich, other than with its own intelligent, healthy and hard-working people? What did the world want to achieve and why?

Goran's head spun from the sudden change. Feeling oddly at liberty to move and order food, he was unable to fully grasp the power of his freedom. Lost in thoughts about his past, incapable to think about his future further than this train ride, he slowly chewed on the sandwich. A small bite every little while, a little sip of beer.

The fresh bread with prosciutto tasted so astonishingly good. He'd forgotten how good fresh bread tasted. In Sarajevo they had eaten stale bread, or a stone-like fake bread that they made at home, quickly, in the pressure cooker to save wood, from oat bran, without yeast. He certainly hadn't seen prosciutto since the war started.

After the train arrived in Rome, Goran phoned Ziza and Šefko's home from the nearest phone booth.

At first Ziza thought he was joking when he said he was calling from Rome. She then explained which metro line to catch to get to their metro station, Laurentina, where Šefko, her husband, would wait for him. She could not wait for Goran to arrive at their place and she phoned me straight away to let me know the news. It was late Friday afternoon. Unaware of Goran's eventful day I was tidying up the house, folding the washing, putting clean dishes in the cupboard. Dario was watching television, Elena playing with her toys.

'Eda, ciao, it's Ziza.' I could hear the joy in her words. 'Goran is in Rome! He's on his way to Laurentina. Šefko will pick him up from there. Did you know he was coming?'

Warmth burst from my chest to my head, making me lightheaded. My vision blurred. I reached with my hand to the nearest wall and leaned on it. After visualising a similar conversation so many times since we left Goran in Sarajevo, I was speechless.

'Eda?' Ziza repeated, unsure if I was still on the line.

'I'm here, I'm here. I just don't know what to say. I can't believe he's finally out. I am so happy, I can't express it with words.'

'We'll call you again soon. I am going to make us something to eat now. Goran must be very hungry. Speak soon.'

The news changed this day from ordinary to extraordinary. We spoke that night at length. Finally the topics of our conversation were more joyous.

We laughed about the young UN soldier's disbelief that Goran was an international journalist, delighted that our plan had worked, that Goran was now free to travel. He just needed a UK visitor's visa organised and he would be on his way to join us.

DAY 511

EARLY on Monday morning Goran went to the British Embassy in Rome to apply for a visitor's visa.

We were a bit nervous about his old Socialist Federal Republic of Yugoslavia passport. The country didn't exist anymore and the passport was deemed to become illegal any day. Hopefully not something that couldn't be resolved with a visa. I had it all planned in my head: Goran would come to Penrith, bring his medicals, we would quickly complete our Australian visa application and be ready to go there by the end of the year. I still had no idea how we would manage to finance the tickets for the trip to Melbourne but I had no time to think about it as yet. There were other more important things to sort out.

At the Embassy they looked at Goran's passport. 'We cannot issue you a visitor's visa. You need to apply for political asylum. The expected wait time for it to be resolved is several weeks.'

We weren't troubled by this—Goran was safe. A few weeks would not make a huge difference.

We talked to each other as often as I could afford to pay. We exchanged letters, which were delivered within a few days from being sent. During the previous eighteen months that had been unimaginable. Goran sent us a few of his photos from Rome: sitting on a bench in a park, basking in the late autumn sunshine, wearing a jumper and a jacket donated by Ziza and Šefko's friends. He looked so painfully thin. He told me he weighed fifty-seven kilograms when he left Sarajevo. With his height of one hundred eighty-three centimetres, that was far too low. I wondered if this delay in reuniting our family had a purpose, albeit a bizarre one, to protect the children and me from seeing him looking abnormally thin, to postpone our reunion until he recovered his weight and strength.

In one of our Bosnian-English gatherings a local woman, a friend of a friend, approached me and said, 'I hear your husband is in Rome waiting for his visa to come to Penrith.'

'Yes, that's right. Goran has applied for political asylum in the UK. It might take a few weeks to have it approved.'

'I have a close friend in Rome,' she continued. 'Caroline is English and married to an Italian man. I'm sure she wouldn't mind helping Goran improve his English while waiting for the visa to be issued.'

'Thank you so much, that would be brilliant.' I couldn't believe our luck, the time spent waiting for a visa would be used to improve Goran's English. How incredible to come across this miraculous opportunity.

'I'll give you her details and your husband can get in touch with Caroline. I'll call her tonight to let her know.'

Goran contacted Caroline and was invited to lunch at their place. They spent hours talking, despite Goran's broken English. He continued to visit Caroline weekly to practise and improve his English.

I relaxed.

Goran was not coming as quickly as I had hoped, but at least we were utilising the waiting time as efficiently as possible.

I updated the Australian Consulate in Manchester with the news and checked that all that was left to do was to send them our medicals. One of the conditions for visa fulfilment was to sit an English test and I assumed that they would ask me to do that. I would've passed the test, I had no doubts—it was only the cost of the travel to a place where I could sit the test, and the cost of the test itself, that worried me. And who would look after Dario and Elena while I was away? Fortunately, the language test was never mentioned. Whether because I sounded fluent enough when I spoke on the phone, or because the application was processed in England, or because of a pure omission, I didn't know. Skipping one step, no matter how small, was of huge importance to me and I was grateful for it.

Jacqui drove the three of us to a clinic in Manchester to complete our medicals and we chatted in her car on the way there. It was the first time since we had met that we could talk about other things, not only about Goran and how to help him get out from Sarajevo. I enquired about her decision to stay at home while the children were young and her plans to go back to her law job. She cheerfully talked about her job before their children were born and about her life at the farm. 'What makes you so happy all the time?' I asked. I found myself still very melancholic even though Goran was safe and I knew we would soon be together again.

'I don't know,' she said. 'I think I am just like that. Despite everything, life is beautiful most of the time.'

I tried to remember what I was like before the war. *Was I also happy most of the time for no apparent reason?* It seemed so long ago that I had felt thoroughly happy and content. *Would wholesome happiness ever return to me?*

Jacqui waited for us while we went through the medical tests. She insisted on paying for it, although I told her I had the money; I'd patiently collected twenty-dollar notes from Madelyn and recently converted them to British pounds. Jacqui took us to lunch and drove us home. A flawless, stress-free day. I hadn't had many like that in the previous eighteen months.

On our return home a local reporter from *Evening News and Star* got in touch with me in search of updates. The newspapers immediately published the great news: 'Phone call ends painful wait for Edita'.

Penrith-based Bosnian refugee Edita Mujkic has had the phone call she has been praying for for 18 months.

She has heard that her husband, Goran, who has been trapped in war-torn Sarajevo, is safe. He flew out of the besieged city to Italy and is staying with Bosnian friends in Rome.

He plans to join Edita and the couple's two children as soon as he has the right papers.

Said Mrs Mujkic: "My whole life has changed now. Everything looks more beautiful."

Madelyn's community cheered when they heard the news and she sent me a card with their best wishes and a bit of money for our phone bills. Everyone was delighted that we would soon be reunited.

But not the British Home Office.

Four weeks after Goran's visa application, the British Embassy in Rome phoned Ziza's place and asked to talk to Goran. They informed him that his visa application had not been approved and asked him to come to the Embassy on November 18 to collect the paperwork.

On the afternoon when Goran called to tell us the news, the three of us were at home. I ran to the phone with a smile on my face, thinking, *That's it, he's finally coming.* Not in my worst nightmare could I have imagined what he told me.

'I have bad news. Unfortunately, the British Home Office is not letting me come to the UK.'

Unbelievable.

Heartless.

Cruel.

'But, why? Why can't you come?' I stuttered.

'You are in a safe country, they told me. Hence I do not qualify to be accepted into the UK as a refugee.'

We were shaken by their decision. The fact that his immediate family had been living in the UK for longer than a year was of no importance. Quite the opposite, the Home Office were most likely afraid that if we reunited in the UK we would permanently stay there and the UK government had no interest in keeping one more Bosnian refugee family within UK borders.

Legs trembling, I moved a step forward and leaned against the chest of drawers near me, unable to grasp the harshness of the decision and its effect on us.

'I don't know what to do now,' I panicked. 'This complicates everything. You know I need to enter Australia first; the visa is in my name. We could try to fly to Rome to meet you there, but I don't think we could afford the extra tickets… I don't know what to do.'

My voice broke; my brain hazy, unable to process the sudden change of an already well-planned scenario.

I glanced at Dario lying on the couch, his hand under his cheek, watching television. One huge tear rolled down his face and onto the cushion underneath, changing its colour from light blue to dark blue.

I immediately regretted my impulsive negative reaction. I should have sounded more positive and said, 'That's okay, we are all safe, we will go to Australia separately, we will meet there.' But after such a long separation, extending it for several months and arranging separate flights to Melbourne seemed to me unbearably complicated. I just needed us to be together. I couldn't tolerate the separation anymore. I had no strength left in me for any new intricate plans. I needed a simple life for a while. I needed us to be like any other ordinary family. I needed normalcy to regain the energy to live.

I tried to comfort Dario after the phone call. 'It's okay, don't worry. The main thing is that dad is safe now. A few more days to wait will not make a big difference. We will sort it out.'

I wasn't sure if my words were enough of a comfort for him. He wanted his dad, not my promises. Elena, luckily too young to understand, was oblivious to our conversation. She just repeated, 'Daddy…' when she heard me mentioning the word *dad*.

DAY 543

HEARING that the Embassy had requested Goran to return on November 18, I thought we could do something to overturn the outcome of his application before this date.

I wrote a three-page heartbreaking letter to Mr S. Rose at the Immigration and Nationality Department in Croydon. I described how difficult the separation was for all of us, how it impacted the children and how much we needed time together to recover before going to Australia. I included a hand written letter from Dario's class teacher at Beaconside Junior School, Susan Kershaw, who presented her view of how the separation from his dad was impacting my son.

I have known Dario since he came to Beaconside Junior School over a year ago.

I am writing this letter on behalf of Dario with his best emotional and educational interests at heart.

Dario is an exceptionally able child who has made remarkable progress since he joined us. Language is no barrier to him—on the contrary, he is highly articulate. His command of English is now superb. He is an excellent mathematician, outstanding in his year group. He is an asset to this school and community.

As his class teacher I have seen his deep suffering. Having been rescued from Sarajevo and come to Penrith as a refugee, he has been separated from his father for more than a year. At the young age of 8 he felt the responsibility of caring for his young sister and his grieving mother. He bears a heavy burden.

The visible signs of stress are to be seen in his face—grimaces of pain, tortured expressions. Should we continue to put a young boy through that?

When Dario heard of his father's escape from Sarajevo, he was elated. His face has become more relaxed. He has been a very happy and cheerful child. How can I explain to him that although his father has reached Italy, he is not allowed to join his family here?

For the wellbeing of Dario Mujkic in particular and the Mujkic family in general, I suggest that Dario's father is given at least a temporary visa to enter this country, so that the family may re-establish themselves in a climate of peace. How can anyone possibly object to that?

We long to see this family re-united within our community and ask that Dario be allowed to complete this academic year without disruption to his education.

Yours sincerely,

Susan Kershaw

(Class Teacher)

Guy phoned the British Embassy in Rome and then sent a fax to Mrs Nicola Hancock there, describing his role in Goran's escape from Sarajevo and emphasising Goran's importance for the continuation of their 'project'. In his fax Guy explained how Goran was in a very dishevelled condition when he came to the Embassy and couldn't explain himself clearly, that he was not looking for refugee status, only to join his family before they continued onto Australia, hence Guy, on behalf of Prometheus Productions, requested a resubmission of Goran's UK visa application.

But all of that didn't help to overrule the original decision. On November 18, Goran was given a Refusal of Entry Clearance and advice on how to appeal, and with it the following short letter signed by the Entry Clearance Officer:

The Secretary of State has considered your application for a visa to enter the United Kingdom as a refugee and has refused it. A notice giving the basis of this refusal, and informing you of your rights of appeal against the decision is attached.

The Secretary of State has also considered whether you should be issued a visa to enter the United Kingdom exceptionally outside the Immigration Rules, but can find no ground to justify this.

Caroline went with Goran to the Embassy, and was extremely upset by their decision. She yelled at the Embassy officials and objected to their decision but they told her that the decision wasn't theirs, that they were only a 'post office' for the Home Office, and they couldn't do anything about it.

We needed to reorganise our plans. As much as I wasn't looking forward to travelling to the other side of the world with two young children on my own, that now seemed inevitable.

I suggested to Dario to write to his dad. Now that we could exchange letters, he could keep his dad up to date with what he did and how he lived.

He typed up a couple of paragraphs in Bosnian, using the old typewriter I borrowed to send the letter to Mr Rose, and hand-signed it with his full name in blue ink.

DEAR DAD,

As you know I have this GAME BOY, but I don't play with it much. I don't have many games so sometimes it gets boring. I received the postcard you sent me.

When Elena and I receive lollies, I take them all and hide them somewhere. Of course she finds them and eats them all.

School is going well. You've already heard that I'm the best in my class.

I LOVE YOU VERY MUCH.

I HOPE YOU WILL SOON COME HERE.

It was sweet and poignant to see some of the most important things in his life mixed up in a few sentences, typed up on the back of an unsent letter I previously typed to send to the Australian Embassy in Manchester, to enquire if our unusual combination of different passports would present an issue for the visa. I cut out Dario's typing to its size and included it with my next letter to Goran.

Not knowing how much longer he would need to stay in Rome before the visa for either the UK or Australia would be finalised, Goran decided to apply for the *Permesso di soggiorno*, permission to stay in Italy. Although that process in Italy could have taken an indefinitely long time, Šefko's sister, who had been living in Rome for twenty years, knew the right people in the right places and, true to the Italian style where connections were more important than rules, the *Permesso* to stay in Italy for a year was issued in record time. At least Goran was not an illegal immigrant in Italy.

Goran mailed his medical examination results to me; I forwarded them to the Australian Consulate in Manchester. A few days later they called to tell me that our visa application was finalised and that they needed our passports for the visa to be stamped in them.

Passports. Hmm. Yet another obstacle to overcome. We all had the old Yugoslav passports, due to become invalid any day; it seemed too risky to use them for the visas.

I phoned the Croatian Embassy in London and enquired about the procedure and the cost of obtaining Croatian passports. It seemed simple, it would be done in London and the passports would be ready in a couple of weeks. Bosnian passports however could only be issued in Paris, they would cost twice as much and it would take much longer to obtain them. The decision was an easy one to make: I would apply for Croatian passports for the children and myself.

But nothing was ever that simple.

As a parent without Croatian citizenship, Goran needed to give his permission for the children to have Croatian passports and the permission had to be authorised by the officials at the Croatian Embassy in Rome.

After arriving at his appointment at the Croatian Embassy, Goran was asked for his passport, and he handed it over. The Embassy official took the passport and, after noticing that it was the old Yugoslav passport, dropped it immediately from his hands as if he had been burnt by its touch. Yugoslavia at that time was reduced to Serbia and Montenegro, with which Croatia was not on good terms due to the war in Croatia and Bosnia. After seeing his passport the Embassy officials became visibly hostile.

Goran restrained himself from any comments, and quietly waited to obtain the authorised permission for the children's Croatian passports. While he was walking out of the embassy, his several-decades-old Timberland shoes, donated by one of Ziza and Šefko's Italian friends, started disintegrating. Goran continued to march, seemingly oblivious to the pieces of their soles left on the Embassy floor, in a hurry to express post the permission to Penrith.

I mailed our passport documents, photos and Goran's permission to the Croatian Embassy in London.

Our new passports arrived a few weeks later.

But that was not enough.

For the Australian visa to be issued we needed Goran's passport too. Goran's old passport was practically not valid any more, and a new, Bosnian passport could not be organised in Italy as at the time the Bosnian Embassy was not yet established in Rome. Sending his Yugoslav passport from Rome to Paris to apply for a Bosnian passport seemed unsafe. We also didn't want to mail his Yugoslav passport from Rome to Penrith and back—the risk of it being lost in the mail was too daunting.

Losing a passport at this stage would prolong and complicate everything. We neither had the time nor money to spend on a new one. We just wanted to finalise the visa and go to Melbourne as soon as we could.

We had no idea how.

DAY 558

IT was almost December, nearly two months since Goran had arrived in Italy.

In Cumbria, Željka and her extended family were preparing to leave for Canada. At their big farewell party numerous people came to congratulate me on Goran's safe escape from Sarajevo, and enquired about the date of his arrival in Penrith. I repeated the same incredible story that he wouldn't be coming as the British Home Office refused his entry.

A woman in her mid-fifties came and introduced herself as Lavinia Howard. She had heard about our unusual family situation and was interested to know more. I briefly summarised the details of our separation, Goran's escape, and the latest news from the Home Office.

'So, you're not planning on staying in the UK?'

'No,' I said. 'We have already completed our visa for Australia. I just want Goran to come here for a month or two, to see the town and get to know the people who helped us and then we will go to Melbourne.'

She said her husband used to know a few people in the Home Office and she would see if he could do something about it.

Although sad to part with Željka, I left the party in a positive mood. Maybe we could turn things around and bring Goran to England after all.

Revived with new hope, a few days later I went to the office of David Maclean, the local MP, to ask for his help. I talked to the MP about our plans. Goran would not request refugee status in the UK and therefore would not be eligible for social security benefits. We would stay in England only a short time, long enough for him to regain his health and for our family to stabilise emotionally before embarking on the trip to Australia. I left the MP's office unsure if he could or would try to make any difference to Goran's entry to the UK.

Shortly after, another article was published in the local newspaper, 'Let my man into Britain'. It detailed our situation, my visit to Mr Maclean and my appeal to let Goran into the UK before we left for Australia. Once again, a light ray of hope lingered in me that the article could attract the attention of someone who could help us bring Goran to England.

Meanwhile, in Rome, Goran helped Ziza with housework to lighten the burden of his prolonged stay. He walked their children to school every morning and took full care of all their ironing, one of the household chores that, over time, he had become confident about.

Ten years earlier, when Dario was born, I returned to work after six months of maternity leave. Having a baby and working full-time made me much busier at home than before and I could not take care of our home as easily as I could until then. Previously, I had ironed a business shirt every evening for Goran to wear the following day, so that it wouldn't crease in the wardrobe if ironed days earlier. After becoming a mum I was far too tired in the evenings to iron so I had to let Goran iron his own business shirts. After the initial struggle and a bit of muttered swearing Goran had slowly become efficient in ironing, in fact better than me. It was natural to him to take over this duty at his hosts' place. Then one day, appreciative of Goran's no-nonsense approach to household tasks, a friend of Ziza and Šefko suggested, 'There is a man at my work who needs regular help with ironing. Would you go and iron for him once a week? He would pay you an hourly rate.'

Unsure of how our plans would unfold and how much longer he needed to stay in Rome, Goran immediately accepted the idea and went to the man's place to iron his clothes for a bit of pocket money. And he continued to visit Caroline for his English lessons.

In one of these visits, Caroline mentioned that her daughter Diana would be travelling to London for the Christmas holidays and Caroline would be visiting her family and friends in the Lakes District area a little bit later.

We saw that as a chance to safely transport Goran's passport to and from England.

We arranged for me to meet Diana in London on the day of her arrival. I made an intricate arrangement with several friends to hand over Dario and Elena from family to family throughout the day, each friend looking after them for a few hours.

On the day of Diana's arrival, I caught the morning train from Penrith and then the tube to meet her. When I emerged from the tube station, the light fog in the cold December air and the misty rain made it all look like one of Monet's paintings of London. But the importance of my mission blurred the beauty of London. Aware of my poor sense of direction, I paid attention only to the street details that would help me trace my way back to the tube station.

I met Diana, she handed me the passport and asked, 'Would you like to have lunch or a coffee in a café nearby?'

Worried about being lost on my way back and missing my train, I politely declined her offer with an excuse that my train to Penrith would be leaving soon. I thanked her for her kindness and hurried back to the train station. I sat there with plenty of time to spare, eating pieces of cheese and spinach *pita* baked the night before, Goran's passport safely tucked in my handbag.

Having all four passports with me, I immediately booked an

appointment with the Australian Consulate in Manchester for the visa to be issued. Anna drove us there.

At the Consulate, they stamped all four passports, our new Croatian ones and Goran's old Yugoslav passport, with the Visa Class 126 Resident stamp while we went out to have lunch. Although this final step could take a couple of weeks, the Consulate understood the complexity of our case and finished it in less than two hours.

We were now eligible to enter Australia on a skilled migrant visa, as independent entrants with permanent residency.

I clutched the valuable passports in my hands all the way to Penrith, almost unable to believe that this lengthy process was finally over, more than two years since we had started the application process. It was incredible that the Australian Consulate kept the file open for so long. Surely there were rules and legislation about the duration of each stage of the application, and we had most likely bent all of them.

I was thankful that the Consulate cared more about people than about rules.

DAY 588

WE spent Christmas with Jacqui's family, at their lovely farmhouse, where we were welcomed to our bedroom with a scene as if from a movie: a big double bed covered in Christmas presents that she had collected for us from her friends and relatives. Loads of new clothes, books and toys for the children. A bottle of expensive perfume, a scarf and a make-up set for me. We were overwhelmed with her extraordinary care. It made us feel special and loved.

After Christmas I went to Appleby to meet Caroline. Very slim, with long light brown hair gathered into a bun and a huge friendly smile, she was full of admiration for the determination with which we had rescued Goran from Sarajevo. She gave me a beautiful red summer dress and a classy French perfume as a Christmas present. I handed her Goran's passport. She was due to return to Rome in a couple of days.

While I was meeting Caroline, Goran received a call from the British Embassy in Rome. They informed him that he was granted a six-month visitor visa, on the condition that he wouldn't apply for political asylum upon his arrival to the UK. They told Goran to come to the Embassy on January 4, between three and four in the afternoon, when his visa would be ready for collection. Luckily, his passport was going to be returned to Rome just in time for this. How incredibly the pieces of the puzzle had finally started slotting into their rightful places.

After picking up his Single Entry visa, Goran and Caroline, who went with him to the Embassy, literally jumped with joy in the elevator.

Almost immediately Goran started searching for a ticket to London. Goran and Šefko decided that they didn't want to waste the money on buying a return ticket. Goran barely had enough money for a one-way ticket. The return ticket seemed an unnecessary waste. One-way was all he needed. But no one would sell them a one-way ticket. With Goran's Yugoslav passport, which was officially not a legal document since January 1, 1994, no agency wanted to take the risk of issuing Goran's one-way ticket in case he wasn't allowed to enter the UK. The two men stubbornly stuck to their principles, and went through travel agencies, one by one, each time going through the same conversation.

'*Buongiorno*. We would like to buy a ticket to London.'

'We have a place available tomorrow. The return ticket cost is…'

'No, not a return ticket,' Goran interrupted. 'I only need a one-way ticket.'

'Right. I need to see your passport. What passport do you have?'

'Yugoslavian. But I have a visa for the United Kingdom. And I also have a visa for Australia.'

'I can't sell you a one-way ticket. If they don't allow you to enter the United Kingdom, the agency will be fined and I will most likely be fired.'

Finally, at Interprisma Viaggi, at Via di S. Nicola da Tolentino, they bought a one-way ticket to London Gatwick for 214,000 lire, around 185 American dollars, for January 9, 1994.

DAY 600

THE night before his departure Goran hardly slept. His flight was at nine-thirty in the morning. Anticipating the possibility of complications, accompanied by Šefko, Goran arrived at the Fuimicino airport several hours before the flight was scheduled to leave. In his hand was a bag of clothes collected during his three-month stay in Rome. Predictably, with a one-way ticket to London and his red Yugoslav passport he was stopped at passport control and asked to step aside. After long questioning, the airport officers decided to call the Home Office in London. After the British Home Office confirmed that Goran's UK visa was valid and that Goran would be allowed to enter the UK, he was finally permitted to board the plane.

At home, restlessly moving around the house since early morning, I impatiently waited to hear that everything was okay and that Goran was allowed to fly to London. As soon as Šefko returned home, Ziza phoned to let us know that Goran was on the plane. A couple of hours later Goran called from London to tell me the arrival time for his train to Penrith that night.

The time seemed to drag more slowly than ever. Every little while I checked the time, and not even an hour would have gone past since the last time I had checked. I tidied the house, cooked dinner and baked a cake, and still had plenty of time left before the arrival of the train.

I declined everyone's offer to drive us to the train station. I didn't want anyone to be with us when we got together after six hundred days of separation. Although I thought that day-by-day I was getting better at hiding my true emotions and worries in front of the children I wasn't sure I could stay calm and suppress tears when I saw Goran. I didn't want additional witnesses to my emotional outbreak.

Thirty minutes before the train was due to arrive, rugged up in warm clothes, the three of us slowly walked to Penrith train station. Approximately one kilometre from our apartment block, it was less than a twenty-minute walk. Night had already fallen; it was dark, cold and misty but we weren't paying attention to that. At the train station I checked the platform where the London train was to arrive. Shortly afterwards the train was announced. Firmly holding Elena's hand, I felt my hand sweating and butterflies in my stomach twirling like crazy as we walked to the platform. Dario was quiet, as always, walking behind me, trying not to add complexity to these emotionally charged moments. We reached the platform. The train was slowing down to a stop, light fog obscuring my view. Only a few people stepped down from the carriages. The train was continuing to Glasgow.

Where is Goran? My heart jumped with the fear that something could have happened during the train ride, or that he'd fallen asleep and missed the stop.

And then we saw him, walking towards us from the far end of the train. I whispered, 'There he is.' Elena heard me and, dressed in her best clothes—white tights, a nice dress and freshly washed jacket—she pulled her hand out of mine and ran towards Goran screaming with joy, 'Daaaaadyyyy…' But she stepped in a puddle, slipped, and fell into it, face down, crying.

Not a picture-perfect welcome for her father, but a very real one.

We gathered around her, and the extreme emotional charge dissolved while we tried to calm her down. We looked like an ordinary family around a young child who had fallen and needed comfort. We cleaned Elena's face, and Goran picked her up.

With Dario holding Goran's other hand we walked towards the taxi stand and went home.

A big poster prepared and illustrated by Dario's school friends waited for us on the biggest wall of our flat: 'Welcome to Penrith!'

TOGETHER AGAIN

EVERYTHING around us appeared to me more beautiful than before. Either I was a different person, or everything around me had dramatically changed. The old and faded grey-blue carpet in our flat, permanently marked with grime spots, changed its colour to silver-blue shades. Our only armchair, with a tall back and ears, its upholstery so old and discoloured that I had to cover it with a random piece of fabric—where I had spent many daytime hours asleep in front of the television to make up for the sleepless nights—became Goran's favourite place. The monotone grey weather, eternally colourless, cold and rainy but never wintery enough to evoke the familiar feeling of fresh snowy winters in Sarajevo, became the charming and poetic English weather. The architectural beauty of the old buildings around us emerged from the haze I had lived in for fifteen months.

Although in many ways Goran and I reconnected in an instant, as if we had never been separated, for my mind it took much longer to understand that we were together again. The anxiety that had rippled throughout my body every morning for almost two years, making me lightheaded even before I woke up, didn't go away easily. Each morning I woke with a tense body even before I opened my eyes, my mind fearing what the day could bring before I remembered that the nightmare was over, that my husband was with me, next to me, in my bed. The piece of me missing for almost two years was back. I would open my eyes and without moving look at him, asleep. I wanted to stretch my hand and touch him, make sure he was really there, it was not just my imagination, but restrained myself—the sleep was as nourishing for him as the wholesome food I served every day to help him recover.

The rhythm that the three of us had established during the long wait for Goran no longer worked. There was now one more person that needed to be consulted when planning or doing anything. Lots of things normally done without many words exchanged between Dario and me needed to be explained and described to Goran. But we all enjoyed this little change in our daily routine; it brought novelty to everything we had been doing since we had arrived in Penrith.

We took Goran to see all the places in the town that were of any importance to us—the house on Old London Road, Dario's school, Elena's crèche, the Meeting House (even though I had completely stopped going there a while earlier).

With my hand snug in his, we wandered the streets of Penrith. I pointed out what-was-what and its meaning to us. We looked at the windows of the Benetton shop, where I had spent many hours daydreaming about buying some of their colourful items. We even walked into Dorothy Perkins, a women's fashion store, much more affordable than Benetton, where I had bought a couple of items of clothing. We paid a visit to the beautiful Bluebell Bookshop in Angel Square, one of the best bookshops in the region, and I introduced Goran to the shop founder and owner, Derek Robinson, who a year-and-a-half earlier initiated the mission to save a dozen Bosnian families by offering them a new home and local residents' support in Cumbria. We checked out all the supermarkets in Penrith and looked for the food Goran had missed the most while trapped in Sarajevo. And that was everything and anything fresh, even frozen, just not canned, and not dry. Strawberries, even frozen, were always at the top of the list. And probably still are. Although he enjoyed many flavoursome meals during his stay with our friends in Rome, his craving for fresh food had not been extinguished. I'd encourage Goran to choose from the fresh food aisle whatever he fancied that day, and we would then figure out what to cook with it.

While I talked a lot about the events and places that had made our lives since we came to Penrith, I did not question Goran much about his life during the war. I knew he had kept a diary. He brought with him several small notebooks packed with notes in his tiny handwriting. After his initial summary of the difficulties of life under siege, the shortage of everything vital and the abundance of danger, we didn't go back to this topic. Undoubtedly Goran didn't enjoy re-living the terrors of his past and preferred to focus on the present and future. Life is too short to waste time on crying about what has happened in the past or to regret doing or not doing something. The past is the past and cannot be changed. We never revisited the details of Goran's life in Sarajevo under siege. We focused our energy on re-connecting with the present and planning the future, even if that was only for the next day.

Gradually our English and Bosnian friends dropped by, everyone wanting to meet Goran, to see the man whose escape from Sarajevo had finally materialised. We hosted dinners, eager for our friends to see the four of us together and happy, as we were before the war. I cooked my best Bosnian meals and cakes, this time not worrying about spending a bit of extra money. Celebrating our reunion was worth every penny.

Not everyone knew the intricate parts of our eventful story; we repeated them countless times. People shook their heads in disbelief on hearing the astonishing details about the international press card and flak jacket, both of which were by then returned to their sources.

When asked about his life in Sarajevo, Goran was laconic. 'It was hard. Shelling from the hills every day and snipers killing people in the streets. We had no food other than cans. The town was without electricity and water for weeks on end. We burned books, furniture and trees from the parks to survive the winter.'

His discomfort with the topic of conversation was obvious and people straightaway switched to happier themes, our life in Cumbria and our plans for Australia.

We went to the homes of our friends and visited places around Penrith. Everyone wanted to get to know this happier version of our family. We enjoyed the time spent at Jacqui's farm and Anna's beautiful cottage, the drives around the Lake District with Anna, bird watching with Jan and her family. We were invited to meals with several families, a couple of them engraved firmly in my memory.

At the Robinsons', after a lovely meal, I offered to help with the dishes. Even after living in Cumbria for longer than a year, I was still puzzled with certain cultural differences—washing the dishes by hand was one of them.

At home, in Sarajevo, from the first day of our life together, Goran and I had a dishwasher. The few dishes that wouldn't fit in it were hand washed with soapy water and then rinsed under a running tap. In Sarajevo no one had ever thought about the need to save water. When I helped with the dishes in the Meeting House for the first time, while washing them under running water, I was told off for wasting water and asked to fill a bowl with hot water and dishwashing liquid. It seemed that no one cared if the dishes were rinsed. So I did as I was told. Since then I hadn't had much of an opportunity to wash dishes in Cumbrian homes as both Jacqui and Anna had dishwashers. At home, of course, I continued to do it my own way, slightly modified, in a bowl for soapy water and then rinsed under running water as quickly as possible.

Faced with the dishwashing process in an English home I was unsure of what to do. Determined to avoid wasting water, and embarrassed about asking my host how to do it, I washed all the dishes, including those used to bake a chocolate cake, in a single bowl of soapy water. In the end the water was brown and thick like mud from all the cocoa, butter and flour. I thought, or imagined, that this perplexed Pauline and her elder daughter standing next to me in the kitchen and talking to me, but I carried on with washing nevertheless. Later on I regretted my ridiculousness. Surely no one washes the dinner dishes and the cake mixing bowls in a single bowl of soapy water. Bosnians definitely do not, but most certainly the English don't either. Fortunately, Pauline didn't take it as a grave faux pas, and never mentioned it, but I kept wondering if they thought I had a weird and unhygienic method for washing dishes.

Another fascinating day, imprinted clearly into my memory, is the day of our visit to Greystoke, an almost thousand-year-old castle. The home of Lavinia Howard and her husband Neville, the castle had housed fourteen generations of Howards. The tranquillity of the castle and its surroundings, its endless green lawn, a lake with a flock of ducks peacefully floating in it, had an instantly calming effect. As we entered the castle and I saw the huge hall with wide stairs in etched dark timber, the thought crossed my mind of how amazing it would be to live in such a place, even as a maid. By now I knew what the word 'maid' meant. A brief tour of the castle included a visit to a huge dollhouse twice Elena's height. She of course wanted to stay there and play, but we continued on and after a few words about its history we sat down to have pre-lunch drinks.

Neville surprised us by saying 'Živjeli!' when we clinked glasses. For a split second Goran and I didn't absorb that the word for cheers had been said in our mother tongue. We looked at each other in surprise and asked Neville where and how he had learned to say cheers in Serbo-Croatian, to which he told us, with a smile, that it was his little secret. We smiled back and left it at that. It matched Goran's idealistic idea that it was Neville who had helped bring Goran to the UK with his Home Office connections. Although I thought that our Australian visa was almost certainly the biggest factor, I liked the fancy idea of a refugee family being helped through personal connections in the Home Office.

Many years later, while exchanging emails with Neville about our past, he told me that despite quite frequent contacts with the Home Office through his work he was not involved in securing Goran's visa as he knew that the British system would react badly to any attempt to interfere. The mystery of what had made it happen remained unresolved.

The days passed, calm and stress-free. We enjoyed our new family life, a long-awaited and well-deserved break from the constant anxiety of the last twenty months.

It was lovely to hear Dario and Elena talking to their dad. Elena brought her picture books for Goran to read, who partly read them in English, and partly made it up in Bosnian, and they both laughed.

Dario showed Goran his school notebooks, talked to him about playing cricket with Steve.

Enchanted, I watched them from the kitchen while preparing our meals, more elaborate than before, as I tried to help Goran put on weight and recover his strength. If only we could have lived like that forever. But we knew we needed to make the move soon; we promised we would and we wanted to.

I explored the cost of our tickets to Melbourne. I still didn't know how we would pay for them; I only had several hundred American dollars saved from Madelyn's letters, converted to British pounds. I called travel agencies and was overwhelmed by the prices. Worried, I mentioned the unaffordability of the tickets to a few people. The information reached a couple whose son worked at a travel agency selling student flights. They immediately tasked him with finding us the cheapest one-way tickets to Melbourne. He surprised us not only with a ticket offer much lower than the other agencies but also with the detail that the cheapest flights were with Alitalia, via Rome. I was immensely excited about this unexpected prospect to see Ziza and Šefko on our last stop in Europe. We decided that if we could have a stopover in Rome without paying extra for the tickets we would certainly do so. Even though the flights were the cheapest possible, they were still three times more than the savings Goran and I had. We could not commit to a departure date. We first had to work out how to pay for it.

Predictably, our English friends wanted to help. A coffee morning was organised at the Meeting House to raise money. I baked a few trays of cakes and many of the English people contributed with cakes, jams and preserves. There were some second-hand goods and books available for sale. Goran told me later on he had seen some people buying their own items brought in earlier that day. Dignified in their help, they preferred to spare us from receiving cash as charity. I translated some of my favourite Bosnian recipes into English, which we printed out at a friend's office, and they were available for sale for two pounds a copy. Still, with the fundraising money and our savings we only scraped together enough for two and a half tickets.

I was thinking of maybe borrowing the rest of the money from Goga, if they could wait a little while for us to repay it. Knowing how much she had already done for us since we had fled Sarajevo, I felt uncomfortable asking for one more favour. I didn't know how long it would take us to find jobs and start earning money in Melbourne. Maybe a few months, maybe longer.

While I was deliberating whether I should ask Goga for the money, totally unexpectedly, a cheque arrived from Madelyn with an enormous amount of money. Some money was accumulated in gifts from her friends and relatives, and a big sum had been promised by a close relative. On that pretence, without delay, Madelyn borrowed from their family savings and included the amount with the collected money. Many years later I discovered that her close relative's promise was never fulfilled and the biggest part of the money ended up coming from Madelyn's own family budget.

Not only did we have the money for all four tickets but a few hundred pounds extra for expenses during the trip and for the first few weeks in Melbourne. I was a little worried that we wouldn't be able to afford any household items when we arrived in Australia, but I pushed these thoughts aside. There wasn't much I could do about it and it was pointless to worry about it in advance. One step at a time.

We booked our tickets, departing from London on March 4, 1994.

A week's stopover in Rome was included with no extra cost. Our final goodbye to Europe and to our dear friends before flying to Melbourne.

FAREWELL

HOW do you pack a household into four suitcases?

From the two bags with which we had fled Sarajevo, during the long twenty-two months of refugee life on a tight budget, we had nonetheless gathered lots of items: clothing, sheets, towels, plates, toys, picture books. I knew we would need all of it in Melbourne, and I would have loved to have it shipped, but we could not afford it. I had to rationalise and pack as much as we could take on the flight, including some sheets and towels, and our best-looking clothes.

The hardest part was deciding what to do with the expensive porcelain dishes that Anna had given me and wanted me to keep. I wanted to keep them too; they were so pretty, so English and so 'Anna'. But each piece was heavy and I could not take them all. In the end I packed a beautiful Portmeirion oval baking dish, a luxurious-looking cake serving dish, and the matching ceramic cake server. Every time I glanced at them they reminded me of Anna and her infinite generosity, the time we spent in Penrith, and the kind Cumbrians who surrounded us and helped us.

A huge food processor, another gift from Anna, and a couple of nice serving plates made their way with us to London. I left them there, as a thank-you gift to our friends with whom we stayed for a couple of nights before continuing to Rome.

Unsure of the future in a faraway land and whether we would ever have an opportunity to come back to London, we wanted Dario to see some of the major monuments in the British capital, a lesson in world history that shouldn't be missed. The decision to leave Elena's stroller behind in Penrith made the idea of visiting the places as a family fairly impossible. The first day I carried our three-and-a-half-year-old in my arms after she quickly became tired from walking and started crying. When we got back to our friends' apartment that evening it was me who almost cried—my arms ached. The following day Elena and I stayed in parks and on nearby benches while Goran and Dario visited as many historic buildings as they could fit in on our last day in London.

Upon landing at Rome airport, the wild butterfly dance in my stomach returned. Excited to see my dearest friend, Ziza, and her family, I was at the same time worried about whether Goran's passport would allow him to enter Italy. Uneasy about possible complications, I almost wished we hadn't stopped in Rome but had travelled straight to Melbourne.

Approaching passport control, I went in first, holding all four passports, my Croatian one on top, then the children's, and tucked at the bottom of the pile Goran's old Yugoslav passport. The immigration officer spread the four passports like playing cards, ignored the Croatian ones, and pulled out the last one, opened it, looked at Goran standing next to me and holding the children's hands and said to him, in Italian, 'You can't enter the country with this passport.'

I didn't understand every word of it, but his tone and the few words I could pick up, 'Non... entrare... passaporto...' were enough for me to start panicking. I tried reasoning with the officer, in English. 'We are only staying for a week, we have tickets for Melbourne and visas for Australia,' but he kept shaking his head and repeating, *'Il suo passaporto non è valido.'* His passport is not valid.

My hands shook and my brain fuzzed with the absurdity of the situation and our helplessness to do anything about it. I knew that if we had to replace our tickets to continue to Melbourne straight away, we wouldn't be able to do so as we hardly had any money left. *What will happen to us in that case?*

'My *Permesso!*' Goran pulled out his *Permesso di soggiorno*, his Italian residence permit, obtained during his stay in Rome after the arrival from Sarajevo. The officer immediately changed his attitude, stamped our passports and we walked into Italy.

The next seven days were spent in a haze of friendship, love, laughter and loads of great food, mixed with visits to famous historic places. It seemed as if we had never separated, as if the war had not happened.

The morning of our departure, when the taxi came to pick us up, Ziza and Šefko came downstairs to help with the luggage and farewell us. As I hugged Ziza goodbye, tears rolled down her face. I had never seen her cry before. She was the most positive person I knew. Even when everything around her indicated that things weren't as great as they should be, she maintained her calm and trusted that in the end it would all be fine. Seeing her cry broke my heart. With a trembling voice I asked, 'Why are you crying?' And she replied, 'Who knows whether I will ever see you again?' Pretending to be strong, disbelieving my own words, I waved her goodbye and said, 'Of course you will, why wouldn't you? It's not like we are going to the end of the world.'

Twenty-two hours later we landed in Melbourne. Once again the uncomfortable sensation in my stomach returned—would Goran's passport cause an issue?

It didn't. All that mattered to Australian immigration was that our visas were valid.

MELBOURNE

AFTER

A message popped up on my phone. 'Edita, I can't believe I found you! Where are you? How are you?'

A long lost friend from school in Sarajevo found me through social media. We had spent twelve years of primary and secondary school in the same class and had been friends until we parted to study for different degrees. Belonging to different circles of friends, we didn't see each other for a few years. Then my marriage and the children happened, I was busy with my own life and only had time for the closest of friends. I thought of her often though; she went through a huge tragedy in her early twenties and I wondered how her life had unfolded after that. Years went by and I had not heard much about her, but I knew that she lived in Sarajevo and that I could get in touch with her whenever I found the time. I didn't count on the fact that the war would sprinkle Sarajevans around the world and that we would permanently lose track of our childhood friends.

Surprised to see her photo with the message, I replied, 'I'm fine, we are all fine, we live in Melbourne. How are you? Where do you live now?'

She updated me on her moves during the war and how she ended up in Sweden, where she lived. Her story was fairly straightforward, she had no husband or children at the time, it was just herself that she needed to save.

When it was my turn to tell our story, I summed up two difficult refugee years in a few sentences.

'I left Sarajevo with Dario and Elena on one of the last convoys, in May. Goran couldn't leave with us; we left it until too late. We stayed five months in Croatia with a friend, and then we moved to England. Goran joined us in January '94. Two months later we came to Melbourne.'

'You know,' she texted, 'it's twenty-five years since we left our home-town.'

I glanced at the date on my phone. One week prior was exactly twenty-five years since Elena, Dario and I had fled Sarajevo. I wished we had remembered to mark the day, but by pure chance no one from my family was in Melbourne—Elena was in Katherine, in the Northern Territory, where she had moved with her teaching job, Dario was in Brisbane on a work trip, Goran was in Europe, managing repairs on the house in Orebić and spending a bit of time with his mum in Sarajevo.

'A quarter of a century! Last week was the anniversary for us. I wish we had done something special to mark it.'

For a while there was no reply. I thought she had left the conversation. It was her daytime in Sweden and she could've been busy.

I messaged her. 'If you're busy let's leave catching up for some other time.'

She replied, 'No, it's fine, I have a cold, I stayed at home today. Are you okay to continue? I would offer to call you, but I have a sore throat and can't talk. What's the time there? Is it too late for you to keep going?'

'It's pretty late here, but it's okay, it's Saturday tomorrow, I can sleep in.'

The house was quiet. I was reading a book before her first message had come. In a way I preferred to exchange messages than to talk, as the topic was emotional for me. I liked the option of re-reading and correcting what I said in my replies. I knew from past conversations with our friends from Sarajevo that we all had different memories from the difficult times during and after the war and sometimes my honest comments on our life in Melbourne were unintentionally misinterpreted. I didn't want anyone to feel sorry for us. It was not easy to start in a new country, but there were so many great things about it too, so many things that we would never have done or seen had we stayed in Sarajevo.

I moved from the couch to use the laptop on the dining table. As I crossed the living room, reminded of our beginnings in this country twenty-three years ago, I looked around our place thinking how at the time we came to Melbourne I thought that I would never again care about what we wore and what we owned. That, as long as we were together, nothing else mattered. Did I still think the same? According to the amount of books and guides stashed on pieces of furniture and overflowing bookshelves, I still believed that education and travel, the source of knowledge and memories that no one can take away from us, are more important than bigger and better cars and houses. But it seems that going through a war and several rough years on the edge of poverty did not destroy my desire for the comfort of a cosy home. The white walls, unassuming furniture and simple selection of colours in our house in Melbourne, in a way, reminded me a lot of our place in Sarajevo.

Then the next message came. 'You spent almost two years on your own. That must've been terribly hard. I can't imagine how worried you were about Goran and your parents. Everything must've been easier after you reunited and started a new life in Melbourne.'

I thought about what to say to that. I also naïvely assumed that everything would be perfect and easy as soon as we were together. But it was not easy. Not for a long time.

For a number of years we struggled, not only financially but also emotionally. We longed for the warmth and love of family and close friends, we longed for a peaceful life, for happy days filled with the joy and fun of life before our ordeal had started. Instead, not yet recovered from the emotional drain caused by the war and family separation, we had a new battle to deal with—finding our place in a world we didn't know, and didn't understand.

For a long time I could not let go of the irrational fear of having to leave the house in an emergency, with no return. All our important documents were stacked in a folder ready to be quickly picked up in case we needed to leave. My mind would verify the location of the folder several times a day. I obsessively made sure that all our clothes were clean and ready to pack if we needed to flee in a hurry. It took a long time to fully accept the stability of our lives.

The war in Sarajevo was still going on and our parents and Goran's sister and her family were still there. Goran's sister died from cancer six months after we arrived in Melbourne—in besieged Sarajevo she could not be treated nor cured. She left behind two young children, a daughter of twelve, and a son of nine. We could do nothing for them; they were behind a thick impenetrable curtain, the siege. We couldn't even phone and talk to them as the lines with Sarajevo were still down. Our pain was so sharp that Goran and I could not even talk about it. And there was no one in Melbourne with whom we could share the pain of this immense loss.

The daily news from Bosnia and the lack of contact with our family prolonged and deepened our emotional strain. The smallest things sparked extreme emotional outbursts.

Once, when I left our second-hand car for a routine service, the mechanic phoned while I was at work to say that the car needed a major repair and had to be kept overnight. I immediately burst into tears. Seeing me crying, a colleague fearfully asked me if everything was okay. I told him about the car and he looked at me puzzled. 'But, why are you crying? It is only a broken car.'

It was not the car that had caused my tears. It was the years of struggle accumulated in me that had made me cry. I had to pick Elena up from childcare by six in the evening. I panicked that I would be late for her. For a second I felt stuck and helpless and my immediate reaction was to burst into tears. A few years later I would have had no distress about it. By then I would learn that being late to collect your child only meant paying a few extra dollars, that leaving work early was not an issue, and that paying for a taxi was not the end of the world. But when you are new to a country, don't know any of the rules and have no one to help you learn and make decisions, it is all overwhelming.

'It wasn't as easy as I thought it would be,' I replied. 'It was easier to go through it together, but still, a tremendous effort to organise a family in a completely new country. It's such a different world here, we had so much to learn at a rapid pace.'

'Did you have much help from the government?'

With no rental history and a limited amount of money, we faced a difficult, tiring and somewhat humiliating process of finding a place to live. Inspecting rental properties without a car meant spending lots of time on trains and hiking. With a map in our hands we paced suburban streets looking for a real estate agency or a house that was open for inspection. Finding an address in a maze of similarly looking streets and houses was hugely challenging. Eventually, we lost patience with the process and rejections and settled on a small and unattractive two-bedroom unit in need of a thorough disinfection. I presumed that no one else wanted it. We cleaned the carpets, painted the walls, and scrubbed the kitchen and bathroom, sticky from years of grime and inadequate cleaning. We bought some cheap Ikea furniture, and second-hand pieces were handed down from friends of our host family.

'We didn't come as refugees; we came on a professional visa. No government help is offered for such cases. After staying with our friends for two months we moved to our own place. Elena was enrolled in full-time childcare, Dario in primary school. I started my full-time job and Goran started going to an English language course and looking for a job at the same time.'

'What about Sarajevan friends there, did they help? There must be some people from Sarajevo there.'

After two years of intense emotional agony, we came to Melbourne as empty shells. What was left inside us was frozen and needed lots of warm care to defrost. We had nothing to offer to friends other than our survival story. They had already heard stories similar to ours; they weren't interested in hearing another one.

Socialising was often too much effort for us. We couldn't offer what people wanted: jokes, and holiday plans. They couldn't offer what we craved: compassion and love. On arrival in Melbourne, an ex-colleague from Sarajevo cheerfully asked me, 'How was London?'

'We didn't live in London,' I said. 'We lived in Penrith, a small town in Northern England, close to Scotland.' He waived his hand as if saying, 'It's all the same, London, Penrith.' Then he added, 'You've changed so much. You used to joke all the time.'

It was pointless to explain why I had changed and why I had nothing to joke about. I wasn't even sure if I would ever be able to joke again.

'We knew a few families from Sarajevo,' I texted back. 'They did help us in the beginning, but they had their jobs, mortgages, and children to raise. I guess we were too hard a case anyway; so emotionally broken that we craved love and friendship far beyond what they could offer. No one had the time to deal with our emotional complexity.'

'Why Australia? It's so far away.'

What if there had been no war? Would we ever have decided to move to another country, learn another language, challenge ourselves by adopting another culture? Would we have had the courage to stay immersed in a society, so foreign to us in many ways, away from everything we knew and everyone we loved, if we didn't have to?

At first seeing the 'new country', its wide spaces and unruly architecture, was a culture shock. Sarajevo is a town with a long and rich history, with beautiful architecture originating from different periods, with the Ottomans and the Austro-Hungarians making the strongest impact on the look of the place. From the middle of the fifteenth-century, Sarajevo had been part of the Ottoman Empire for four hundred years. Many beautiful mosques and the old bazaar Baščaršija, with its narrow alleyways and single-storey shops and stalls, originate from that period. During the much shorter period that followed, under the Austro-Hungarian empire, Sarajevo went through a period of fast development when beautiful buildings in neo-Gothic and Romanesque styles were built. The first tram in Europe made it look like a true European capital. The mix of styles gives the town an exotic and unusual look. A mix of Istanbul and Vienna in a way.

Seeing the strip of shops in a Melbourne suburb on our second day in Australia, with the box-like flat-roofed buildings in different sizes, with faded facades and mismatched bricks confused me. I had a weird feeling of going back in time. The look of the shoe-store we entered, a few foldable tables lined up against the wall and shoe-boxes stuck up on them, nearly brought tears to my eyes. *What is this place? Where have we come to?* Slowly we learned to love Melbourne, its modern city centre, and the unusual messy mix of building styles that changes from suburb to suburb, its climate, and the proximity to great beaches.

'We had applied for an Australian Visa before the war, we knew people who had moved here and liked it. I must admit, several years after settling in, I started wondering if Melbourne was the right place for us, and if not, where that perfect place would be. Of course, I dreamed of living in France… But no place in the world is better than the other. The right place is where we choose to live, and we chose Melbourne, or Melbourne chose us. We are happy here.'

'What about your work? Did you manage to find work easily?'

How lucky I had been with finding work! The company for which I worked in Sarajevo was one of the few software providers in the world that ran their business on a particular type of mainframe computer. And another one like that existed in Melbourne. Only three days after we arrived, on a Saturday morning, Mario, our friend who had generously offered that we stay with his family until we found our own place, spotted a job advertisement in *The Age* newspaper. He yelled from the kitchen, 'Hey, have a look at this! This job is made for you!'

We quickly put my résumé together and sent it the following day. In less than a week, I had a job interview with an agent, followed shortly after by an interview with the potential employer. I was offered the job and started working a month after we arrived. The job was at a lower position than the one I had held in Sarajevo, but I accepted it without hesitation. There was no time to look for a better job or higher pay. We needed the money straight away.

'Yes,' I replied to her. 'I was really lucky with that. Found a job in less than a month, similar to what I did in Sarajevo.'

'I guess you came from England with decent English. I had to learn Swedish from scratch. It was very difficult in the beginning.'

It was difficult for me too. Although more than fine in day-to-day conversations, my English was inadequate for a professional environment. Partaking in work meetings or any other quick conversation was exhausting. I remembered coming out of my first business meeting with five or six colleagues, where the quick exchange of words was way too fast for me to follow. My brain worked hard and converted English words into a combination of pictures and Bosnian words, whatever was found first in the big library of my brain, but if no match was found, my brain, not yet trained to deduce meaning without understanding each word, would halt right there, repeatedly searching harder and harder, and eventually giving up. In the meantime the conversation moved on and I would miss a few important sentences, which made the rest of the conversation even more difficult to understand. We left the meeting, everyone commented on the discussion, and they all laughed while my poor brain buzzed in circles, unstoppable, still trying to make sense of what I had heard.

'Well, it wasn't really at a great level when we came, I struggled a bit at times, but I managed.'

'What do you speak at home, Bosnian or English? In so many

Sarajevan families here the children hardly speak Bosnian.'

My thoughts went to December the year we came to Melbourne, when four-year-old Elena fell off a wall at a Melbourne beach and seriously crushed her left elbow. She had a long and difficult operation, wore a splint and a cast.

That's when my conversations with Elena could no longer be carried out in Bosnian. Annoyed and edgy from the pain and discomfort, she could not understand when I told her, '*Lezi na ledja*', to help her find a more comfortable position to fall asleep. I did not have the energy and the patience to explain the simple phrase using other Bosnian words (if that is possible at all for such a short sentence), so I said it in English, 'Lie on your back,' and since that moment I fully switched to talking to her in English.

Elena and I didn't exchange a word in Bosnian for many years. Whether that was the right decision or not, I will never know. I wanted her to become fully fluent in English before she started school. I was concerned that starting school and not understanding the language could cause stress and potentially make Elena dislike school, which could have lifelong consequences. I was concerned that alternating languages would confuse and tire her. I guess I transposed my own experience from the time in Penrith when it was extremely tiring for me to switch from English to Bosnian all the time. Perhaps for a child of four that would be natural and easy, not tiring. They say that children easily absorb as many languages as they are immersed in. But I could only believe things I experienced. I imagined that the first steps of bilingualism would be hard for anyone, even a child. I wanted to protect Elena from that, thinking that when the time was right she would absorb Bosnian anyway, as Goran kept speaking it at home. We often had a situation where Goran would try to explain something to little Elena in Bosnian, she would stare at him, confused, and then turn her head towards me, and I would repeat what her dad had said, in English. I slowly started using more English with Dario as well. But his Bosnian was already well established and he seemed to be handling two languages easily and without any confusion.

In 1998, when I went back to Sarajevo for the first time, I regretted not insisting on speaking Bosnian with the children. Elena, almost eight at the time, went with me on the trip. She could not speak Bosnian at all, other than a few everyday words like *dodji* (come here), *ručak* (lunch), *obuci se* (put some clothes on). It was painful seeing my dad talking to Elena with love in his eyes, about her grandmother, about her mum, and about how cute she, his granddaughter, was, while Elena could barely understand a word or two of what he was telling her.

Over time, though, through many visits to Sarajevo and Orebić, Elena learned to speak Bosnian, albeit with a foreign accent. Old enough when we left Sarajevo, Dario preserved his mother tongue and his Sarajevan accent too.

'We mix the two languages. Goran only speaks Bosnian at home, I suppose it keeps him closer to his origins. I used to speak only English to the children, I thought it was better for them, but nowadays, they don't mind whether we speak English or Bosnian, they speak both.'

'Your mum and dad, are they still in Sarajevo?'

When my mum died in Sarajevo in 1997, at the age of seventy, I was totally unprepared for it and was for a long time in a state of shock and disbelief. Although not in the best health during the last two decades of her life, she died unexpectedly after a short and acute illness. I never had the chance to see her stretching *yufka* and baking *pita* again. At the time we still didn't have Australian passports. I could not even make it to Sarajevo quickly enough to attend my mum's funeral.

All the questions I had strung in my head since I had last seen her in March 1992—about her life before me, her four brothers, her mum's illness and many other details I wanted to pass onto my children—too complicated for short and expensive weekly phone calls, saved for when I could see her face-to-face, remained unanswered. My family history never to be completed, our family tree forever missing leaves.

At that time my ex-employer from Sarajevo requested that my dad move out of our flat, back to their flat in Grbavica, completely destroyed during the war and uninhabitable. Our flat had been given to me by my employer with the intention to keep me, and my professional skills, in the company for longer. In the former Yugoslavia not many people owned their own houses and flats. In the great socialist tradition, flats were mostly owned by companies and allocated to their employees for indefinite use. By allocating me a flat they were guaranteeing that I would stay with them for at least ten years as otherwise I would not be able to keep the flat. When Goran was about to leave Sarajevo during the war, he checked with a few lawyers if my parents were safe to stay there. He was assured that they had the full right to live in their daughter's flat.

Nevertheless, it seemed the war had changed this law and my dad had to move out. I could not find a logical or a lawful explanation behind such an inhumane and unjust request. By all accounts, I had the right to keep the flat—I had worked for the company for longer than ten years before leaving Sarajevo. I felt that Sarajevo was rejecting me, with full force, taking away from me something that was truly mine, a place to which I could go back—reinforcing our decision to stay in Melbourne. I was stressed beyond comprehension that I could not be there to help my dad ease the painful transition. We sent as much money as we could to replace the broken windows and missing doors in his flat, to have the water and electricity fixed, to pay people to help him move.

When I went back to Sarajevo during the European summer of 1998, more than two years after the war had finished, a year and a half after my mum had died, I found my dad alone and unwell, living in extremely modest conditions. A few inside doors were still missing. Seeing him like that overwhelmed me with sadness and pain.

I spent two weeks cleaning the flat, washing his clothes and sheets, cooking and freezing food and buying household items to help him simplify his daily routine. I knew I could not make much long-term difference and hoped that he would accept occasional assistance from someone who could clean and cook for him a few times a week.

On the last day before our departure we sat in his kitchen, my dad smoking a rolled cigarette. Eight-year-old Elena, not used to people smoking near her, looked noticeably uncomfortable, surrounded by the floating clouds of smoke. While Elena waved her hands in the air in an attempt to change the flow of the smoke that seemed to go straight to her face, I tried to negotiate with my dad for a cleaner to come once every two weeks—I would pay for it. He smiled and nodded, agreeing to everything, but I knew that he would not call the cleaner. After avoiding the subject for two weeks, I finally mentioned my mum. I knew it would distress him. Thinking about the two wars that she had lived through, her poor health, the intense headaches she had had most of her life, and several strokes, I said, 'My poor mum, she didn't have much of a life, did she?' And my dad said, 'What makes you think that? She was very happy. She had me, she loved me, she had you, and she loved you immensely. What else do you need for a happy life?'

In the years to follow I thought of his words many times. What else do we need to be happy other than to give and receive love?

My mum and dad were both born in a small town in the south of Bosnia and Herzegovina. Both went through the hardship of losing their respective fathers early. Consequently, both of them had to leave school after eight years of primary school. My dad became an accomplished furniture maker, an incredibly talented one, who made all the amazing pieces in my parents' flat. He came up with astonishing designs and had an incredible eye for detail. Had he lived in a different time he could have become a rich and famous furniture designer. My mum, although an elite student, had to stop her education to stay at home and look after her four younger brothers after their mum became ill.

My mum and dad were incredibly in love and had dated for seven years before getting married and moving to Sarajevo. Dad found a job in a private carpentry business. My mum worked from home as a dressmaker. When I was born, all their dreams were fulfilled. They wanted a girl, and they had a girl. Uncertain if their incomes would be adequate to provide for two children and send them to university, they decided to not have more than one child. My mum told me that if they had had a boy they would have probably had another child, but after having me they decided that one child was enough for their happiness.

There weren't many families around me with one child; two was the norm in those days, and I knew no one else who was an only child because their parents had so decided. I never felt that I missed out on anything for not having any siblings. What you don't know you can't miss. As a child I was annoyed when adults asked me if I would have preferred to have a sibling. As if they had asked me, 'Would you prefer to live on Mars?' *How would I know? I've never tried it.* Being an only child was all I knew.

In my adulthood I sometimes ponder about which of my personality traits had been shaped by not having siblings. Some of the life skills that I think I'm not strong at are likely those that would be learned from an early age in a home with more than one child. I am not good at arguing, or responding quickly in accusatory situations. These skills are easily learned if there is someone in the house to argue with or to defend yourself from. I'm also not that great at sensible sharing. At times I give too much, in gifts, in time, or care, and then, thinking that I'm overwhelming the other person, I withdraw, which can be confusing in friendships. On the other hand, my independence and self-sufficiency, ability to spend an endless amount of time by myself, in complete silence or in the company of books does not seem to be a common quality of my friends with siblings. Of course, this could all be just who I am and have nothing to do with being or not being an only child.

'Unfortunately,' I replied to my friend, 'my mum and dad are not with us anymore. My mum died shortly after the war finished, in 1997, my dad three years later.'

'Do you still have friends and other family in Sarajevo? Do you go back?'

After that first trip in 1998, we regularly went back to Sarajevo every year or two, depending on our work and school commitments. Partly, it was to visit Goran's mum who, after both Goran's dad and my dad died, was the only grandparent our children had. Partly, it was to try and maintain our children's connection to their place of birth and with their only cousins, Goran's niece and nephew. But mainly it was because we missed Europe, its architecture and our friends who lived there, because we missed summertime at the Croatian seaside and the amazing cuisine both Bosnia and Croatia have to offer.

Every return to Sarajevo though brought an apprehension and unease. In the beginning I was nervous to see my hometown for the first time after the war; I didn't know in what state I would find our parents, relatives and friends after four years of struggle under the siege. The subsequent visits felt awkward at times, sometimes even sad. There was a deep void between us, those who had left Sarajevo many years ago, and those who had stayed. We had all changed. Our friendships had changed too. They seemed the same, but somehow they were different. We felt the same love for one another, but we had become different people.

In the beginning they could not imagine how we lived; the cultures and lifestyles were so significantly different. Neither better nor worse from the life in Sarajevo before the war, just completely different. Starting from the decision we had to make about where and what type of house to buy: closer to the central business district, or further away, bigger or smaller, new or old, in a residential area or closer to shops—the options were endless. Then to which school to send our children: private, public, single-sex, mixed, more alternative, more traditional, academic, sporty, or musically-inclined. No less difficult are the decisions about all different kinds of insurance and retirement fund options. None of this existed in pre-war Sarajevo, and in a way much of it still doesn't.

After a while, explaining lost its importance. And if you can't talk about your life with your friends, what do you talk about? We weren't reading the same books, no longer holidaying in the same places; there wasn't much we had in common other than our shared history. Once you drop the detailed connectivity with someone you have less and less to talk about. After a quick scan of who was where and what they were

241

doing, there wasn't much more to chat about. We still deeply loved and cared about one another, but the time spent together stopped having the remedial effect that profound friendships bring.

My return visits to Sarajevo felt bittersweet, like going back to an old boyfriend. Memories of the good times together brought the desire to see each other to an almost unbearable level. But after the first few moments of happiness, after recognising the unique silhouette and the familiar smell in the air, the hope that things could be like before would be irreversibly destroyed. And the happiness bubble would burst, reminding me why we weren't made for each other anymore.

Nevertheless I keep going back, if only to walk down the main streets and taste the local food. And this despite the fact that I became gluten intolerant many years ago. The two best known Bosnian national dishes, *pita* and *somun*, a special Bosnian flat bread in which *ćevapi* are served, bring about a dose of discomfort I am willing to go through for the sake of bringing back the memories and tastes of my earlier life in Sarajevo.

Knowing that the majority of my friend's family is still in Sarajevo, and her connection to the city is different to mine, I carefully measured my words.

'We go back often, as often as we can. There is nothing like going back to your place of birth, so many memories emerge every time.'

'Hope we can see each other in Sarajevo one day, I'm there at least once every year.'

'That would be phenomenal, after all these years. Let's work on it!'

I closed my laptop and went to bed. I tossed and turned for a long time. The tumultuous emotions kept me awake while different details of our story went through my head again and again.

How extraordinarily lucky we had been to have escaped in time, and unharmed. It wasn't easy, but in a way the journey we went through enriched our lives. The *what if* scenarios went through my head as they had many times in the last twenty-five years. *What if Elena hadn't been a little baby when the war started and if I had not decided to leave*

Sarajevo? Would we have all survived and how would we live now in our birthplace, changed so much since the war? What would my children have been like growing up in post-war Sarajevo? What if something had happened to Goran during the war, if he had been injured or killed? How would that have affected me and our children? What if we had decided to change our original destination and move to Canada instead of Australia? What if we had insisted on staying in England?

My mind went to a moment when, while driving our brand-new car on my way to work in Melbourne, an image from Sarajevo before the war had flashed through my head.

Our second-hand car had broken down the day before and I left it at the car service. That morning, while I was at work, the mechanic called to tell me that the car was beyond repair. Annoyed with the news, I could not believe that we had picked a second-hand car in such poor condition that it only lasted us a year. As nothing could be done about it, I went on to finish up my work assignment, and ended up being even more annoyed when I was told to wait my turn for a PC. Although we all had our own terminals for the main computer, PCs were still a rarity. We only had a few for the department and we had to book time and wait for our turn. I tried to fill the wait by working on my English to Bosnian translation of an IT book. While I could understand perfectly the technical side of it, I struggled with the sentence structures and word order. Unsure how to translate a paragraph, fed up with it all, I went to have a coffee with my work colleagues. Already gathered for a coffee break, they were chatting, laughing, teasing each other, and exchanging jokes. I arrived and sat, fuming.

Seeing me visibly tense, someone asked, 'What's wrong? Why are you so angry?'

I told them what had happened that morning and without thinking much I said, 'I have only three wishes: to drive a new car, to have a PC on my desk and to be fluent in English.'

Many years and a war later, in Melbourne, on my way to work, I realised my wishes had been granted. Perhaps the old saying, 'Be careful what you wish for' is more than just a saying.

But what I had truly always wished for was only harmony and love in my life.

A broken car and a lack of material things are only external factors that can temporarily affect how we feel. Deep down it is unimportant—it does not matter. No cars or objects can replace the feeling of offering love, of being loved.

It's absurd that people spend their lives trying to earn more, to have more, to buy more, only to look more powerful in their own eyes. It's even more absurd that a human being can believe that an enormous amount of money or power is so important that they choose to kill their fellow human beings to prove the supremacy of their religion or their ethnicity over others.

Looking back I can only assume that the road we travelled was in some way necessary; it made us who we are today. It made us all, Dario and Elena especially, more resilient than an average person. Despite complex and challenging life conditions, they grew up to be competent and confident adults, courageous and curious, with a deep sense of social justice. They speak Bosnian, they frequently travel to Europe and never miss visiting their place of birth and the holiday house in Orebić, but in all aspects of their lives they are so very Australian.

When the four of us are together, when I watch our adult children talking and laughing, that's when I feel truly happy. After a long journey from there to here, we have restored our harmony.

I now understand what my dad meant when he said that my mum had had a good life.

It is only love that truly matters.

ACKNOWLEDGEMENTS

EACH and every person mentioned in this story played an important role in shaping it to be as it is told here—a story about the pain war brings to people, and the persistence, resilience and love that can change its outcome. My huge thanks to everyone who helped me make it a tale about love.

Special thanks to the following people: Goga Mešin and her family for bravely inviting us to be their guests at the beginning of the war in Bosnia, for sharing their family home with us and supporting us emotionally and financially for five months; Kanita Aljović for lending us her car; Željka Pavić for insisting that we move to England and for being the supportive friend I needed, then and now; Derek Robinson and his crew for coming to Croatia in October 1992 to rescue a few Bosnian refugee families, and to offer them a new life in Cumbria.

My immense and eternal gratitude to Anna Walker and her family for their love and infinite generosity, to Guy Forrester for relentlessly pressing the UNPROFOR in Sarajevo until we achieved what we wanted, and alongside him to Máire Morgan and to the late Clem Shaw who both had special roles in it.

I am forever indebted to a number of people in Cumbria who offered their unreserved help and support while we lived there, with everything they could and even more: Derek and his family for being at the heart of it all; Jan Barnard, for making sure we had what we needed before I even mentioned it; Jacqui Findlay, for cheering me up regularly with her happy laugh and having us over at her farm; Charlotte and Adam Hill for being the lovely next door neighbours I could count on; Monica Tweddell, for looking after us even if she wasn't able to visit very often; and Steve, for the regular entertainment and for the flak jacket. They cared and loved us and made my pain and worries more bearable.

Big thanks to Željka's American friend Liza Michaelson who visited Cumbria in December 1992 and connected me with Madelyn Altman, whose regular letters, love, support, care and money arriving from

Friday Harbour, on the other side of the world, brought light to my days, so necessary to survive the darkness I was in. I am immensely grateful to Madelyn for that. And for teaching me English, one letter at a time.

Enormous thanks to John B for delivering all the important documents and the precious flak jacket to Goran in Sarajevo.

I am incredibly grateful to Ziza Derviškadić, her husband Šefko and their children, for offering their home and their love to Goran when he needed it most, and for our unique friendship for many years before and after that. A big thank you to Caroline C and her family for everything they did for Goran while he lived in Rome.

Thank you to all my friends who listened to the story about our family's escape from Sarajevo and said, 'You have to write that down.' Thank you to Julie Nelsen, my first reader who said, after reading the first thirty or so pages many years ago, 'I want to hear more.' Also thank you to Julian Murphy who read one of the early versions and provided valuable and insightful input. And of course, a big thank you to Dario and Elena who patiently read, reread and corrected numerous drafts over many years. Even though at first the story brought tears to Elena's eyes, as she could not remember anything and could not relate to that little girl, who in her own words 'caused so much pain to her mum', she bravely persisted in reading it and always provided the well-measured corrections and encouraging feedback of an English teacher. Dario, with the well-trained eye of an editor and lawyer, offered sharp corrections, important and precious.

This book would stay as a family record and nothing more if it wasn't for the encouragements received from several writing competitions over the years. I am particularly grateful to the Deborah Cass Writing Prize, and to Dan Cass for his support and encouragements. I am also indebted to Varuna, the National Writers' House—the week of residency for manuscript development offered priceless time to write and write only when I needed it the most. And finally, huge thanks to Hawkeye Publishing for shortlisting my story

Courage and publishing it in their 2020 Sydney Hammond Short Story Anthology.

Finding a publisher who can see a good story in an unusual topic is not an easy task. I am grateful to Carolyn Martinez from Hawkeye Publishing for taking the time to read my manuscript and for her immediate understanding of the importance of sharing it. I am extremely appreciative of Carolyn's valuable input with the manuscript improvements, but even more so of her professionalism and prompt responses to my never-ending questions.

To Dario and Elena, my endless love and gratitude for who you were then and who you are now. Seeing in you the people you have become makes everything worthwhile.

And finally, to Goran, my husband, my love: thank you for not giving up then and for supporting me now in telling our story. I am grateful to have you.

ABOUT THE AUTHOR

EDITA Mujkić was born and raised in Sarajevo, in what was then Yugoslavia, and now is Bosnia and Herzegovina. After the war broke out in her home country, she fled Sarajevo in May 1992 with her two children. After five months in Croatia, Edita and her children moved to England where she was an interpreter for other Bosnian refugees, although at the time she could barely speak English. Two years later, in 1994, the family arrived in Melbourne.

Edita's eventful family history prompted her to create a written record about it. While she worked on her memoir, Edita submitted extracts to several writing competitions and was longlisted, shortlisted, a runner-up and a winner. This encouraged her to persist with shaping the story for publishing. *Between Before and After* is her first book.

Awards:
Shortlisted for the 2020 Sydney Hammond Memorial Short Story
Winner of the 2017 Varuna Mentorship Award
Runner-up in the 2016 Deborah Cass Writing Prize
Longlisted for the 2016 Richell Prize for Emerging Writers

Book reviews can make or break a book. If you liked what you read, please do consider posting a review on Goodreads or your favourite forum.

Between Before and After is available at www.hawkeyebooks.com.au and all good bookstores and libraries.

Lightning Source UK Ltd.
Milton Keynes UK
UKHW020610130922
408762UK00009B/2501

TREES
OF BRITAIN AND EUROPE

PHOTOGRAPHIC FIELD GUIDE

TREES
OF BRITAIN AND EUROPE

BOB PRESS and DAVID HOSKING

NEW
HOLLAND

The publishers, author and photographic consultants gratefully acknowledge the assistance of all those involved in the compilation of this book. Photograph sources are as listed below:

Frank Lane Picture Agency Ltd: Heather Angel 6, 127tl, 179tr, 189bl, 21 lbr, 213mr, 221tl,ml, 231t,m, 233tl; Ray Bird 91tr, 195ml,mr; Sdeuard Bisserot 51tl, ll5br, 137tl, 173tr, l8lbr, 187b, 205tl, 207bl, 213br, 221tr Daniel Bohler (Silvestris) 211ml; B. Borrel l8ltl; Mike Clark 143bl; Paul Davies 173br, 187tr; Justus De Cuveland (Silvestris) 173bl; Robin Fletcher 175bl; Bob Gibbons 55tl, 61tr, 63tr, 71hr, 85tl, 103ml, 103mr, ll5ml, 117b, 119tr, 125mr,bl, 141tr, 145b, 147tl,ml, 149bl, 153bl, 159bl, 161tl,bl, 171tr, 177bl, 181bl, 187tl 197ml,mr, 201mr, 203bl, 205br,bl, 217br, 223tr,bl, 227tl,tr, 231bl, 233tr; Frank Lane 14, 115tl; A.R. Hamblin 181mr; E.H. Herbert 11, 65tl, 67tr, 69tr, 77bl, 81tl, 89tl, 91tl, 95tl,tr, 99ml,mr, 107bl, 123tl,bl,br, 127bl, 137ml,bl, 155tl,tr, 157tl, 159tl, 189tl, 191tl, 193m, 197bl, 219ml,mr, 225ml; Mike Hollings 89ml, 143tr, 199br; David Hosking 10, 49bl, 55tr, 59tl, 65bl,br, 71mr,bl 73br, 75tl,bl, 81mr,bl, 83br, 85tl, 87mr 93tl,bl, 97tl, l0ltr,br, 103bl,br, l05bl, lllbr, 121tr,b, 123tr, 125tl, 129tl, 131bl,br, 133tr, 135bl, 139tl, 143ml, 145tl, 149tl, 153tr, 155bl, 157bl,br, 159tr, 161tr,br, 165m,br, 167tr,mr,br, 169tl, 179bl, 181ml, 185t, 189ml,mr, 193tr, 197br, 207mr,br, 215bl, 217tr,mr, 219bl,br, 221mr,br, 225tl,bl, 227ml,mr; Wilhelm Irsch (Silvestris) 203tl; Karl Heinz Jakobi (Silvestris) 51ml, 181tr; Eva Lindenburger (Silvestris) 137br; Malcolm MacCachlon 103mr; Mark Newman 53tl; M. Nimmo 47tr, 49tl,ml,mr,br, 51tr,mr,br, 53tr,hr, 55hl, 57tl,ml,bl, 59tr,bl, 61ml, 63tl, 67tl,bl,br, 73tr, 75ml, 77tr, 81br, 83tl,tr, 87tl,tr,ml,br, 89bl,br, 99tl,tr, l0lbl, 103tl,tr, l05br, 109tl, llltl,mr, 113tl, 117tr, 119tl,ml,bl,br, 125tl,tr,ml, 131tl,tr 133tl, 137tr,mr, 141tl, 143mr,br, 147tr,br, l51tr,br,bl, 153br, 157tr, 159ml,mr, 161ml, 165bl, 167tl,ml, 169bl, 175tr, 177mr, 179ml,br, 183tl,tr,ml,mr, 185m, 191ml mr,bl, 203tr, 207tl, 211tl,tr, 215tl, 217tl, 219tl, 225tr,mr, 229tr, 233bl; J.R. Press 61tl, 79bl, 91bl,br, 93tr,br, 95bl,135br, 145tr, 169mr, 175tl, 179mr, 193b, 211bl, 215ml,mr,br, 223tl; M.C.F. Proctor 107br, lllml 197tr, 217bl; lan Rose l0ltl, 113ml, 117tl, 189tr, 195tr, 199tr, 227bl; Michael Rose 63m, 109bl, llltr, 195bl; MJ. Short; 171br, 173tl, 231br; Harry Smith 47tl, 55br, l05tr 119mr, 147bl, 149br, 153tl, 161mr 163m, 167bl 171bl,tl, 175br 179mr, 187m, 191br, 199ml,bl, 201tl, 209tl,tr,bl, 211mr, 213tl,tr; A. Stevens 59mr, 69br, 97bl, 155br, 169tr,br; D.A. Sutton 121tl, 129tr,m,b, 135tr, 145mr, 165t, 171ml,mr,bl, 177tl,ml, 185bl,br, 203br, 209br, 221bl, 225br, 227br, 233br, 235tl,br; B.R. Tebbs 95br, ll5bl; M.J. Thomas 61br, 107tl; Roger Tidman 71tl, 73tl, 113tr; N.J. Turland 81ml, ll5tr,mr, 117m, 127bl, 133bl, 139bl,br, 151tl, 183br, 223br, 235tr,ml,mr,bl; D. Warren 213ml; J. Watkins 149tr; L. West 109br; A.Wharton 229tr; Dr. Wilson 141mr,bl,br; P. Wilson 191tr.

N.J. Turland 15, 47bl, 51bl, 57tr, 59ml,br, 63b, 65tr, 69tl,bl, 73bl, 75tr,mr,br, 77tl,br, 79tl,tr,bl, 83bl, 99bl,br, 107tr, 109tr, lllbl, 113bl, 121m 133br, 135tl, 141ml, 143tl, 159mr, 163tl,tr, 199mr, 207tr,ml, 213bl, 215tr, 217ml, 229tl; Bob Gibbons 12,47br, 53bl, 57br, 61mr,bl, 71tr,ml, 81tr, 85bl,br, 89tr,mr, 97tr,bl, l05tl, 113br, 127tr, 139tr, 163b, 169tl, 177tr,br, 183bl, 189br, 193tl, 219tr, 229br; Wildlife Matters (Dr John Feltwell) 145m.

(t = top; tl = top left; tr = top right; m = middle; ml = middle left; mr = middle right; b = bottom; bl = bottom left; br = bottom right.)

This edition first published in 2002 by
New Holland Publishers (UK) Ltd
Garfield House, 86-88 Edgware Road , London W2 2EA
www.newhollandpublishers.com

First published in 1992
10 9 8 7 6

ISBN 1 84330 131 8 (flexiback)

Commissioning Editor: Charlotte Parry-Crooke
Editors: Ann Baggaley, Caroline Taggart
Design: ML Design, London
Artwork: Margaret Tebbs

Typeset by ML Design, London
Reproduction by Scantrans Pte Ltd, Singapore
Printed and bound in Singapore by Tien Wah Press (Pte) Ltd

CONTENTS

INTRODUCTION
— *page 6* —

How to Use the Guide
— *page 8* —

Distribution and History of Trees in Europe
— *page 11* —

How to Identify Trees
— *page 16* —

Glossary
— *page 20* —

Tree Names and Classification
— *page 21* —

Families of Trees
— *page 22* —

Key to Trees
— *page 29* —

THE TREES OF BRITAIN AND EUROPE
— *page 45* —

Field Equipment
— *page 236* —

Conservation
— *page 237* —

Organisations
— *page 238* —

Arboreta
— *page 239* —

BIBLIOGRAPHY
— *page 241* —

INDEX
— *page 242* —

INTRODUCTION

Like all living things, trees come in many shapes and sizes. In fact only their woodiness and generally large size unite them as a single group of plants. They are, however, an important group. Wherever they occur, trees can dominate the landscape, whether *en masse* in forests or standing in solitary, magnificent splendour. Certainly they hold an attraction which is more than a merely economic one, in

part because they convey both fragile beauty and resilient strength. This attraction is enhanced by an understanding of how and why trees grow where they do, and by the ability to put a name to each specimen encountered. This book is intended to help you in both areas by providing a complete guide to identification, along with information on structure, distribution and other aspects of the lives of trees.

Sugar Maple in autumn colour

Trees are often defined as having a single large and well-developed trunk which branches well above ground level, while shrubs have a smaller and more diffuse habit with several stems branching at or near the ground. These differences are largely artificial and this book includes species normally regarded as shrubs which frequently also form trees. There are also a few species which are not trees but which are popularly thought of as trees, and mistaken for them. (An example is the Banana, which is really a giant herb.) The book covers all but the rarest of trees native or naturalised in Europe, as well as foreign trees which are grown on a large scale, as orchard, timber or crop trees, and those commonly used in amenity plantings and as ornamentals in towns and streets or parkland. Only those trees confined to gardens and specialist collections are omitted.

Trees are influenced by physical boundaries such as mountain ranges rather than by lines on maps, so although Europe in a floristic sense has some resemblance to the political outline of the continent there are some major differences. As defined in this book, Europe extends from the Arctic tundra south to the Mediterranean Sea, and from the Atlantic Ocean eastwards to a line running down the Ural Mountains to the Caspian Sea, including the Crimean Peninsula but excluding the Caucasus Mountains, Anatolian

Turkey and the countries south of it, as well as the island of Cyprus. The Atlantic islands of the Azores, Madeira and the Canaries have a distinctive flora of their own and are also omitted.

The main guide runs from page 46 to page 235 and contains photographs and descriptions of the trees. Each species is illustrated and described – on the opposite page – in detail. Extra photographs of many species are included, further illustrating details of foliage, flowers and fruits. Where very similar species exist these are also described and illustrated with a marginal drawing to show the differences. How to use this guide is described on pages 8 to 10.

The remaining introductory sections provide further information on trees. *Distribution and history of trees in Europe* explains why different trees grow where they do and the influence of man and nature on our forests. *How to identify trees* describes the various structures of a tree, what characteristics to look for and their diagnostic importance; this section is followed by a *Glossary* of botanical terms. *Tree names and classification* explains how trees are classified and the use of both popular and scientific names. *Families of trees* gives a brief summary of the main features of each family into which the European trees included here are divided. Finally, there are *Keys* to help you to identify any specimen before turning to the descriptions to confirm your choice.

At the end of the book are short sections covering other points of interest. *Field equipment* tells you what tools you need to identify trees in their natural habitat. *Conservation* explains the role of trees in the natural world and examines some of the measures taken to preserve them. *Organisations* lists the names and addresses of the main bodies concerned with the protection and understanding of trees and *Arboreta* gives a list of places to visit all across Europe where you can see fine collections of trees. The *Bibliography* suggests selected books which will help you to take your study of trees further, and the two *Indexes* contain all the trees mentioned in the book under their common and scientific names.

How to Use the Guide

The trees covered in this guide are arranged according to the families described on pages 22 to 28. This follows the usually accepted botanical order, beginning with the conifers and ending with the palms. Wherever possible, each genus is followed by that most similar to it.

Each of the main species in the guide is illustrated by one or more photographs and described in detail. Where the description begins 'Closely resembles **x**' then, apart from any particular characters noted, the tree matches species **x** (which has a full entry elsewhere). Additional species are described at the end of some of the main entries. These trees are either so similar as not to warrant a separate entry of their own or are similar to, but much less commonly encountered than, the described tree. For these additional species the main features and distribution are given and they are illustrated with a marginal figure. All the elements relating to each species are displayed together for ease of use.

Full text describes the trees, their origins and distribution.

Marginal figures provide further detailed information or illustrate similar species.

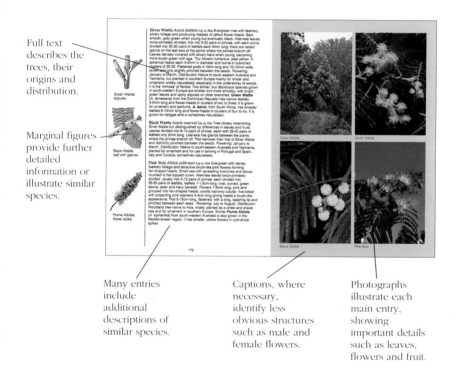

Many entries include additional descriptions of similar species.

Captions, where necessary, identify less obvious structures such as male and female flowers.

Photographs illustrate each main entry, showing important details such as leaves, flowers and fruit.

The Descriptions

The descriptions provide detailed information about each tree. The popular, or common, name is printed in **bold**; some trees have no common name in English. The scientific name is printed in *italics*. This is followed by the height the tree normally achieves. The emphasis here is on the word normally; some individuals may be smaller or larger, but most will fall within the range given. The tree is deciduous unless otherwise stated.

Common name   Scientific name   Height   Main diagnostic features

Willow-leaved Pear *Pyrus salicifolia* Up to 10m Slender, elegant tree with distinctive silvery leaves. Trunk straight, with dark, smooth, silver-grey bark. Crown domed, with horizontal main branches and drooping, densely white-woolly twigs. Alternate leaves 3.5-9cm long, narrow, pointed, grey-green with silver down on both sides at first, the upper surface becoming glabrous and glossy green. Flowers in tight clusters appear with the leaves. Petals five, white, each about 10mm long, notched or rounded at the tip. Fruit 2.5cm long, pear-shaped or cylindrical, brown when ripe, with a white, woolly stalk; flesh sour, firm and gritty in texture. *Flowering:* April. *Distribution:* A native of the Caucasus Mountains, Siberia and Iran to Asia. Widely cultivated as an ornamental. The weeping variety cv 'Pendula' is often more common in cultivation.

Uses

Flowering period   Country of origin   Distribution   Frequency

The order of the text is the standard one used in describing plants: trunk, crown, bark, branches and twigs; leaves and stipules; inflorescence and flowers; fruits. Like the height, the flowering period given represents a range only. It can vary widely for any given species depending on where in the continent an individual tree is growing as well as local fluctuations in the timing of the seasons. The greatest variation occurs with trees which have a broad north-south geographical range, or which are found from the mild Atlantic coasts to the more continental climate of eastern and central Europe. The description ends with an indication of the distribution of the tree in Europe and, for introduced species, their country of origin, plus the relative frequency and any relevant ecological factors and major uses.

The Photographs and Captions

Quince

Each main entry is illustrated with at least one photograph. Important details of leaves, flowers, fruits or bark are shown in additional photographs. Less obvious structures such as male and female flowers or immature fruits are identified in the captions. By virtue of their size and where they grow, trees are not always easy to photograph in their natural surroundings and some specimens are depicted in arboreta. Many of the species included in this book are seldom illustrated outside specialist scientific publications and, for this reason, a few photographs which are not of the highest quality are deemed worth their place here.

The Marginal Figures

Hybrid Larch:
needle rosette

The marginal figures provide further, detailed illustrations. These are usually of the additional species mentioned at the end of the text entries and almost all such species are illustrated. The only exceptions are where the identifying features are based solely on size, colour or flowering time. A few of the figures depict species already shown in photographs if additional illustrations are useful. Again captions clarify precisely what is being shown.

Distribution and History of Trees in Europe

Like all plants, trees show a definite pattern in their natural distribution. Most are confined to either the northern or southern hemisphere. A few families occur in both hemispheres but are represented in each area by different groups of closely related species (genera). A typical example is the Beech family Fagaceae, which has the Beech genus (*Fagus*) north of the equator and the Roble Beech genus (*Nothofagus*) south of the equator. Similarly, within the northern hemisphere, the Old and New Worlds have many genera in common but the species found in each area differ. The only tree widespread in both the Old and New Worlds is the Juniper. Many trees extend across Europe and large parts of Asia or North Africa, but some are unique to Europe, sometimes to very small areas. Spanish Fir, for example, is confined to a small area of limestone mountains near Ronda in south-western Spain, while Abelitzia is found only on the island of Crete. These species are said to be endemic to a particular region. The occurrence of trees is very much influenced by variations in local conditions and the requirements of individual species. Europe presents a wide variety of climates, soils and habitats and supports a rich and diverse tree flora. Despite this, the forests and woodlands can be divided into just three major forest types, coniferous, broad-leaved temperate and Mediterranean.

Coniferous forest

Coniferous forests occur in both the north and the south of the continent. Northern coniferous forest or taiga stretches across northern Europe from the Scottish highlands and the coast of Norway to eastern Siberia and Japan. It also occurs in northern North America. Along the Atlantic coast of Europe it extends well into the Arctic Circle but does not reach so far north in the colder continental land mass, ending at the treeless landscape of the Arctic tundra. The southern limits are more vague, often extending into the broad-leaved temperate regions down major mountain chains such as the Urals. Even further south coniferous forest occurs at high altitudes, generally above 2,000m, in isolated mountain ranges, principally the Pyrenees, Alps, Auvergne massif, Apennines, Carpathians and Balkan mountains. These forests are dominated by evergreen conifers, in particular species of Fir, Pine and Spruce. Deciduous Larches dominate

11

Broad-leaved temperate forest

the highest areas where even evergreens struggle in the dry, cold winters. The only widespread broad-leaved trees in these regions are Birches.

Broad-leaved temperate forests occupy a broad but irregular belt from the Atlantic to the Russian steppe, extending north to the Scottish lowlands, Denmark and southern Scandinavia and south to a line from the Pyrenees through Venice to the Black Sea. The northern limit is set by a daily minimum growing-season temperature of 6 °C, the southern limit by the amount of summer rainfall. These forests are adapted to a clear-cut annual cycle of seasons and require a relatively high level of rainfall throughout the year. They are dominated by tall, deciduous, broad-leaved trees. In the north of the belt these are species of Birch. In the central portion, on the better soils and at lower altitudes, they are species of Oak, while on the poorer soils, especially calcareous ones, and at slightly higher levels they are Beech. Other trees may dominate over smaller areas or in more specialised habitats, principally Willows and Alders on wet ground, Elms on rich soils, and also Maples and Limes.

Mediterranean evergreen forests occupy the most southerly parts of Europe where the summers are hot and dry and the winters warm, wet and humid. They can withstand severe frosts but not over prolonged periods. The dominant broad-leaved trees are principally evergreen species of Oak, and to a lesser extent Olive, Buckthorn and Strawberry-tree. Among coniferous trees, species of Pine, Cedar and Cypress are important. Although conifers are often thought of as more typical of cold climates, their drought-resistant adaptations make them well suited to Mediterranean and even subtropical regions.

History of European Trees

The last ice age which began some one million years ago had a great influence on the distribution of trees in Europe. As the ice advanced, trees were forced southwards. The major European mountain ranges run east-west and some species, prevented by these mountains from retreating at their preferred altitudes, were probably wiped out. As the final retreat of the ice began, around 11,000 years ago, the trees were able to expand their range northwards behind it. In some mountain areas populations of cold-tolerant trees were left behind, isolated as the lands around warmed and confined them to 'islands' in the higher, cooler altitudes. Species of many predominantly northern genera have survived within such mountain refugia. As the lands became warmer still, less hardy trees were able to expand their territory or to emerge from warm refugia where they had survived. This probably occurred in Britain, where a few species more typical of the southern flora, such as the Strawberry-tree, had probably survived in the south-west. However, the British Isles were cut off from the continent around 6,000 years ago, so only trees which had already reached the area of modern France are present, slower-colonising trees arriving too late to take a place in the flora before the land connection was severed.

Man's Influence

A major factor affecting recent forests is the activity of man. The extent and timing of man's influence is often misunderstood. Common and firmly held beliefs include the 'facts' that Europe was heavily and extensively wooded up to medieval times and beyond, with large hunting forests preserved in their original 'wildwood' state; that woods were destroyed in later periods in the causes of house- and ship-building; that the last ancient woods, at least in Britain, were mainly destroyed during the two world wars. None of these so-called facts is correct.

The northern coniferous forests have generally been the least disrupted, since they tend to occur on poorer soils of lesser agricultural potential. They do have considerable value as a source of timber and even in early times timber was exported to other parts of Europe. As one of the most densely wooded remaining parts of Europe, Scandinavia maintains a healthy timber industry.

Further south, the broad-leaved temperate forests were much more at risk since, after clearance and ploughing, they provide rich soils. In these areas disruption was much greater as land was claimed for agriculture. Man's interference in the broad-leaved forests probably began on a large scale around 4000 BC when populations of elms all over Europe suddenly declined. One theory for this is that a plague of Dutch Elm disease was encouraged by agricultural activities. Forest clearance continued from this time, probably through a combination of felling, ploughing and browsing by farm stock.

Whatever the exact means employed, clearance was rapid and effective and took place much earlier than is often supposed. In England, for example, little forest remained by the time of the Domesday Book (1086) and much of what did remain had ceased to be 'wildwood'. Indeed, the present distribution of Britain's forests was largely in place before Roman times. Many large forests of later periods occupied areas previously cleared but allowed to revert to forest; these do not represent part of the original tree cover. Britain is now one of the least wooded areas in Europe.

Nevertheless, during this clearance many areas both large and small were left as forest or woodland of varying kinds, most of them intensively managed, for timber was a valuable resource. They also provided grazing, foraging for pigs and cover for game.

In these woods coppicing was particularly important. This is a management system in which trees are cut on a regular cycle. The stumps produce suckers which after a few years grow into sizeable trunks which can be harvested in turn; the cycle then begins again. Coppicing does no lasting harm; indeed it prolongs the life of the tree, or at least of the stool, which is the part remaining after felling, almost indefinitely. A by-product of coppicing is the abundance of wild flowers which flourish in the increased light of a recently coppiced wood. As the trees regenerate and shade deepens, so the flowers decrease, flourishing again when the trees are next cut.

Many hedgerows also represent remnants of ancient wildwood, deliberately left both as boundary marks and as a source of timber and fuel in their own right. Such hedgerows are rich in species, both trees and woodland flowers. Recently planted hedgerows are much poorer and less varied.

Hedgerows

Mediterranean evergreen forests suffered most of all. Although some were managed, the majority have been so completely ravaged that it is now difficult to find any great extent remaining. A major problem here was grazing by goats, which are especially destructive to trees. Degraded forests of this type form one of two vegetation types. Maquis, which occurs mainly on limestone, is dominated by aromatic shrubs such as sunroses with only a scattering of stunted evergreen trees. Garigue is poorer still, with small shrubs but no trees at all. Fires would also have caused damage. Unlike the deciduous trees of the wetter regions, evergreens will burn while alive, flaring like torches in wind-fanned fires. In the taiga this would not be a major problem, since many of the species there actually need regular burning to maintain healthy forests, but in the Mediterranean region regeneration may have been more difficult. Natural fires have always been a hazard. To this must now be added the modern

Mediterranean evergreen forest

phenomenon of the arsonist.

As well as destroying some native trees, man has helped to spread others and introduced foreign species from various countries, greatly increasing the number and diversity of European trees. Early introductions, either from one European area to another or from other continents, had mostly food or medicinal uses. An example is the Carob, which was introduced to some countries so long ago that its native distribution is almost completely obscured. Others are Sweet Chestnut, Date Palm, Medlar, Azarole and Orange. Some trees were introduced to support particular industries, such as the White Mulberry which is the food for silkworms. In later times timber and ornamental trees have been very much to the fore. Large numbers of conifers have been introduced in the interests of providing cheap timber, while the Australian genus *Eucalyptus* is the latest in a number of successful large-scale introductions. Some of these alien species compete poorly with native trees and survive only while they receive care. Others readily escape from cultivation, spreading and establishing themselves in the wild. When they do so they are classed as naturalised trees.

How to Identify Trees

As in any group of living organisms, trees differ from one another in various ways and to a greater or lesser degree depending on the species. When identifying trees it is important to recognise the structures you are examining and to be sure you are comparing like with like. Similarly, the main diagnostic features for species within one group of trees may not have the same importance for species of another group. For example, the leaves and fruits provide the major clues to distinguish species of Oaks, while in Tamarisks the flowers and bark show the most important characteristics. Knowing which are the appropriate features for which group comes with experience. Nevertheless, a basic understanding of the structures and their variation is essential and this section describes the various parts of a tree and explains some of the terms used in the descriptions.

Trunk and Bark

Trees are woody plants with a well-developed trunk or bole which, together with the main branches, is covered in a layer of bark which protects the tree from the outside environment. Trees grow in girth as well as height, adding additional layers of woody tissue each year – the so-called annual rings seen when a trunk is cut across and which can be used to calculate the age of the tree. To accommodate this expansion in girth the bark may stretch and rupture, often cracking in distinctive patterns or flaking to show differently coloured layers beneath. It is constantly renewed to maintain protection of the tree. Palms are unusual in achieving more or less their full girth shortly after germination, thereafter increasing only in height. There may be a single trunk or several, especially in trees that produce suckers, shoots which grow from around the base of the trunk or even from roots and eventually form thickets of stems around the parent tree.

Crown

As it grows the tree branches to form a crown and the branching pattern can be distinctive. So, too, can the shape of the crown, although this may change dramatically during the life of the tree. Young Cedars-of-Lebanon, for example, are spire-shaped but old trees are flat-topped and spreading. Conifers tend to grow quickly, often producing regular whorls of branches around the trunk, creating a conical shape. Broad-leaved trees are frequently slower growing, branching irregularly and producing a variety of crown shapes. There are exceptions, such as Sumach which has regularly forked branches. Again palms are unusual in having no branches: the crown is composed solely of leaves crowded at the top of the trunk.

Twigs also vary with age, first-year twigs often being a different colour to older growth, or covered with protective hairs which may be lost as the twig matures.

Leaves

Leaves are the sites for food production and gas-exchange and as such are vitally important. The shape and arrangement of the leaves are often characteristic of particular trees. Most have leaves alternating on the twig, but some have opposite pairs or whorls of leaves. Compound leaves are divided into separate leaflets. In pinnate leaves the leaflets lie in two parallel rows, usually with an odd leaflet at the tip. Twice-pinnate leaves have each initial division (pinna, plural pinnae) itself pinnately divided. In palmate leaves the leaflets radiate from the petiole or leaf-stalk like fingers on a hand.

Simple leaves have a single blade, although this may be pinnately or palmately lobed without being completely divided into leaflets. The shape of the blade ranges from very long and narrow to circular and even squarish, and the leaf margin may be entire, i.e. unbroken, or variously toothed. Leaves also vary in colour, texture and hairiness. They are generally paler and hairier on the underside. Conifers have leathery leaves which are either narrow and needle-like or scale-like, overlapping and pressed against the shoot.

Stipules are leaf-like growths at the base of the petiole. They are present in a number of species but often fall early.

An obvious distinction is between deciduous and evergreen trees. Deciduous trees shed all their leaves annually at the onset of the harshest season. In Europe this is usually winter but for trees from warm areas it may be the dry season. Actively growing trees with a full canopy of leaves require a generous supply of water. In winter this is locked up in the form of ice, so by shedding their leaves and entering a prolonged period of dormancy deciduous trees avoid the problems of

Leaf Types

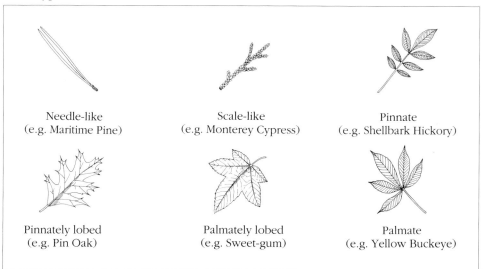

Needle-like (e.g. Maritime Pine)	Scale-like (e.g. Monterey Cypress)	Pinnate (e.g. Shellbark Hickory)
Pinnately lobed (e.g. Pin Oak)	Palmately lobed (e.g. Sweet-gum)	Palmate (e.g. Yellow Buckeye)

both drought and cold. Leaf-fall is also a mechanism for eliminating the build-up of waste products which are lost with the leaves, causing the bright autumnal colours produced by some trees. New leaves are produced each spring.

Evergreens also shed their leaves, but more gradually, constantly replacing them so that there is a full canopy of foliage throughout the year. The advantage of retaining leaves is greatest for trees where the growing season is short or likely to be disrupted, since they are able to take full advantage of the time available with no delay while new leaves develop. Whenever the growing period ceases, even only briefly, these trees enter a period of dormancy until growth can resume again. The leaves of evergreen trees are tough and leathery, often small or narrow with inrolled margins, the surfaces waxy and frequently bluish-green; all adaptations to reduce water-loss.

A few trees are semi-evergreen, normally retaining their leaves but shedding them like a truly deciduous tree in extreme conditions. A very small number such as Mount Etna Broom have dispensed with leaves altogether, the leaves developing but rapidly lost, their functions taken over by green stems.

Flowers

These are the reproductive organs of trees. They are made up of successive whorls of sepals, petals, stamens and ovaries, although any of these parts may be modified or absent. Sepals (collectively the calyx) and petals (the corolla) provide most clues to identity, especially in their number, size and colour. The parts of either of these whorls may be fused in varying degrees. Where the sepals and petals are

Flower Types

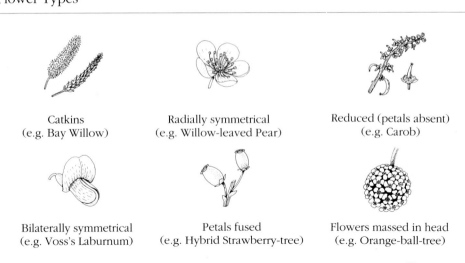

| Catkins (e.g. Bay Willow) | Radially symmetrical (e.g. Willow-leaved Pear) | Reduced (petals absent) (e.g. Carob) |
| Bilaterally symmetrical (e.g. Voss's Laburnum) | Petals fused (e.g. Hybrid Strawberry-tree) | Flowers massed in head (e.g. Orange-ball-tree) |

indistinguishable from each other, they are referred to as perianth-segments (the perianth). Stamens are the male parts of the flower, ovaries are the female parts and flowers may be male, female or hermaphrodite. Male and female flowers are sometimes borne in separate clusters or even on separate trees. The flowers may be solitary or grouped in a variety of clusters, spikes or heads. Trees pollinated by insects tend to have brightly coloured flowers and often produce scent and nectar. Wind-pollinated trees have reduced or inconspicuous flowers massed in slender catkins which often appear before the leaves to allow the unrestricted spread and reception of pollen.

Cone-bearing trees or conifers have male and female cones instead of flowers and fruits. Male cones are small and yellow when shedding pollen. The larger female cones are more noticeable and consist of scales bearing egg-cells. When ripe they are generally woody but can be fleshy and berry-like as in Junipers.

Trees rarely flower until well-established or even not until into old age as in the Pagoda-tree, so it not particularly unusual to find specimens with few, if any, flowers.

Fruits

Fruits of non-coniferous trees fall into two broad categories, fleshy and juicy or dry. Fleshy and juicy fruits include all berries and berry-like fruits as well as firm fruits such as apples. Dry fruits include pods, capsules and nuts. A few have woody, cone-like fruits resembling those of conifers. Fruits or seeds may be winged or have a parachute of hairs to aid in dispersal by the wind.

Fruit Types

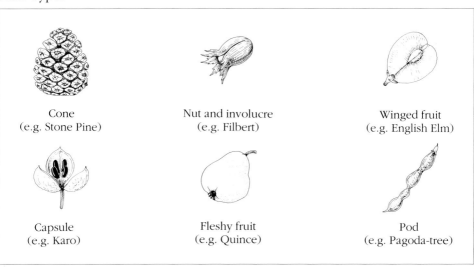

Cone (e.g. Stone Pine)	Nut and involucre (e.g. Filbert)	Winged fruit (e.g. English Elm)
Capsule (e.g. Karo)	Fleshy fruit (e.g. Quince)	Pod (e.g. Pagoda-tree)

Glossary

Alternate	With one leaf at each joint of the stem.
Anther	Fertile part of a stamen, containing pollen.
Aril	Fleshy layer covering the seed of some trees.
Bract	Leaf-like organ beneath a flower or inflorescence, sometimes modified or very reduced in size.
Burrs	Numerous short, twiggy outgrowths from the trunk.
Calyx	All the sepals of a flower.
Capsule	Dry fruit splitting when ripe to release seeds.
Catkin	Slender inflorescence of small, usually wind-pollinated flowers.
Corolla	All the petals of a flower.
Crown	All the branches of a tree.
Cultivar	Type of plant developed by gardeners, not originating in the wild.
Cupule	Cup-shaped structure enclosing a fruit or fruits.
Deflexed	Bent backwards.
Glabrous	Smooth and hairless.
Inflorescence	A group of flowers and their particular arrangement e.g. a spike or cluster.
Involucre	Leaf-like structure enclosing a flower.
Lenticel	Pore in a trunk, twig or sometimes fruit, allowing the passage of gases to and from the tissues.
Opposite	With a pair of leaves at each joint of the stem.
Ovary	Female organ of a flower containing ovules which, after pollination, form seeds.
Palmate	With lobes or leaflets spreading from a single point.
Papillae	Slender outgrowths resembling hairs.
Perianth	The sepals and petals of a flower, especially when these are not distinguishable from one another.
Petiole	Leaf stalk.
Pinna	One of the main (primary) divisions of a pinnate leaf; in twice-pinnate leaves the pinnae are themselves pinnate.
Pinnate	With two parallel rows of lobes or leaflets.
Rachis	Central axis of a pinnate leaf to which leaflets are attached.
Sepals	Outermost whorl of floral parts, often green.
Stamen	Male organ of a flower.
Stigma	Sticky area on ovary receptive to pollen.
Stipule	Leaf-like organ at the base of a petiole.
Sucker	New shoot growing from the roots of the parent tree.
Style	Elongated part of the ovary bearing the stigma.
Trifoliate	With three leaflets.

Tree Names and Classification

All plants, including trees, can be divided into groups based on characters common to all members, and the groups arranged in a hierarchy or classification. The most frequently used ranks are described below.

The basic unit is the species, generally regarded as a group of individuals which possess common characteristics clearly distinguishing them from other groups and which are capable of breeding together to produce viable offspring. Within this unit there may be considerable minor variation between individuals; if sufficiently marked and consistent these differences are used to define subspecies or varieties. Cultivars are horticulturally derived trees with characters, such as variegated leaves, not found in naturally occurring populations. Unlike animals, plant species are frequently able to interbreed and produce viable offspring. Many new species are thought to have arisen this way and it is one of the complications of classifying trees. There are even examples of hybrids between different genera e.g. Leyland Cypress (*Cupressus* x *Chamaecyparis*).

Closely related species are grouped into a genus and genera into a family, a useful division widely used by botanists when referring to plants. Some families contain only tree species, others contain annual and perennial herbs as well as shrubs and trees.

All families belong to one of two divisions, gymnosperms and angiosperms. The gymnosperms are plants with naked seeds and include all the cone-bearing trees such as Pines and Cypresses. The angiosperms have seeds protected by an ovary and include all plants commonly referred to as flowering plants. The trees in this group are generally referred to as broad-leaved.

A tree often has two names, a popular or common name and a scientific or Latin name. Both have their drawbacks, but the scientific name is more reliable and frequently more informative. All trees have a scientific name consisting of two elements, showing the genus and the species to which the tree belongs. Thus White Poplar *Populus alba* and Aspen *Populus tremula* are separate species both belonging to the Poplar genus *Populus*. The names indicate the relationship of the trees to each other and often describe diagnostic characters, in this case *alba* for white leaves and *tremula* for the fluttering motion typical of Aspen leaves. Scientific names are the international currency of plant nomenclature.

Many trees also have one or even several common names. These, of course, vary in different languages and are not always applied consistently. They can be misleading, too. Norway Maple is native and common in many countries besides Norway, and Box-elder is neither a box nor an elder but a species of ash. Sometimes the same name is given to two different trees. *Ceratonia* and *Robinia* are both sometimes called Locust-tree. Conversely, some trees have no common name, often because they are too little known to have acquired one. However, common names are more easily remembered than scientific names. They are often quite evocative, such as Tree-of-Heaven and Foxglove-tree, and have aptness and charm.

Families of Trees

The trees covered in this guide are grouped into 52 families whose essential characteristics are described here. Not all the family names may be familiar but all the European genera within each family are listed at the end of the description. Some of the families also contain annual or perennial herbs but the description applies only to the trees.

Pines Family Pinaceae pp. 46-72

Coniferous trees with needles. In Pines the needles form bundles with a sheathing base. The needles of Firs and Douglas-firs leave sucker-like scars on the twigs after falling. Those of Spruces and Hemlock-spruces are borne on persistent peg- or cushion-like bases. Larches - the only deciduous genus - and Cedars have needles in rosettes on short spur-shoots. Cones are generally large and may be pendulous or erect. They often take several years to mature. Genera: *Abies, Cedrus, Larix, Picea, Pinus, Pseudotsuga, Tsuga.*

Swamp-cypresses Family Taxodiaceae pp. 74-6

Coniferous trees with needles. Most are evergreen but Swamp-cypress and Dawn Redwood are deciduous. Cones are globular or broadly ovoid. Genera: *Cryptomeria, Taxodium, Metasequoia, Sequoia, Sequioadendron.*

Monkey Puzzles Family Araucariaceae p. 76

Evergreen coniferous trees from the southern hemisphere. The leaves are needle-like or broad, in Monkey Puzzle itself resembling large, overlapping scales and giving a curious and very distinctive spiky-cylindrical appearance to the branches. Male cones are cylindrical, females usually large and globose, disintegrating when mature. Many species are ornamentals. Genus: *Araucaria.*

Cypresses Family Cupressaceae pp. 76-84

All are evergreen coniferous trees or shrubs. Most have overlapping, scale-like leaves but some Junipers have needles as well as, or instead of, scale leaves. In False Cypresses the foliage forms flattened sprays. Cones are globular, with scales touching edge to edge; in Junipers they are fleshy. Genera: *Chamaecyparis, Cupressus, Juniperus, Thuja* and the generic hybrid x *Cupressocyparis.*

Yews Family Taxaceae p. 86

Evergreen trees with needles and fleshy, berry-like fruits. Genera: *Taxus, Torreya.*

Yellow-woods Family Podocarpaceae p. 86

Important evergreen forest trees, mainly from the southern hemisphere but extending into Central America and Japan. The leaves are needle-like or scaly (in non-European species). Fruits are fleshy and berry-like with a single seed. Genus: *Podocarpus.*

Maidenhair-tree Family Ginkgoaceae p. 86

A deciduous tree with fan-shaped leaves and fleshy, berry-like fruits. Genus: *Ginkgo.*

Willows Family Salicaceae pp. 88-100

Deciduous trees or shrubs, many of them Arctic or alpine species. The alternate leaves often have large stipules at the base of the petiole. The flowers lack a perianth and are borne in male and female catkins on different trees. The seeds are tufted with white hairs. Genera: *Populus, Salix.*

Walnuts Family Juglandaceae pp. 102-4
Deciduous trees which exude latex from broken twigs. The alternate leaves are pinnate and usually aromatic. The flowers are in separate male and female catkins on the same tree; males lack a perianth. The seeds, edible in some species, are enclosed in a hard outer husk. Genera: *Carya, Juglans, Pterocarya.*

Birches Family Betulaceae pp. 106-10
A large family of deciduous trees or shrubs, mainly from the northern hemisphere. The leaves are broad and alternate. The flowers, in separate male and female catkins, lack a perianth. In Birches and Alders the small, winged nutlets are borne in cylindrical, cone-like catkins. Hazels and Hornbeams have large, woody nuts, each attached to a leafy, often ragged or lobed involucre. Genera: *Alnus, Betula, Carpinus, Corylus, Ostrya.*

Beeches Family Fagaceae pp. 112-22
A very large family of forest trees important in both hemispheres. They are deciduous or evergreen with alternate, often lobed or spiny leaves. The wind-pollinated flowers are small, the males in catkins, the females in clusters of one to three. Nuts or nut-like fruits (the acorns of Oaks) are partly or wholly enclosed in a scaly or spiny cup. Many trees in this family are major sources of timber, food for both humans and animals, and tannins. Genera: *Castanea, Fagus, Nothofagus, Quercus.*

Elms Family Ulmaceae pp. 124-6
Deciduous trees. The alternate leaves are often markedly assymmetrical at the base. The small wind-pollinated flowers are either hermaphrodite or unisexual. Fruits nut-like or berry-like and edible. Elms have seeds surrounded by a papery wing. Several are important timber or fruit trees. Many produce a slippery mucilage. Genera: *Celtis, Ulmus, Zelkova.*

Mulberries Family Moraceae p. 128
Deciduous, occasionally evergreen, trees with alternate, toothed or deeply lobed leaves. Many exude a milky latex. Sometimes male and female flowers are borne on different trees. There are four perianth-segments. In Fig the flowers are tiny and enclosed in a hollow, fleshy receptacle. The usually berry-like fruit is formed from the whole flower-head. The family contains climbers and herbs as well as trees. Genera: *Broussonetia, Ficus, Maclura, Morus.*

Laurels Family Lauraceae p. 130
Evergreen trees with alternate, aromatic leaves with numerous oil-glands. The flower parts are usually in multiples of three, sometimes in multiples of two. The fruit is berry-like and sometimes fleshy. This family contains many important spice trees. Genera: *Laurus, Persea.*

Pokeweeds Family Phytolaccaceae p. 130
Mostly trees, shrubs and climbers from tropical and warm regions. The leaves are alternate, entire and often succulent. There are four to five sepals and petals but the petals are sometimes absent. The fruit is usually juicy, berry-like and segmented. Genus: *Phytolacca.*

Planes Family Platanaceae p. 132
Deciduous trees with flaking bark and alternate, deeply palmately lobed leaves. The flowers are four- to six-petalled in separate male and female, globular heads. The seeds have a tuft of hairs at the base. Genus: *Platanus.*

Witch-hazels Family Hammamelidaceae p. 132
Deciduous trees or shrubs, often with stellate hairs. The leaves are alternate and often palmately lobed. The flowers usually have prominent sepals and petals but in Sweet-gums the male flowers are reduced to stamens and the females have a perianth of tiny scales. The fruit is a capsule. Some species produce extracts used for medicine or perfume. Genus: *Liquidambar.*

She-oaks Family Casuarinaceae p. 134
A curious group of trees found mainly in very dry parts of Australia. They are evergreen but the leaves have been reduced to little more than scales on the drooping twigs. The flowers are wind-pollinated, males and females sometimes on different trees. Male flowers are reduced to a single stamen and crowded in catkin-like spikes. Females are similarly reduced to a single ovary, the heads forming cone-like fruits. Often used as sand-binders. Genus: *Casuarina.*

Pittosporums Family Pittosporaceae p. 134
A family of evergreen trees mainly from warm regions, especially Australia. The alternate, leathery leaves are usually entire. The flowers are usually hermaphrodite but are male and female in some species. They have five sepals and five petals and are often scented. The fruit is a capsule or (in some non-European trees) a berry. Many are ornamental and perfumed oils are derived from the scented flowers. Genus: *Pittosporum.*

Magnolias Family Magnoliaceae p. 136
Evergreen or deciduous trees or shrubs with alternate leaves. Large, solitary flowers have five or more petal-like perianth-segments and numerous stamens. The fruits form a slender, cone-like structure. Genera: *Liriodendron, Magnolia.*

Roses Family Rosaceae pp. 136-68
Deciduous or evergreen trees or shrubs. The alternate leaves are entire, lobed or pinnate. The usually showy flowers are five-petalled. The fruit is fleshy and firm as in Apples, Pears and Quince, or juicy, and is frequently crowned with the withered remains of the sepals. It contains one to several often stony seeds. This very large family occurs worldwide but especially in the temperate northern hemisphere, and contains many species of herbs. It includes some of the most widely grown fruit-trees in the world. Many others are important in the wild as sources of food for animals and birds; some are widely cultivated as ornamentals. Genera: *Amelanchier, Cotoneaster, Crataegus, Cydonia, Eriobotrya, Malus, Mespilus, Prunus, Pyrus, Sorbus.*

Peas Family Leguminosae pp. 170-8
Deciduous or evergreen trees with alternate, often pinnate leaves. The five-petalled flowers are small in Wattles and Albizias, but larger and with a very characteristic form in the other genera where the upper petal is erect, the side pair spreading and the bottom pair fused to form a boat-shaped keel enclosing the stamens and ovary. In Carob the petals are absent. The fruit is also characteristic of the whole family, being a dry, slender, many-seeded pod called a legume. A very large family also containing numerous annual and perennial herbs. Along with the Rosaceae it is one of the most important families of crop plants, but only a few of the trees are grown for food and some are poisonous. The main commercial use is for timber and ornament. Genera: *Acacia, Albizia, Caragana, Ceratonia, Cercis, Genista, Gleditsia, Laburnum, Robinia, Sophora.*

Citruses **Family Rutaceae** pp. 178-80
A family of mainly evergreen trees and shrubs, some deciduous, all highly aromatic. Many have spiny twigs. The flowers are usually white with four to five petals and are often fragrant. The fruits are rather variable but in European trees are either berry-like, in *Citrus* with a leathery rind and juicy pulp derived from modified hairs, or nut-like with a papery wing. Commercially a very important family of orchard trees. Some species are also used in the perfume industry. Genera: *Citrus, Phellodendron, Ptelea.*

Soapberries **Family Sapindaceae** p. 182
A large family of mainly tropical trees. The alternate leaves are usually pinnate. The flowers, borne in large inflorescences, have four or five petals. The fruit may be dry or fleshy and is often edible although most species contain toxic, oily saponins which can be used as soap substitutes and fish poisons. Many members of this family are woody climbers. Genus: *Koelreuteria.*

Quassias **Family Simaroubaceae** p. 182
A family of mainly tropical trees and shrubs with alternate, usually pinnate leaves. The flowers are often unisexual, or functionally so, and have five sepals and five petals. The fruit is usually winged or a capsule. Genus: *Ailanthus.*

Mahoganies **Family Meliaceae** p. 182
A large family of tropical and subtropical trees important elsewhere in the world for their timber. The leaves are usually pinnate or twice pinnate. The flowers have three to five sepals, three to seven petals and stamens forming a tube. The fruit is berry-like or a capsule. Genera: *Cedrela, Melia.*

Cashews **Family Anacardiaceae** pp. 184-6
Family including Pistachios and Sumachs. Deciduous or evergreen trees or shrubs, with usually alternate and pinnate leaves. The flowers are borne in large, often branched clusters and have five, or occasionally no, petals. The fruit is small and berry- or nut-like. Many of the species exude irritant toxins which can produce an allergic skin reaction. Genera: *Pistacia, Rhus, Schinus.*

Maples **Family Aceraceae** pp. 188-92
Trees with often peeling bark. The majority are deciduous. The leaves are opposite and mostly deeply palmately-lobed, in a few species simple or pinnate. The flowers are hermaphrodite or male and female, with five sepals and five petals, although the latter may be absent. The winged fruits form pairs. Many are ornamental or timber trees and some North American species yield sugar. Genus: *Acer.*

Horse-chestnuts **Family Hippocastanaceae** p. 194
Large deciduous trees. The leaves are opposite and palmate. The large flowers have four or five petals and long, curved stamens. The fruit consists of one to several nuts in a spiny case. Genus: *Aesculus.*

Boxes **Family Buxaceae** p. 196
Evergreen trees or shrubs. The leaves and twigs are paired. The unisexual flowers are inconspicuous, the males only with a perianth. The fruit is a woody capsule. Genus: *Buxus.*

Hollies Family Aquifoliaceae p. 196

Evergreen trees or shrubs with alternate, usually spiny leaves. The flowers are white and four-petalled, with males and females on separate trees. The fruit is berry-like. Genera: *Ilex.*

Spindles Family Celastraceae p. 198

Deciduous trees or shrubs with opposite leaves and twigs. The flowers are four- or five-petalled and the fruit is a four-lobed capsule. Genus: *Euonymus.*

Buckthorns Family Rhamnaceae pp. 198-200

A large and more or less worldwide family of small trees and shrubs. Most are deciduous and frequently spiny or thorny. The leaves are opposite or alternate. The flowers are hermaphrodite or unisexual with males and females on different trees; they have four or five petals. The fruit is berry-like or a hard nut. Genera: *Frangula, Paliurus, Rhamnus, Zizyphus.*

Oleasters Family Elaeagnaceae p. 202

Small, deciduous and often thorny trees or shrubs with alternate leaves. The male and female flowers are on different trees; they have two or four petal-like and partly fused sepals, but lack petals. The fruit is berry-like. All parts of the tree are covered with minute silvery or occasionally shiny reddish scales which give a distinctive silvery sheen to the plant. Genera: *Elaeagnus, Hippophae.*

Mallows Family Malvaceae p. 202

A very large family, mostly of herbs and shrubs but containing a few trees. The leaves are alternate. The showy flowers have an outer whorl of sepal-like segments (the epicalyx) as well as usually five sepals and five large petals. The numerous stamens are fused to form a long central column. The fruit is variable, depending on the genus. As well as many ornamental plants this family includes cotton. Genus: *Hibiscus.*

Tamarisks Family Tamaricaceae p. 204

Small, slender trees or shrubs with wand-like twigs and tiny, scale-like, clasping leaves. The flower-parts are in whorls of four or five and the fruit is a small capsule releasing seeds with a tuft of hairs at one end. A taxonomically difficult family, not easy to identify with certainty. Some species, especially one from Asia Minor, are a source of manna. Genus: *Tamarix.*

Limes Family Tiliaceae p. 206

A large and widespread family of deciduous trees with alternate, usually heart-shaped leaves. Fragrant, five-petalled flowers hang in clusters beneath a wing-like bract. The fruit is a small nut. A number of Lime species are important timber and ornamental trees and one was once a major forest tree in Britain. Genus: *Tilia.*

Myrtles Family Myrtaceae pp. 208-12

A very large family of evergreen trees, many of them from Australia. The description here is of the most important genus in Europe, the Gums (*Eucalyptus*). The bark is frequently peeling, shredding or fibrous. The highly aromatic leaves are of two kinds; juveniles are paired and often bluish, while adult leaves are alternate and dull green. The perianth-segments of the flowers are fused to form a lid or bud-cap which falls when the flower opens. The fruit is a woody capsule. Dominant forest trees in Australia and famous as the food of koalas, in Europe they are now important timber trees. Genus: *Eucalyptus.*

Pomegranate Family **Punicaceae** p. 212

Small deciduous trees or shrubs with opposite, entire leaves. The flowers are large and solitary with five to seven petals. The fruit is a berry with a leathery rind. Genus: *Punica.*

Dogwoods Family **Cornaceae** p. 214

Small deciduous trees or shrubs. The leaves are opposite and entire. The usually small, clustered flowers have four petals and the fruit is berry-like. Genus: *Cornus.*

Ebonies Family **Ebenaceae** p. 214

A family of mainly tropical trees with only one genus widely grown in Europe. The leaves are alternate. The flowers, often males and females on different trees, have a persistent calyx which enlarges in fruit, and a three- to seven-lobed corolla. The fruit is a berry, often edible. As well as fruit, the family yields the highest quality timber. Genus: *Diospyros.*

Storaxes **Styracaceae** p. 214

Deciduous trees and shrubs with resinous bark. The leaves are alternate. The flowers have five petals, usually joined at the base into a short tube. The fruit is a capsule. All parts of the tree are usually covered with a scurf of stellate hairs. A number of species are ornamentals and Storax yields a fragrant gum. Genus: *Styrax.*

Heaths Family **Ericaceae** p. 216

A very large family of trees and shrubs, most of them evergreen. The alternate or whorled leaves may be small and narrow to needle-like as in heaths and heather or broad and leathery. The flowers may be small or very large and are urn-shaped or funnel-shaped with five free or fused petals. The fruit is a capsule or a warty berry. Most members of the family require acid soils. Many are typical of and dominant on northern temperate moorland and heathland. Others are Mediterranean plants and occur in areas of southern Europe, North Africa and the Cape Province of South Africa. Rhododendrons are forest or mountain trees most abundant in the Himalayas and New Guinea. Most species are ornamental. Genera: *Arbutus, Erica, Rhododendron.*

Olives Family **Oleaceae** pp. 218-22

Evergreen or deciduous trees or shrubs. The leaves are opposite and either entire or pinnate. Petals, if present, are four, joined in a tube. The fruit is either a berry or dry and winged. The family contains many ornamentals as well as timber trees and the commercially important Olive. Genera: *Fraxinus, Ligustrum, Olea, Phillyrea, Syringa.*

Buddleias Family **Loganiaceae** p. 222

A family of mostly tropical trees, shrubs, climbers and herbs. The only trees occurring in Europe are Buddleias, to which this description applies. Trees with usually stellate hairs and opposite or alternate leaves. The flowers have tubular, four-lobed corollas and are massed in globular or spike-like heads. The fruit is a capsule. Genus: *Buddleia.*

Potatoes Family **Solanaceae** p. 222

A very large, worldwide family of herbs, climbers, shrubs and a few trees. The leaves are variable, usually alternate and entire, lobed or pinnate. The flowers have five petals forming either a flat, spreading corolla or a tubular one. The fruit is a berry or a dry capsule. This family contains many major fruit and vegetable crops such as tomatoes and potatoes as well as tobacco and various ornamentals. Genus: *Nicotiana.*

Bignonias Family Bignoniaceae p. 224
Deciduous trees with large, usually opposite leaves which are usually pinnate or twice pinnate, less often undivided. The flowers have a tubular, five-lobed corolla. The pod-like fruit releases winged seeds. Genera: *Paulownia, Catalpa, Jacaranda.*

Myoporums Family Myoporaceae p. 226
A family of small trees and shrubs, mostly from Australia. They are usually evergreen. The leaves are alternate, rarely opposite, and usually gland-dotted. Both calyx and corolla are five-lobed. The fruit is berry-like but rather dry. Genus: *Myoporum.*

Honeysuckles Family Caprifoliaceae pp. 226-8
Small trees, shrubs or woody climbers, mostly deciduous. The opposite leaves are pinnate, deeply lobed or undivided. Five-petalled flowers are borne in large clusters. The fruit is a berry. Many species are ornamentals. Genera: *Sambucus, Viburnum.*

Agaves Family Agavaceae p. 230
Evergreen trees with an often straight or forked trunk with or without thick branches. The leaves are large, sword-shaped, and all crowded in rosettes at the tips of the trunk or branches. The flowers have six petal-like perianth-segments. The fruit is berry-like. Genera: *Cordyline, Dracaena, Yucca.*

Bananas Family Musaceae p. 230
Bananas are not really trees at all but giant herbs which produce soft, trunk-like pseudostems formed by the sheathing leaf-bases. The true stem lies underground. The complex inflorescence contains whorls of flowers, the males above the females. The fruit is an elongated, fleshy berry. Genus: *Musa.*

Palms Family Palmae pp. 232-4
Evergreen trees with a single trunk but no branches. The leaves are large, divided, fan- or feather-shaped, and all crowded at the top of the trunk. The flowers have six perianth-segments, often in two whorls of three. The fruit is fleshy or dry. Genera: *Chamaerops, Jubaea, Phoenix, Trachycarpus, Washingtonia.*

Key to Trees

A deliberate attempt has been made to restrict the characters used in the keys to ones which are readily observed. If this has made them a little unwieldy in parts it is hoped that this will be outweighed by a reduction in the experience needed for their successful use. Inevitably, the keys will sometimes ask questions referring to characters unavailable in a particular specimen. Therefore, following the numbered keys is a further key which provides a synopsis of all the trees divided solely on their leaf characters. You can use this as a ready reference to pin-point the small group of trees in which your specimen is mostly likely to be found.

Numbered Keys

Every step in the key consists of two (occasionally three or four) contrasting statements. Look at your tree and see which is true. The next numbered stage is indicated at the end of the line. The next stage may be another key, or the next numbered section in the same key (set in **bold** type). Follow the series of correct statements until you arrive at a name and page number or numbers where you can check your identification. The first key will lead you to secondary keys, and these to species. Sometimes a tree will fit both statements. These few trees are keyed out twice, so it does not matter which statement you choose. After using the key to decide which species your tree is, turn to the appropriate page and use the description and illustrations to confirm your selection. Even if you find the keys a little daunting at first, persevere. They are an essential identification tool.

1	Crown of very large leaves only, all in tufts at the top of the trunk or of thick branches	*Key 1*
	Crown of twigs and branches with evenly distributed leaves	**2**
2	Leaves either needle-like, or scale-like and often overlapping, or absent	*Key 2*
	Leaves broader, not scale-like or overlapping	**3**
3	Leaves in opposite pairs on shoots	*Key 3*
	Leaves alternate on shoots	**4**
4	Leaves divided into separate leaflets	*Key 4*
	Leaves simple or lobed but not divided into leaflets	**5**
5	Leaves evergreen	*Key 5*
	Leaves deciduous	**6**
6	Fruits fleshy or juicy	*Key 6*
	Fruits dry	*Key 7*

KEY 1 Leaves very large, in tufts

1	Leaves undivided, sword-shaped or oar-shaped	**2**
	Leaves divided; trunk unbranched	**4**
2	Leaves oar-shaped; trunk undivided, soft and green	Banana p. 230
	Leaves sword-shaped; trunk divided or branching to form a crown	**3**
3	Crown dense, umbrella-shaped	Dragon-tree p. 230
	Crown open, irregular or trunk not branching to form a crown	Cabbage-tree p. 230, Spanish Bayonet p. 230
4	Leaves fan-shaped, palmate	**5**
	Leaves feathery, pinnate	**7**
5	Tree up to 14m high, the trunk covered with a thatch of dead leaves, at least near the crown	**6**
	Tree rarely more than 2m high, the trunk covered with old leaf-bases and fibres only	European Fan Palm p. 232
6	Leaf-segments with numerous long threads	Petticoat Palm p. 232
	Leaf-segments stiff, lacking threads	Chinese Windmill Palm p. 232
7	Trunk lead-grey, clean and smooth except for old leaf-scars	Chilean Wine Palm p. 234
	Trunk brownish, usually covered at least in parts by old leaf-bases	Date Palms p. 234

KEY 2 Leaves needle- or scale-like

1	Leaves usually absent; fruit a small pod	Mount Etna Broom p. 178
	Leaves present though sometimes tiny; fruit usually a woody cone or berry-like	**2**
2	Leaves scale-like, pressed against the stem	**3**
	Leaves needle-like, usually wide-spreading	**9**
3	Scale-leaves at least 30mm long, rigid and sharp-edged	Monkey Puzzle p. 76

	Scale-leaves less than 10mm long, not rigid or sharp	**4**
4	Scale-leaves minute, in whorls around the nodes of the twigs	She-oak p. 134
	Scale-leaves sometimes small but alternate or paired, never in whorls	**5**
5	Wispy-foliaged, pink- or white-flowered tree	Tamarisks p. 204
	Densely foliaged, coniferous tree	**6**
6	Fruiting cone fleshy and berry-like	Junipers pp. 82-4
	Fruiting cone with woody scales	**7**
7	Cone ovoid, with overlapping scales	Western Red Cedar p. 76, Wellingtonia p. 74
	Cone more or less globose, scales meeting edge to edge	**8**
8	Leafy shoots forming flattened sprays	False Cypresses p. 78, Leyland Cypress p. 78
	Leafy shoots not forming flattened sprays	Cypresses p. 80, Leyland Cypress p. 78, Japanese Red Cedar p. 76
9	Needles all pressed close against the shoot with only their tips spreading; bark spongy	Wellingtonia p. 74
	At least some needles widespreading; bark hard	**10**
10	At least needles of side-shoots in two flat, parallel rows	**11**
	All needles whorled or parted on either side of shoot, but not in flat rows	**13**
11	Deciduous; fruiting cone woody	Swamp-cypress p. 74
	Evergreen; fruiting cone berry-like	**12**
12	Needles dark, dull green; fruit scarlet	Yew p. 86
	Needles light, bright green; fruit yellowish	Plum-fruited Yew p. 86
13	Needles all borne singly	**14**
	Most needles borne in distinct whorls, pairs or bundles of two or more	**17**

14	Female cones erect on branches; needles with a sucker-like base	**15**
	Female cones pendulous on branches; base of needles not sucker-like	**16**
15	Needle-base circular, leaving a flat scar	Firs pp. 46-8
	Needle-base elliptical, leaving a raised scar	Douglas-firs p. 56
16	Needles with persistent, peg-like bases	Spruces pp. 50-4
	Needles with cushion-like bases	Hemlock-spruces p. 56
17	Most needles in bundles of two to five	**18**
	Most needles in whorls of either three, or ten or more, rarely in pairs	**19**
18	Needles in bundles of two	Pines pp. 58-62
	Needles in bundles of three	Pines pp. 64-6
	Needles in bundles of five	Pines pp. 66-8
19	Needles on all shoots in whorls of three or four, occasionally in pairs	**20**
	Needles on short shoots in whorls of ten or more	**21**
20	Needles in whorls of three or in pairs; coniferous trees	Junipers pp. 82-4
	Needles in whorls of four; flowering tree	Tree-heath p. 216
21	Deciduous tree	Larches p. 70
	Evergreen tree	Cedars p. 72

KEY 3 Leaves broad, opposite

1	Leaves twice-pinnate	Jacaranda p. 224
	Leaves pinnate	**2**
	Leaves not divided into leaflets	**4**
2	Tall trees with smooth or slightly furrowed bark; fruits dry, winged	**3**
	Small trees with ridged, corky bark; fruit a berry	Elders p. 226
3	Fruits one per stalk	Ashes p. 218
	Fruits paired on stalks	Box-elder p. 192

4	Twigs all green, mostly leafless; flowers pea-like	Mount Etna Broom p. 178
	Older twigs brown or blackish; flowers not pea-like	**5**
5	Flowers in catkins appearing before the leaves	Purple Willow p. 96
	Flowers not in catkins, appearing after the leaves	**6**
6	Flowers with four or fewer sepals or petals	**7**
	Flowers with five or more sepals or petals	**15**
7	Evergreen tree	**8**
	Deciduous tree	**12**
8	Petals absent; fruit a woody capsule	**9**
	Petals four; fruit a berry	**10**
9	Tall trees with usually bluish-green leaves smelling of eucalyptus; bark often shredding	Gums pp. 208-12
	Small trees with dark or light green non-aromatic leaves; bark not shredding	Box p. 196
10	Leaves silvery-green; trunk often with numerous cavities	Olive p. 220
	Leaves not silvery; trunk without cavities	**11**
11	Leaves of two kinds, those of young growth oval and toothed, those of mature growth lance-shaped and entire; petals joined only at the base	Phillyrea p. 220
	Leaves all oval and entire; petals joined below in a tube at least as long as the lobes	Glossy Privet p. 220
12	Leaves entire	**13**
	Leaves toothed	**14**
13	Flowers yellow, appearing before the leaves; fruit a red berry	Cornelian Cherry p. 214
	Flowers pink or white, appearing after the leaves; fruit a capsule	Lilac p. 222
14	Twigs spiny; flowers greenish-white, in small clusters	Buckthorn p. 200
	Twigs not spiny; flowers lilac, in dense conical clusters	Buddleia p. 222

15	Evergreen tree	Laurustinus p. 228
	Deciduous tree	**16**
16	Scarlet flowers and globose fruits solitary or paired	Pomegranate p. 212
	Flowers and fruits in clusters	**17**
17	Flowers 5cm or more; fruit a pod-like capsule	**18**
	Flowers less than 5cm; fruit a berry, winged or a lobed capsule	**19**
18	Flowers mainly blue or purplish; capsule less than 5cm long	Foxglove-tree p. 224
	Flowers white; slender capsule 10cm or more long	Indian Bean-tree p. 224
19	Flowers white; fruit a berry	**20**
	Flowers yellowish, red or pink; fruit winged	**21**
20	Leaves entire; flowers in small loose clusters	Alder-buckthorn p. 200
	Leaves lobed or toothed; flowers in large, branched and domed heads	Guelder-rose p. 228, Wayfaring-tree p. 228
21	Leaves palmately lobed (except Tartar Maple); fruit winged	Maples pp. 188-92
	Leaves not lobed; fruit a four-lobed capsule	Broad-leaved Spindle p. 198

KEY 4 Leaves alternate, compound

1	Leaves palmate, the leaflets radiating from the petiole	**2**
	Leaves pinnate, the leaflets in two rows	**4**
	Leaves twice-pinnate	**18**
2	Leaflets three	**3**
	Leaflets five to seven	Horse-chestnuts p. 194
3	Leaves odourless; flowers pea-like, with bright yellow, unequal petals	Laburnums p. 178
	Leaves foul-smelling when crushed; flowers with greenish, equal petals	Hop-tree p. 178
4	Young twigs stout and densely velvet-hairy	Sumachs p. 184
	Young twigs not velvet-hairy	**5**

| 5 | Evergreen tree | **6** |
| | Deciduous tree | **8** |

| 6 | Leaves aromatic; fruit nut- or bead-like | **7** |
| | Leaves not aromatic; fruit a long pod | Carob p. 176 |

| 7 | Foliage weeping; leaves smelling of pepper | Pepper-tree p. 184 |
| | Foliage not weeping; leaves smelling of resin | Mastic-tree p. 186 |

| 8 | Flowers pea-like, with five unequal petals | **9** |
| | Flowers not pea-like, petals equal or absent | **12** |

| 9 | Twigs spiny | **10** |
| | Twigs unarmed | **11** |

| 10 | Spines of twigs in pairs; leaves ending in an odd leaflet | False Acacia p. 174 |
| | Spines of twigs in threes; leaves ending in a spiny point | Honey Locust p. 176 |

| 11 | Leaves ending in an odd leaflet; flowers white | Pagoda-tree p. 174 |
| | Leaves ending in a slender point; flowers bright yellow | Siberian Pea-tree p. 174 |

| 12 | Flowers in catkins or unbranched clusters; cut twigs leaking latex | **13** |
| | Flowers in large, branched clusters; cut twigs not leaking latex | **15** |

| 13 | Leaves aromatic | Walnuts p. 102 |
| | Leaves not aromatic | **14** |

| 14 | Twigs with a chambered pith; catkins solitary; fruit winged | Caucasian Wingnut p. 104 |
| | Twigs with a solid pith; catkins in clusters of three or more; fruit not winged | Hickories p. 104 |

| 15 | Leaflets toothed, at least in the upper half; flowers pure white or yellow | **16** |
| | Leaflets entire, or with a few teeth in the lower half; flowers greenish or brownish | **17** |

| 16 | Leaflets hairy beneath; flowers white | Rowans pp. 154-6 |
| | Leaflets glabrous; flowers yellow | Golden-rain-tree p. 182 |

| 17 | Leaflets entire; fruit nut-like | Pistachios p. 186 |
| | Leaflets with at least a few teeth; fruit winged | Tree-of-Heaven p. 182 |

18	Trunk and twigs armed with clusters of spines	Honey Locust p. 176
	Trunk and twigs unarmed	**19**
19	Evergreen tree; leaves silvery-hairy becoming	
	bluish-green; flowers yellow	Wattles p. 172
	Deciduous tree; leaves neither silvery nor	
	bluish; flowers pink or lilac	**20**
20	Leaflets less than 2.5cm; flowers pink, in	
	brush-like heads	Pink Siris p. 172
	Leaflets more than 2.5cm long; flowers	
	lilac in large clusters	Persian Lilac p. 182

KEY 5 Leaves alternate, simple, evergreen

1	Leaves spiny (sometimes entire in young trees)	**2**
	Leaves sometimes toothed but not spiny	**3**
2	Fruit an acorn; flowers green, males in catkins	Oaks p. 114
	Fruit a berry; flowers white, in clusters	Hollies p. 196
3	Leaves densely covered with rusty hairs beneath	**4**
	Leaves glabrous or with white hairs beneath	**5**
4	Leaves toothed; flowers about 1cm long	Loquat p. 146
	Leaves entire; flowers up to 25cm long	Evergreen Magnolia p. 136
5	Petiole winged; twigs spiny	Citruses p. 180
	Petiole not winged; twigs unarmed	**6**
6	Leaves either aromatic or with wavy or rolled-under margins	**7**
	Leaves neither strongly aromatic, nor with	
	wavy or rolled-under margins	**8**
7	Leaves smelling of eucalyptus (rarely of	
	lemon), margins flat	Gums pp. 208-12
	Leaves smelling of almonds, margins rolled under	Cherry Laurel p. 168
	Leaves smelling of bay, margins wavy	Sweet Bay p. 130
	Leaves not aromatic, margins wavy	Pittosporums p. 134
8	Flowers white, greenish or yellow;	
	fruit a berry or a long pod	**9**
	Flowers large, red or purple; fruit a	
	short capsule	**14**
9	Flowers bright yellow or creamy, tiny and	
	massed in spherical heads or short spikes;	
	fruit a long pod	Acacias p. 170

| | Flowers white or greenish-yellow, solitary, in clusters or long spikes; fruit a berry | **10** |

| 10 | Bark red, flaking or shredding; flowers urn-shaped; berries red | Strawberry-trees p. 216 |
| | Bark not flaking or shredding; flowers with spreading petals; berries blackish | **11** |

| 11 | Leaves toothed | Portugal Laurel p. 168 |
| | Leaves entire | **12** |

| 12 | Flowers in spikes much longer than the leaves; berries segmented | Phytolacca p. 130 |
| | Flowers solitary or in clusters much shorter than the leaves; fruit not segmented | **13** |

| 13 | Petals white, spotted with purple | Waterbush p. 226 |
| | Petals absent; sepals greenish-yellow | Mediterranean Buckthorn p. 200 |

| 14 | Leaves toothed; flowers red | Hibiscus p. 202 |
| | Leaves entire; flowers purple | Rhododendron p. 216 |

KEY 6 Leaves alternate, simple, deciduous; fruits juicy

| 1 | Leaves fan-shaped | Maidenhair-tree p. 86 |
| | Leaves not fan-shaped | **2** |

| 2 | Twigs with paired spines, one curved and one straight in each pair | Jujube p. 198 |
| | Spines, if present, not paired | **3** |

| 3 | Leaves and twigs covered with minute silvery scales | Sea-buckthorn p. 202, Oleaster p. 202 |
| | Leaves and twigs without silvery scales | **4** |

| 4 | Flowers yellow, greenish or brownish | **5** |
| | Flowers pure white or pink | **8** |

| 5 | Leaves entire | **6** |
| | Leaves toothed or lobed | **7** |

| 6 | Flowers bright yellow, solitary or in small clusters; fruit yellow or purplish black | Date-plum p. 214 |
| | Flowers greenish-yellow, in globular heads; fruit yellow with a pitted rind | Osage Orange p. 128 |

| 7 | Leaves coarsely toothed; flowers solitary | Nettle-trees p. 126 |
| | Leaves medium- to fine-toothed and at | |

| | least some also deeply lobed; flowers in catkins | Mulberries p. 128 |
| | Leaves palmately lobed, the margins of the lobes entire; flowers inside a hollow, fleshy receptacle | Fig p. 128 |

| 8 | Leaves lobed | **9** |
| | Leaves entire or toothed but not lobed | **11** |

| 9 | Twigs thorny or spiny | Hawthorns pp. 148-52 |
| | Twigs unarmed | **10** |

| 10 | Leaves three-lobed, the lobes themselves sometimes lobed | Apples p. 144 |
| | Leaves with more than three lobes | Whitebeams p. 156, Wild Service-tree p. 158 |

| 11 | Flowers solitary | Quince p. 144, Medlar p. 146 |
| | Flowers in clusters | **12** |

| 12 | Leaves entire | Himalayan Tree Cotoneaster p. 146, Cherry Laurel p.168 |
| | Leaves toothed | **13** |

| 13 | Sepals deciduous, absent on fruit; single seed stony | Cherries pp. 160-8 |
| | Fruit crowned by withered sepals (except Plymouth Pear); seeds several | **14** |

| 14 | Fruit less than 2cm long | **15** |
| | Fruit usually more than 2cm | Apples p. 142, Pears pp. 136-40 |

| 15 | Fruit blue-black | Snowy Mespil p. 152 |
| | Fruit orange or red | **16** |

| 16 | Twigs thorny | Hawthorns p. 150 |
| | Twigs unarmed | Whitebeams p. 158 |

KEY 7 Leaves alternate, simple, deciduous; fruits dry

| 1 | Twigs zigzag, spiny | Christ's Thorn p. 198 |
| | Twigs not zigzag or spiny | **2** |

| 2 | Leaves lobed | **3** |
| | Leaves not lobed | **6** |

| 3 | Leaves cut square or notched at the tip; flowers large, up to 5cm long, solitary | Tulip-tree p. 136 |
| | Leaves rounded or pointed at the tip; flowers much smaller, in clusters or catkins | **4** |

| 4 | Leaves pinnately lobed; fruit an acorn | Oaks pp. 116-22 |
| | Leaves palmately or irregularly lobed; seeds silky plumed | **5** |

| 5 | Leaves white-felted below | White Poplar p. 98 |
| | Leaves smooth or sparsely hairy below | Planes p. 132, Oriental Sweet-gum p. 132 |

| 6 | At least male flowers in cylindrical catkins | **7** |
| | Flowers single or in clusters | **14** |

| 7 | Male and female flowers in the same catkin; fruits spiny | Sweet Chestnut p. 112 |
| | Male and female flowers in separate catkins; fruit not spiny | **8** |

| 8 | Fruit a capsule releasing silky-plumed seeds | **9** |
| | Fruit a nut or winged nutlet | **10** |

| 9 | Leaves broadly oval to heart-shaped, margins bluntly toothed | Poplars pp. 98-100 |
| | Leaves usually narrowed to a long point, (if broad then with two ear-shaped stipules at the base), entire or sharply toothed | Willows pp. 88-96 |

| 10 | Nut enveloped in a leafy involucre | **11** |
| | Nutlets winged, in cylindrical or cone-like catkins | **13** |

| 11 | Nuts single or in small clusters | Hazels p. 110 |
| | Nuts in long catkins | **12** |

| 12 | Involucre three-lobed | Hornbeam p. 110 |
| | Involucre unlobed | Hop-hornbeam p. 110 |

| 13 | Fruiting catkins cylindrical, pendulous | Birches p. 108 |
| | Fruiting catkins oval, not pendulous | Alders p. 106 |

| 14 | Leaves entire | **15** |
| | Leaves toothed | **17** |

15	Leaves oval to oblong, densely covered with white stellate hairs; white flowers bell-shaped	Storax p. 214
	Leaves almost circular, glabrous; pink flowers pea-like	Judas-tree p. 176
	Leaves oval to elliptical, glabrous or with a few silky hairs; flowers yellow or brownish	**16**

| 16 | Leaves matt bluish-green with inconspicuous | |

veins; flowers with a long, tubular corolla   Shrub Tobacco p. 222
Leaves dark glossy green with conspicuous
veins; perianth not tubular; fruit spiny   Beech p. 112

17   Leaves symmetrical at the base   Limes p. 206
      Leaves asymmetrical at the base   **18**

18   Flowers solitary; fruit spiny; broadly conical tree   Roble Beech p. 112
      Flowers solitary; fruit with four narrow
      wing-like ridges; short-trunked tree
      with a broom-like crown of erect branches   Caucasian Elm p. 126
      Flowers in clusters; fruit with a broad
      papery wing; usually long-trunked,
      spreading tree   Elms p. 124

Leaf Key

The trees covered in the main entries in this book are broken down here into groups based on their leaf types. These types are presented as a series of headings. Using a leaf from the tree you wish to identify, run down the headings to find which group it best fits. Trees with leaves which fit in more than one group are listed under each applicable heading. It may be difficult to decide if a leaf is narrow or broad, shallowly lobed or merely toothed; some deciduous leaves are leathery and can appear evergreen, so you may have to check more than one category. Finally there is a list of trees with spiny twigs.

Leaves absent

Mount Etna Broom

Scale leaves: all evergreen

Monkey Puzzle; Red Cedar; False Cypresses; Leyland Cypress; Cypresses; Junipers (some); She-oak; Tamarisks

Narrow leaves: more than twice as long as broad

Needles, less than 5mm broad
  evergreen or deciduous: round, three- or four-sided in cross-section
Spruces (some); Douglas-fir; Pines; Larches; Cedars; Japanese Red Cedar; Wellingtonia

  evergreen or deciduous: flattened
Firs; Spruces (some); Hemlock-spruces; Swamp-cypress; Coast Redwood; Junipers (some); Yew; Plum-fruited Yew; Tree-heath

Leaves more than 5mm broad
  evergreen: entire or toothed
Oaks (some); Sweet Bay; Avocado; Pittosporums; Loquat; Cherry Laurel; Acacias; Gums (adult foliage); Olive; Phillyrea; Cabbage-tree; Yucca; Dragon-tree; Banana

  deciduous : entire
Willows (some); Pears (some); Medlar; Sea-buckthorn; Oleaster; Pomegranate; Date-plum; Shrub Tobacco; Banana

  deciduous: toothed
Willows (some); Sweet Chestnut; Algerian Oak; Cherries (some); Spindle-tree; Jujube; Buddleia

Broad leaves: less than twice as long as broad

Evergreen: entire
Holm Oak; Citruses (some); Cretan Maple; Box; Gums (juvenile foliage); Rhododendron; Eastern Strawberry-tree; Phillyrea; Laurustinus

Evergreen: toothed
Oaks (some); Portugal Laurel; Lemon; Hollies; Mediterranean Buckthorn; Hibiscus; Strawberry-tree; Phillyrea

Deciduous: entire
Maidenhair-tree; Beech; Osage Orange; Pears (some); Quince; Medlar; Himalayan Tree
Cotoneaster; Judas-tree; Pistachio; Tartar Maple; Cornelian Cherry; Date-plum; Storax; Lilac;
Shrub Tobacco; Foxglove-tree; Indian Bean-tree

Deciduous: toothed
Willows (some); Poplars; Alders; Birches; Hornbeam; Hop-hornbeam; Hazels; Roble Beech;
Oaks (some); Elms; Caucasian Elm; Nettle-trees; Mulberry; Paper Mulberry; Pears (some);
Apples (some); Service-trees (some); Snowy Mespil; Hawthorns (some); Cherries (some);
Broad-leaved Spindle-tree; Christ's Thorn; Buckthorn; Limes; Wayfaring-tree

Leaves deeply lobed: evergreen or deciduous

Pinnately lobed
Oaks (some); Apples (some); Service-trees (some)

Palmately or irregularly lobed
White Poplar; Hazels; Black Mulberry; Paper Mulberry; Fig; Planes; Oriental Sweet-gum;
Tulip-tree; Hawthorns; Whitebeam; Maples; Indian Bean-tree; Foxglove-tree; Guelder-rose;
Palms (some)

Leaves twice pinnate: evergreen or deciduous

Wattles; Pink Siris; Honey-locust; Persian Lilac; Jacaranda

Leaves pinnate: evergreen or deciduous

Leaves ending in an odd leaflet
Walnuts; Hickories; Caucasian Wingnut; Service-trees; False Acacia;   Pagoda-tree;
Siberian Pea-tree; Golden-rain-tree; Tree-of-Heaven; Sumachs; Pepper-tree; Pistachios (some);
Box-elder; Ashes; Elders; Palms (some)

Leaves ending in a sharp or blunt point
Siberian Pea-tree; Honey-locust; Carob; Tree-of-heaven; Pepper-tree; Mastic-tree

Leaves palmate: evergreen or deciduous

Leaflets three (trifoliate)
Laburnums; Hop-tree; Pistachio

Leaflets five or more
Horse-chestnut; Palms (some)

Leaves spiny

Oaks (evergreen species); Hollies; Date Palms

TREES

OF BRITAIN AND EUROPE

Common Silver Fir *Abies alba* Up to 50m Tall, evergreen tree with spiky, ragged crown, often reduced to upper branches only in old trees. Pyramidal to narrowly conical in shape with smooth, greyish bark cracking with age. Young twigs densely hairy. Leathery but flexible needles 15-30 x 1.5-2mm, flattened and slightly notched, blue-green, with two silvery bands below. Lateral needles on the shoot spread horizontally, but shorter upper ones grow up and out, forming a distinct parting above the shoot. Cones 10-20cm long, erect, cylindrical, green ripening to brown, with a deflexed bract below each scale. *Distribution:* Forms extensive natural forests from northern Spain to eastern Poland and the Balkans; widely planted for timber in northern and western Europe but being superseded by species more resistant to pollution and disease. An almost identical tree, thought to be wild in Calabria in Italy and planted in France, is sometimes separated as **A. pardei**. It differs only by the centrally placed resin canals within the needles.

Caucasian Fir *Abies nordmanniana* Up to 70m More densely branched and broadly pyramidal than Common Silver Fir, and often much taller. Evergreen, retaining its branches almost to the ground, even in old age. Young twigs sparsely hairy. Needles resemble those of Common Silver Fir but all curve up and forwards, not leaving a central parting above the shoot. Cones 10-20cm long, erect, cylindrical, ripening dark brown, with a long, deflexed bract beneath each scale. *Distribution:* Native to the Caucasus and mountains of northern Turkey, widely planted in central Europe and elsewhere for timber. Similar **Sicilian Fir** (*A. nebrodensis*) is almost extinct in the wild in its native Sicily but is now being planted elsewhere. It has smooth twigs and needles only 8-13mm long, spreading to leave a parting both above and below the shoot.

Sicilian Fir

Grecian Fir *Abies cephalonica* Up to 30m Stiff- and prickly-leaved tree with stout and pyramidal crown. Young twigs glabrous; buds very resinous. Thick, flattened needles 15-35mm long are rigid and spine-tipped, spreading evenly out on either side of the shoot to leave a distinct parting above, a less distinct parting below. Cones 12-16cm long, erect, with a deflexed bract beneath each scale. *Distribution:* Native to high mountains in Greece, also planted for timber in Italy. **A. borisii-regis** is probably a hybrid between Common Silver Fir and Grecian Fir and occurs in the Balkan Peninsula. Intermediate between the parents, it has densely hairy young twigs, resinous buds and rigid, spine-tipped needles. Cones are rarely produced.

Spanish Fir *Abies pinsapo* 20-30m Closely resembles Grecian Fir but the smaller needles, 10-15mm long, spread out all around the shoot. Cones are narrower, only 3-4cm wide, and have bracts concealed by the cone-scales. *Distribution:* Native only to limestone mountains in south-western Spain but planted for timber, mainly in Portugal and Austria. **Algerian Fir** (*A. numidica*) from Algeria has larger, less rigid needles banded with white on the underside; sometimes grown for timber. **A. x insignis** is a hybrid between Spanish and Caucasian Firs, often used as a park tree. Twigs hairy; blunt needles often parted beneath the shoot. Cones have bracts just visible beneath the lower cone-scales.

Abies x *insignis*

Common Silver Fir

Caucasian Fir

Grecian Fir

Spanish Fir: ♂ cones

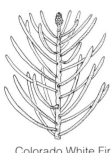

Colorado White Fir

Siberian Fir

Abies balsamea:
needle underside

Grand Fir *Abies grandis* Up to 100m, often less Large, fast-growing
evergreen with symmetrical, narrowly conical crown of aromatic
foliage. Young twigs olive green, with sparse, minute hairs. Needles
dark, glossy green, flattened and notched, of various lengths from
20-60 x 1.5-2mm, with two silvery bands below. They spread out to
either side of the shoot leaving a parting down the centre. Erect dark
brown cones 5-10cm long, cylindrical but taper at the tips. Bracts
concealed by cone-scales. *Distribution:* Native to western North
America, disease-resistant and widely planted for timber in the wetter
areas of northern and central Europe. **Colorado White Fir**
(*A. concolor*) has longer, fleshy needles which curve upwards away
from the shoot; they are often bluish, sometimes green on the upper
surface. Also from western North America and planted for timber
in Europe.

Noble Fir *Abies procera* 40-50m, sometimes more This fir has
characteristic large cones almost hidden by the long, deflexed bracts.
Stout, narrowly conical tree with horizontally spreading branches and
smooth, pale grey bark. Young twigs reddish hairy; buds resinous only
at their tips. Flattened, blunt, bluish-green needles10-35mm long,
pressed against the shoot before curving upwards, leaving a parting
below the shoot. Cones 12-20cm long, erect, with long, deflexed
bracts. *Distribution:* A western North American species tolerant of
exposed sites and poor soils, planted in northern and western Europe
for timber and ornament.

Alpine Fir *Abies lasiocarpa* Up to 48m Similar to Noble Fir, this
species has a more slender trunk, narrowly pyramidal crown and
much smaller cones. Needles 15-40mm long, point forwards and
curve upwards, with no parting above the shoot. Cones 5-10cm long,
with the bracts concealed by the cone-scales. *Distribution:* A western
North American species, planted for timber in Iceland and parts of
Scandinavia. Similar **Siberian Fir** (*A. sibirica*) forms extensive forests
in Siberia, extending west to Russia, and is planted for timber in
Scandinavia. It differs mainly in the thinly hairy twigs; the very resinous
buds; narrow, flexible needles and much smaller cones.

Nikko Fir *Abies homolepis* Up to 27m Relatively small tree with
roughly triangular but irregular crown. Young twigs glabrous; buds
very resinous. Needles short, rather stiff and flattened, about 25mm
long, rounded or notched at the tips, with two white bands beneath.
They spread straight out to leave a distinct parting above the shoot.
Cones 8cm long, erect, ripening from purple to brown, often streaked
with white resin; bracts concealed by the cone-scales. *Distribution:* A
native of Japan often planted in or near towns as it is pollution-
resistant. **A. balsamea** is similar but has needles with two grey
bands beneath and violet-purple cones with smaller scales. A short-
lived species of wet ground in North America, occasionally planted in
Europe.

Grand Fir

Grand Fir

Noble Fir

Noble Fir

Alpine Fir

Nikko Fir

Siberian Spruce

Norway Spruce *Picea abies* subsp. *abies* Up to 65m Conical evergreen with sweeping, curved branches, the upper ascending, the lower drooping. Smooth reddish-brown bark develops fine cracks. Twigs sometimes have sparse, minute hairs. Dark green needles 10-25mm long spread out and up to reveal the lower side of the shoot. Stiff, prickly and four-sided, they are borne on short, peg-like bases which persist on the shoot after the needles fall. Male cones crimson. Cigar-shaped female cones 10-18cm long, dark red and erect at first, ripening red-brown and becoming pendulous. Cone-scales square or irregularly notched at the tips. *Distribution:* A major forest tree in northern Europe and in mountains as far south as the Alps and Balkan Peninsula. Extensively planted for timber in many areas, it is the species commonly used for Christmas trees. **Siberian Spruce** (*P. abies* subsp. *obovata*) differs from the more common subspecies in the dense and minute hairs on the twigs, often shorter needles and shorter, ovoid to cylindrical, shiny brown cones. It is found mainly in Scandinavia and Russia.

Oriental Spruce *Picea orientalis* Up to 40m or more Very similar to both Norway and Siberian Spruces but has even smaller needles. Twigs densely hairy. Needles, the smallest of any spruce, are only 6-10mm long with rounded tips, crowded and loosely pressed to the shoot. Pendulous cones 6-9cm long, tapered at both ends, slightly curved, with broad, rounded scales. *Distribution:* Native to south-western Asia, but grown for timber in a few parts of Europe, mainly Austria, Belgium and Italy; also planted in gardens.

Brewer's Weeping Spruce *Picea breweriana* 10-20m Sheets of blackish-green, weeping foliage hang vertically from the upswept or spreading branches of this attractive evergreen. Smooth pinkish to purplish bark breaks into scales. Slender twigs finely hairy. Stiff, fleshy needles 20-35mm long, flattened and curved, spreading out all around the shoot. They are dark bluish-green, with two white bands beneath and leave woody peg-like bases when they fall. Narrow, cylindrical cones 10-12cm long, pendulous, ripening from purple to brown, often streaked with white resin. Scales rounded. *Distribution:* Slow-growing tree native only to mountains in California and Oregon; widely planted in European parks and gardens for its beautiful weeping habit. **Morinda** (*P. smithiana*), from the Himalayas, is the only other spruce which may be confused with Brewer's Weeping Spruce. It has similar but less marked weeping foliage. The shoots are glabrous, the bright green needles four-sided and the cones broader. It is also planted for ornament.

Morinda: needle

Norway Spruce

Norway Spruce: ♂ cones (above) & ♀ (below)

Norway Spruce

Oriental Spruce

Brewer's Weeping Spruce

Brewer's Weeping Spruce: ♂ and ♀ cones

Sitka Spruce *Picea sitchensis* Up to 60m Vigorous and fast-growing evergreen with stiff and slightly pendulous small side-shoots and bluish foliage. Conifer with conical crown and stout trunk, sometimes with buttresses. Bark grey, peeling in thin scales or plates. Main branches ascending or level. Needles flattened, stiff and pointed, 15-30mm long, dark green above, with two conspicuous bluish-white bands beneath; they are borne on persistent peg-like bases; radiate all around the shoot at first, but the upper become pressed to the shoot while the lower ones spread to leave a parting below. Mature cones 6-10cm long, pendulous, bluntly cigar-shaped, with diamond-shaped, papery scales irregularly toothed at the tips. *Distribution:* Native to western North America, and thrives on a wide range of soils, especially wet ones. Planted on a large scale for timber in north-western and parts of central Europe.

Colorado Spruce *Picea pungens* Up to 30m Evergreen with stiff and prickly needles, usually grey-green but some forms have blue leaves. Crown narrowly conical with regular whorls of branches held horizontally. Bark dark brown and scaly. Yellow-brown twigs glabrous and rough with persistent peg-like leaf-bases. Rigid, four-sided needles 20-30mm long spread out around the shoot before curving up and forwards. Mature cones 6-10cm long, pendulous, broadly cylindrical, with scales which narrow to blunt and slightly ragged tips. *Distribution:* Native to western North America, planted for timber on drier soils in northern and central Europe. Blue-leaved forms of this tree are widely grown for their striking foliage. The best known is **Blue Spruce** (cv. 'Glauca').

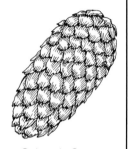

Colorado Spruce

Dragon Spruce *Picea asperata* Up to 20m Similar to Norway Spruce in habit and to Colorado Spruce in foliage. Sturdy tree with down-curved branches. Bark greyish-brown, rough and peeling in thin flakes. Twigs mostly glabrous. Four-sided needles, 12-18mm long, stiff and prickly, spread all round the shoot. Pendulous mature cones 7.5-12.5cm long ripen from fawn-grey to chestnut brown. The cone-scales are variable, either rounded, cut straight across or rhombic at the tips. *Distribution:* A mountain tree widespread in western China, planted on a small scale in Europe.

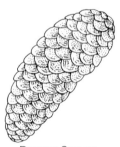

Dragon Spruce

Sitka Spruce

Sitka Spruce: young, ripening & mature cones

Colorado Spruce

Dragon Spruce

Black Spruce

Tiger-tail Spruce

Engelmann Spruce *Picea engelmannii* Up to 50m Evergreen conifer similar to Colorado Spruce but foliage less harsh and pleasantly aromatic, smelling of menthol when crushed. Twigs have dense but minute glandular hairs. Four-sided, blue-green needles 15-25mm long spread to leave a parting below the shoot; they are soft and flexible with persistent, woody, peg-like bases. Pendulous ripe cones are only 3.5-7.5cm long with squared-off, ragged-tipped scales. *Distribution:* Native to western North America and planted for timber in northern Europe, mainly in Scandinavia. Two similar North American species, both with short needles and cones, are planted on a small scale in Europe. **Red Spruce** (*P. rubens*) has yellowish-green needles 10-15mm long and cones 3-4cm long. **Black Spruce** (*P. mariana*) has bluish needles 6-18mm long radiating on all sides of the shoot, the upper pressed forwards. Cones are 2-3.5cm long.

Tiger-tail Spruce *Picea polita* Up to 20m Stouter and sharper than those of any other spruce, the sickle-shaped needles of this tree are painful to grasp. Conical evergreen with horizontal branches; grey-brown bark is rough and flaking, glabrous twigs pale and shiny. Bright, rather yellowish-green needles 15-20mm long, four-sided, rigid and extremely sharp-pointed, radiate on all sides of the shoot and curve forwards. They have persistent, woody, peg-like bases. Ripening from grey-green to cinnamon brown, the pendulous mature cones, 10cm in length, are broadly cylindrical and blunt. Broad, rounded cone-scales have distinctive pale margins. *Distribution:* Native to the Japanese island of Honshu; in Europe grown mainly in parks.

Serbian Spruce *Picea omorika* Up to 30m Slender evergreen with spire-like crown of blue-green foliage retained almost from the ground. Red-brown bark falls away in flakes. Twigs densely hairy and rough with old woody, peg-like leaf-bases. Flattened, blunt needles 8-18mm long have two broad, whitish bands beneath. The upper needles are pressed forward on the shoot, the lower spread out to leave a parting below the shoot. Crimson young cones reach 3-6 x 1.5-2.5cm when ripe and resemble those of Tiger-tail Spruce but taper to a point. The rounded scales lack a pale margin. *Distribution:* Native only to the Drina River Basin in central Yugoslavia but planted for timber in parts of Scandinavia and widely grown elsewhere as an ornamental.

White Spruce *Picea glauca* Up to 30m Striking evergreen whose intense bluish foliage usually gives off a strong, unpleasant smell when crushed. Narrowly conical crown becomes rounded in older trees; branches turn up at the tips. Bark cracks into rounded plates. The four-sided needles, 12-13mm long, are stiff, bluntly tipped and pale bluish-green with persistent, woody, peg-like bases. They spread out from the sides and top of the shoot leaving a parting below. Pendulous, orange-brown mature cones 2.5-6cm long, cylindrical to shortly cigar-shaped with rounded scales. *Distribution:* Native to North America and often planted for its attractive foliage; also grown as a timber tree in northern Europe.

Engelmann Spruce

Tiger-tail Spruce

Serbian Spruce

White Spruce

Mountain Hemlock-spruce

Eastern Hemlock-spruce

Large-coned Douglas-fir

Western Hemlock-spruce *Tsuga heterophylla* Up to 70m Graceful evergreen with distinctive drooping tips to the branches and leading shoot. Irregular whorls of branches clothe the trunk almost to the ground. Bark grey, becoming purple-brown and flaking. Young twigs have long, light brown hairs. Blunt, hard, flattened needles of irregular lengths from 6-20mm are dark green above with two broad white bands below. They spread horizontally to either side of the shoot and have prominent, cushion-like bases which persist after the needles fall. Male cones red. Female cones only 2-2.5cm long, drooping, ovoid to cylindrical, red-brown when ripe and composed of few, rounded scales. *Distribution:* Native to the west coast of North America; grown as a timber tree in northern Europe from Ireland to Germany and Denmark. **Mountain Hemlock-spruce** (*T. mertensiana*), also from the west coast of North America, has blue-green needles radiating all around the shoot and larger cones 5-7.5cm long. It is sometimes planted in parks.

Eastern Hemlock-spruce *Tsuga canadensis* Up to 30m Very similar to Western Hemlock-spruce but with a much broader, bushier crown and needles 8-18mm long with two narrow white bands below. The central row of needles on the upper side of the shoot is twisted, clearly showing the pale underside. Ripe cones 1.5-2cm in length hang from short stalks. *Distribution:* Native to the east coast of North America; in Europe occasionally planted on a small scale for timber, more commonly as an ornamental.

Douglas-fir *Pseudotsuga menziesii* Up to 55m, sometimes more Very tall evergreen, though seldom reaching its maximum height of 100m in Europe. Crown conical, with irregular whorls of branches. Ridged, somewhat corky bark becomes grey or dark purplish-brown with age. Hairy twigs bear projecting, elliptical scars of fallen needles. Needles 20-35mm long, very narrow, sharp-pointed but otherwise soft, dark green and grooved above, with two white bands below. They mostly spread to leave partings both above and below the shoot and give off a pleasantly aromatic scent when crushed. Cones 5-10cm long, ovoid and pendulous, ripening from red or green to brown. Distinctive three-pronged bracts protrude well beyond the broad cone-scales. *Distribution:* Native to western North America; extensively planted in much of Europe as a high-grade timber tree. **Large-coned Douglas-fir** (*P. macrocarpa*) from northern California is sometimes used as a park tree. It has large cones, 9-12.5cm or more long, and slightly curved needles radiating to all sides of the shoot.

Western Hemlock-spruce

Eastern Hemlock-spruce

Douglas-fir

Western Hemlock-spruce: ripening and mature ♀ cones

Douglas-fir

Shore Pine *Pinus contorta* Up to 30m Evergreen conifer with short, contorted branches and twisted needles borne in pairs. Often a short tree, the crown is bushy in young specimens, but becomes tall and narrow in old ones. Bark brown, cracking into corky squares. Paired needles 30-70 x about 1mm, twisted, sharply pointed and yellowish-green. Cones occur in clusters of two to four, 2-6cm long; symmetrically ovoid, they ripen from red to pale shiny brown in the second year. Cone-scales tipped with a slender, fragile spike. *Distribution:* Native to the west coast of North America, it grows well on wet or poor soils and is widely planted for timber in north-western and central Europe. Similar **Lodgepole Pine** (*P. contorta* var. *latifolia*) has a narrower crown and brighter green needles.

Bosnian Pine *Pinus leucodermis* Up to 30m Stout pine with paired needles, found on very dry limestone soils. Pyramidal crown dense and regular, with down-curved branches. Smooth grey bark cracks to reveal yellowish patches. Glabrous twigs have an ash-grey bloom. Paired blackish-green needles 70-90mm long, stiff, sharp-pointed, cover the shoot densely except at the base of the current year's growth which is bare for a short way leaving a cup-shaped tuft of needles at the tip. Cones 7-8cm long, ovoid and slightly shiny, ripening from blue to brown in the second year; exposed ends of cone-scales pyramidal with a short, recurved spine. *Distribution:* Native to Italy and the Balkan Peninsula, growing on light, dry soils.

Bosnian Pine

Pinus heldreichii Up to 20m Very similar in most respects to Bosnian Pine but shorter and with a more rounded crown. Twigs retain their ash-grey bloom for the first year only, turning brown in the second year. Paired needles 60-90mm long are brighter green than Bosnian Pine. Mature cones are paler brown, the exposed ends of the cone-scales flat with a straight spine. *Distribution:* Native to mountains in the central Balkan Peninsula.

Pinus heldreichii

Austrian Pine *Pinus nigra* subsp. *nigra* Up to 50m The very dense, hard and rough foliage gives a dark overall appearance to this evergreen conifer. Young specimens pyramidal, old ones flat-topped. Bark grey-brown to black and very rough. Yellowish-brown twigs rough with persistent leaf-bases. Stiff, very dark green needles 100-150mm long, in pairs grouped in whorls on twigs, toothed and thickened at the tips. Cones of 5-8cm, usually in pairs, ripen in the second year from pink to pale, shiny brown; the exposed ends of the spreading scales are keeled and spine-tipped. *Distribution:* Found on alkaline and neutral soils in central Europe and coasts of southern Europe; also widely planted.

Corsican Pine *Pinus nigra* subsp. *laricio* Up to 40m or more Very similar to its close relative Austrian Pine, but this subspecies has fewer, shorter branches and sparser foliage. Slender, grey-green needles soft and flexible, often twisted in young trees. *Distribution:* Endemic to Corsica, southern Italy and Sicily. Valuable timber tree, widely planted in much of Europe. Similar **Red Pine** (*P. resinosa*) from eastern North America is grown on a small scale in Europe. It has reddish bark, orange twigs and long, slender, lemon-scented needles 100-150mm long.

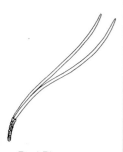

Red Pine:
needle-bundle

Shore Pine

Shore Pine

Bosnian Pine

Pinus heldreichii

Austrian Pine

Corsican Pine

Scots Pine *Pinus sylvestris* Up to 35m The long, bare trunk of this evergreen conifer has conspicuously reddish upper bark and supports a small, flat, often lop-sided crown. Young trees conical with whorled branches, older trees with bare lower trunks, branching only at the top of the trunk. Bark reddish-brown and fissured, lighter and papery at the top. Paired grey or bluish-green needles 25-80mm long, twisted and finely toothed with a long, greyish sheath around the base of each pair. Male cones yellow or red. Female cones short-stalked and in clusters of one to three, each 2-8cm long, ovoid to conical and ripening from pinkish-purple to dull grey-brown in the second year. Cone-scales have exposed ends flat or slightly pyramidal with a short spine. *Distribution:* Common tree forming forests on poor, light soils on high ground throughout Europe.

Dwarf Mountain Pine

Dwarf Mountain Pine *Pinus mugo* Up to 3m, rarely more Dwarf and shrubby, this upland pine hugs the ground and seldom reaches its maximum height of 10m, although it can form a small conical tree. Evergreen tree or more commonly shrub with numerous crooked, spreading stems and branches. Twigs initially green, becoming brown. Paired needles 30-80 x 1.5-2mm, bright green, stiff and curved. Ovoid cones of 2-5cm in clusters of one to three, ripening shiny brown in the second year. The exposed end of each scale is usually flat with a central boss bearing a small spine. *Distribution:* Native to high mountain slopes of central Europe and the Balkan Peninsula, but often planted in northern Europe as a sand-binder and as a wind- or avalanche-break elsewhere.

Mountain Pine: old cone

Mountain Pine *Pinus uncinata* Up to 25m Closely resembling Dwarf Mountain Pine, and sometimes included in that species, this tree is most obviously distinguished by its much greater height. It forms an erect tree with a single trunk. Mature cones are larger, 5-7cm long, with the exposed ends of the cone-scales, especially the lower ones, hooked or curved downwards. *Distribution:* A mountain species found in the Alps, Pyrenees and mountains of central Spain.

Maritime Pine: needle-bundle

Maritime Pine *Pinus pinaster* Up to 40m Long and bare, the trunk of this evergreen conifer supports an open crown of wide-spreading branches bearing very long, stiff needles. Bark red-brown and deeply fissured. Twigs reddish-brown. Pairs of greyish-green needles 100-250 x 2mm, stiff and spiny. Young female cones pink, in clusters of three to five at the tips of shoots. Mature cones 8-22cm long, symmetrically conical to oval and pale, shiny brown. They ripen in the second year and persist on the tree. Exposed end of each cone-scale is rhomboidal and keeled with a prickly point. *Distribution:* Found on light and sandy soils near the sea around the Mediterranean, also planted elsewhere for timber and shelter.

Scots Pine

Scots Pine

Scots Pine: ♂ and ♀ cones

Dwarf Mountain Pine

Mountain Pine

Maritime Pine: ♂ and ♀ cones

Stone Pine

Aleppo Pine:
winged seed

Jack Pine

Stone Pine *Pinus pinea* Up to 30m Radiating branches and a flattened, spreading crown give this stout pine a very distinctive umbrella-shape. Evergreen conifer with bare trunk; bark deeply fissured and flaking to reveal reddish-orange patches. Twigs greyish-green, eventually brown. Paired needles 100-200 x 1.5-2mm, slightly twisted. Male cones orange or brown. Female cones 8-14cm long ripen from yellowish-green to shiny brown over three years. Exposed end of each scale weakly pyramidal. Seeds have a wing less than 1mm long. *Distribution:* Found on light soils all around the Mediterranean coasts and planted both for ornament and for the edible seeds.

Aleppo Pine *Pinus halepensis* Up to 20m Sparse but very bright, shiny green foliage clothes the often twisted branches of this evergreen conifer. Trunk stout and, like branches, often twisted. Bark pale grey, becoming reddish-brown, fissured and flaking. First year twigs grey, older ones brown. Clear green needles 60-150 x 0.7mm, stiff, curved and spiny-tipped; borne in pairs. Shiny, reddish-brown cones of 5-12cm are borne on thick, scaly, recurved stalks and ripen in the second year. Exposed ends of the cone-scales are convex. Seeds have a wing about 20mm long. *Distribution:* Drought-resistant and common in hot, dry parts of the Mediterranean; often planted as a windbreak and soil-stabiliser.

Jack Pine *Pinus banksiana* Up to 25m A thin crown of crooked branches and distinctive curved cones identify this pine. Crown rather variable in shape, oval with ascending branches in young trees, broader and spreading in old trees. Reddish-brown bark deeply fissured into narrow vertical ridges; glabrous yellowish twigs turn reddish in the second year. Paired olive-green needles 20-40mm long, stiff and curved or slightly twisted, with pointed tips and minutely toothed margins. Yellowish cones 2.5cm long, borne in pairs or threes, erect, strongly curved with the scales on the outer side much larger than those on the inner; they may remain unopened on the tree for many years. *Distribution:* Native to northern parts of North America and very hardy but short-lived; planted for timber, mainly in central Europe.

Stone Pine

Aleppo Pine

Aleppo Pine

Jack Pine

Monterey Pine:
needle-bundle

Monterey Pine *Pinus radiata* Up to 40m Among the three-needled pines this tree is distinguished by its slender, bright green needles and large cones which remain on the tree for many years. High-domed, with spreading lower branches which may reach to the ground. Bark thick, dark brown and deeply ridged in old trees. Twigs glabrous, reddish-brown. Very slender, straight, bright green needles 100-150mm long, borne in threes and densely crowded on the shoots. They are pointed, with finely toothed margins. Cones 7-14cm long, ovoid, very asymmetric at the base, borne in clusters of three or five, ripening shiny brown; they curve back on the stalk when mature and remain closed on the branches and trunks for many years. Cone-scales broad, especially on the larger side of the cone. *Distribution:* Native to coastal hills in Monterey County in California. It withstands salt winds and is grown for both timber and shelter in western Europe.

Northern Pitch Pine *Pinus rigida* Up to 25m This pine is peculiar in developing tufts of needles directly on the trunk and main branches as well as on the shoots. A rather broad evergreen with an open, irregular crown. Glabrous twigs prominently ridged, changing from green to orange-brown in the second year. Stiff, slightly twisted needles 80-90mm long, or up to 120mm in the additional tufts, are borne in threes; they are grey-green, thick, with a horny point and finely toothed margins. Ovoid, symmetrical cones of 3-7cm are clustered, ripening shiny yellowish-brown and persisting on the tree for many years. Cone-scales thin and flat with a recurved spine. *Distribution:* Forest tree native to eastern North America, thriving on poor soils and planted for timber on a small scale in Europe.

Canary Island Pine

Canary Island Pine *Pinus canariensis* Up to 30m Slightly weeping evergreen with spreading yellow twigs, very long needles and large cones. Tree with spreading branches. Pendulous twigs glabrous, prominently ridged, yellow. Flexible, pointed needles 200-300mm long, borne in threes and densely crowded on the shoot. Solitary or clustered cones 10-20cm long, ovoid to conical, bent back on a short stalk when mature. Exposed ends of the cone-scales pyramidal with a central dimple. *Distribution:* Endemic to the Canary Islands and once widespread on dry slopes there; now much reduced in the wild, it is planted for timber in Mediterranean countries, principally Italy.

Loblolly Pine

Loblolly Pine *Pinus taeda* Up to 30m or more Very adaptable species, seeding and spreading freely; something of a nuisance in the wild where it often invades abandoned farmland. Evergreen with a rather stout trunk and reddish bark breaking into broad, scaly ridges. Twigs are glabrous, waxy green at first, later yellowish-brown and ridged. Stiff, slightly twisted needles 120-250mm long, borne in threes, pale green with horny tips and minutely toothed margins. Cones 6-10cm long, roughly cylindrical and stalkless. Exposed ends of cone-scales have a raised, horizontal ridge and a stout, recurved spine. *Distribution:* Native to southern and eastern North America, grown on a small scale for timber in Europe.

Monterey Pine

Northern Pitch Pine

Canary Island Pine

Loblolly Pine

Jeffrey's Pine

Arolla Pine: needle-bundle

Weymouth Pine: needle-bundle base

Western Yellow Pine *Pinus ponderosa* Up to 75m The tallest pine commonly planted in Europe, this evergreen has stout needles borne in threes. Trunk stout with very thick, scaly, yellowish or dark reddish-brown bark. Crown conical, spire-like, the drooping branches upturned at the tips. Twigs glabrous, orange-brown or green turning to nearly black. Stiff, stout, curved needles 100-250mm long, borne in threes, rarely in pairs or fives. They are deep yellowish-green and aromatic, with horny tips and minutely toothed margins. Solitary or clustered ovoid cones 8-15cm long, ripen reddish-brown and spread away from the shoot or turn downwards. When shed they often leave the lowest few cone-scales on the tree. Exposed ends of the cone-scales have a transverse ridge and a central boss tipped with an erect spine. *Distribution:* Native to western North America, sometimes planted in Europe for timber, more frequently for ornament. Two similar North American species are occasionally grown in Europe. Both have large cones 15-25cm long. **Jeffrey's Pine** (*P. jeffreyi*) is often confused with Western Yellow Pine but has bright red bark, bluish-green needles and cone-scales with a recurved spine. **Digger Pine** (*P. sabiniana*) grows to 25m with scanty foliage and grey-green needles 200-300mm long.

Arolla Pine *Pinus cembra* 25-40m A densely foliaged pine which retains its branches, even the lowest ones, so that the trunk is almost completely hidden. Evergreen conifer with short, level branches. Scaly bark marked with resin blisters. Twigs covered with brownish-orange hair. Stiff, shiny green needles 50-80 x 1mm grouped in erect bundles of five and crowded on the twigs. Male cones purple or yellow. Short-stalked female cones 5-8cm long, ovoid, ripening from bluish to purplish-brown over three years. Cone-scales rounded, thickened at the tips with minute hairs. Seeds wingless. *Distribution:* Mountain species native to the Alps and Carpathians at altitudes of 1500-2400m. Planted for timber in parts of northern Europe.

Weymouth Pine *Pinus strobus* Up to 50m Evergreen conifer with dense, horizontally held, flexible bluish-green needles, 50-140mm long, arranged in bundles of five with a distinctive tuft of hairs at the base of the bundle-sheath. Eventually broadly pyramidal in outline. Bark of young trees greyish-green, of mature trees brown and fissured. Young shoots have tufts of reddish-brown down below the needle bundles. Large, pendulous, sticky female cones 8-20cm long, cylindrical, but often curving towards the tip. They ripen in the second year. Seeds have a wing 18-25mm wide. *Distribution:* A North American species formerly widely planted for timber, but susceptible to blister rust and less commonly grown nowadays.

Western Yellow Pine

Arolla Pine

Arolla Pine

Weymouth Pine

Bristle-cone Pine:
needle-bundle

Bristle-cone Pine *Pinus aristata* Up to 15m Small tree or even a sprawling shrub, this pine has needles with conspicuous white flecks of resin and bristly cones. Trunk very short with thin, smooth bark becoming ridged and scaly with age. Twigs yellowish-brown with minute reddish hairs. Stiff, incurved, pointed needles 20-40mm long borne in fives, densely crowded and long persistent on the shoot; they are deep green with conspicuous white dots of resin and smell of turpentine when crushed. Cones 4-9cm long, cylindrical, ripening in the second year. Each cone-scale is tipped with a long, slender spine giving the whole cone a bristly appearance. *Distribution:* Native to high altitudes in the Rocky Mountains and planted on a small scale for timber in Europe.

Macedonian Pine *Pinus peuce* Up to 30m Compact, narrowly conical evergreen somewhat resembling Bhutan Pine. Thin grey bark cracks into small scales. Twigs glabrous, shiny green at first, brownish-grey later. Stiff, slender needles 70-120mm long, sharp-pointed, minutely toothed. Borne in fives, they are crowded and forward pointing. Solitary or clustered cones 8-15cm long, curved, brown and resinous when ripe. Cone-scales broadly wedge-shaped. *Distribution:* Endemic to mountains in the Balkan Peninsula and planted on a small scale in Germany.

Bhutan Pine

Bhutan Pine *Pinus wallichiana* Up to 50m A five-needled pine with wide-spreading needles and smooth cones, this is an elegant evergreen with an open crown of wide-spreading, drooping branches. Bark smooth or shallowly fissured, greyish-brown. Twigs grey-green with a purplish waxy bloom when young, darkening with age. Flexible, grey-green needles 80-200mm long, sharp-pointed, toothed and borne in fives. Those on young shoots are erect; on older shoots they droop and spread widely. Cones 15-25cm long, solitary or in clusters of two or three, cylindrical and pendulous, pale brown and resinous when ripe in the second year. Exposed ends of cone-scales are grooved lengthwise, the lowest scales usually recurved. *Distribution:* Native to cool zones of the Himalayas. It is pollution-resistant and is planted in Italy for timber, elsewhere in Europe for ornament.

Bristle-cone Pine

Macedonian Pine

Macedonian Pine

Bhutan Pine

Siberian Larch

European Larch *Larix decidua* Up to 35m Deciduous conifer with needles which turn yellow in autumn before falling. Conical crown becomes broader with age, the branches irregularly whorled and horizontal or pendulous. Bark grey to pale brown, becoming thick, especially towards the base of the trunk, before cracking away. Pendulous twigs yellowish, knotted and roughened with old leaf-bases. Shoots are of two types: long shoots bear scattered needles; short spur-like shoots bear needles in tufts of 30-40. Flattened needles 12-30mm in length, soft and pale green. Young cones appear just before new leaves, males yellow, females red. Mature cones, 2-3cm long, ovoid, with 40-50 close-pressed, softly hairy scales; they persist on the twigs for several years after shedding seeds. *Distribution:* A fast-growing but short-lived tree native to the Alps and Carpathian Mountains; widely planted for timber throughout northern and central Europe. Similar **Siberian Larch** (*L. russica*) is a Siberian species planted for timber from Sweden to Russia. It has hairy twigs and larger cones with incurved scales.

Dahurian Larch *Larix gmelinii* Up to 30m Closely resembling European Larch, this tree has yellow or reddish and often hairy twigs. Needles 30mm long and bright green. Mature cones, 2-2.5cm long, have only about 20 glabrous scales. *Distribution:* Native to eastern Asia; grown as a timber tree in Denmark and Scandinavia.

Japanese Larch *Larix kaempferi* Up to 40m Resembles European Larch but has a distinct blue-green cast to the foliage. Upper part of the trunk may twist spirally, especially in young trees. Crown broader than that of European Larch, with wide-spreading branches and waxy, orange twigs. Bark reddish-brown. Blue- or grey-green needles have two distinct white bands beneath. Young female cones are creamy yellow, with green bracts. Mature cones, 1.5-3.5cm long, have softly hairy scales; upper edges of the scales curve outwards. *Distribution:* Native to Japan; an important timber tree in much of northern Europe from the British Isles and France to Russia. **Hybrid Larch** (*L. x eurolepis*) is a vigorous hybrid between European and Japanese Larches, with features intermediate between both parents. It is planted for timber in various parts of Europe.

Hybrid Larch: needle rosette

European Larch

European Larch: ♂ & young ♀ cones

European Larch

Dahurian Larch

Japanese Larch: young cones

Japanese Larch

Deodar *Cedrus deodara* Up to 60m Pale green needles are borne in tufts like those of larches, but are evergreen. A relatively stout trunk supports a triangular crown with downswept branches and a drooping leading shoot. Twigs densely hairy. Shoots are of two types: long or short and spur-like. Needles 20-50mm long, three-sided and scattered along long shoots, in rosette-like tufts of 15-20 on short shoots. Cones large and erect; males 5-12cm long, yellow; females greenish, ripening in the second year. Ripe cones 8-12 x 5-8cm, barrel-shaped, rounded at the top, eventually breaking up to leave a persistent central spike. *Distribution:* Native to the Himalayas; planted for timber in southern Europe.

Atlantic Cedar

Atlantic Cedar *Cedrus atlantica* Up to 40m Closely resembles Deodar but has upwardly angled branches and a stiff, erect leading shoot. Young twigs downy. Needles only 10-30mm long, usually green, sometimes blue-green, in tufts of 10-45 on short shoots. Male cones are 3-5cm long; female cones, measuring 5-8 x 3-5cm, have a flat or dimpled top and ripen in the second year. *Distribution:* Native to the Atlas Mountains of North Africa; planted as a timber tree in southern Europe and as an ornamental elsewhere, especially the blue-leaved forms.

Cedar-of-Lebanon: needle rosette

Cedar-of-Lebanon *Cedrus libani* Up to 40m Conical only when young; old trees develop massive trunks and characteristic large, level branches with flat, shelf-like masses of foliage. Twigs glabrous; dark green needles form tufts of 10-15, but otherwise generally resemble those of other cedars. Barrel-shaped ripe cones, 7-12cm long, have rounded tops and ripen from purple to brown in the second year. *Distribution:* A slow-growing, long-lived tree, native to Turkey, Syria and the Lebanon; used for timber in Europe but often seen as a park tree.

Deodar

Deodar

Atlantic Cedar

Cedar-of-Lebanon

Dawn Redwood

Coast Redwood:
leading shoot

Swamp-cypress *Taxodium distichum* Up to 50m A deciduous conifer which sheds both leaves and smaller side-shoots in autumn, this tree may be narrowly conical, triangular or domed with a fluted trunk and reddish, stringy and peeling bark. Stump-like pneumatophores or breathing roots often project up to 1m above the ground around the base of the trunk, especially in waterlogged soils. Shoots are of two kinds: persistent terminal shoots and short, alternate and deciduous side-shoots. Needles 8-20mm long, flattened, pointed and pale green, borne spirally on terminal shoots and in two rows on short shoots. Tiny yellow to purplish male cones form slender clusters. Thick-stalked female cones 12-30mm long, globular, ripening from green to purple. Bluntly diamond-shaped cone-scales each have a short, hooked central spine. *Distribution:* Native to swampy woods in south-eastern North America, often planted in similar soils in southern Europe for ornament and timber. Similarly deciduous **Dawn Redwood** (*Metasequoia glyptostroboides*) has paired side-shoots and needles, and cones without spines on the scales. Previously known only from fossils, it was discovered as a living tree in China in 1941 and is now planted in European parks.

Coast Redwood *Sequoia sempervirens* Up to 112m The tallest tree in the world, with a correspondingly large trunk clad with very soft and thick, fibrous, reddish bark. Narrowly columnar evergreen conifer with downwardly angled lower branches. Dark outer bark flakes away, leaving reddish, fibrous inner layers. Needles on the leading and cone-bearing shoots are 6mm long, scale-like and spirally arranged; those of the paired side-shoots are 6-20mm, narrow, flattened, pointed and often curved, with two white bands beneath, and form two rows along the shoot. Mature in the second year, cones of 1.8-2.5 x 1.2cm are ovoid, each of the 15-20 cone-scales having a sunken centre. *Distribution:* Native to the Pacific coast of North America, planted for ornament and sometimes for timber in western Europe.

Wellingtonia *Sequoiadendron giganteum* Up to 90m Shorter than Coast Redwood but more massive, this evergreen conifer has a trunk up to 7m in diameter, even when measured above the thickly buttressed base. Narrowly conical tree with downswept branches turning up at their tips. Bark thick, spongy, red-brown. Needles rather scale-like, 4-10mm long, oval to awl-shaped, spirally arranged and pressed against the shoot, the bases of the blades joined to the shoot but the tips spreading. Cones 5-8 x 3-4.5cm, ovoid and blunt, ripening in the second year. The 25-40 wrinkled cone-scales each have a sunken centre, often bearing a small spine. *Distribution:* Native to the Sierra Nevada mountains of California, occasionally planted for timber in parts of Europe, but more often grown as a park or avenue tree.

Swamp-cypress

Swamp-cypress

Swamp-cypress: winter

Coast Redwood

Coast Redwood

Wellingtonia

Chinese Fir: needle
underside

Japanese Red Cedar *Cryptomeria japonica* Up to 35m Narrowly
conical evergreen with irregularly whorled branches and shoots
hidden by narrow, awl-shaped needles. Pale red bark soft and thick,
peeling in long strips. Sparsely branched green twigs often droop.
Spirally arranged on the shoot, bright green needles 6-15mm long are
narrow, awl-shaped, incurved and roughly four-sided. Orange male
cones clustered at tips of shoots. Female cones, borne on stout side-
shoots, 1.2-3cm long when ripe, globular, with 20-30 cone-scales
each with five hooked spines in the centre. *Distribution:* Native to
China and Japan; introduced into parts of Europe for timber, most
notably in the Azores, where it thrives in the damp climate, but also
grown for ornament elsewhere. A Chinese species planted in parks,
Chinese Fir (*Cunninghamia lanceolata*), is a sparsely branched
evergreen. Its much longer needles have two white bands beneath
and mature cones have sharp-pointed, overlapping scales.

Monkey Puzzle *Araucaria araucana* Up to 25m Impossible to mistake
for any other tree, the stiff shape and intricate branches covered with
large overlapping leaves make Monkey Puzzle instantly recognisable.
Erect evergreen with distinct whorls of branches. Side branches may
point up or down and are shed after a few years. Leaves 30-40mm
long, broadly triangular, rigid and sharp-pointed, arranged in close-
set, overlapping whorls completely hiding the shoot. They remain
green for 10-15 years but may persist on the tree long after turning
brown and dying. Male and female cones borne on different trees.
Brownish male cones 10cm long form clusters at tips of shoots.
Globular female cones solitary, erect on the upper side of the shoot,
10-17cm long, with numerous golden-tipped, leafy scales. They ripen
in the second year before breaking up on the tree. Large brown seeds
edible. *Distribution:* Native to coastal mountains of Chile and
Argentina, widely planted in western Europe as an ornamental, garden
curiosity and even as a street tree. The related **Norfolk Island Pine**
(*A. heterophylla*), from Norfolk Island in the Pacific, is a popular
ornamental tree in Mediterranean countries. It is tall, with whorls of
small, soft, needle-like leaves giving the shoots a plumose
appearance.

Norfolk Island Pine

Western Red Cedar *Thuja plicata* Up to 65m Otherwise resembling
Lawson Cypress, this pyramidal or conical evergreen is very erect, the
leader and foliage never drooping. Tall tree with a stout, often fluted
trunk and reddish, shredding bark. Resin-scented foliage forms
flattened sprays. Scale-like leaves 2-3mm long, glossy green above,
faintly marked with white below. They are pressed against the shoot in
alternating pairs, the lateral pairs larger than the vertical pairs. Female
cones ovoid, 12mm long, ripening green to brown. They have 10-12
rather leafy, overlapping cone-scales, each with a hook on the inner
side of the tip. *Distribution:* Native to western North America, planted
in cool, damp parts of western and central Europe and sometimes
naturalised. Similar **White Cedar** (*T. occidentalis*) has yellowish,
apple-scented foliage. Native to eastern North America; various
cultivars are planted in Europe, especially dwarf ones.

White Cedar

Japanese Red Cedar

Monkey Puzzle

Western Red Cedar

Western Red Cedar: small ♂ and ripening ♀ cones

Sawara Cypress

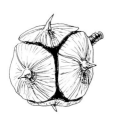

Nootka Cypress

Hinoki Cypress *Chamaecyparis obtusa* Up to 36m Very similar to the more widespread Lawson Cypress, this broadly conical tree has reddish bark peeling in long strips. Flattened sprays of foliage give a sweet, resinous scent when crushed, unlike the distinctive parsley scent of Lawson Cypress. Scale leaves blunt, not pointed, with X- or Y-shaped white markings on those beneath the shoot. Cones resemble those of Lawson Cypress. *Distribution:* Native to Japan, commonly planted in Europe as an ornamental tree. A second Japanese ornamental, **Sawara Cypress** (*C. pisifera*), is very similar. It has slender, drooping shoots and pointed leaves with spreading tips.

Lawson Cypress *Chamaecyparis lawsoniana* Up to 45m Pendulous sprays of foliage and a nodding leading shoot give the whole tree a drooping appearance. Dense evergreen with dark grey-brown bark, cracking into plates. Parsley-scented, light green shoots form flattened, pendulous sprays. Alternating pairs of tiny, pointed, scale-like leaves about 2mm long, closely pressed against the shoot; those on the upper side are dark green, those on the lower have whitish marks. Male cones blackish-red. Female cones, 8mm in diameter, globular and bluish-green, made up of eight scales which touch edge to edge. Each scale has a ridge in a central depression and ripens pale brown. *Distribution:* Native to western North America, widely planted in Europe and sometimes naturalised. Similar **Nootka Cypress** (*C. nootkatensis*) has cone-scales with curved spines. Also from North America, it is sometimes planted for ornament.

Leyland Cypress x *Cupressocyparis leylandii* Up to 35m Remarkable for its rapid growth, this generic hybrid is now one of the most commonly planted evergreen conifers for hedges and gardens. Narrow, columnar crown, with dense, upwardly angled branches from base to tip, leaving little if any bare trunk. Leading shoot leans but does not droop. Shoots form sprays of foliage which are flattened in some but not all forms. Pointed, scaly leaves 0.5-2mm long, dark green above, yellowish beneath, in alternating pairs pressed against the shoot. Female cones globular, green when young, 2-3cm long and brown and woody when ripe. Cone-scales few, meeting edge to edge, each with a blunt central spine. *Distribution:* A garden hybrid between Nootka and Monterey Cypresses; widely cultivated. Two forms of Leyland Cypress are common; cv. 'Hagerston Grey' (female parent Nootka Cypress) has greyish leaves while cv. 'Leighton Green' (female parent Monterey Cypress) has greener leaves and flattened sprays of foliage.

Hinoki Cypress

Lawson Cypress

Lawson Cypress: small purplish ♂ and
globular ♀ cones

Leyland Cypress

Monterey Cypress

Mexican Cypress

Rough-barked
Arizona Cypress

Monterey Cypress *Cupressus macrocarpa* Up to 35m Evergreen conifer with markedly upswept branches bearing ropy or cord-like foliage. Crown narrow and pointed when young but broadly domed or flat-topped in old trees. Bark ridged, yellowish-brown. Blunt, scaly leaves 1-2mm long, closely pressed against the shoot in alternating and overlapping pairs. Cones borne at the tips of shoots; males 3-5mm long and yellow; females 20-30mm, globose to ellipsoid, ripening from green to brown in the second year. The 8-14 cone-scales meet edge to edge, each scale with a pointed central boss. *Distribution:* Native to southern California; salt-resistant and favoured for coastal shelter and ornamental plantings in western and southern Europe.

Italian Cypress *Cupressus sempervirens* Up to 30m A dark, sombre evergreen, differing from Monterey Cypress mainly in shape, leaf size and cone colour. Wild trees (forma *horizontalis*) are low with spreading branches but the more commonly seen cultivated form (forma *sempervirens*) is a dense, spire-like tree with sharply upswept branches giving a characteristic narrowly columnar crown. Bark greyish, often with spiral ridges. Scaly, blunt leaves only 0.5-1mm long, dark green and pressed against the shoot in alternating pairs. Ellipsoid-oblong cones of 2.5-4cm diameter have 8-14 scales meeting edge to edge; each scale has a short, blunt central point and is often wavy at the edges. They ripen from green to yellowish-grey in the second year. *Distribution:* Native to the Aegean region but anciently cultivated in southern Europe, especially Italy, and now naturalised in many Mediterranean countries.

Mexican Cypress *Cupressus lusitanica* Up to 25m A variable tree closely resembling Monterey Cypress but with spreading branches and drooping twigs and leading shoot. Scaly leaves 1.5-2mm long, green to waxy blue-green and pointed. Female cones 10-15mm long, blue-green when young, with six to eight cone-scales. *Distribution:* Native to Central America from Mexico to Guatemala; grown both for timber and ornament in France, Italy and the Iberian Peninsula.

Smooth Arizona Cypress *Cupressus glabra* Up to 20m The greyish- or bluish-green foliage of this evergreen has a rather unpleasant smell, reminiscent of grapefruit, when crushed. Crown even and rather rounded cone shape, with strongly upswept branches. Purple bark blisters and flakes to leave paler patches. Scaly leaves greyish- to bluish-green, dotted with resin, often with a central white spot. Male cones prominent all through winter; female cones 15-25mm long, ripen glossy brown and persist on the shoots for some years. Cone-scales meet edge to edge, each with a small, curved central spine. *Distribution:* Slow-growing tree native to central Arizona but increasingly planted in Europe in parks and gardens.

Rough-barked Arizona Cypress *Cupressus arizonica* Up to 30m Very similar to, and often confused with, Smooth Arizona Cypress, differing mainly in having rough, stringy, greenish-brown bark and much greener leaves usually lacking the central white spot. *Distribution:* Native to southern USA and northern Mexico, planted on a small scale for timber in parts of Europe, principally Italy.

Monterey Cypress

Monterey Cypress

Italian Cypress

Mexican Cypress: ♂ cones

Smooth Arizona Cypress

Rough-barked Arizona
Cypress

Juniper *Juniperus communis* Up to 6m Small tree, often no more than a low shrub, with prickly evergreen foliage studded with dull, blue-black, berry-like cones. Bark reddish, shredding. Twigs slender, angled. Needle-like leaves, all juvenile, are 8-30mm long. Arranged in whorls of three, they are stiff, prickly and bluish with a broad white band above. Male and female cones borne on different trees. Males small, yellowish; fleshy females oval to globular, 6-9mm long. Initially green they ripen blue-black with a dull bloom in second or third year and contain three seeds. *Distribution:* Found scattered throughout Europe, especially on lime-rich soils, but mainly on mountains in the south.

Syrian Juniper:
needle whorl

Prickly Juniper *Juniperus oxycedrus* Up to 14m Resembles Common Juniper but makes a taller tree and has needles 4-25mm long with two whitish-blue bands on the upper side. Fleshy female cones 6-15mm long ripen from yellow to red or reddish-purple in the second year. A very variable tree, especially in needle and cone size, and cone colour. Several distinct subspecies have been recognised on the basis of these and other characteristics. *Distribution:* Native throughout southern Europe; widespread in dry hills and on maritime sands. The similar **Syrian Juniper** (*J. drupacea*) has cones 20-25mm long ripening brown or blue-black and containing three tiny seeds united to form a single stone. A western Asian species which extends into southern Greece.

Phoenician
Juniper

Phoenician Juniper *Juniperus phoenicea* Up to 8m Evergreen with foliage of two distinct kinds, cord-like shoots with scaly leaves and young growth bearing needles; this is a small tree, sometimes no more than a spreading shrub. Twigs round in cross-section. Juvenile leaves of young growth up to 14mm long, needle-like, wide-spreading, in whorls of three; scaly adult leaves only 1mm long, blunt with pale margins and closely pressed to the shoot in pairs or threes. They have a gland set in a furrow on the back. Fleshy female cones 6-14mm long, blackish at first, becoming green, then yellowish, finally ripening dark red in the second year. Each contains three seeds. *Distribution:* Widespread throughout coastal Mediterranean regions.

Juniper

Juniper

Prickly Juniper

Phoenician Juniper

Grecian Juniper *Juniperus excelsa* Up to 20m Tree with almost entirely cord-like foliage, needles rarely occurring on mature trees. Conical evergreen, the crown broadening with age. Twigs round in cross-section. Scaly adult leaves 1-1.5mm long, pointed with a central gland on the back, and borne in alternating pairs to form four ranks of overlapping leaves closely pressed to the shoot. If present, needle-like juvenile leaves are like those of Phoenician Juniper but 5-6mm long and borne in pairs, not threes. Globose, fleshy female cones 8mm long, dark purplish-brown with a waxy bloom, ripen in the second year. *Distribution:* Native to the Balkan Peninsula, Crete and the Crimea; sometimes used for timber but not cultivated.

Spanish Juniper

Stinking Juniper *Juniperus foetidissima* Up to 17m Often confused with the similar Grecian Juniper, but easily distinguished by the unpleasant smell given off by the crushed foliage. Evergreen with a straight trunk and crown remaining narrowly conical. Twigs stouter than Grecian Juniper and four-angled in cross-section. Scaly adult leaves also like those of Grecian Juniper but less closely pressed to the shoot, especially at the tips, and lacking a central gland. Fleshy female cones are 7-12mm long, waxy only when young, ripening dark red-brown to nearly black in the second year. *Distribution:* Mountain tree with a similar distribution to that of Grecian Juniper, but absent from Crete. **Spanish Juniper** (*J. thurifera*) differs in having regularly forked twigs, scale-like leaves with a central gland and dark purple ripe cones 7-8mm long; foliage does not smell unpleasant. This species is confined to the French Alps and mountains of central and southern Spain.

Chinese Juniper: fleshy cone

Pencil Cedar *Juniperus virginiana* Up to 30m The tallest of the junipers commonly seen in Europe, with a narrowly pyramidal and spire-like crown. The crushed foliage smells unpleasant. Twigs four-angled in cross-section. Scaly adult leaves 0.5-1.5mm long with all but the pointed tips pressed closely against the shoot; a small gland is often present on the back of each leaf. Needle-like juvenile leaves 5-6mm long with two white bands below are usually present on adult trees. Both adult and juvenile leaves are borne in alternating pairs. Fleshy female cones only 4-6mm long, ovoid, ripening from bluish-green to brownish-violet in the second year. *Distribution:* Native to eastern and central North America. In Europe it is planted for timber in central and southern regions, and many of the numerous cultivars are grown elsewhere as ornamentals. **Chinese Juniper** (*J. chinensis*), from China and Japan and widely grown for ornament, is similar but smaller and has juvenile leaves banded white above and borne in threes.

Grecian Juniper

Stinking Juniper

Pencil Cedar

Pencil Cedar

California Nutmeg

Yew *Taxus baccata* Up to 25m Sprays of dark, sombre needles contrast with reddish bark and matt scarlet berry-like fruits. Evergreen tree or shrub with a thick trunk and rounded crown. Bark reddish, flaking and peeling. Although spirally arranged on the twig, the flattened, sharp-pointed needles, 10-30mm long, spread out to form two lateral rows. They are dark dull green above, yellowish beneath. Male and female flowers borne on different trees, the males yellow, the females greenish. Berry-like fruit consists of a seed 6-7mm long surrounded by a fleshy, dull scarlet, cup-like structure – the aril – up to 1cm long. *Distribution:* Shade-tolerant and common in woods and scrub, especially on limestone, throughout most of Europe; in the past often planted in enclosed areas such as churchyards. **California Nutmeg** (*Torreya californica*) has whorls of horizontal branches, stiff needles banded with white beneath and green fruits streaked with purple when ripe. Native to California, it is planted as a park tree.

Plum-fruited Yew *Podocarpus andinus* Up to 15m Resembles Yew but has less sombre foliage and yellow-green, plum-like fruits. Conical evergreen tree or large shrub with several trunks, especially in cultivation. Bark smooth, dark brown, fading to grey with age. Young twigs green. Needles up to 5cm long, spirally arranged but spreading to either side of the shoot to form two forward-pointing rows. They are narrow, flattened, straight or slightly curved, bright green above and turned to reveal the paler lower surface by a twist in the short stalk. Male and female flowers usually occur on different trees. Males form erect, yellow, catkin-like clusters grouped at the tips of the shoots; slender green females form clusters of two to six on a short stalk in the axils of the needles. Fleshy fruits 15-20mm long, yellowish and flecked with white; each contains a single stony seed. *Distribution:* Native to the Andes in southern Chile; planted in Europe as an ornamental and for hedges.

Maidenhair-tree

Maidenhair-tree *Ginkgo biloba* Up to 30m The very leathery, pliant leaves are distinctive: they are notched, fan-shaped with radiating veins, and measure 12 x 10cm. Irregularly conical tree with one or more trunks. Shoots are of two kinds: long shoots have widely spaced leaves; spur-like short shoots have clusters of leaves. Male and female flowers borne on short shoots on different trees, males in thick, erect catkins, females singly or in pairs, on long stalks. Fleshy, oval fruit 2.5-3cm long, yellowish when ripe. It is edible but smells unpleasant and contains a single stony seed. *Distribution:* Native to China but probably extinct in the wild; an attractive ornamental widely planted in parks and gardens in much of Europe.

Yew

Yew: ♂ flowers

Yew: ripe fruits

Plum-fruited Yew: ♂ flowers

Maidenhair-tree

Maidenhair-tree

Bay Willow: catkins

Bay Willow *Salix pentandra* 5-7m, rarely up to 17m Highly glossed leaves and shiny twigs give a varnished appearance to this shrub. May be small or tall with spreading branches. Twigs reddish-brown, glabrous and very shiny. Alternate leaves, 5-12cm long and less than three times as long as wide, are elliptical to oval, pointed, leathery, dark and very shiny above, paler below. Yellow glands tip the minute marginal teeth. Hairy-stalked catkins appear with the leaves, male and female on different trees. Dense, cylindrical male catkins, 2-5cm long, pale yellow; greenish females shorter. Capsules up to 8mm long release silky-plumed seeds. *Flowering:* May to June. *Distribution:* Common along waterways and in wet soils in most of Europe except the Mediterranean islands.

Almond Willow: leaf and stipules

Almond Willow *Salix triandra* Up to 10m Small bushy tree or robust shrub with smooth, dark grey bark which flakes to reveal large reddish-brown patches. Twigs olive-brown, rather shiny, glabrous, ridged or angled when young, becoming cylindrical with age; they are rather brittle at the base. Alternate leaves, 4-11cm long and more than three times as long as wide, may be widest above the middle, elliptical or even very narrow; they are long-pointed and have a thickened, toothed margin, glabrous, dark dull green above, green or slightly bluish beneath. The short petiole has a pair of large, toothed, ear-shaped and persistent stipules at the base. Erect catkins appear with or just before the leaves, males and females on different trees. Yellow males are 2.5-5cm long, cylindrical and fragrant; females are shorter and denser. Capsule about 3mm long releases silky-plumed seeds. *Flowering:* April to May. *Distribution:* Very variable tree usually found on wet soils, native to most of Europe except the far north; scattered in the Mediterranean region.

Salix x *rubens*

Crack Willow *Salix fragilis* Up to 25m Brittle where they join the branches, the twigs of this stout willow easily break away. Tree with a short, thick and often leaning trunk and broad, rounded crown. Twigs glabrous and olive-brown. Alternate leaves 9-15cm long, lance-shaped, long-pointed, hairy at first but soon completely glabrous and dark shiny green above, bluish-grey beneath; margins have coarse, even, gland-tipped teeth. Similar-looking male and female catkins 4-6cm long with short, hairy stalks borne on different trees, appearing with the leaves; males pale yellow, females greenish. Capsule 4-5mm long releases silky-plumed seeds. *Flowering:* April to May. *Distribution:* Found on deep, wet, lowland soils, especially on the fringes of farmland where it is often planted. Occurs throughout most of Europe but patchily distributed in the Mediterranean region. Very similar **S.** x ***rubens*** has dull leaves often retaining some silky hairs, and more tapered at the tips. A hybrid between Crack and White Willows, more common and widespread than Crack Willow and often cultivated.

Bay Willow

Bay Willow: fruiting catkins

Almond Willow: ♂ catkins

Almond Willow

Crack Willow

Crack Willow: ♀ catkins

White Willow *Salix alba* var. *alba* 10-25m Distinctive even when seen from a distance, this tree has silvery grey leaves, a well-defined trunk and upswept branches usually forming a narrow crown. Young twigs with silky, close-pressed hairs become glabrous and olive to brown. Narrow, pointed and minutely toothed leaves 5-10cm long and more than three times as long as wide, alternate, at first covered with silky, silvery hairs but the upper surface eventually becomes dull green and naked. Erect to spreading catkins on densely hairy stalks appear with the leaves, males and females on different trees. Pale yellow, cylindrical males 4-5cm long, greenish females shorter and more slender. Capsule about 4mm long releases silky-plumed seeds. *Flowering:* April to May. *Distribution:* Widespread throughout Europe, usually found by running water.

Golden Willow *Salix alba* var. *vitellina* Up to 25m A variety of White Willow, differing in the leaves and female catkins, and especially in the twigs. One-year-old twigs bright yellow or orange, in some cultivars even bright red, and very noticeable in winter. Leaves almost identical to those of White Willow but bright, shiny green above, not dull green. Female catkins have short ovaries in the angles of longer scales, giving the catkin a ragged effect. *Flowering:* April to May. *Distribution:* Of obscure origin, but commonly planted in some areas, mainly for the ornamental effect of the colourful young twigs. Very similar **Cricket-bat Willow** (*S. alba* var. *caerulea*) lacks the brightly coloured twigs and has broader leaves often 10-11cm long, with margins conspicuously toothed. Leaves are covered initially with dense, close-pressed silvery hairs which soon fall, leaving mature leaves dull blue-green above and bluish beneath. It is essentially a tree of south-eastern England, where it is common and widespread, apparently little known or overlooked in the rest of Europe.

Cricket-bat Willow

Weeping Willow: ♀
catkin

Golden Weeping Willow *Salix* x *sepulcralis* Up to 12m Beautiful tree with long, weeping branches almost sweeping the ground and forming a broad, leafy dome. Twigs very slender, golden yellow, thinly hairy at first, but soon becoming glabrous. Alternate, narrowly lance-shaped and pointed leaves 7-12cm long, more than three times as long as wide, finely and evenly toothed. Young leaves hairy, but mature to become smooth, bright green above, bluish below. Catkins on shaggy hairy stalks appear with the leaves, males and females on different trees. They are 3-4cm long, narrowly cylindrical and often curved. Trees are usually male. *Flowering:* April. *Distribution:* Of hybrid origin, this is the most common of several weeping willows widely planted for ornament. One of the parents of Golden Weeping Willow, the very similar **Weeping Willow** (*S. babylonica*), is a Chinese species with smooth twigs and shorter, stalkless catkins. It is much less common.

White Willow: fruiting catkins

Golden Willow: winter

Golden Weeping Willow

Golden Weeping Willow

Dark-leaved Willow *Salix myrsinifolia* Up to 3m Very variable, at most a small tree, often only a low and sprawling shrub, but always bushy and open. Dull brown or greenish twigs have dense white hairs when young, retaining at least a few hairs into the second year or beyond. Alternate leaves, 2-6.5cm long and less than three times as long as wide, are broadly oval or widest above the middle, short-pointed with irregularly toothed and sometimes recurved margins; there may be two hairy, ear-shaped auricles at the base of the petiole. Both leaf surfaces thinly hairy at first, becoming more or less glabrous with age except for the midrib beneath. Short, dense and cylindrical catkins 1.5-4cm long appear with the leaves, males and females on different trees. Males are rather shorter and broader than females. Stalked capsule 7mm long releases silky-plumed seeds. *Flowering:* April to May. *Distribution:* Native and widespread in northern Europe eastwards to Siberia; also in mountains in central Europe. Similar **S. borealis** is an Arctic species whose twigs have more dense white hairs and elliptical, leathery leaves, more densely hairy when young. **S. pedicellata** has young twigs with dense grey hairs, leaves up to 11cm long, with toothed or entire margins, more or less glabrous above but thinly hairy beneath. It is native to wet habitats in the Mediterranean region.

Salix borealis

Salix appendiculata: leaf and stipules

Salix appendiculata Up to 3m Small tree or shrub similar to Dark-leaved Willow, with short, wide-angled branches. Young twigs have short hairs, becoming glabrous; peeled twigs have few, indistinct ridges. Alternate leaves up to 14 x 1-3cm, very variable in both size and shape, usually widest above the middle with entire or indistinctly toothed margins. Upper surface glabrous and dark green, lower surface paler and hairy. Paired stipules at the base of the petiole large, almost heart-shaped and coarsely toothed. Loosely flowered catkins about 3cm long appear with or just before the leaves, males and females on different trees. Stalked capsule releases silky-plumed seeds *Flowering:* April to May. *Distribution:* Mountain tree native to the eastern Alps, Apennines and Balkan mountains at altitudes above 500m.

Salix x smithiana Up to 9m Small spreading tree or robust shrub. Dark brown twigs hairy for the first year, showing narrow ridges when peeled. Alternate leaves 6-11cm long, narrowly lance-shaped, shortly pointed, with minutely toothed margins rolled under. They are dull green above with silky grey hairs beneath, mostly shed with age. The crescent- or ear-shaped stipules at the base of the petiole are often well-developed and persistent. Catkins, appearing before the leaves and crowded towards the twig tips, have grey hairs, the males densely so and black flecks. Males are 2-3cm long, ovoid, females longer and more slender; they are borne on different trees. *Flowering:* March to April. *Distribution:* A common natural hybrid between Osier and either Grey or Rusty Sallow, widespread throughout Europe. When Rusty Sallow is a parent the hairs may be reddish.

Dark-leaved Willow: ♀ catkins

Salix appendiculata: ♂ catkins

Salix appendiculata

Salix x *smithiana*: ♂ catkins

Rusty Sallow

Grey Sallow *Salix cinerea* subsp. *cinerea* Up to 10m Small tree or tall shrub with both leaves and young twigs felted with grey hairs. Crown broad with spreading branches. Twigs gradually become glabrous, usually in the second year; peeled twigs have long, conspicuous ridges. Alternate leaves, 2-16cm long, vary in size and shape but are less than three times as long as wide, usually broadly oval or widest above the middle, with regularly warty-toothed, rolled-under margins; two broad, ear-shaped stipules at the base of the petiole; they are dull green with short hairs above, grey felted below. Stalkless male and female catkins appear before the leaves on different trees. Erect, 2-3cm long and cylindrical to oval, they are densely covered in grey hairs with darker flecks. Capsule up to 10mm long releases silky-plumed seeds. *Flowering:* March to April. *Distribution:* Common in wet fenland and marshes in most of Europe, but absent from Iberia and some Mediterranean islands. Closely related **Rusty Sallow** (subsp. *oleifolia*), native to a wide range of habitats in Atlantic Europe from Portugal to Britain, has red-brown twigs and leaves with stiff, rusty hairs below.

Goat Willow *Salix caprea* Up to 10m Small tree or tall shrub with an open, spreading crown and very soft, furry grey catkins borne on bare branches. Thick, stiff twigs, thinly hairy when young, soon becoming glabrous and yellowish-brown; peeled twigs smooth, almost circular. Alternate leaves 5-12cm long, broadly oval to elliptical, oblong or almost circular, and shortly pointed. Dull green and thinly hairy above, grey-woolly below, they have margins with irregular, gland-tipped teeth; petiole sometimes has two small, ear-shaped, wavy-toothed stipules at the base. Male and female catkins, borne on separate trees, appear before the leaves. Crowded at the ends of twigs, they are 1.5-2.5cm long, erect, ovoid, stalkless and silky silver-grey. Thinly hairy capsule up to 10mm long releases silky-plumed seeds. *Flowering:* March to April. *Distribution:* Grows along hedgerows and edges of woods, often in quite dry places; native throughout Europe.

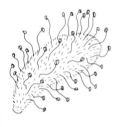

Osier: ♂ catkin

Osier *Salix viminalis* 3-6m Small tree or tall shrub frequently cropped to provide a 'head' of long, straight, pliant twigs; the naturally formed crown is rather narrow. Long, straight twigs flexible, with dense grey hairs at first, later glabrous and shiny olive or brown. Narrow, tapering leaves 10-15cm in length, alternate, dull green above, densely covered with silvery silky hairs below; margins often wavy and rolled under. Male and female catkins on separate trees appear before the leaves. Crowded at the tips of twigs, they are 1.5-3cm long, erect or curved, ovoid and densely hairy, the males yellowish, females brownish. Hairy capsule up to 6mm long releases silky-plumed seeds. *Flowering:* February to April. *Distribution:* Native and common throughout lowland Europe but mainly planted for the withies or twigs, or a relict of cultivation in the west.

Grey Sallow

Goat Willow: ♀ tree

Goat Willow: fruiting catkins

Osier

Salix elaeagnos:
♀ catkin

Purple Willow:
♂ catkins

Violet Willow

Salix elaeagnos Up to 6m, rarely to 16m Slender tree with extremely narrow leaves which are hairy but, unlike other willows, matt white beneath and not at all shiny or silky. Small tree or erect shrub. Young twigs densely covered with white or grey hairs, older twigs glabrous and yellowish- or reddish-brown. Alternate, crowded leaves, 5-15cm long, are very narrow, usually less than 1cm wide, with entire margins. Slightly leathery, they are dark shiny green above when mature, with dense white hairs beneath. Catkins appear just before the leaves, crowded towards tips of twigs and slightly reddish, males and females on different trees. Males are up to 3cm long, dense and spreading; females slightly shorter and more erect. Capsule up to 5mm long releases tufted seeds. *Flowering:* April to May. *Distribution:* Native to central and southern Europe and sometimes cultivated elsewhere.

Purple Willow *Salix purpurea* Up to 5m, often less This small willow, frequently only a very low spreading shrub, is unusual in that its leaves are often paired. Bark smooth, grey and acrid; twigs slender, flexible, glabrous, yellowish or grey, sometimes tinged with red. Leaves often in opposite pairs or nearly so, very variable in size and shape, 2-8 x 0.5-3cm and usually narrowly oblong with short teeth towards the tips. Thinly hairy at first or glabrous, they are usually dull dark green above, paler beneath. Stalkless catkins 1.5-3cm long appear before the leaves, erect and paired on the twigs, males and females on different trees. Males have red or purple anthers. Ovoid capsule up to 4mm long releases tufted seeds. *Flowering:* March to April. *Distribution:* Widespread but scattered by streams and on wet soils throughout most of Europe except the extreme north of Scandinavia.

Salix daphnoides 6-12m Small tree or large shrub whose twigs have a waxy blue bloom and showy black-flecked catkins. Erect or spreading branches form a rounded crown. Glabrous, dark red-brown twigs have a thick, waxy blue bloom when young; buds are dark crimson: Alternate leaves, 7-12cm long and more than three times as long as wide, are oblong or widest above the middle, pointed, the margins with even, gland-tipped teeth. There is usually a pair of toothed, glandular stipules at the base of the petiole. Young leaves thinly woolly, soon becoming glabrous, dark, shiny green above, bluish beneath. Catkins appear before the leaves, 2-4cm long, erect and rather crowded on the twigs, males and females on different trees. They are densely hairy, the tips of the scales showing as blackish flecks, especially in male catkins. Small, narrowly ovoid capsule about 4mm long releases silky-plumed seeds. *Flowering:* February to March. *Distribution:* Native to much of central Europe from the Baltic southwards to Italy and from France to the Balkans, but patchy. **Violet Willow** (*S. acutifolia*) is similar but has drooping waxy twigs turning violet in winter, and longer, much narrower, shiny leaves green on both sides. It is a Russian species sometimes planted in gardens and by streams.

Salix elaeagnos: ♀ catkins

Purple Willow: fruiting catkins

Salix daphnoides: ♂ catkins

Salix daphnoides: fruiting catkins

White Poplar:
♀ catkin

Grey Poplar:
leaf underside

Big-toothed Aspen

White Poplar *Populus alba* Up to 20m, rarely to 40m A spreading tree, the often leaning trunk suckering at the base, the White Poplar frequently forms groves and is conspicuous by its bi-coloured leaves. Fissured grey bark has horizontal rows of black lenticels. Twigs have dense white hairs for the first year or so, then become glabrous. Alternate leaves 3-9cm long, irregularly lobed; those near the twig tips often have three to five deep lobes; dark green above, pure white on the thickly hairy underside; petioles cylindrical. Hairy catkins appear well before the leaves on different trees, males 4-7cm long, with purple anthers; females 3-5cm with greenish stigmas, lengthening when in fruit. Capsules 3mm long. *Flowering:* February to March. *Distribution:* A widespread tree favouring soft, wet ground, native from central to south-eastern Europe but ornamental and introduced to many areas.

Grey Poplar *Populus x canescens* Up to 30m or more Tall, robust tree of hybrid origin, sharing similarities with both the parents, White Poplar and Aspen. Grey bark with horizontal rows of black lenticels. Young twigs densely hairy, becoming glabrous. Alternate leaves of two distinct types; those of side-shoots resemble Aspen, 3-6cm long, almost circular with irregular, wavy-toothed margins, more or less glabrous, petiole laterally flattened and glabrous; those of leading shoots and suckers 6-8cm long, oval to broadly triangular, coarsely and often doubly toothed, grey hairs beneath, petiole cylindrical and thickly covered in hairs. Catkins similar to Aspen, appearing well before the leaves. Capsules and seeds rarely produced. *Flowering:* March. *Distribution:* Native or introduced to much of Europe. Male trees appear to be much more common than females.

Aspen *Populus tremula* Up to 20m, often less Pale looking tree, the light, fluttering motions of the leaves accentuated by the flashing of their pale undersides. Freely suckering with a broad crown. Bark smooth, greyish. Young twigs thinly hairy, becoming glabrous and dull grey-brown. Leaves alternate, 1.5-8cm long, broadly oval to almost circular, bluntly and coarsely toothed, dark green above but very pale beneath; leaves of suckers more heart-shaped and thinly hairy. Petiole flattened on both sides, enabling the leaf to twist easily. Often crowded on the tips of twigs, catkins 5-8cm long appear well before the leaves on different trees, males with reddish-purple anthers, females with pink stigmas. Capsules about 4mm long. *Flowering:* February to March. *Distribution:* A short-lived tree, native and common on poor soils throughout Europe but restricted to mountains in the south; often forms groves. Two North American species are very similar. **American Aspen** (*P. tremuloides*) has yellowish bark and finely toothed leaves. **Big-toothed Aspen** (*P. grandidentata*) has young twigs with dense grey hairs, and large-lobed leaves with dense grey hairs beneath and square or wedge-shaped bases.

White Poplar

White Poplar: ♂ catkins

White Poplar: ♀ catkins

Grey Poplar

Aspen

Aspen

Balm-of-Gilead

Black Poplar *Populus nigra* Up to 35m Robust tree with a broad, rounded crown, and numerous burrs and large rough swellings on the trunk. Dull grey bark coarsely fissured. Twigs glabrous and shiny orange-brown. Leaves alternate, 5-10cm long, rhombic, triangular-oval with fine, blunt teeth on the margins, lower surface only slightly paler than the upper; petiole flattened on both sides. Loose-flowered catkins 3-5cm in length appear before the leaves on different trees, males with crimson anthers, females with greenish stigmas, becoming longer when in fruit. Capsules 5-6mm long. *Flowering:* March to April. *Distribution:* Native and widespread in most of Europe. Two commonly planted North American species similar to Black Poplar can easily be distinguished from it by their strongly balsam-scented leaves, conspicuously paler on the underside. **Balm-of-Gilead** (*P. candicans*) has broad, heart-shaped leaves. **Western Balsam Poplar** (*P. trichocarpa*) has leaves with gradually tapering tips and bases cut straight across.

Lombardy Poplar *Populus nigra* var. *italica* Up to 35m Very distinctive variety of Black Poplar, differing from the normal tree only in its shape, the strongly upswept to nearly vertical branches giving a tall, narrow crown. Trees are always male. *Flowering:* March to April. *Distribution:* Originating in northern Italy and one of the most widely planted of several fastigiate (i.e. columnar) poplars. It is frequently seen along roads and avenues in many parts of Europe.

Hybrid Black Poplar *Populus* x *canadensis* Up to 30m Hybrid often very similar to, and in some areas more common than, its European parent, Black Poplar. Spreading or narrow tree. Crown sometimes narrow or fastigiate. Trunk without swellings or burrs, bark greyish and coarsely fissured. Twigs greenish or sometimes reddish.
Leaves alternate, like Black Poplar, but more sharply and distinctly toothed and fringed with short hairs. Catkins and capsules, if produced, similar to Black Poplar. The name Hybrid Black Poplar actually covers several clones, all originating as hybrids between the North American Cottonwood and Black Poplar. *Flowering:* March to April. *Distribution:* Very fast-growing trees, the various clones are extensively planted, mainly in central Europe but also in western and southern regions. **Cottonwood** (*P. deltoides*) from North America is a spreading tree with larger leaves 10-18cm long with fringes of dense hairs and glandular teeth. Grown for timber and as a roadside tree, mostly in northern Europe; sometimes naturalised.

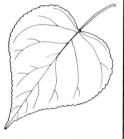

Cottonwood

Black Poplar

Black Poplar

Lombardy Poplar

Hybrid Black Poplar

Walnut

Walnut *Juglans regia* Up to 30m Large, wide-spreading tree with divided, leathery and aromatic leaves, thick trunk and spreading crown of tortuous branches. Bark smooth, grey, eventually fissured. Twigs have a central pith divided into chambers and distinctive Y-shaped scars where leaves have fallen. Alternate leaves pinnately divided into seven to nine entire leaflets each 6-15cm long, those towards the tips of the leaf larger than the others. Male flowers in solitary, pendulous catkins 5-15cm long on old wood, female flowers in spike-like clusters of two to five on new growth. Roughly globular, green fruit 4-5cm long contains an oval, wrinkled stone, the familiar walnut. *Flowering:* May to June. *Distribution:* Native to the Balkans and parts of Asia, but planted since ancient times in many parts of Europe and widely naturalised.

Black Walnut *Juglans nigra* Up to 50m Large, fast-growing tree similar to Common Walnut but with finer, more abundant foliage. Domed crown; bark black or brown, deeply fissured into diamond-shaped ridges. Twigs have a central pith divided into chambers and large Y-shaped leaf-scars. Alternate leaves pinnately divided into 15-23 leaflets, each 6-12cm long, oval to lance-shaped, pointed and irregularly fine-toothed and hairy beneath. The terminal leaflet is sometimes absent. Male flowers in catkins 5-15cm long, female flowers in spike-like clusters of five. Globular or slightly pear-shaped fruit 3.5-5cm long is green and hairy, containing an oval, ridged stone. *Flowering:* May to June. *Distribution:* A native of North America, widely planted for timber in eastern parts of central Europe.

Butter-nut *Juglans cinerea* Up to 30m Generally similar to Black Walnut but with paler bark, larger leaves and characteristic leaf-scars. Slender, conical crown and purplish-grey bark split into flat-topped ridges. Leaf-scars have a prominent, hairy fringe along the upper edge. Large alternate leaves pinnately divided into 11-19 leaflets each 6-12cm long, thinner and brighter green than in Black Walnut. Flowers like Black Walnut. Fruit 4-6.5cm long, ovoid to almost globose and sticky as well as hairy. *Flowering:* April to June. *Distribution:* A woodland tree native to eastern North America, occasionally planted for timber, mainly in Denmark and Romania.

Butter-nut: leaf scars

Walnut

Walnut: ♂ catkins

Black Walnut

Butter-nut

Butter-nut: ♂ catkin

Butter-nut: ♀ flowers

Shagbark Hickory *Carya ovata* Up to 40m Broad tree with a markedly shaggy trunk as the grey bark splits into long strips or scales; few, widespreading branches. Twigs usually glabrous, reddish-brown with a solid pith. Buds have 10-12 overlapping scales, at least the outer ones dark. Alternate leaves pinnately divided into five or seven pointed leaflets 10-20cm long, the upper three much larger than the others. All hairy and glandular beneath when young, becoming glabrous but retaining dense hairs on the marginal teeth. Male and female flowers on the same tree; male catkins in clusters of three or more, each many-flowered and drooping; female flowers small, greenish, in two- to ten-flowered spike-like clusters. Fruit 3.5-6cm long, more or less globose, with a thick, yellowish husk splitting to the base to release a white, stony seed. *Flowering:* April to May. *Distribution:* Native to eastern North America. Edible nuts used commercially in America but the tree is planted only for timber in central Europe. Two other, similar, North American species are planted on a small scale. **Shellbark Hickory** (*C. laciniosa*) has orange twigs and seven to nine leaflets. **Mockernut Hickory** (*C. tomentosa*) has hairy young twigs and lacks the distinctive shaggy bark.

Shellbark Hickory

Bitternut Hickory *Carya cordiformis* Up to 30m Easily recognised in winter by the bright yellow buds. Bark light brown, with fine ridges, never distinctly shaggy. Twigs slender, more or less glabrous, with a solid pith. Buds have four to six paired, bright yellow scales. Leaves alternate, pinnately divided into 5-11 pointed and toothed leaflets 8-15cm long which are hairy beneath when young. Male and female flowers similar to those of Shagbark Hickory. Fruit 2-3.5cm long, almost globose to almost cylindrical with four wings in the upper half. Husk thin, splitting to below the middle to release a grey, stony seed. *Flowering:* June. *Distribution:* Native to eastern North America, planted for timber in Germany. **Pignut Hickory** (*C. glabra*), also from eastern North America and planted in Germany, has buds with overlapping scales, five glabrous leaflets, and ovoid fruits splitting to the middle to release a brown seed.

Pignut Hickory: buds

Caucasian Wingnut *Pterocarya fraxinifolia* Up to 30m Broad-crowned, short-trunked tree with pinnate leaves and conspicuous long catkins of winged nuts hanging from the twigs in autumn. There may be one to several trunks with numerous suckers around the base. Grey bark is deeply fissured. Twigs and smaller shoots crowded and twisted, with chambered pith. Pale brown buds are stalkless and lack scales. Alternate leaves pinnately divided into from 21-41 narrowly oval, pointed leaflets; the middle ones, up to 18cm long, are largest. All are unequal at the base, toothed, slightly forward pointing and overlapping; bright, shiny green with long brown or white hairs along the midrib beneath, they turn yellow in autumn. Male and female catkins solitary, many-flowered and pendent; yellowish males 5-12cm long, green females 10-15cm, lengthening to 50cm when in fruit. Fruit is a green, broadly winged nut. *Flowering:* March to April. *Distribution:* Native to the Caucasus Mountains and northern Iran, widely planted in European parks. A less frequently planted Chinese species, **Chinese Wingnut** (*P. stenoptera*), differs mainly in the hairy young twigs and conspicuously winged leaf-axis.

Chinese Wingnut

Shagbark Hickory

Shagbark Hickory

Bitternut Hickory

Caucasian Wingnut

Italian Alder

Smooth Alder

Green Alder:
winged nutlet

Common Alder *Alnus glutinosa* Up to 20m Easily recognised during winter when the old cones are conspicuous on bare twigs, this is a small, broadly conical tree with sticky young twigs covered with orange warts. Winter buds stalked. Alternate leaves bright green, 4-10cm long, round or widest above the middle, doubly toothed, the tip often shallowly notched. Five to eight pairs of veins have long, yellow hairs in the axils. Flowers in catkins appear before the leaves: pendulous males 2-6cm long are initially purple, later yellowish; ovoid females 1.5cm long are grouped in stalked clusters of three to eight, purplish becoming green. Woody fruit 1-3cm long resembles a small cone containing narrowly winged nutlets. *Flowering:* February to March. *Distribution:* Common throughout most of Europe, especially in wet places and beside water. **Italian Alder** (*A. cordata*), endemic to Corsica and southern Italy but planted in other southern areas, has leaves with blunter teeth and female catkins in clusters of only one to three.

Grey Alder *Alnus incana* Up to 10m, rarely to 25m A more or less Arctic-alpine tree, frequently only a shrub, generally rather similar to Common Alder. Smooth bark grey or, in Arctic trees, yellow and translucent. Winter buds shortly stalked. Young twigs hairy, sometimes densely so, but not sticky. Alternate leaves similar to Common Alder but more oval and pointed, grey-green and hairy beneath, with 7-12 pairs of veins. Male and female catkins also similar to Common Alder but the females are stalkless. Seeds broadly winged. *Flowering:* February to March. *Distribution:* Native or naturalised throughout northern Europe, extending south to mountains in Italy, Albania and Romania. Similar **Smooth Alder** (*A. rugosa*) is a North American species widely planted and naturalised in central Europe. It is most easily distinguished by the toothed, not doubly toothed, leaves with reddish hairs in the axils of the veins beneath.

Green Alder *Alnus viridis* Up to 5m Resembling a small Common Alder, this close relative grows in mountainous areas. Small tree or shrub. Twigs smooth or with minute hairs. Winter buds without stalks. Sticky when young, the alternate, elliptical to roughly circular leaves 4-9cm long have sharply double-toothed margins and hairs in the vein axils beneath. Flowers appear with the leaves. Yellow male catkins 5-12cm long; females, in clusters of three to five with several leaves at the base of the stalk, 1cm long, initially green, later reddish. Woody, cone-like fruit 1.5cm long contains broadly winged nutlets. *Flowering:* April. *Distribution:* Mountain species mainly occurring in central and eastern Europe but extending to France and Corsica.

Common Alder: winter

Common Alder: fruiting catkins

Grey Alder: fruiting catkins

Green Alder: ♂ and ♀ catkins

Downy Birch:
fruiting catkin (a)
and scale (b)

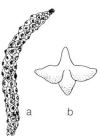

Silver Birch:
♂ catkin (a) and
fruiting scale (b)

Downy Birch *Betula pubescens* Up to 25m Small tree or often a shrub, especially in Arctic regions where it forms extensive low woods and thickets. Very variable with spreading branches and smooth, brown or grey bark. Young twigs lack resin glands but are covered with downy white hairs. Alternate oval leaves up to 5.5cm long, rounded or triangular at the base, with regularly, coarsely toothed margins. Pendulous clusters of male catkins 3-6cm long appear at tips of twigs in winter but mature in spring. In the leaf-axils female catkins, 1-4cm long, are composed of scales with spreading or upswept lateral lobes and female flowers; they eventually break up to release narrowly winged nutlets. *Flowering:* April to May. *Distribution:* Short-lived species, growing mainly on wet soils. Cold-tolerant and common throughout northern and central Europe, and on mountains in the south.

Silver Birch *Betula pendula* Up to 30m Slender, elegant tree with distinctive, silvery-white bark abruptly broken into dark, rectangular plates at the base of the trunk. Branches pendulous towards the tips. Young twigs warty with pale resin glands. Alternate leaves usually 2.5-5cm long, oval to triangular, with the base cut straight across or slightly heart-shaped, and sharply and unevenly double-toothed margins; thin in texture, dark glossy green above, glabrous when mature. Clusters of two to four male catkins 3-6cm long, drooping from tips of twigs, brown in winter but yellowish when opening in spring. Axillary female catkins only 1.5-3.5cm long, made up of scales with down-curved lobes and female flowers; they eventually break up to release broadly winged nutlets. *Flowering:* April to May. *Distribution:* Short-lived pioneer species on light, sandy soils, often forming woods where other trees are cut down before being shaded out by other species. Native throughout much of Europe, but absent or confined to mountains in the south.

Paper-bark Birch *Betula papyrifera* Up to 27m Tree with bark peeling in long strips, sometimes brown in young trees, but usually white like that of Silver Birch. Small to medium-sized tree with strongly ascending branches. Peeling bark horizontally banded with rows of lenticels. Twigs rather hairy as well as warty. Leaves similar to those of Silver Birch but very variable in size, from 4-10cm long, more oval and longer pointed, thick in texture, matt green above with hairs in the axils of veins beneath and on the petiole. Male and female catkins as in Silver Birch but males longer, up to 10cm. Scales of female catkins have erect lobes. *Flowering:* April to June. *Distribution:* Native to young forests of north-eastern North America and planted in European parks and gardens.

Downy Birch

Silver Birch

Silver Birch: ♂ catkins

Paper-bark Birch

Eastern Hornbeam: nut and involucre

Eastern Hop-hornbeam: nut and involucre

Filbert: nut and involucre

Turkish Hazel: nuts and involucres

Hornbeam *Carpinus betulus* Up to 30m Often coppiced or pollarded, Hornbeams frequently have twisted or fluted trunks and branches; twigs densely covered with thick hairs. Bark smooth, pale grey, sometimes fissured. Alternate, oval leaves 4-10cm long, sharply pointed, rounded at the base with sharply double-toothed margins. The underside has about 15 pairs of prominent, hairy, parallel veins. Pendulous yellow male catkins up to 5cm long; green female catkins 2cm, reaching 5-14cm when in fruit. Each pair of nuts is attached to a leaf-like, three-lobed involucre up to 4cm long. *Flowering:* April to May. *Distribution:* Common hedgerow and woodland species. Native to most of Europe. Similar **Eastern Hornbeam** (*C. orientalis*) is smaller with toothed, but not lobed, involucres. Native to south-eastern Europe west to Italy and Sicily.

Hop-hornbeam *Ostrya carpinifolia* Up to 12m Papery, fruiting heads resemble clusters of hops and become conspicuous in late summer. Slender tree, sometimes shrubby and with several trunks. Brown bark cracks and peels. Twigs hairy, with orange warts. Alternate, oval, long-pointed leaves 5-8cm long, sharply double-toothed with 12-15 pairs of veins. Flowers appear with the leaves; pendulous yellow male catkins up to 10cm long, the female catkins much shorter. In fruit the female catkins are dense and roughly cylindrical, 3-5cm long, composed of many pale green or whitish, leaf-like involucres, each enclosing a single nut. *Flowering:* April. *Distribution:* Occurs in the more southerly parts of Europe from France and Corsica eastwards. **Eastern Hop-hornbeam** (*O. virginiana*) has glandular-hairy twigs; larger, less conspicuously veined leaves downy beneath; and longer, hairier fruit-stalks. Native to North America and planted for ornament in Europe.

Hazel *Corylus avellana* Up to 12m Small tree with a short trunk, but often only a shrub. Twigs have reddish, glandular hairs. Stiffly hairy leaves 10cm long, alternate, almost circular, with a heart-shaped base and sharp, double-toothed margins. Flowers appear before the leaves; male catkins up to 8cm long, pendulous, bright yellow; spike-like females 5mm long have bright red styles. Hard-shelled nut 1.5-2cm long enveloped within a ragged, leafy, cup-like involucre about as long as the nut. The edible kernel is the familiar hazelnut. *Flowering:* January to April. *Distribution:* Common in hedges and woods, often coppiced. Native throughout almost all of Europe. **Filbert** (*C. maxima*) is very similar but the involucre completely encloses the nut. Native to the Balkans but widely planted and naturalised elsewhere.

Turkish Hazel *Corylus colurna* Up to 22m Similar to Common Hazel but usually a tree not a shrub, larger in all its parts, with distinctive fruits. Bark rough; branches spreading. Alternate leaves up to 12.5cm long, broadly oval, abruptly pointed, heart-shaped at base. Margins double-toothed or shallowly lobed. Male catkins reach 12cm long. Nut larger than that of Common Hazel; leafy, cup-like involucre surrounding it has very deeply divided, ragged and toothed lobes. *Flowering:* February. *Distribution:* Native to south-eastern Europe and Asia Minor, and introduced to many other parts of Europe.

Hornbeam

Hornbeam

Hop-hornbeam

Hazel: ♂ catkins

Hazel

Turkish Hazel: ♂ catkins

Sweet Chestnut *Castanea sativa* Up to 30m In summer the clusters of erect male catkins of this tree are visible from some distance, giving a yellowish cast to the otherwise bright green foliage. Bark greyish, often spirally fissured. Alternate leaves 10-25cm long, narrowly oblong with a pointed tip, broadly wedge-shaped base and sharply toothed margins. Slender, erect catkins have numerous yellowish male flowers in the upper part and female flowers grouped in threes towards the base. Each female cluster is surrounded by a green, spiny cupule which forms the protective outer husk of the fruit, splitting irregularly to release one to three shiny, reddish-brown nuts. *Flowering:* June to July. *Distribution:* Found mainly on well-drained, acid or neutral soils. Native to southern Europe but widely planted elsewhere for its edible nuts and naturalised in many places.

Oriental Beech

Beech *Fagus sylvatica* Up to 40m Forming dense-canopied woods, beeches create a deep litter of decay-resistant dark brown leaves which discourages ground plants. Broadly domed tree with smooth, grey bark. Alternate, oval to elliptical leaves 4-9cm long have wavy margins and seven to eight pairs of parallel veins. Both margins and undersides of veins have silky hairs. Male and female flowers yellowish. Males, in drooping long-stalked heads, have four to seven perianth-lobes. Paired female flowers surrounded by a stalked, spiny, four-lobed involucre which in fruit reaches a length of 2-5cm, the lobes eventually spreading to release two triangular brown nuts. *Flowering:* April to May. *Distribution:* Common throughout western and central Europe on well-drained soils and characteristic of chalk and limestone; often planted for timber and ornament. The very similar **Oriental Beech** (*F. orientalis*) has leaves widest above the middle with 8-12 pairs of veins. It grows in sheltered sites in south-eastern Europe and Asia Minor.

Rauli: fruit

Roble Beech *Nothofagus obliqua* Up to 23m Similar to its Northern hemisphere relative Common Beech but dislikes lime-rich soils. Tree with a tall, open crown of arching branches. Grey bark initially smooth, later rough and cracked. Leaves similar to those of Common Beech but unequal at the base, tips less pointed, margins irregularly toothed and veins in 7-11 pairs. Dark green above, paler beneath, the leaves turn yellow or red in autumn. Male and female flowers borne in axils of leaves. Males solitary, borne towards tips of shoots; females usually in threes enclosed by a single stalkless, spiny, four-lobed involucre. Fruiting involucre reaches 8mm long, the lobes spreading to release the three nutlets, each 5mm long. *Flowering:* February to March. *Distribution:* Native to South America, from Chile to northern Argentina. A remarkably fast-growing tree, planted for timber in Britain and increasingly popular as an ornamental. The related **Rauli** (*N. procera*) has a similar native distribution and is also planted in parks and gardens. It has leaves with finely toothed, wavy margins and 14-20 pairs of veins, and nutlets about 10mm long.

Sweet Chestnut

Sweet Chestnut

Sweet Chestnut

Beech

Beech: fruit

Roble Beech: ♂ flowers

Evergreen Oak:
♂ catkin

Round-leaved Oak

Kermes Oak

Cork Oak

Evergreen Oak *Quercus ilex* Up to 25m Evergreen superficially resembling a holly tree, but with much less stiff and spiny foliage. Broadly domed tree, sometimes shrubby, with nearly smooth bark. Twigs grey-brown, hairy. Alternate leaves 3-7cm long, elliptical to oval, thick and leathery but not stiff, glossy green above, white- to green-felted beneath, with 7-11 pairs of veins. Leaves are often entire but those on low shoots and suckers have wavy margins with short spiny teeth. Flowers have narrow, pointed perianth-lobes. Clusters of one to three, bitter-tasting acorns ripen in the first year. Cup 12mm in diameter with close-pressed, felted scales encloses a third to a half of the acorn. *Flowering:* June. *Distribution:* Native to the Mediterranean but a widely planted ornamental elsewhere, sometimes naturalised in western and southern Europe.

Round-leaved Oak *Quercus rotundifolia* Up to 20m Closely resembles Evergreen Oak, differing in the broader leaves and sweet acorns. Leaves broadly oval to almost circular, grey-green above with only five to eight pairs of veins. Flowers have broad and blunt, not narrow and pointed, perianth-lobes. Acorn sweet-tasting and edible, the cup with shorter and thicker scales than in Evergreen Oak. *Flowering:* June. *Distribution:* Native to France, Spain and Portugal, where it tends to replace Evergreen Oak.

Kermes Oak *Quercus coccifera* Up to 5m Small evergreen closely resembling a holly bush in its stiff and spiny leaves. Densely branched tree, frequently only a low shrub with numerous ascending branches. Young twigs yellowish, with star-shaped hairs. Alternate leaves 1.5-4cm long, oval to oblong, sometimes heart-shaped at the base, glossy, stiff and leathery, with wavy and spine-toothed margins; petiole only 1-4mm long. Acorns usually solitary, ripening in the second year. Shallow acorn-cups have stiff, more or less spiny and spreading scales. *Flowering:* April to May. *Distribution:* Widespread throughout the Mediterranean, especially in the hotter, drier parts, but absent from much of Italy.

Cork Oak *Quercus suber* Up to 20m Evergreen tree whose extremely thick, furrowed outer bark yields commercial cork. When stripped away it reveals the thin, bright orange inner bark beneath. Young twigs have yellow hairs. Alternate leaves of 3-7cm, oblong-oval, dark green above, white-hairy below, with wavy and toothed margins; petiole 8-15mm long. Acorns of early-flowering trees ripen in the first year, those of late-flowering trees in the second year. Cup of 12-18mm diameter has long, spreading scales in the upper half, close-pressed scales in the lower; it encloses half the acorn. *Flowering:* May to June. *Distribution:* Common in southern Europe, often planted there and elsewhere for commercial cork and for ornament.

Evergreen Oak

Evergreen Oak

Round-leaved Oak: young ♂ flowers

Kermes Oak

Cork Oak: outer cork harvested

Cork Oak

Quercus crenata

Turkey Oak *Quercus cerris* Up to 35m Large, spreading tree with dull, blackish bark cracking into plates. Twigs rough, brown or grey with short hairs; buds surrounded by persistent, fringed scales. Rather variable leaves alternate, usually 5-10cm long, oblong but tapering at both ends, with four to seven pairs of narrow lobes, rough and dull above, woolly below; petiole 8-15mm long. Acorns in clusters of one to five, ripening in the second year, half to two-thirds enclosed in woody cups 15-22mm in diameter with thick, pointed, outward-curving scales. *Flowering:* May to June. *Distribution:* Native to southern half of Europe except Spain and Portugal, and widely introduced elsewhere. Similar **Q. crenata**, found scattered through southern Europe, has smaller leaf-lobes tipped with a short point and smaller acorn cups with narrower, softer scales.

Valonia Oak *Quercus ithaburensis* subsp. *macrolepis* 10-15m Semi-evergreen tree sometimes shedding its leaves in harsh conditions. Twigs densely yellow or grey-hairy, becoming glabrous. Dull alternate leaves 6-10cm long, oval to nearly oblong, pointed, densely hairy beneath with three to seven pairs of large triangular, bristle-tipped lobes which may themselves be lobed; petiole 15-40mm long. Acorns ripening in the second year. Woody cup up to 50mm in diameter with thick, flat and wide-spreading scales, enclosing half the acorn. *Flowering:* April. *Distribution:* Native to the central and eastern Mediterranean, from southern Italy to the Balkans and Aegean; formerly cultivated for the acorn cups which yield tannin.

Macedonian Oak *Quercus trojana* Up to 15m Semi-evergreen or completely deciduous tree, sometimes an erect shrub. Young twigs grey or brown with minute hairs. Alternate leaves 3-7cm long, oblong to widest above the middle, glabrous and shiny on both sides, with 8-14 pairs of lobes each tipped with a short or bristle-like point; petiole 2-5mm long. Acorns ripen in the second year. Cup 15-22mm in diameter and enclosing two-thirds of the acorn has the lower scales close-pressed and the upper spreading or curving inwards. *Flowering:* April. *Distribution:* Native to south-eastern Italy and western parts of the Balkan Peninsula.

Macedonian Oak

Turkey Oak

Turkey Oak

Valonia Oak

Macedonian Oak: immature acorns

*Quercus
dalechampii*

Sessile Oak *Quercus petraea* Up to 40m Similar to Pedunculate Oak with which it often dominates in woods, it has hairier leaves and stalkless acorns. Tree with a long trunk leading through to the top of the domed crown, and smooth, purplish-grey bark. Twigs glabrous. Alternate leaves 7-12cm long, widest above the middle, with five to eight pairs of rounded lobes, pale undersides with fine, close-pressed hairs plus reddish tufts in the vein axils; petiole 10-16mm long, yellowish. Acorns in clusters of one to six, almost stalkless, ripening in the first year. Shallow, stalkless cups 12-18mm in diameter have thin, downy scales. *Flowering:* May. *Distribution:* Common on light soils and often a dominant woodland tree. Widespread throughout Europe except for parts of the Mediterranean. Similar **Q. dalechampii**, from south-eastern Europe reaching to Austria, Italy and Sicily, has hairless leaves and warty acorn-cups.

Quercus polycarpa Up to 25m Small, rather leathery-leaved tree. Twigs glabrous. Alternate leaves 6-10cm long, elliptical, glabrous, with wavy margins and divided into seven to ten pairs of regular, shallow and blunt lobes; petiole 15-35mm long, grooved. Acorns ripen in the first year. Cup 10-15mm long, brown with broadly oval, pointed and very warty scales with minute hairs. *Flowering:* May. *Distribution:* Native to south-eastern Europe westwards to Hungary. **Q. mas**, native to southern France and northern Spain, is very similar but has leaves with narrow, forward-pointing lobes; the fruit stalks have silky hairs.

*Quercus
pedunculiflora*

Pedunculate Oak *Quercus robur* Up to 45m Massive, spreading tree, often dominating woodland; many individuals are very long-lived. Deeply furrowed bark dark grey. Young twigs brownish, sometimes hairy. Alternate leaves 10-12cm long, oblong to widest above the middle with five to seven pairs of irregular lobes plus small ear-shaped projections at the base of the blade; petiole not more than 5mm long. Acorns in clusters of one to five, on a stalk 4-8cm long, ripening in the first year. Scales of the shallow, 11-18mm diameter cups are fused together except for their tips. *Flowering:* May to June. *Distribution:* Common in most of Europe and frequently a dominant woodland tree on heavy, alkaline soils. Similar **Q. pedunculiflora**, from the Balkans and Crimea, has yellow-grey hairs on the undersides of leaves and on the acorn cups.

Sessile Oak

Sessile Oak: ♂ flowers

Sessile Oak

Quercus polycarpa

Pedunculate Oak

Pedunculate Oak

Hungarian Oak

Quercus brachyphylla

Quercus virgiliana

Portuguese Oak

Hungarian Oak *Quercus frainetto* Up to 30m Domed tree with long, straight branches, stout trunk and deeply fissured bark. Young twigs downy at first, later glabrous. Large buds surrounded by persistent scales. Leaves alternate, crowded towards the tips of twigs, 10-20cm long, widest above the middle and tapering towards the base, deeply divided into seven to nine pairs of oblong lobes which are often themselves lobed, grey- or brown-hairy beneath; there are two ear-shaped lobes at the base of the blade. Acorns in clusters of two to five, ripening in the first year. Cup 6-12mm long, with oblong, blunt and hairy scales loosely overlapping, enclosing about one third of the acorn. *Flowering:* May. *Distribution:* An eastern European species, extending from the Balkans to Hungary and southern Italy.

Pyrenean Oak *Quercus pyrenaica* Up to 20m Medium-sized tree producing numerous suckers. Twigs hairy and pendent. Alternate leaves 8-16cm long, oblong or widest above the middle, deeply divided into four to eight pairs of narrow, pointed lobes, glabrous above with dense white hairs beneath; petiole up to 22mm long. Acorns ripen in the first year. Cup up to 15mm long, with loosely overlapping, narrow but blunt scales. *Flowering:* May. *Distribution:* A western European species, from the Iberian Peninsula to France and northern Italy. **Q. congesta**, endemic to southern France, Sardinia and Sicily, is very similar but the leaves have grey-green hairs beneath. **Q. brachyphylla** from Greece, Crete and the Aegean is sometimes semi-evergreen; leathery leaves have overlapping lobes hairy or glabrous beneath, and acorn-cups have warty lower scales.

Downy Oak *Quercus pubescens* Up to 25m, often less Small, grey-leaved tree, often broader than it is tall, sometimes only a shrub. Twigs have dense grey hairs. Alternate leaves 4-12cm long, usually elliptical with four to eight pairs of shallow, forward-pointing lobes. Undersides of young leaves have grey, velvety hairs, and gradually become glabrous. Acorns in clusters of one to four, very short stalked, ripen in the first year. Shallow cups of 15mm diameter, with close-pressed and grey-woolly scales, enclose about one third of the acorn. *Flowering:* May. *Distribution:* Native to dry limestone hills in south-central and western Europe. Similar **Q. virgiliana** has larger, oblong leaves with large, broadly toothed lobes and sweet, edible acorns on a single long, hairy stalk, the cups 30mm in diameter with loosely overlapping, slightly warty scales. Native to southern Europe from Corsica east to Asia Minor.

Algerian Oak *Quercus canariensis* Up to 30m Semi-evergreen tree with both twigs and young leaves densely woolly before becoming glabrous. Young twigs grooved. Alternate leaves 6-18cm long, elliptic to oval, margins with 9-14 pairs of slightly pointed teeth, green above, bluish beneath, glabrous when mature; petiole 8-30mm long. Acorns in clusters of one to three on a single short stalk ripen in the first year. Cup 12-20mm long, with narrowly oval, warty lower scales and smaller, loosely pressed upper scales, half enclosing the acorn. *Flowering:* April to May. *Distribution:* Native to Portugal and Spain. It often forms hybrids with Downy Oak. **Portuguese Oak** (*Q. faginea*) is a similar tree or shrub from Iberia and the Balearics. It has slightly smaller leaves, 4-10cm long, which remain hairy beneath.

Hungarian Oak

Pyrenean Oak

Downy Oak

Algerian Oak

Red Oak

Scarlet Oak

Pin Oak

Red Oak *Quercus rubra* Up to 35m Oak with striking autumn leaves of scarlet or deep blood red. Broadly domed tree with stout, dark red twigs and smooth, silvery bark. Alternate leaves 12-22cm long, oblong, divided about halfway to the midrib into lobes each with one to three slender teeth, matt green above and grey with a few brownish hairs in the vein-axils beneath; petiole 25-50mm long. Acorns ripen in the second year. Cup of 18-25mm diameter is very shallow, the closely pressed, oval scales thin with fine hairs. *Flowering:* May. *Distribution:* Native to eastern North America and one of several species widely planted in Europe for their rich autumn colours.

Scarlet Oak *Quercus coccinea* 20-25m Open tree with leaves turning bright scarlet in autumn. Twigs hairy when young, becoming glabrous and yellowish-brown. Alternate leaves 9-15cm long, oblong to elliptical with three or four pairs of spreading, toothed lobes, bright glossy green above, paler and glabrous but for tufts of hairs in the vein-axils beneath; petiole 30-60mm long. Acorns solitary, on a short stalk, ripening in the second year. Cup 15-20mm in diameter with scales closely pressed together and enclosing half the acorn. *Flowering:* May. *Distribution:* Ornamental tree grown in streets and parks for its very bright autumn foliage.

Pin Oak *Quercus palustris* 20-40m Similar to Red Oak and also producing good autumn colours. Trunk straight. Crown conical, with low-hanging branches and stiff, rather pendent twigs. Leaves like Red Oak but 10-15cm long, more deeply cut with jagged-toothed lobes, bright green on both sides, turning red in autumn; petiole 20-50mm long. Flowers and fruits like Red Oak but acorn-cup only 10-15mm in diameter, enclosing one third of the acorn. *Flowering:* May. *Distribution:* Native to eastern North America and planted for timber, mainly in eastern Europe from Denmark and Germany to Hungary and Romania.

Red Oak: autumn

Scarlet Oak: autumn

Scarlet Oak: immature acorns

Pin Oak: immature acorns

Wych Elm *Ulmus glabra* Up to 40m Broad tree with toothed, asymmetric leaves and clusters of papery winged fruits. Broader than other elms with widespreading branches: young twigs stout and stiffly hairy. Rounded to elliptical and long-pointed leaves 10-18cm in length are alternate, with stiff hairs above and softer hairs beneath; each leaf has 10-18 pairs of veins. Asymmetric leaf-base has one side curved to overlap and conceal the leaf-stalk. Purplish-red flower clusters appear before the leaves. Perianth has four to five lobes. Fruit 15-20mm long has the seed centrally placed in the papery wing. *Flowering:* February to March. *Distribution:* Found on rich, damp soils in hilly areas, especially by water. Native to most of Europe but absent from Mediterranean islands. Somewhat resistant to Dutch Elm disease, unlike other species, and now the only common elm in Britain and northern Europe. **Dutch Elm** (*U.* x *hollandica*) is very similar, but has shiny leaves and often suckers freely. Commonly planted in northern Europe but much reduced by disease in recent years. **U. elliptica**, native to the Crimea and occasionally planted, is also very similar. It has broader leaves fringed with long hairs and fruits which are hairy in the centre. **English Elm** (*U. procera*) is a narrower tree with persistently hairy twigs, greenish flowers with red anthers and fruits 10-17mm long with the seed set near the tip of the wing. Best known in Britain, although it occurs in other parts of western and central Europe.

English Elm: winged fruit

Small-leaved Elm *Ulmus minor* Up to 30m Narrow tree with sharply ascending branches and long, pendulous, glabrous young twigs. Suckers often present. Alternate leaves 6-8cm in length, usually widest above the middle, pointed, and smooth on both sides; there are 7-12 pairs of veins and the long side of the asymmetric leaf-base makes a 90-degree turn to join the stalk. Clusters of small flowers open before the leaves appear. Perianth is four- to five-lobed, anthers red. Fruits 7-18mm long have the seed set near the top of the papery wing. *Flowering:* March. *Distribution:* Prefers deep, moist soils along roadsides and hedgerows; native to most of Europe except Scandinavia; also widely planted. Hybrids with Wych Elm are often planted for ornament. A very variable species with many distinctive local populations and sometimes divided into several separate species. Very similar **U. canescens** from central and eastern Mediterranean regions has young twigs with dense white down, leaves with grey down beneath and 12-16 pairs of veins.

Ulmus canescens: leaf underside

European White Elm *Ulmus laevis* Up to 35m Clusters of long-stalked flowers flutter in spring on the bare twigs of this tall, open tree. Crown tall and wide-spreading. Bark initially smooth, becoming deeply ridged with age. Twigs softly downy or glabrous. Oval to nearly round leaves 6-13cm in length, alternate, usually glabrous above but often downy grey beneath, with 12-19 pairs of veins and a very asymmetric leaf-base. Clusters of reddish, long-stalked flowers with four to five perianth-lobes appear before the leaves. Pendulous fruits 10-12mm long have a centrally positioned seed and a fringe of white hairs on the papery wing. *Flowering:* May. *Distribution:* Native to central and south-eastern Europe, mainly in river valleys, occasionally planted for shelter elsewhere.

European White Elm: flower cluster

124

Wych Elm

Wych Elm

Wych Elm

Small-leaved Elm

Small-leaved Elm

European White Elm

Caucasian
Nettle-tree

Southern Nettle-tree *Celtis australis* Up to 25m Rounded tree with leaves which resemble those of the nettle in size, shape and toothing, but do not sting. Bark grey or brown. Alternate, narrowly oval, sharply toothed leaves 4-15cm long have a rounded or heart-shaped base, often wavy margins and taper to the often twisted tip. The upper surface has stiff hairs, the lower white down, especially on the veins. Flowers appear with the young leaves; solitary in the leaf-axils, they are dull brownish-green, with four to five perianth-lobes. Fleshy, edible, berry-like fruits of about 1cm are long stalked, ripening from brownish-red to black, and contain a very rough, knobbly stone. *Flowering:* May. *Distribution:* Native to southern Europe, especially the central region from Italy to Yugoslavia, but planted elsewhere as a street tree and ornamental. **Caucasian Nettle-tree** (*C. caucasica*), from Asia but also occurring in Bulgaria and possibly Greece, is a smaller tree with leaves with wedge-shaped bases and a slightly roughened stone. **C. glabrata** from the Crimea is a small tree or shrub 3-4m in height with entirely hairless leaves and a slightly roughened stone.

Celtis tournefortii 1-6m Small tree, frequently only making a large shrub. Young twigs are reddish-brown but also have white downy hairs. Alternate leaves 5-7cm long, oval with a rounded base, short tapering tip and slightly rounded teeth tipped with a short point. Dark green upper leaf surface may be roughened with short stiff hairs; paler lower surface is downy. Flowers like those of Southern Nettle-tree. Ovoid fruits 0.7-1.1cm long ripen browny-yellow and contain a four-ridged stone. *Flowering:* May to June. *Distribution:* Native to Sicily, the Balkan Peninsula and the Crimea.

Keaki

Caucasian Elm *Zelkova carpinifolia* Up to 30m Unusual tree instantly recognisable by its broom-like crown. Trunk very short and stout, usually only 1-3m high. There are often several trunks, which sometimes sucker. Bark grey-brown, smooth but flaking to reveal orange patches. Branches numerous and almost erect, giving a dense, ovoid crown. Twigs slender, grey- or green-brown with white hairs. Alternate leaves 5-10cm long, oval to elliptical, pointed, coarsely toothed, slightly unequal at the base and almost stalkless. Both sides have stiff hairs, those on the lower surface on either side of the veins. Male and female flowers borne on the same twig, the males on the lower, leafless part, the females solitary in the axils of leaves near the twig-tip. Both sexes have five partially fused perianth-segments. Nut-like fruit 5mm long, rounded and ridged. *Flowering:* April to May. *Distribution:* Slow-growing, long-lived tree native to the Caucasus Mountains. It is planted purely as an ornamental tree, mainly in central and western Europe. Similar **Keaki** (*Z. serrata*), from Japan, is also grown for ornament. It has more spreading branches, more sharply toothed leaves which turn rich yellow and red in autumn, and fruits without ridges. **Abelitzia** (*Z. abelicea*) is the only native European species of *Zelkova*, endemic to the mountains of Crete and rarely cultivated. It is often a large shrub 3-5m in height, with leaves 2.5cm long, scented white flowers and hairy fruits.

Southern Nettle-tree

Southern Nettle-tree

Celtis tournefortii

Caucasian Elm

White Mulberry:
♂ catkin

India Rubber-tree

Paper Mulberry

Osage Orange:
♂ flowers

Black Mulberry *Morus nigra* Up to 12m Bushy-headed tree with short, often leaning trunk and twisted, rough branches. Young twigs hairy and exuding milky latex when cut. Alternate heart-shaped, toothed or lobed leaves 6-20cm in length, rough above with soft hairs beneath. Male and female flowers borne on the same tree in catkin-like spikes, the males 2.5cm long, the females about half this length. Four perianth-segments, those of female flowers becoming fleshy in fruit. Soft, fleshy fruits 2-2.5cm long, dark red or purplish, very tart until fully ripe. *Flowering:* May. *Distribution:* Originating in central Asia but long cultivated in Europe as a fruit tree, and now widely naturalised, especially in southern Europe. Similar **White Mulberry** (*M. alba*) has leaves smooth and glossy above, hairy only on the veins beneath, and white or pinkish fruits. Native to eastern Asia, sometimes planted as a roadside tree and naturalised in south-eastern Europe.

Fig *Ficus carica* Up to 8m Large, long-stalked leaves and fleshy fruits make this low, wide-spreading tree difficult to confuse with any other. Thick and leathery alternate leaves, 10-20cm long and broad, are palmately divided into three to five rounded lobes. They are sparsely bristly and distinctly rough to the touch. Flowers are borne on the inside of a hollow, fleshy and swollen pear-shaped structure which forms the young fig. Fruit ripens in the second year and when fully developed is 5-8cm long and brownish or violet-green. *Flowering:* June to September. *Distribution:* Native to south-western Asia and possibly to the Mediterranean, where it is widely grown for fruit and shade, often seen as an isolated tree among fields; sometimes grown for ornament in northern Europe. **India Rubber-tree** (*F. elastica*), a tall evergreen with glossy, oblong, entire leaves, is also grown as a shade tree in Mediterranean countries.

Paper Mulberry *Broussonetia papyrifera* Up to 15m Small tree with spiky, orange fruits. Young twigs have shaggy hairs. Alternate leaves 7-20cm long, oval, sharply toothed and sometimes deeply lobed, rough above with dense, short grey hairs beneath. Male and female flowers borne on different trees, males in catkins, females in dense, globose, woolly heads. Perianth four-lobed in male flowers; having four small teeth in females, becoming fleshy and pulpy when in fruit. Rather spiky fruiting head is about 2cm in diameter, orange with red individual fruits. *Flowering:* April to May. *Distribution:* Native to eastern Asia and uncommon there, planted and sometimes naturalised in southern Europe.

Osage Orange *Maclura pomifera* Up to 14m Small, spiny, irregularly domed tree with twisted branches. Bark rough, rather orange in colour. Dark, glossy green, alternate leaves 5-12cm long, oval, long-pointed with a wedge-shaped base and entire margins. Male and female flowers borne on different trees. Males greenish-yellow, in long-stalked clusters 1.5-2.5cm across; numerous females form globular yellowish heads 2-2.5cm across. Both sexes have a four-lobed perianth. Fruit 10-14cm long is formed by the whole female flower-head and consists of a tough, pitted rind ripening yellow or orange and enclosing stringy, white, inedible flesh. *Flowering:* June. *Distribution:* Native to southern and central North America, cultivated for ornament and hedges and naturalised in southern Europe.

Black Mulberry

Fig

Paper Mulberry

Osage Orange

Sweet Bay *Laurus nobilis* Up to 20m Bushy, densely branched evergreen with leaves spotted with numerous oil glands – appearing as tiny translucent dots – which give off a strong, spicy scent when the leaves are bruised. Broad, conical crown of ascending branches and slender, hairless twigs. Bark smooth, grey or dull black. Alternate, narrowly oblong to lance-shaped leaves 5-10cm long, leathery with wavy margins and dotted with numerous tiny oil glands. The short petiole is dark red. Four-petalled flowers are borne in small clusters, yellowish males and greenish females on different trees. Ovoid green berries 1-1.5cm in length turn black when fully ripe. *Flowering:* April to June. *Distribution:* Native to dry areas of the Mediterranean and sometimes naturalised further north. Widely cultivated as a pot herb in much of Europe and often grown as a clipped shrub.

Avocado *Persea americana* 7-9m, sometimes more Dense evergreen with large, leathery, aromatic leaves and fleshy, pear-shaped fruits. Rounded, much-branched tree up to 18m in the wild but considerably smaller in cultivation. All parts of the tree, but especially the leaves, are densely dotted with oil glands. Alternate leaves 10-20cm long, elliptical to oval, shortly pointed, entire and glabrous. Leathery in texture, dark green above and slightly bluish below, they are aromatic when crushed. Flowers 2cm in diameter, greenish with grey hairs, borne in elongated clusters. Perianth six-lobed, the three outer lobes sometimes smaller than the inner three. Fruit about 10cm long, usually pear-shaped but sometimes oblong or globose, with a smooth or warty skin which may be green, yellow, brownish or purple when ripe. Thick, creamy-white flesh surrounds a single large stone. *Flowering:* February to May. *Distribution:* Exact origin obscure but assumed to be native to Central America. Grown commercially in Mediterranean Europe for the edible fruits which vary in size, colour and skin texture depending on the cultivar.

Avocado

Phytolacca: fruits

Phytolacca *Phytolacca dioica* 3-8m Small evergreen tree with long cylindrical clusters of juicy, deep purple fruits. Old trees develop a characteristic trunk spreading into a broad, irregular plate-like base at ground level. Crown broad with stout, spreading branches. Bark smooth, greyish-brown. Twigs stout, rather fleshy and hairless. Alternate leaves 6-12cm long, elliptical to oval, with wedge-shaped bases, pointed tips and entire margins, bright green in colour with a prominent pale midrib. Greenish-white flowers borne in drooping cylindrical clusters 8-15cm long, males and females on different trees. Males 1.5cm long, with five pointed, petal-like perianth-segments; females slightly larger with blunt perianth-segments. Fruit is a compressed globe 3mm long and 7.5mm across, made up of seven to ten segments joined at the base and ripening from green to deep purple. Each segment contains a single seed. *Flowering:* June to August. *Distribution:* Native to warm parts of South America, grown as an ornamental and shade tree in Mediterranean countries and sometimes naturalised.

Sweet Bay

Sweet Bay

Avocado

Phytolacca

London Plane

London Plane *Platanus x hispanica* Up to 35m Tree with thin, grey bark regularly flaking away from the trunk to reveal a mosaic of large buff and yellow patches. Broad, spreading tree, the old branches twisted and held horizontally. Large alternate leaves up to 25 x 25cm, palmately divided to less than halfway to the midrib into five triangular lobes with forward-pointing teeth. Flowers form strings of globose heads, the males in two to six yellowish-green heads, the females usually in two, rarely as many as five, crimson heads. Fruiting heads 2.5cm long are brown, remaining on the tree until the following spring before breaking up to release abundant, white-haired seeds. *Flowering:* June. *Distribution:* Of hybrid or perhaps cultivated origin, vigorous and pollution-tolerant; one of the most common street trees in Europe.

Oriental Plane *Plantanus orientalis* Up to 30m Closely resembling, and possibly one of the parents of, London Plane. It has less colourful bark but differs principally in the leaves and flower-heads. Leaves cut to two-thirds of the way to midrib into five to seven narrow lobes. Lobes usually coarsely toothed, can sometimes be entire. Flower-heads hang in clusters of three to six. *Flowering:* April to June. *Distribution:* Native to the Balkans and Crete and extending into western Asia. It is often planted as an ornamental and park tree.

Sweet-gum

Oriental Sweet-gum *Liquidambar orientalis* Up to 7.5m Superficially resembling a plane tree, this is very much smaller and does not have such colourful bark. Small tree with a dense crown of spreading branches. Bark dark orange-brown, fissured and corky. Alternate leaves 4-6cm long, deeply palmately five-lobed, the lobes oval with the middle lobe larger than the others. Margins coarsely toothed and glandular. Flower-heads globular. Yellow males consist of stamens and small scales and are clustered in catkins 5-10cm long. Greenish females 1-1.5cm long consist of beaked ovaries and small scales, and are solitary or paired. Prickly fruiting head 2-3.5cm long is made up of numerous slender capsules, each with one or two seeds. *Flowering:* May. *Distribution:* Native to Asia Minor but grown in Europe as a source of liquid storax, a fragrant resin obtained from the inner bark. **Sweet-gum** (*L. styraciflua*) from North America has larger, brighter and less deeply lobed leaves. It is an ornamental producing splendid autumn colours.

London Plane

London Plane: fruit

Oriental Plane: fruit

Oriental Sweet-gum: flowers

Drooping She-oak:
fruiting head

Pittosporum

Karo:
fruit and seeds

Horsetail She-oak *Casuarina equisetifolia* Up to 20m Tree of arid land, with curious whip-like foliage consisting of tiny, scaly leaves set in whorls around the shoots. Evergreen with conical or columnar crown of slender, upswept branches. Bark greyish-brown, peeling in strips. Twigs tough, pendulous, very slender and green. Minute, grey-green, scaly or tooth-like leaves arranged in whorls of six to eight around the shoot. Male flowers form a brownish spike of 1-1.5cm long, each flower consisting of a single stamen. Female flowers form a dense, reddish head 3-4mm long which eventually becomes the cone-like fruiting head 1-1.5cm long with woody scales. Individual fruits nut-like and winged. *Flowering:* February to March. *Distribution:* Native to Australia. Drought-resistant and salt-tolerant, it is planted in Mediterranean countries for shelter, soil stabilisation and ornament. Similar **Drooping She-oak** (*C. stricta*), also from Australia, is more cold tolerant and has much larger flower-heads.

White Holly *Pittosporum undulatum* Up to 20m Evergreen tree with a pyramidal crown, sometimes a large shrub. Bark smooth, grey; twigs green. Alternate, shiny green leaves 7-13cm long, oval to lance-shaped, pointed, the margins entire but distinctly wavy and crinkled. Evening-scented, white, five-petalled flowers borne in branched, few-flowered clusters. Fruit a smooth, ovoid capsule 1-1.2cm long, tipped with a short point. Orange when ripe, it splits in two, revealing seeds embedded in a sticky substance. *Flowering:* May to June. *Distribution:* Native to south-eastern Australia, widely cultivated as an ornamental in southern and western Europe and naturalised in places. **Pittosporum** (*P. tenuifolium*) is similar but has shorter, oblong and blunt leaves and solitary purplish flowers. Native to New Zealand, grown in Europe as a foliage plant.

Karo *Pittosporum crassifolium* Up to 10m Small, erect evergreen with a narrow crown, sometimes only a shrub. Bark black. Alternate leaves 5-8cm long, oblong or widest above the middle, blunt and very leathery, dark green above, with dense white hairs beneath. Male and female flowers in separate, few-flowered clusters, all the stalks arising from the same point. Each flower has five dark red to purplish-black, oblong petals. Fruit a globose capsule of 2-2.8cm, woody and white-hairy, opening by four valves when ripe. *Flowering:* March. *Distribution:* Native to New Zealand, grown for ornament and shelter and naturalised in warm parts of western Europe. **P. tobira** from China and Japan is also grown for ornament. It has hairless leaves and fragrant white or yellowish flowers.

Horsetail She-oak

Horsetail She-oak

White Holly

Karo

Chinese Tulip-tree

Tulip-tree *Liriodendron tulipifera* Up to 45m Tall tree with stout, straight trunk; crown slender and straight-sided when young, becoming domed. Bark grey, brown or slightly orange, becoming ridged with age. Distinctive alternate leaves 7-12cm long have two, rarely one or three, spreading lobes on each side and a square or shallowly notched tip. Bright green above, slightly bluish and waxy beneath, they turn butter-yellow in autumn. Flowers are cup-shaped and resemble yellow-green tulips; nine petal-like perianth-segments are about 5cm long, the inner six with an orange band near the base. Fruit 5-8.5cm long, narrow and cone-like. *Flowering:* May to June. *Distribution:* Native to North America and preferring deep, moist soils; widely planted in Europe for both ornament and timber. Similar **Chinese Tulip-tree** (*L. chinense*) has more deeply and narrowly lobed leaves unfolding copper-coloured before turning green. Native to China and planted for ornament.

Evergreen Magnolia *Magnolia grandiflora* Up to 30m Evergreen tree with large, spreading branches making a conical crown. Smooth bark dull grey. Young twigs have thick reddish down. Leaves 8-16cm long, alternate, thick and leathery, entire, sometimes wavy-edged, very shiny on the upper surface but covered with rusty hairs beneath. Flowers fragrant, up to 25cm in diameter and composed of six petal-like segments, solitary at the tips of shoots, produced a few at a time. Initially conical, the flowers gradually open almost flat. Single-seeded fruits form a cone-like structure 5-6cm long. *Flowering:* July to November. *Distribution:* Native to eastern North America and a widely grown ornamental in mild regions. Several other magnolias are also commonly grown in Europe as ornamentals. One of the most common is **M.** x **soulangiana**, a small deciduous tree or shrub with pink or purple-tinged flowers appearing before the leaves.

Common Pear *Pyrus communis* Up to 20m A narrow, suckering tree, with leaves turning yellow to dark red in autumn. Young twigs slightly hairy, soon glabrous and reddish-brown, usually becoming spiny in older trees. Alternate leaves 5-8cm long, pointed, oval to elliptical, finely toothed on the margins; densely hairy when unfurling, they soon become glabrous. Flowers in clusters appear with the leaves. Five petals white, 12-14 mm long; anthers reddish-purple. Fruit ranges from 4-12cm in length, pear-shaped to globose, and yellowish to brown. It has characteristically gritty flesh, due to the presence of stone-cells, and it may be sweet or tart. *Flowering:* April. *Distribution:* Originating in western Asia, anciently introduced to Europe and now widespread in woods, hedgerows and thickets. The cultivated pear of gardens is var. *culta*.

Tulip-tree

Tulip-tree

Evergreen Magnolia

Common Pear

Common Pear

Common Pear

Snow Pear *Pyrus nivalis* Up to 20m Medium-sized, stout tree with ascending, usually spineless branches. Twigs stout, densely woolly when young, becoming glabrous and darker. Alternate leaves 5-9cm long, widest above the middle, densely hairy beneath, entire or slightly toothed at the tip with the margins of the blade running down the petiole; petiole 1-2cm long, densely hairy. Flowers, in dense clusters, appear slightly after the leaves. Five white petals, 14-16mm long, styles hairy at the base. Fruit 3-5cm long, more or less globose, on a long stalk, greenish-yellow with purple spots. Flesh sweet when overripe. *Flowering:* April to May. *Distribution:* Sunny places and dry open woods in central Europe from Austria to Yugoslavia. Two other, similar species are cultivated and sometimes naturalised outside their native ranges. **Austrian Pear** (*P. austriaca*) has more or less erect branches, lanceolate leaves toothed at the apex with yellowish-grey wool beneath, and glabrous styles. It is a tree of open spaces, native to central Europe from Switzerland to Russia. **Sage-leaved Pear** (*P. salvifolia*) is spreading and spiny; lanceolate or elliptical, entire leaves have grey wool beneath. The bitter fruit is 6-8cm long, on a long, woolly stalk. Usually an isolated tree on sunny, grassy slopes and in dry woods from France and Belgium to Romania and Russia, its fruit is used to make perry.

Sage-leaved Pear

Wild Pear *Pyrus pyraster* 8-20m Very like Common Pear but distinguishable by its more bushy spiny growth, and much smaller hard fruits. Trunk short and straight; bark rough and cracked. Branches spreading or angled upwards, with grey to brown, usually spiny twigs, forming a round crown. Leaves alternate, 2.5-7cm long, elliptical, oval or circular, pointed with a wedge- or heart-shaped base; margins toothed at the apex. Young leaves hairy, soon becoming glabrous. Flowers in clusters of four to five, each with five pure white, slightly crinkled petals 10-17mm long. Fruit globular or top-shaped, 1-3.5 cm long, fleshy, firm, gritty, ripening to yellow, brown or black. *Flowering:* April to May. *Distribution:* Usually single trees in thickets and open woods, found through much of Europe. Similar **Caucasian Pear** (*P. caucasica*) is a rare tree of Greece, Crimean Russia and Turkey. It is taller, with entire leaves and dull brown, stoutly stalked fruits.

Almond-leaved Pear *Pyrus amygdaliformis* Up to 6m Dense shrub or small slender tree, with spreading, sometimes spiny branches. Twigs dull grey, slightly woolly when young, becoming glabrous. Alternate leaves 2.5-8cm long, usually lanceolate or widest above the middle, with a faintly toothed or entire margin, shiny above and rough beneath when mature; petiole 2-5cm long. Flowers, up to eight in a cluster, appear with or before the leaves. Five petals, each 7.5mm long, white, usually notched. Fruit globular, 1.5-3cm in diameter, yellowish-brown when ripe, with a thick stalk. *Flowering:* April. *Distribution:* A tree of dry and rough places, usually as a single specimen. Native to the Mediterranean, from Spain to Yugoslavia. Similar **P. bourgaeana** has oval to heart-shaped, toothed and glabrous leaves 2-4cm long, petals up to 10mm long. It is an uncommon tree native to the Iberian Peninsula, usually found near temporary water-courses.

Pyrus bourgaeana

Snow Pear

Wild Pear

Almond-leaved Pear

Almond-leaved Pear

Willow-leaved Pear

Pyrus elaeagrifolia

Willow-leaved Pear *Pyrus salicifolia* Up to 10m Slender, elegant tree with distinctive silvery leaves. Trunk straight, with dark, smooth, silver-grey bark. Crown domed, with horizontal main branches and drooping, densely white-woolly twigs. Alternate leaves 3.5-9cm long, narrow, pointed, grey-green with silver down on both sides at first, the upper surface becoming glabrous and glossy green. Flowers in tight clusters appear with the leaves. Petals five, white, each about 10mm long, notched or rounded at the tip. Fruit 2.5cm long, pear-shaped or cylindrical, brown when ripe, with a white, woolly stalk; flesh sour, firm and gritty in texture. *Flowering:* April. *Distribution:* A native of the Caucasus Mountains, Siberia and Iran to Asia. Widely cultivated as an ornamental. The weeping variety cv 'Pendula' is often more common in cultivation.

Pyrus elaeagrifolia Up to 10m Small slender tree or shrub, with spreading, often spiny branches. Twigs have grey hairs. Alternate leaves 3.5-8cm long, more or less lanceolate, toothed at the tip or entire, covered with dense grey-white wool even when mature; petiole short. Flowers appear with the leaves, in more or less stalkless clusters. Petals five, white, each 10mm long. Fruit about 1.3cm long, pear-shaped or globular, green when ripe, with a thick stalk. *Flowering:* April. *Distribution:* An isolated tree of dry habitats, native to the Balkans, Russia and Turkey.

Plymouth Pear *Pyrus cordata* Up to 8m Small, slender tree, sometimes only a shrub, with spreading, normally spiny branches and purplish, almost glabrous twigs. Alternate leaves 2.5-5.5 cm long, oval or heart-shaped, with a toothed margin, hairy only when young and often glabrous from the first; petiole 2.5cm long. Flowers in slender clusters appear with the leaves. Petals five, white, each 6-8mm long; sepals deciduous. Fruit pear-shaped, red and shiny when ripe, without persistent sepals and with a slender stalk. *Flowering:* April. *Distribution:* Uncommon or rare tree of woods and hedgerows. Native to Britain, France and the Iberian Peninsula.

Willow-leaved Pear

Willow-leaved Pear

Pyrus elaeagrifolia

Plymouth Pear

Plymouth Pear

Plymouth Pear

Malus dasyphylla:
flower (2 petals
removed)

Crab Apple: flower
(2 petals removed)

Siberian Crab
Apple

Cultivated Apple *Malus domestica* Up to 15m Well-known orchard tree producing the familiar large, edible fruits. Small, with brown bark and downy twigs. Leaves alternate, oval or elliptical, pointed and slightly toothed 4-13cm long, sparsely hairy above; more densely woolly below even when mature. Flowers five-petalled, usually pink but occasionally white, 3-4cm in diameter, appearing in clusters with the leaves. Both the flower-stalks and the outer surface of the persistent sepals are densely hairy. Firm, usually sweet-tasting fruit, exceeding 5cm long, varies in colour from green to red or brown. *Flowering:* May to June. *Distribution:* Of hybrid origin and divided into thousands of cultivars, it is the best known orchard tree grown throughout Europe; often escapes and becomes naturalised. Similar **Paradise Apple** (*M. pumila*), from Asia Minor but widely cultivated, is only 2m high and produces numerous sweet, green fruits 3-5cm long. **M. dasyphylla**, sometimes considered the same species as Paradise Apple, is endemic to the Danube Basin. It is spiny and has sour, yellowish fruits.

Crab Apple *Malus sylvestris* 2-10m Spiny wild trees have white flowers, the unarmed descendants of domesticated trees have pink-tinged flowers. Small, spreading tree often with a dense crown and large, twisted branches. Bark brown, cracked into scales. Toothed leaves 3-11cm long, alternate, oval, elliptical or almost circular; glabrous on both surfaces when mature. Flowers five-petalled, 3-4cm in diameter, white or pinkish, appearing in clusters with the leaves. Persistent sepals have thick hair on the inner surface. Fruit 2.5-3cm long is smaller than that of cultivated apple; yellow-green flushed with red, it is hard and sour. *Flowering:* May to June. *Distribution:* Native to chalky, hilly regions in much of Europe; anciently domesticated, no longer used as a fruit tree but widely naturalised.

Japanese Crab Apple *Malus* x *floribunda* 6-9m Free-flowering tree producing masses of pink and white blossom in spring. Small with low, rounded crown of numerous branches. Bark greyish-brown. Twigs somewhat pendulous, reddish when young, densely hairy. Alternate leaves, 4-8cm long, oblong to oval, pointed, toothed or sometimes even lobed. Underside downy at first, soon becoming glabrous. Fragrant flowers appear in clusters with or just after the leaves; deep pink in bud, they open paler pink and fade to white. Petals five, oblong and blunt; deciduous sepals hairy on the inner surface. Globular fruit up to 2.5cm long but often smaller, ripening bright yellow and produced in great numbers. *Flowering:* April to May. *Distribution:* Probably originating as a garden hybrid in Japan and one of the most commonly planted ornamental crab apples in Europe. Several other species are also widely grown, including **Siberian Crab Apple** (*M. baccata*), with white flowers and bright red fruit persisting on the twigs until spring, and **Purple Crab Apple** (*M.* x *purpurea*), with purplish flowers and fruits.

Cultivated Apple

Cultivated Apple

Cultivated Apple

Crab Apple

Crab Apple

Japanese Crab Apple

Malus florentina

Malus florentina Up to 4m An apple with lobed leaves and very small, red fruits. Small tree, the twigs lacking spines or thorns. Alternate leaves 3-6cm long, broadly oval in outline, base heart-shaped or cut straight across, margins toothed with several sharp, irregular lobes on each side. Upper leaf surface dark green, lower with dense white hairs; petiole short, only 0.5-2cm long. Flowers 1.5-2cm long, white, five-petalled, with deciduous sepals. Fruit about 1cm long, ellipsoid to pear-shaped, red when ripe and with gritty flesh. *Flowering:* April to May. *Distribution:* An endemic species scattered through Italy, southern Yugoslavia, Albania and northern Greece.

Malus trilobata Up to 10m Small tree or tall shrub generally resembling *M. florentina*. Alternate leaves 4-10cm long may be broader than long and have three deep lobes; the lobes themselves are two- or three-lobed. Light green turning red in autumn, they have at most sparse hairs beneath; petioles 2-7cm long. White flowers 3.5cm across. Yellowish-green to red, pear-shaped fruits 2-3cm long bear persistent sepals. *Flowering:* May. *Distribution:* Native to Asia Minor and extending into Greece and Bulgaria, where it grows in evergreen scrub.

Quince *Cydonia oblonga* Up to 7.5m Small tree or shrub with large, solitary flowers and very hard, sweet-smelling fruit. Trunk short, slender, with greyish-brown bark. Young shoots spiny and woolly, becoming glabrous later. Oval leaves, 5-10cm long, alternate, entire, with grey wool below. Pink or white flowers solitary on short, hairy stalks, 4-4.5cm long, cup-shaped, the five broad, blunt or notched petals much longer than the persistent sepals. Globose or pear-shaped fruits only 2.5-3.5cm long in wild plants but reach 12cm in cultivated ones; they are downy, yellow and fragrant when ripe but with very woody flesh. *Flowering:* May. *Distribution:* Native to Asia but cultivated in much of Europe and naturalised in places, especially in the south.

Quince

Malus florentina

Malus trilobata

Quince

Quince

Loquat

Loquat *Eriobotrya japonica* Up to 10m Evergreen with a dense covering of velvety, rusty brown hairs on the twigs and undersides of the leaves. Small tree or shrub with coarse foliage. Bark grey, rough. Alternate, strongly veined leaves 10-25cm long, elliptical to oblong or widest above the middle and with toothed margins; the dark, glossy green upper side contrasts strongly with the densely hairy red-brown underside. Fragrant flowers, about 1cm long, borne in tightly branched, pyramidal clusters at the tips of shoots. Five yellowish-white, notched petals may be almost hidden by dense reddish hairs. Sweet, edible fruits 3-6cm long ripen deep yellow; they resemble small apricots with a crown of persistent sepals and contain several seeds. *Flowering:* November to April. *Distribution:* Native to China; widely cultivated in southern Europe as a fruit tree and ornamental.

Medlar *Mespilus germanica* Up to 6m Small tree or spreading shrub with unusual fruits resembling very large, brown rose-hips. Crown dense and tangled; bark grey-brown, cracked. Young twigs densely covered with white hairs, older twigs black and glabrous. Leaves alternate, dull yellowish-green and crinkled, 5-15cm long, lance-shaped to widest above the middle with distinctly sunken veins and may be entire or minutely toothed; they are felted with white hairs below. Large white flowers of 3-6cm diameter solitary, the narrow sepals longer than the five broad petals. Dull brown fruits 2-3cm in length, globose with a depression surrounded by persistent sepals; fruits persist on the tree and are very hard, only becoming edible when overripe. *Flowering:* May to June. *Distribution:* Native to moist, open woodlands of south-eastern Europe but cultivated for the fruit and widely naturalised in central and western areas.

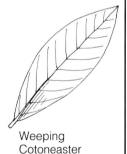

Weeping Cotoneaster

Himalayan Tree Cotoneaster *Cotoneaster frigidus* Up to 15m Semi-evergreen usually retaining both leaves and fruits well into winter. Small tree, often with several trunks and wide-arching branches. Leaves 6-12cm long, elliptical or widest above the middle, leathery, deep dull green above, with grey or white wool beneath but glabrous by late in the season. Leaves of young erect twigs alternate and spirally arranged, those of other twigs forming two ranks. Flowers about 8mm in diameter have five white, erect petals, in dense, flattened clusters 5cm across. Fruits numerous, 5mm long, globose, bright red, crowned with withered sepals and containing two seeds; fruits persist on branches well into winter. *Flowering:* June. *Distribution:* Native to the Himalayas; grows well in towns and widely cultivated as an ornamental. **Weeping Cotoneaster** (*C.* x *watereri*) is a name covering a group of commonly grown garden hybrids. They are very variable in habit, leaf-size and fruit-colour; some closely resemble Himalayan Tree Cotoneaster, but few are as tall and robust.

Loquat

Loquat

Medlar

Medlar

Himalayan Tree Cotoneaster

Himalayan Tree Cotoneaster

Crataegus calycina

Hawthorn *Crataegus monogyna* Up to 18m Very thorny tree with deeply lobed leaves, masses of white flowers and red fruits. Naturally forming a dense tree, it is often cut back to form hedges and prevented from reaching its full height. Bark pale grey to brown, cracking into small plates. Twigs with numerous thorns up to 15mm long. Alternate, shiny leaves 1.5-4.5cm long, one and a half times as long as broad, divided into three to seven lobes reaching more than halfway to the midrib; lobes entire or toothed near the tip. Flowers of 8-15mm diameter five-petalled, white to pale pink, each with a single style. Dark or bright red fruits 7-14mm long, globose to ovoid, containing a single seed. *Flowering:* May to June. *Distribution:* Native throughout Europe; very common in woods and thickets, especially on alkaline soils. Often seen as a hedging plant in northern Europe. Similar **C. calycina** has leaves with toothed lobes reaching only one third of the way to the midrib; the lowest lobe is often deeper than the others. Fruits roughly cylindrical. Native to both deciduous and evergreen woods, mainly in northern and central Europe and replacing Hawthorn in the more extreme climates.

Midland Hawthorn: flower (2 petals removed)

Midland Hawthorn *Crataegus laevigata* Up to 10m Shade-tolerant and less thorny than its relative the Hawthorn, this smaller tree grows in woods. Trunk fluted. Thorns few, 6-15mm long. Rather leathery leaves 1.5-6cm long, only three-quarters as broad as long, with three to five lobes which rarely reach halfway to the midrib; lobes toothed at the base. Flowers of 15-24mm diameter, five-petalled, white, each with two or three styles. Deep red fruits of 6-13mm, globose, containing two seeds. *Flowering:* May to June. *Distribution:* Usually found in oak woods on heavy, moist soils. Native to central Europe as far west as France and Britain. Red, double-flowered forms are common street trees.

Oriental Hawthorn

Oriental Hawthorn *Crataegus laciniata* Up to 10mThe young twigs, leaves and flower-stalks of this hawthorn are all covered with long, white hairs. Small tree, often a shrub. Bark grey-brown with a reddish colour showing through the cracks. Young twigs have white hairs, becoming glabrous and blackish. Spines few. Alternate leaves 1.5-4cm long, oval to triangular, slightly longer than broad and deeply divided into three to seven narrow, toothed lobes. Dull green above and leathery, they have long hairs on both surfaces. Flower-clusters compact, with up to 16 flowers of 1.5-2cm diameter on white-haired stalks. Petals five, white; sepals with a hooked tip; styles four to five, rarely three, spreading. Fruits 15-20mm long and broader than this, hairy when young, ripening brick red or yellowish-orange, each containing three to five seeds. *Flowering:* June. *Distribution:* Native to south-eastern Europe, Sicily and Spain, growing on mountain slopes among scrub and on woodland margins.

148

Hawthorn

Hawthorn

Midland Hawthorn

Oriental Hawthorn

Azarole

Azarole *Crataegus azarolus* Up to 8m Resembles Oriental Hawthorn but the twigs, leaves and flower-stalks are covered with dense, short hairs. Small tree or shrub. Young twigs densely hairy, becoming smooth and glabrous, and with stout spines up to 1cm long. Alternate leaves 3-5cm long, oval to triangular, deeply divided into three to five narrow lobes which are entire or have a few teeth; the base of the leaf blade often continues on to the petiole. Both surfaces have dense, short hairs. Flowers in compact clusters of 3-18, each flower 1.2-1.8cm in diameter, white, five-petalled and with one to three styles. Greenish-yellow to orange-red fruits, 20-25mm long, globose, resembling small apples; each contains one to three seeds. *Flowering:* March to April. *Distribution:* Native to Crete and western Asia but anciently cultivated in southern Europe for the edible fruits; naturalised in much of the Mediterranean region.

Cockspur Thorn *Crataegus crus-galli* Up to 10m Small tree armed with very long and sharp thorns, turning bright orange in autumn. Short trunk and low, spreading crown. Bark greyish-brown, smooth or finely cracked. Smooth, purplish twigs bear numerous sharp spines 7-10cm long. Alternate leaves 5-8cm long, much longer than broad, widest above the middle, with toothed margins and glabrous on both surfaces, turning bright orange in autumn. Flowers 1.5cm in diameter on glabrous stalks form loose clusters. Five white petals; two styles. Bright red fruits 10-12mm long, globose, persisting on the twigs throughout winter; each contains two seeds. *Flowering:* May. *Distribution:* Native to north-eastern North America, widely planted in Europe as an ornamental and street tree.

Broad-leaved
Cockspur Thorn

Hybrid Cockspur Thorn *Crataegus x lavallei* Up to 21m Sturdy, leafy tree similar to Cockspur Thorn but with fewer spines. Young twigs downy. Alternate leaves oval or widest above the middle and irregularly toothed, dark green, glossy above, downy beneath. White flowers 2cm across have very woolly stalks and sepals, five petals and one to three styles. Fruits 16-18mm long, orange-red speckled with brown, globose to pear-shaped, and persisting through the winter. *Flowering:* June. *Distribution:* Probably a hybrid with Cockspur Thorn as one of the parents, it first arose in cultivation in Paris in 1880. A handsome tree, widely planted as an ornamental. A second, similar, ornamental hybrid, **Broad-leaved Cockspur Thorn** (*C.* x *prunifolia*), has broader leaves and densely hairy flower-clusters.

Azarole

Cockspur Thorn

Cockspur Thorn

Hybrid Cockspur Thorn

Five-seeded
Hawthorn

Hungarian
Hawthorn

Five-seeded Hawthorn *Crataegus pentagyna* Up to 8m Small, graceful tree or shrub with few, stout thorns, usually dull black fruits and arching branches. Bark light brown. Young twigs have sparse, cobwebby hairs at first, becoming grey-brown and glabrous. Stout spines 1cm long. Alternate leaves 20-60mm long and as wide, oval and deeply divided into three to seven sharply toothed lobes, the lowest lobes often wide-spreading; leathery, dark olive-green and nearly glabrous above, paler with sparse cobwebby hairs beneath. Flowers numerous in loose, branched clusters, each 12-15mm in diameter with five white petals, and four to five styles. Dull black, blackish-purple or, on occasion, reddish fruits 10-15mm long, globose to ovoid, containing four to five seeds. *Flowering:* May to June. *Distribution:* A tree of scrubland and forests, native to eastern Europe, reaching to Russia and the Balkan Peninsula.

Hungarian Hawthorn *Crataegus nigra* Up to 8m Closely resembles Five-seeded Hawthorn, differing mainly in the leaves and fruits. Leaves 4-8cm long, oval to triangular and less leathery, divided into 7-11 lobes. Flowers few, in unbranched clusters. Fruit ripens shiny black with green flesh. *Flowering:* April to May. *Distribution:* Endemic to woodlands in central Europe, from Czechoslovakia and Hungary to Albania.

Juneberry *Amelanchier lamarckii* Up to 10m Attractive tree producing colourful spring and autumn foliage as well as drifts of white flowers. Small, slender tree or shrub with an open crown. Bark smooth, grey-brown. Young twigs have shaggy white hairs before becoming smooth and glabrous. Alternate leaves up to 8cm long, oval-oblong to elliptical with a round or heart-shaped base, pointed tip and finely sharp-toothed and slightly upturned margins. Young leaves coppery-red with silky hairs when unfolding in spring; autumn leaves turn shades of yellow and red. Flowers appear with the leaves in loose clusters on hairy stalks 2-3.5cm long. Five white, erect petals blunt and strap-shaped; sepals hairy on the inner surface and joined below to form a bell-shaped tube. Sweet, edible fruits about 1cm long and crowned with persistent sepals ripen purplish-black with a grape-like bloom; each contains four to ten seeds. *Flowering:* April to May. *Distribution:* Probably a natural hybrid arising in the wild in North America but long established in Europe, both as an ornamental and as a naturalised tree in Britain, Holland and Germany. Very similar **Snowy Mespil** (*A. ovalis*) is a shrub up to 5m tall, native to limestone regions of southern and central Europe.

Five-seeded Hawthorn

Hungarian Hawthorn

Juneberry

Juneberry

True Service-tree *Sorbus domestica* Up to 20m Tree with pinnately divided leaves, domed clusters of white flowers and very hard fruits resembling tiny pears. Crown domed, with spreading to horizontal branches. Bark shredding. Alternate leaves pinnately divided into six to eight pairs of oblong leaflets each 3-5.5cm long, the blade symmetrical at the base, toothed towards the tip with soft hairs beneath, mainly on the veins. Flowers in domed, branched clusters, each flower 16-18mm in diameter, with five white or creamy petals and five styles. Pear-shaped fruits 20mm or more in length, green or brownish, very astringent until frosted, after which they are edible. *Flowering:* May. *Distribution:* Mainly found in dry, deciduous woods. Native to southern Europe and the Mediterranean region; often planted in other parts of Europe as an ornamental or fruit tree and sometimes naturalised.

Japanese Rowan (a) and Sargent's Rowan (b)

Rowan *Sorbus aucuparia* 5-20m Tree with pinnate leaves, clusters of white flowers and bright scarlet fruits. Somewhat bushy with rounded, open crown and spreading branches. Bark smooth. Alternate leaves pinnately divided into five to ten pairs of oblong leaflets, each 3-6cm long, leaflet blades toothed in the upper part, asymmetric at the base with grey hairs below. Flowers 8-10mm in diameter, with five white petals and three to four styles. Globose or oval fruits 6-9mm long, scarlet. *Flowering:* May. *Distribution:* In woods or open places on all but waterlogged soils; common on mountains. Native to most of Europe and frequently planted as a street tree. Two similar Asian species with colourful autumn foliage are planted as ornamentals and street trees. **Japanese Rowan** (*S. commixta*), from Japan, has six to seven pairs of glossy leaflets and reddish-orange fruits. **Sargent's Rowan** (*S. sargentiana*), from China, has four to five pairs of leaflets and red fruits 6mm long.

Vilmorin's Rowan

Hupeh Rowan *Sorbus hupehensis* Up to 14m Closely resembles Rowan, differing in the leaves and fruits. Slightly drooping leaves pinnately divided into five to six pairs of oblong, bluish-green leaflets each 3.7-7.5cm long and sharply toothed towards their tips. Leaf-axis reddish and grooved. Leaves turn red in autumn. Globose fruits about 6mm long, white or pale pink, persisting on the twigs into winter. *Flowering:* May. *Distribution:* Native to western China, planted as an ornamental in parks and gardens. **Vilmorin's Rowan** (*S. vilmorinii*) also has dark pink fruits which fade as they ripen. It has 9-12 pairs of small, narrow leaflets. Ornamental, native to China.

True Service-tree

True Service-tree

Rowan

Hupeh Rowan

Sorbus meinichii

Sorbus mougeotii

Sorbus umbellata

Broad-leaved
Whitebeam

Bastard Service-tree *Sorbus hybrida* Up to 14m Tree with leaf-blades divided into several leaflets at the base and a lobed upper portion. Crown dense and ovoid. Alternate leaves 7.5-10.5cm long, oval and pinnately divided into two, rarely four, pairs of completely separate leaflets at the base, each leaflet toothed towards the tip; remainder of leaf lobed, with deepest lobes reaching to the midrib. Leaves leathery, grey-green above with dense grey or white wool beneath. White, five-petalled flowers of about 1cm diameter form branched clusters. Globose fruits 10-12mm long, red, speckled with a few small lenticels. *Flowering:* May. *Distribution:* Native to south-western Scandinavia, sometimes planted as an ornamental. Similar **S. meinichii** is a rare species from Norway which has four to five pairs of leaflets below the lobed portion of the leaf.

Swedish Whitebeam *Sorbus intermedia* Up to 15m Rounded tree with a short trunk and domed crown. Young twigs densely hairy, glabrous later. Alternate leaves 6-12cm long have elliptical lobes, those near the base of the blade cut one third of the way to the midrib, those towards the tip progressively shallower, eventually reduced to coarse teeth; glossy green above, felted with yellowish-grey hairs beneath; there are seven to nine pairs of veins. Flowers 12-20mm in diameter, white, five-petalled, in flattened, branched clusters. Oblong to ovoid fruits 12-15mm long, scarlet, speckled with a few lenticels. *Flowering:* May. *Distribution:* Native to Scandinavia and the regions around the Baltic; tolerant of air pollution, it is commonly used as a street tree. Two mountain trees are similar: **Austrian Whitebeam** (*S. austriaca*), endemic to the eastern Alps, Carpathians and mountains of the Balkan Peninsula, has leaves densely covered beneath with dull white hairs and fruits speckled with many large lenticels.
S. mougeotii, endemic to the western Alps and Pyrenees, has leaves lobed only a quarter of the way to the midrib and fruits with few small lenticels.

Sorbus umbellata Up to 7m Small tree, sometimes a shrub, very variable in size, shape and lobing of the leaves. Alternate leaves 4-7cm long, sometimes larger, usually broad, widest above the middle to almost round with shallow lobes reducing to coarse teeth towards the tip, green and glabrous above, thickly felted with woolly white hairs beneath. Flowers of 1.5cm diameter white, five-petalled, in loose clusters. Globose fruits 1.5cm long, yellowish. *Flowering:* May to June. *Distribution:* Native to south-eastern Europe.

Broad-leaved Whitebeam *Sorbus latifolia* Up to 18m Rounded tree. Young twigs hairy, becoming shiny red-brown and glabrous. Alternate, rather leathery leaves 5-10cm long, broadly elliptical with shallow, triangular lobes and sharply, sometimes doubly, toothed margins, upper surface gradually becoming glabrous, lower surface retaining densely grey-haired veins in seven to nine pairs. Flowers of 2cm diameter, white, five-petalled, on woolly stalks forming branched clusters. Globose fruits 12-15mm long, yellowish-brown, speckled with numerous large lenticels. *Flowering:* May. *Distribution:* Widespread woodland tree occurring from Portugal and Spain east to Germany and Sweden.

Bastard Service-tree

Swedish Whitebeam

Sorbus umbellata

Broad-leaved Whitebeam

Wild Service-tree *Sorbus torminalis* Up to 25m Deeply lobed leaves and brown fruits distinguish this from other species of *Sorbus*. Domed tree, sometimes only a large, spreading shrub. Bark scaly, twigs shiny brown. Alternate leaves 5-10cm long, oval with three to five pairs of toothed, pointed lobes, the lowest pair deeper and more wide-spreading than the others; dark green above, hairy beneath when young but almost glabrous when mature. Flowers 10-15mm in diameter, white, five-petalled, each with two styles, borne on woolly stalks in branched clusters. Brown fruits 12-18mm long, widest above the middle, fleshy and dotted with numerous lenticels. *Flowering:* May to June. *Distribution:* Scattered but widespread in deciduous woods, usually on clay soils. Native to all but the far north of Europe.

Whitebeam

Whitebeam *Sorbus aria* Up to 25m Pallid tree standing out from its surroundings, especially in spring when the white undersides of the leaves are most noticeable. Trunks often several. Alternate leaves 5-12cm long, oval with irregular teeth curving towards the rounded tip; bright green above, white felted beneath; veins in 10-14 pairs. Flowers 10-15mm in diameter, white, five-petalled, in branched clusters. Ovoid fruits 8-15mm long, scarlet with many small lenticels. *Flowering:* May to June. *Distribution:* Native to woods and rocky places in most of Europe, mainly on limestone; it is confined to mountains in the south. One form with yellow-flecked fruits and another with silvery leaves are common street trees.

Rock Whitebeam

Greek Whitebeam *Sorbus graeca* 4-5m Generally similar to Whitebeam but a small tree or only a shrub. Alternate, rather leathery leaves 5-9cm long, broad, widest above the middle to almost circular, doubly toothed with sharp, even and spreading teeth, underside thickly felted with greenish-white wool; veins in 9-11 pairs. Flowers and fruits like those of Whitebeam but fruits generally less than 12mm long. *Flowering:* May to June. *Distribution:* Mainly found in eastern Europe, extending to Italy, Sicily and the eastern Mediterranean. Very similar **Rock Whitebeam** (*S. rupicola*), from Britain and Scandinavia, has leaves 8-14.5cm long with forward-pointing teeth and fruits 12-15mm long with numerous lenticels.

Wild Service-tree

Wild Service-tree

Wild Service-tree

Whitebeam

Whitebeam

Greek Whitebeam

Peach *Prunus persica* Up to 6m In autumn, large, globular, red-flushed fruits distinguish this bushy, straight-branched tree from the similar Almond. Alternate, lance-shaped, finely toothed leaves 5-15cm long, folded lengthways into a V-shape. Flowers usually solitary, appearing as the leaf-buds open; flower-tube as broad as it is long; five petals 10-20mm long, deep pink, occasionally pale pink or white. Sweet, juicy fruit 4-8cm long, globular, yellow flushed with red, and downy. *Flowering:* March to May. *Distribution:* Origin obscure, but possibly native to China; cultivated in Europe in orchards and gardens, often trained as an espalier. The **Nectarine** (cv. 'Nucipersica') is a smooth-fruited cultivar.

Almond *Prunus dulcis* Up to 8m One of the first to flower in spring, this open-crowned tree or shrub has profuse pink or white blossom. Ascending branches spiny and very twiggy in wild trees, unarmed and straight in cultivated trees. Alternate leaves 4-13cm long, finely toothed, folded lengthways to form a shallow V-shape. Flowers mostly in pairs appear before the leaves; they have a short, bell-shaped tube and five spreading, pale pink or rarely white petals 15-25mm long. Pink flowers fade to white with age. Oblong-oval, flattened grey-green fruit 3.5-6cm long, velvety with thin flesh. Large pitted stone is the familiar almond nut. *Flowering:* March to April. *Distribution:* Probably native to Asia; cultivated for the seeds (almonds) throughout southern Europe and as an ornamental in the north. **P. webbii** resembles wild Almond but has smaller parts: leaves 3.5-9cm long, pink petals 10mm, fruits 20-25mm and not flattened, the stones hardly pitted. It occurs in southern parts of Italy and the Balkan Peninsula, and in Crete.

Prunus webbii

Apricot *Prunus armeniaca* 3-10m Small, rounded tree with reddish-brown twigs and young leaves. Branches twisted, twigs smooth. Alternate, nearly circular, finely toothed leaves 5-10cm long have abruptly pointed tips and straight or heart-shaped bases; mature leaves dull green above and greenish-yellow beneath; red petiole usually has two glands near the top. Flowers short-stalked, solitary or paired, appear before the leaves. Hairy flower-tube bell-shaped; five petals 10-15mm long, white or pale-pink. Initially tart, sweet ripe fruit 4-8cm long is round, yellow to orange, and downy. *Flowering:* March to April. *Distribution:* Native to central Asia and China; widely grown as a fruit tree, mainly in southern Europe.

Apricot

Cherry Plum *Prunus cerasifera* Up to 8m Spreading easily by means of suckers, this small round-headed tree or shrub readily forms thickets or hedges. Slender, sometimes spiny; branches numerous. Young twigs green, smooth and glossy. Alternate, oblong to oval leaves 4-7cm long taper at both ends and have small, rounded teeth; smooth and glossy above, downy on veins beneath. Solitary flowers appear before the leaves. Five petals 8-10mm long, white or pale pink. Smooth, globose fruit 3.5cm long, yellow or red. *Flowering:* March. *Distribution:* Native to thickets in the Balkan Peninsula; widely planted and naturalised elsewhere. A red-leaved form (var. *pissardii*) is common as a street tree. **Briançon Apricot** (*P. brigantina*) is an alpine tree closely resembling Cherry Plum but with boldly and irregularly sharp-toothed leaves and flowers in clusters of two to five; it is endemic to dry slopes in the French and Italian Alps.

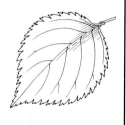

Briançon Apricot

Peach

Peach

Almond

Apricot

Cherry Plum

Cherry Plum

Blackthorn *Prunus spinosa* Up to 6m Black and thorny, the branches of this small tree or shrub are dense and wide-spreading. Trunks produce numerous suckers. Intricately branched, thorny twigs are downy when young, becoming glabrous and smooth with age. Alternate, toothed leaves 2-4.5cm long, widest above or below the middle, dull and glabrous above, but hairy on the veins beneath. Numerous flowers solitary, appearing well before the leaves. Five white petals 5-8mm long. Very astringent fruit 1-1.5cm long, short-stalked and bluish-black with a greyish, waxy bloom. *Flowering:* March to April. *Distribution:* Native everywhere except in the extreme north of Europe. It grows in hedges and thickets, often forming these itself by means of suckers.

Bullace

Plum *Prunus domestica* Up to 10m Thorny in the wild, this white-flowered tree is usually unarmed in cultivation. Branches straight, twigs dull and more or less glabrous. Alternate leaves 3-8cm long are toothed, dull green and glabrous above, downy beneath. Flowers short-stalked, in clusters of two to three appearing with the leaves. Five petals 7-12mm, greenish-white. Pendulous fruits 2-7.5cm long and not as wide, blue-black, red or purple, may be sweet or acid-tasting. *Flowering:* March to May. *Distribution:* Of hybrid origin (probably between Blackthorn and Cherry Plum), plums are cultivated for fruit throughout Europe and widely naturalised, often in hedgerows and almost always close to houses. This species includes several different kinds of fruit tree besides Plums. The wild **Bullace** and cultivated **Damson** and **Greengage** (all subsp. *institia*) have densely hairy and often spiny twigs, pure white petals and yellow, red or purple fruits.

Saint Lucie Cherry

Saint Lucie Cherry *Prunus mahaleb* Up to 10m A cherry with clusters of small, very fragrant flowers, followed by bitter black fruits. Small, rather spreading tree, often only a shrub, with grey-brown bark. Alternate broadly oval to rounded leaves 4-7cm long, cut straight across, rounded or weakly heart-shaped at the base, abruptly pointed at the tip, margins have small, rounded teeth. Upper surface dark and glossy, lower more bluish, with downy hairs on the midrib. Short clusters of fragrant white flowers tip short, leafy shoots. Flower-tube bell-shaped, petals 5-8mm long. Fruits 6-10mm long, glossy black when ripe, with thin, bitter flesh. *Flowering:* April to May. *Distribution:* Widespread, mainly in open woods and thickets on dry slopes. Native to hilly parts of central and southern Europe, naturalised in the north, often grown for ornament.

Blackthorn

Blackthorn

Plum

Saint Lucie Cherry

Yoshino Cherry

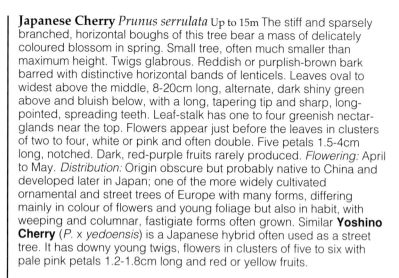

Japanese Cherry *Prunus serrulata* Up to 15m The stiff and sparsely branched, horizontal boughs of this tree bear a mass of delicately coloured blossom in spring. Small tree, often much smaller than maximum height. Twigs glabrous. Reddish or purplish-brown bark barred with distinctive horizontal bands of lenticels. Leaves oval to widest above the middle, 8-20cm long, alternate, dark shiny green above and bluish below, with a long, tapering tip and sharp, long-pointed, spreading teeth. Leaf-stalk has one to four greenish nectar-glands near the top. Flowers appear just before the leaves in clusters of two to four, white or pink and often double. Five petals 1.5-4cm long, notched. Dark, red-purple fruits rarely produced. *Flowering:* April to May. *Distribution:* Origin obscure but probably native to China and developed later in Japan; one of the more widely cultivated ornamental and street trees of Europe with many forms, differing mainly in colour of flowers and young foliage but also in habit, with weeping and columnar, fastigiate forms often grown. Similar **Yoshino Cherry** (*P.* x *yedoensis*) is a Japanese hybrid often used as a street tree. It has downy young twigs, flowers in clusters of five to six with pale pink petals 1.2-1.8cm long and red or yellow fruits.

Sargent's Cherry *Prunus sargentii* Up to 25m Generally similar to Japanese Cherry and, like that species, often not attaining its full height in cultivation. Leaves 9-15cm long, more oblong than in Japanese Cherry; dark red, grooved petiole has two reddish nectar-glands near the top. Rose-pink petals, only 15-20mm long, lack the notched tip of Japanese Cherry. Fruits 7-11mm long, ovoid and blackish-crimson, not often produced in cultivation. *Flowering:* April. *Distribution:* Native to the island of Sakhalin and to mountains in Japan, widely grown in Europe as an ornamental in streets, parks and gardens.

Tibetan Cherry *Prunus serrula* Up to 20m Most like Spring Cherry but flowers later. Bark one of the most attractive of all cherries, purplish-black but peeling away in bands to leave a highly glossed, reddish mahogany colour beneath. Leaves more narrowly oval than in Spring Cherry, with petioles only 6-7mm long. White flowers appear with the leaves, on stalks about 4cm long. Fruits 4-12mm long, ripening bright red. *Flowering:* April to May. *Distribution:* Native to western China, widespread as a park and garden tree, mainly grown for its striking bark.

Tibetan Cherry

Japanese Cherry

Japanese Cherry

Sargent's Cherry

Tibetan Cherry

Spring Cherry

Wild Cherry

Spring Cherry *Prunus subhirtella* Up to 20m Principally a spring-flowering tree, this species also includes autumn-flowering forms. Dense and bushy-crowned, seldom attaining its full height in cultivation. Twigs slender, crimson and downy. Alternate leaves about 6cm long, oval to narrowly oblong, drawn out to a long-pointed tip, sharply and irregularly toothed, downy on the veins below and on the crimson petiole. Short-stalked flowers appear before leaves, in clusters of two to five. Flower-tube urn-shaped, petals 8-12mm long, pale to rose-pink and notched. Globose to ellipsoid fruit 7-9mm long ripens purplish-black. *Flowering:* March to April. *Distribution:* Native to Japan but widespread throughout Europe as an ornamental tree in streets and gardens. Trees which flower from October to April are distinguished as **Autumn Cherry** (cv. 'Autumnalis').

Wild Cherry *Prunus avium* Up to 30m Larger than most other cherries, Wild Cherry has a well-developed trunk with shiny, red-brown bark peeling in horizontal bands. Oval to oblong leaves 8-15cm long, alternate, abruptly pointed with blunt, forward-pointing teeth. Undersides have prominent veins with tufts of hairs in the angles. Petioles have two prominent nectar-glands near the top. Flowers of 2-3cm diameter appear just before leaves in clusters of two to six. Five white petals 1-1.5cm long. Sweet or bitter fruits 9-12mm long are usually dark red but sometimes yellowish, bright red or black and hang on long stalks. *Flowering:* April to May. *Distribution:* Common in mixed and deciduous woods, especially in hilly regions. Native almost throughout Europe and widely cultivated for the fruit.

Sour Cherry *Prunus cerasus* Up to 8m Round-headed tree or large shrub, similar to Wild Cherry, but smaller and with a poorly defined, short or branched trunk. Suckers often produced. Slightly leathery leaves 3-8cm long, alternate, abruptly pointed at the tip; margins have small, rounded teeth; dark, glossy green above; paler, prominently veined underside downy when young, becoming glabrous. Petiole may have several greenish nectar-glands. Five-petalled flowers appear just before leaves in clusters of two to six. Long-stalked, acid-tasting fruits 1.8cm long and bright red. *Flowering:* April to May. *Distribution:* Native to south-western Asia; introduced to Europe for the edible fruit, widely planted and naturalised in many places.

Spring Cherry

Spring Cherry

Wild Cherry

Wild Cherry

Sour Cherry

Sour Cherry

Bird Cherry *Prunus padus* Up to 17m The bark of this small tree is smooth, grey-brown and has a strong, unpleasant smell. Branches ascending. Slightly leathery, oblong to elliptical leaves 6-10cm long, alternate, dark green above, paler or bluish below, with a tapering point and sharply fine-toothed margins. Petiole has two or more greenish nectar-glands. Flowers appear after leaves in elongated spikes of 7-15cm containing 15-35 white, almond-scented flowers with five petals 6-9mm long. Tart, astringent fruits 6-8mm long and shiny black. *Flowering:* May. *Distribution:* Grows in woods, thickets and hedgerows in damp soils and by streams in limestone areas. Native to most of Europe except the Mediterranean, it replaces Wild Cherry in the far north; sometimes planted for ornament.

Rum Cherry *Prunus serotina* Up to 30m Spreading tree with a stout trunk covered with smooth, peeling grey bark which is bitter and distinctly aromatic. Alternate leaves 5-14cm long, inverted-oval to oblong or elliptical with a short, tapering point; fine teeth on the margins flattened and forward-pointing. Upper surface dark and shiny, lower paler and slightly downy. Flowers and fruits similar to those of Bird Cherry but petals only 3-5mm long and minutely toothed on the margins; calyx persistent in fruit. *Flowering:* May to June. *Distribution:* Native to eastern North America, planted for timber in central Europe, grown elsewhere as an ornamental and sometimes naturalised. Native to the same area, **Choke Cherry** (*P. virginiana*) is very similar but usually only a shrub reaching 5m, without aromatic bark. Dull leaves have conspicuous veins and spreading teeth and the calyx is deciduous. Planted and naturalised in central and western Europe.

Choke Cherry

Cherry Laurel *Prunus laurocerasus* Up to 8m Small, spreading evergreen which has glossy, stiff and leathery leaves smelling of almonds when crushed. Young shoots green. Alternate, oblong to lance-shaped leaves 10-20cm long, leathery, dark and glossy green above, yellowish-green below with rolled-under, entire or minutely toothed margins; petioles green. Flowers fragrant, in upright spikes equal in length to the leaves. Five petals, white, about 4mm long. Globose red fruits 2cm long ripen shiny black. *Flowering:* April. *Distribution:* Native to the Balkan Peninsula but grown for ornament in much of Europe and commonly naturalised in open woods.

Cherry Laurel

Portugal Laurel *Prunus lusitanica* Up to 8m, rarely to 20m Generally similar to Cherry Laurel although it can exceptionally reach 20m in height. Unscented leaves more elliptical than in Cherry Laurel, always toothed, softer, very dark green above. Both young shoots and petioles red. Flower spikes contain up to 100 flowers and are considerably longer than the leaves. Fruit can be ovoid or globose, ripening purplish-black. *Flowering:* June. *Distribution:* Native to the Azores and Iberian Peninsula, west to southern France. Frequently planted in mild parts of western Europe, mainly for hedges, and often naturalised.

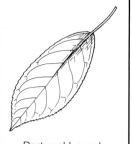

Portugal Laurel

Bird Cherry

Bird Cherry

Rum Cherry: flowers in bud

Cherry Laurel

Cherry Laurel

Portugal Laurel

Swamp Wattle: leaf

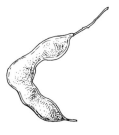

Blackwood: fruit

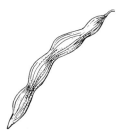

Sydney Golden
Wattle: fruit

Golden Wreath *Acacia saligna* Up to 10m Drooping evergreen with blue-green foliage and flowers in numerous bright yellow pom-poms. Small tree or shrub with suckering stems, weeping bluish-green twigs and smooth grey bark. Pendulous, alternate leaves variable in size and shape, but usually 10-20cm long and straight or sickle-shaped; dull or shiny and blue-green, with a single vein. Flowers tiny but grouped into pendulous clusters of one to eight showy, bright yellow, spherical heads 1-1.5cm in diameter. Straight, narrow and flattened pods 6-12cm long and 4-8mm wide pinched between each white-stalked seed. *Flowering:* March to May. *Distribution:* Native to western Australia, widely planted in southern Europe and one of several *Acacia* species grown in Europe as sand-stabilisers. Two similar, widely planted species are also sometimes naturalised in southern Europe. Both have upwardly curved branches. **Golden Wattle** (*A. pycnantha*) has bright green leaves and fragrant flower-heads in clusters of 20-30. **Swamp Wattle** (*A. retinodes*) has leaves less than 2cm wide and scarlet seed-stalks.

Blackwood *Acacia melanoxylon* Up to 15m, occasionally to 40m Erect, robust evergreen with a straight, rough-barked trunk. Bark brown, furrowed. Dull, dark green alternate leaves 6-13cm long, lance-shaped but blunt and slightly curved, with three to five prominent veins. Occasionally feathery, pinnately divided leaves may also appear, especially on young trees. Flowers very small but massed into creamy-white, spherical heads each 10mm in diameter and borne in axillary clusters. Red-brown pods 70-120mm long and 8-10mm wide, flattened and twisted; seeds have conspicuous scarlet stalks. *Flowering:* July to October. *Distribution:* Native to south-eastern Australia and Tasmania, planted for timber and naturalised in south-western Europe.

Sydney Golden Wattle *Acacia longifolia* Up to 10m Bushy, spreading evergreen with shiny foliage and erect spikes of bright yellow flowers. Slender tree or tall shrub with broad, bushy crown of stiff, glabrous twigs. Bark smooth, grey. Alternate leaves 7-15cm long, narrowly oblong, bright shiny green with prominent, parallel veins. Flowers very small, bright yellow and strong-smelling, grouped in erect, cylindrical spikes up to 5cm long. Narrow, cylindrical pod of 7-15cm long may be straight or twisted and curled; it is pinched between each white-stalked seed. *Flowering:* April to May. *Distribution:* Coastal tree native to Australia (New South Wales), grown in much of south-western Europe as a dune-stabiliser and ornamental.

Golden Wreath

Golden Wreath

Blackwood

Blackwood

Sydney Golden Wattle

Sydney Golden Wattle

Green Wattle:
stipules

Black Wattle:
leaf with glands

Plume Albizia:
flower spike

Silver Wattle *Acacia dealbata* Up to 30m Evergreen tree with feathery, silvery foliage and producing masses of yellow flower-heads. Bark smooth, grey-green when young but eventually black. Alternate leaves twice-pinnately divided, first into 8-20 pairs of pinnae, with each pinna divided into 30-50 pairs of leaflets each 5mm long; there are raised glands on the leaf-axis at the points where the pinnae branch off. Leaves densely covered with silvery hairs when young, becoming more bluish-green with age. Tiny flowers numerous, pale yellow, in spherical heads each 5-6mm in diameter and borne in branched clusters of 20-30. Flattened pods 4-10cm long and 10-12mm wide, brown and only slightly pinched between the seeds. *Flowering:* January to March. *Distribution:* Native to south-eastern Australia and Tasmania, but planted in southern Europe mainly for timber and ornament; widely naturalised, especially in the understorey of woods. It is the 'mimosa' of florists. Two similar, but deciduous species grown in south-western Europe are smaller and more shrubby, with bright green leaves and spiny stipules on older branches. **Green Wattle** (*A. farnesiana*) from the Dominican Republic has narrow leaflets 3-5mm long and flower-heads in clusters of two to three; it is grown for ornament and perfume. ***A. karoo***, from South Africa, has broader leaflets 6-10mm long and flower-heads in clusters of four to six. It is grown for hedges and is sometimes naturalised.

Black Wattle *Acacia mearnsii* Up to 15m Tree closely resembling Silver Wattle but distinguished by differences in leaves and fruits. Leaves divided into 8-14 pairs of pinnae, each with 25-40 pairs of leaflets only 2mm long. Leaf-axis has glands between the points where the pinnae branch off. Pod narrower than that of Silver Wattle and distinctly pinched between the seeds. *Flowering:* January to March. *Distribution:* Native to south-eastern Australia and Tasmania, planted for ornament and for use in tanning in Portugal and Spain, Italy and Corsica; sometimes naturalised.

Pink Siris *Albizia julibrissin* Up to 14m Evergreen with dense, feathery foliage and attractive brush-like pink flowers forming fan-shaped heads. Small tree with spreading branches and dense, rounded to flat-topped crown. Alternate leaves twice-pinnately divided, usually into 5-12 pairs of pinnae, each divided into 35-50 pairs of leaflets; leaflets 1-1.5cm long, oval, curved, green above, paler and hairy beneath. Flowers 7-9mm long, pink and grouped into fan-shaped heads; corolla narrowly tubular, five-lobed with projecting pink stamens 3-4cm long giving heads a brush-like appearance. Pod 5-15cm long, flattened, with a long, tapering tip and pinched between each seed. *Flowering:* July to August. *Distribution:* Woodland tree native to Asia, widely planted as a street and shade tree and for ornament in southern Europe. Similar **Plume Albizia** (*A. lophantha*) from south-western Australia is also grown in the Mediterranean region. It has smaller, yellow flowers in cylindrical spikes.

Silver Wattle

Silver Wattle

Black Wattle

Pink Siris

Clammy Locust :
fruit

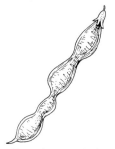

Pagoda-tree: fruit

Siberian Pea-tree:
fruit

False Acacia *Robinia pseudacacia* Up to 25m Open-crowned tree with spirally ridged bark and yellowish-green, pinnate leaves. Trunk short, often several. Branches brittle, twisted. Young twigs dark red-brown. Alternate leaves 15-20cm long, pinnate with three to ten pairs of oval to elliptical yellowish-green leaflets; petiole has two woody, spiny stipules at the base, and each leaflet also has a tiny stipule at the base of its petiole. White, fragrant, pea-like flowers form dense, hanging clusters 10-20cm long. Calyx tubular, two-lipped; petals unequal, the upper erect, the side pair overlapping the fused, boat-shaped lower pair. Smooth pods 5-10cm long persist on the tree for some time. *Flowering:* June. *Distribution:* Native to open woods of North America, widely planted as a street tree, naturalised in parts of southern Europe. Similar **Clammy Locust** (*R. viscosa*) from North America has pink flowers and sticky, hairy pods. It is planted as an ornamental in central and southern Europe.

Pagoda-tree *Sophora japonica* Up to 25m Pinnately leaved tree only producing flowers in old age. Bark furrowed. Crown open with twisted branches. Young twigs hairy, bluish-green, becoming glabrous and green. Alternate leaves 15-25cm long, pinnate with three to eight pairs of oval, pointed leaflets, dark shiny green above, bluish or hairy beneath. Pea-like flowers 10-15mm long, white or pale pink in large clusters of 15-25cm across at the tips of twigs, with five unequal petals, the upper erect, the side pair overlapping the fused, boat-shaped lower pair; calyx tubular, slightly two-lipped. Pod 5-8cm long, greenish, distinctly pinched between each seed. *Flowering:* August to September. *Distribution:* Native to eastern Asia, planted for ornament in Europe and sometimes naturalised.

Siberian Pea-tree *Caragana arborescens* Up to 7m Small tree, often a shrub. Alternate leaves pinnate with four to six pairs of leaflets, each 10-35mm long, elliptical to oblong or widest above the middle; there is usually no terminal leaflet, the leaf-axis ending in a very slender spine-like tip. Pea-like flowers 15-22mm long, yellow, in small clusters of two to five. Five petals unequal, the upper erect, the side pair overlapping the fused, boat-shaped lower pair; calyx a bell-shaped tube with five triangular teeth. Pod 3-6cm long but only 2-5mm wide, splitting to release numerous seeds. *Flowering:* May. *Distribution:* Native to northern Asia, often grown as an ornamental and naturalised in parts of France.

False Acacia

False Acacia

Pagoda-tree

Siberian Pea-tree

Carob: ♀ flowers

Honey Locust:
flowers

Carob *Ceratonia siliqua* Up to 10m Low evergreen tree with a domed, bushy, thickly branched crown. Alternate leaves pinnate with two to five pairs of leathery leaflets but no terminal leaflet. Each leaflet 3-5cm long, oval to almost circular, notched at the tip, dark, shiny green above and pale beneath, often with wavy margins. Tiny flowers grouped in short, green, unisexual spikes with males and females borne on the same or different trees. They lack petals and the five sepals soon fall, leaving only a central disc bearing either stamens or a style. Ripe pods 10-20cm long, violet-brown with seeds embedded in a white pulp. *Flowering:* August to October. *Distribution:* Native and common in the drier parts of the Mediterranean where it is also grown for fodder.

Honey Locust *Gleditsia triacanthos* Up to 45m Tall tree armed with numerous large, sharp spines, those on the trunk and main branches in large groups, those on the smaller twigs characteristically in threes. Bark brown with vertical cracks. Alternate leaves either pinnate with 7-18 pairs of leaflets each 20-30mm long, or twice-pinnate, each pinna with 8-14 pairs of leaflets only 8-20mm long; there is no terminal leaflet, the leaf-axis ending in a spine. Flowers, 3mm long, may be male, female or hermaphrodite, forming dense axillary clusters; the three to five oval petals are greenish-white. Pods 30-45cm long, flattened and curved, often also twisted, contain numerous seeds. *Flowering:* June. *Distribution:* Native to central North America around the Mississippi River, widely cultivated in southern and central Europe and naturalised in some areas.

Judas-tree *Cercis siliquastrum* Up to 10m Attractive tree with pink-purple pea-like flowers borne directly on the trunk and main branches as well as on the twigs. Slender and spreading, often with several trunks. Crown thin and irregular. Alternate leaves 7-12cm long, almost circular, heart-shaped at the base, bluish-green when young, turning dark or sometimes yellowish-green above. Pink flowers 15-20mm long have five unequal petals, the upper erect, the side pair overlapping the fused, boat-shaped lower pair; they appear with or before the leaves. Pods 6-10cm long ripen purplish-brown. *Flowering:* May. *Distribution:* A tree of dry, rocky areas, native to the Mediterranean, but often grown as an ornamental elsewhere. It grows well on dry, chalky soils in northern Europe, but is susceptible to the cold.

Carob: ♂ flowers

Carob

Honey Locust

Honey Locust

Judas-tree

Judas-tree

Voss's Laburnum:
flower

Laburnum *Laburnum anagyroides* Up to 7m Free-flowering tree
decked with numerous pendulous yellow flower-clusters in summer.
Small and slender with ascending or arching branches. Both twigs
and leaves grey-green with silky, close-pressed hairs. Alternate leaves
trifoliate, the elliptical leaflets each 3-8cm long. Pea-like flowers, each
about 2cm long, yellow and fragrant, forming pendulous clusters
10-30cm long. Five petals unequal, the upper erect, the side pair
overlapping the fused, boat-shaped lower pair. Pods 4-6cm long,
smooth and dark brown when ripe; they persist on the tree after
splitting, exposing the paler inner surfaces and poisonous black
seeds. *Flowering:* May to June. *Distribution:* Short-lived tree of upland
woods and thickets, native to southern and central Europe and one of
the most widely planted ornamental trees, often naturalised. **Voss's
Laburnum** (*L.* x *watereri*) is a hybrid between Laburnum and Scotch
Laburnum with the early flowering time of the first and the long flower-
clusters of the second. It is the most commonly planted laburnum in
some areas.

Scotch Laburnum *Laburnum alpinum* Up to 5m, sometimes more Small
tree, frequently only a shrub, very similar to Laburnum and most easily
distinguished by the glabrous and green twigs and leaves. Trifoliate
leaves 3-8cm long, glossy on both surfaces and light green beneath.
Flower-clusters 15-40cm long, dense-flowered and pendulous; flowers
about 1.5cm long. Pod glabrous with a wing 1-2mm wide where the
two halves join on the upper side. Seeds brown. *Flowering:* June.
Distribution: Mountain tree native to southern parts of central and
eastern Europe, also planted along roadsides.

Mount Etna Broom:
leafy twig

Mount Etna Broom *Genista aetnensis* Up to 5m Small tree, often a
low shrub, with opposite, somewhat weeping, branches and twigs.
Small, opposite leaves fleeting and rapidly shed, their function taken
over by the green twigs. Profuse flowers yellow, about 12mm long,
with five unequal petals, the upper erect, the lateral pair overlapping
the fused, boat-shaped lower pair; calyx tubular with blunt upper teeth
about 1mm long and minute lower teeth. Pod ovoid, flattened,
containing one or two seeds. *Flowering:* June. *Distribution:* Endemic to
dry hills in Sardinia and Sicily, sometimes planted as an ornamental
and then reaching heights up to 10m.

Amur Cork-tree

Hop-tree *Ptelea trifoliata* Up to 8m Trifoliate leaves resemble those
of Laburnum but smell unpleasant when crushed, as do the bark and
young fruits. Small tree or shrub with brown bark and rounded crown.
Twigs dark brown, shiny. Alternate leaves trifoliate, each leaflet
6-12cm long, oval to elliptical, sometimes minutely toothed, glabrous
and shiny. Flowers unisexual or hermaphrodite, borne in clusters at
the tips of twigs. Four or five greenish-white petals narrowly oval and
hairy on the inner surface. Small, single-seeded nut-like fruit
surrounded by a broad, disc-like papery wing 15-25mm in diameter,
notched at the tip. *Flowering:* June to July. *Distribution:* Native to
eastern North America, planted in parks and elsewhere for ornament,
sometimes naturalised in central Europe. The Chinese **Amur Cork-
tree** (*Phellodendron amurense*), also grown in parks and gardens, is
somewhat similar but has leaves with 5-11 leaflets and black, berry-
like fruits.

Laburnum

Laburnum

Scotch Laburnum

Mount Etna Broom

Hop-tree

Hop-tree

Sweet Orange

Sweet Orange *Citrus sinensis* Up to 10m Very glossy-leaved evergreen often bearing both flowers and fruits simultaneously. Small, rounded and often bushy tree. Young twigs angled, sometimes with thin, blunt spines. Alternate leaves 7.5-10cm long, oval to elliptical, dark glossy green above, firm, leathery and dotted with shiny oil glands; petiole short with a prominent narrow wing. Large, white, fragrant flowers solitary or in loose clusters in the leaf-axils; the numerous stamens are erect. Fruit is the well-known orange, about 7.5cm in diameter, thick-skinned and with sweet, juicy flesh. *Flowering:* Mainly May, but can flower at almost any time of year depending on the variety. *Distribution:* Native to eastern Asia, but grown in orchards and gardens all around the Mediterranean. There are many similar species, differing mainly in their fruits, including the sour **Seville Orange** (*C. aurantium*); **Tangerine** (*C. reticulata*) which has thin, loose rind; **Bergamot Orange** (*C. bergamia*) with yellow, pear-shaped fruits which yield bergamot oil; and less well-known local species.

Grapefruit

Grapefruit *Citrus paradisi* Up to 8m Small, spiny evergreen, similar to Sweet Orange but with large, pale yellow fruits. Leathery leaves 10-15cm long, broadly elliptical or widest above the middle with a rounded or heart-shaped base; petiole has a broad wing up to 15mm wide at the top, tapering towards the base. Flowers solitary or in clusters in leaf-axils or at tips of twigs. Fruit 10-15cm in diameter, more or less globular or slightly flattened, pale yellow when ripe with a thick rind and slightly tart, juicy flesh. *Flowering:* Mainly March. *Distribution:* Native to China, cultivated in Mediterranean regions. The similar **Pomelo** (*C. grandis*) is a larger, less spiny tree with hairy twigs and leaf-midribs and more narrowly winged petioles; fruits even larger than those of Grapefruit, up to 25cm in diameter.

Lemon

Lemon *Citrus limon* Up to 10m Very similar in overall appearance to the Sweet Orange, but bearing oval, pale yellow fruits. Leathery leaves about 10cm long have minutely toothed margins; there is usually a thick, stiff spine at the base of the short petiole, which lacks a wing. Small white flowers flushed purple or reddish on the outside. Fruit 6.5-12.5cm long, oval, with a protruding apex, yellow when ripe, the juicy flesh remaining sour. *Flowering:* More or less throughout the year. *Distribution:* Origin obscure, but widely cultivated throughout the Mediterranean. Similar **Citron** (*C. medica*) has very large, yellow fruits, while **Sweet Lime** (*C. limetta*) has greener, sweeter fruits.

Sweet Orange

Sweet Orange

Grapefruit: young fruits

Grapefruit

Lemon

Lemon

Golden-rain-tree *Koelreuteria paniculata* Up to 15m Tree with large clusters of yellow flowers and distinctive papery fruits. Trunk and branches stout and twisted, crown rather thin. Deeply cracked bark brown with an orange underlayer. Twigs downy when young, soon becoming glabrous. Alternate leaves 15-40cm long, pinnately divided into 9-15 pairs of leaflets; each leaflet 3-8cm long, oval to oblong, deeply toothed or lobed towards the base, glabrous, dark green above, paler beneath. Flowers yellow, in large branched clusters up to 40cm long at tips of twigs, each flower about 1cm across, with four sepals, four narrow, pointed petals and usually eight stamens. Fruit 5.5cm long, a conical, inflated and papery capsule with conspicuous red veins; when ripe it splits into three valves to release black seeds. *Flowering:* July to August. *Distribution:* Native to eastern Asia, frequently planted as an ornamental and street tree in various parts of Europe but mainly in the south and naturalised in places as far north as Britain.

Downy Tree-of-Heaven

Tree-of-Heaven *Ailanthus altissima* 20-30m Fast-growing tree with a very straight trunk and strongly ascending branches. Trunk suckering at the base. Bark grey. Rank-smelling, alternate leaves of 45-60cm long pinnate, with 13-25 pairs of leaflets, usually, but not always, ending with an odd leaflet. Leaflets 7-12cm long, narrowly oval with two to four small teeth near the base; unfolding red, the leaves become dark green above, paler beneath. Flowers 7-8mm in diameter, five-petalled, greenish-white and strongly scented; males and females occur in large, branched clusters on different trees. Fruits 3-4cm long have a twisted, membranous wing. *Flowering:* July. *Distribution:* Native to China; prefers dry, light soils and is tolerant of air pollution; widely planted in Europe as a street tree or soil-stabiliser and often naturalised. Similar **Downy Tree-of-Heaven** (*A. vilmoriniana*) has leaves with red petioles and entire leaflets hairy beneath. Native to China, also grown for ornament in Europe.

Chinese Cedar: flower

Persian Lilac *Melia azederach* Up to 15m Graceful, open, small tree with persistent bead-like yellow fruits. Trunk often short, bark dark grey and furrowed, crown spreading. Alternate leaves up to 90cm long, twice-pinnate, the pinnae with numerous glossy leaflets each 2.5-5cm long, narrowly oval to elliptical with toothed or lobed margins. Large, loosely branched axillary flower-clusters 10-20cm long. Flowers fragrant, lilac, with five to six narrow, spreading petals each about 18mm long and an erect tube of fused stamens. Globose or ovoid fruit 6-18mm long, pale yellow, containing a single hard seed. *Flowering:* June. *Distribution:* Short-lived mountain tree native to dry parts of southern and eastern Asia, commonly planted for ornament and shade, especially along roads in southern Europe and naturalised in the Balkans and Crete. **Chinese Cedar** (*Cedrela sinensis*), from China, is also planted for ornament. It has shaggy bark, leaves only once-pinnate and lacking a terminal leaflet; flowers white.

Golden-rain-tree

Golden-rain-tree: fruit

Tree-of-Heaven

Tree-of-Heaven

Persian Lilac

Persian Lilac

Stag's-horn Sumach *Rhus typhina* Up to 10m Small tree or shrub with regularly forked branches covered with thick, velvety hair. Crown rounded; often suckering or with several trunks. Young twigs curved and also with thick velvety hair. Alternate leaves pinnately divided into 11-29 drooping leaflets, each 5-12cm long, narrowly oval, pointed, toothed and softly hairy, turning bright orange and red in autumn. Flowers five-petalled, males greenish, females red, in conical heads 10-20cm long and usually on different trees. Fruit nut-like, about 4mm long, in dense, dull crimson and hairy heads up to 20cm long which remain on the bare tree through winter. *Flowering:* May to July. *Distribution:* Native to North America but a common ornamental in Europe and naturalised in northern and central parts.

Varnish-tree:
♂ flowers

Common Sumach *Rhus coriaria* Up to 3m Small, semi-evergreen tree or shrub with ascending branches. Young twigs stout and thickly covered with hairs. Alternate leaves pinnately divided into 7-21 leaflets, each 1-5cm long, oval to oblong, coarsely toothed and sometimes with small lobes near the base; leaf-axis hairy and narrowly winged. White flowers with five petals 3-4mm in diameter, borne in dense, compactly branched conical clusters about 10cm long at the tips of the twigs, males and females on different trees. Fruit nut-like, 4-6mm long, covered with dense, short, purplish-brown hairs. *Flowering:* May to July. *Distribution:* Native to dry rocky areas in southern Europe. **Varnish-tree** (*R. verniciflua*), native to Japan, is planted for ornament. It forms a domed, deciduous tree up to 14m tall with thick, aromatic, entire leaflets, loosely branched clusters of yellowish flowers and pale brown, poisonous fruits.

Pepper-tree *Schinus molle* Up to 12m Weeping evergreen tree with slender, drooping twigs and long, hanging clusters of flowers and fruits. Alternate leaves pinnately divided into 7-13 pairs of leaflets, leaf-axis flattened but not winged and usually ending in a spiny point, sometimes in a terminal leaflet; leaflets each 20-60mm long and 3-8mm wide, smelling of pepper when crushed. Creamy five-petalled flowers 4mm in diameter, borne in loose, pendulous clusters up to 25cm long at the tips of the twigs. Bead-like fruits 7mm in diameter, shiny pink when ripe. *Flowering:* June to December. *Distribution:* A mountain species, native to Central and South America. Grown as an ornamental in southern Europe and sometimes naturalised there. **Brazilian Pepper-tree** (*S. terebinthifolia*), from Brazil and Paraguay, is similar but does not have weeping foliage. Leaflets are broader, on a winged axis, and fruits are bright red. It is sometimes grown for ornament.

Brazilian
Pepper-tree

Stag's-horn Sumach: autumn

Stag's-horn Sumach: winter

Common Sumach

Pepper-tree

Mastic-tree

Mastic-tree *Pistacia lentiscus* Up to 8m Bushy, spreading evergreen with highly aromatic leaves and fruits. Twigs glabrous but warty with raised lenticels. Alternate leaves pinnately divided into three to six pairs of leaflets; narrowly winged leaf-axis ending in a short spine; petiole downy. Leaflets 1-5cm long and 0.5-1.5cm wide, narrowly oval to oblong, and tipped with a short spine; dark green, leathery. Flowers in dense, spiky, axillary heads 2-5cm long, yellow-tinged to purplish, lacking petals. Aromatic fruits 4mm long, globose with a slender spike-like tip, bright red when young but ripening black. *Flowering:* April. *Distribution:* Native to the Mediterranean and Portugal, on rocky slopes, in open thickets and on the edges of woods.

Pistachio *Pistacia vera* Up to 6m Small tree or shrub with rough, ridged bark. Alternate leaves may be undivided or pinnate with three or sometimes five leaflets and a very narrowly winged leaf-axis; petiole glabrous. Leaflets 3.5-9cm long, broadly oval to oblong, thin-textured, grey-green, initially downy but soon glabrous. Flowers similar to those of Turpentine-tree. Hard-shelled fruits 2-2.5cm long, ovoid, tipped with a slender point, pale reddish-brown when ripe, containing a single seed. *Flowering:* April. *Distribution:* Native to western Asia but widely grown in the Mediterranean region for its edible seeds and naturalised in places.

Turpentine-tree *Pistacia terebinthus* Up to 10m Grey-barked tree with stickily resinous twigs and resin-scented leaves. Small tree, often only a shrub. Alternate leaves pinnately divided into three to nine leaflets, the leaf-axis cylindrical, not winged and ending in a leaflet; petiole glabrous. Leaflets leathery, dark and shiny, each 2-8.5cm long, oval to oblong and tipped with a slender spine. Flowers in loose and long-branched clusters appear with the leaves, males and females on separate trees; they are green to brownish-purple and lack petals. Fruits 5-7mm long, pear-shaped, tipped with a slender point; coral red when young but ripening brown. *Flowering:* March to April. *Distribution:* A species of scrub and thin woodland, preferring dry and rocky, chalky soils. Native to the Mediterranean, Portugal and south-western Asia. Similar **P. atlantica** has narrower, blunt-tipped leaflets, narrowly winged leaf-axes and minutely hairy petioles. It is native from Greece eastwards to the Crimea.

Pistacia atlantica

Mastic-tree

Mastic-tree

Pistachio

Turpentine-tree

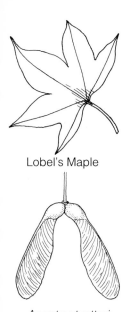

Lobel's Maple

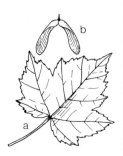

Acer trautvetteri:
fruit

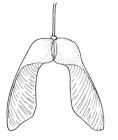

Red Maple: leaf (a)
and fruit (b)

Sycamore *Acer pseudoplatanus* Up to 35m A very fast-growing, invasive tree, the wide-spreading crown often broader than it is high. Twigs grey-green. Opposite leaves 10-15cm long, with five coarsely toothed lobes. Flowers greenish-yellow, appearing with the leaves and hanging in separate male and female clusters 6-12cm long. Fruits in pairs 3.5-5cm long, the grey-brown wings making an angle of 90 degrees. *Flowering:* April to May. *Distribution:* Native to central and southern Europe, also widely planted, often naturalised. Similar **Lobel's Maple** (*A. lobelii*), a rare mountain tree of central and southern Italy, has a columnar shape, leaves with entire lobes, erect flower-clusters and fruits with horizontally spreading wings.

Heldreich's Maple *Acer heldreichii* Up to 25m Tree with a high, domed crown. Twigs red-brown. Opposite leaves 5-17cm long, with three to five toothed lobes, the central lobe separated almost to the leaf-base. Flowers few, yellow-green, in clusters appearing with the leaves. Fruits 2.5cm long, paired, the curved reddish wings making a wide angle. *Flowering:* May. *Distribution:* Mountain tree native to the Balkan Peninsula. Similar **A. trautvetteri**, from Turkey and the Caucasus, has the central leaf-lobe separate only two-thirds of the way to the base; fruit has almost parallel wings.

Silver Maple *Acer saccharinum* Up to 35m Elegant tree, with tall spreading crown and numerous slender, upwardly arching branches. Trunk short and stout, with smooth grey-brown bark, flaking and becoming shaggy with age. Twigs brown or purplish. Opposite leaves 9-16cm long, with five deeply and irregularly toothed lobes, green above, with silver hairs beneath. Red or greenish flowers appear before the leaves, males and females in separate clusters of four to five, males short stalked, females long stalked; both sexes lack petals. Fruits 5cm long, paired, the green, strongly veined wings diverging at a narrow angle. *Flowering:* March. *Distribution:* Native to North America, commonly planted as a street tree.

Sugar Maple *Acer saccharophorum* Up to 35m A tall, stately tree, resembling Norway Maple. Opposite leaves up to 16cm long, normally five-lobed, occasionally with downy veins beneath. Flowers greenish-yellow, on thin stalks 2.5cm long, males and females in separate clusters; both sexes lack petals. Fruits 2.5cm long, paired, the wings making an angle slightly less than 90 degrees. *Flowering:* April. *Distribution:* Native to eastern North America, planted as a street or park tree, but the brilliant autumn red found in native trees is often not developed in Europe. Similar **Red Maple** (*A. rubrum*), from North America, is widely planted on moist soils. Twigs, buds, young leaves, five-petalled flowers and fruits are all red, as are the autumn leaves.

Tartar Maple *Acer tataricum* Up to 10m Shrub or small tree, with smooth brown bark and pale stripes on the trunk. Opposite leaves 6-10cm long, usually undivided, oblong, heart-shaped at the base, with finely toothed margins. Flowers greenish-white, males and females in separate, obliquely erect clusters of 20-30. Fruits 2.5cm long, paired, wings more or less parallel and deep red with green edge. *Flowering:* May. *Distribution:* Native to southern and central Europe, from Austria and the Balkans to the Crimea.

Tartar Maple: fruit

Sycamore

Sycamore

Heldreich's Maple

Silver Maple

Sugar Maple: autumn

Tartar Maple: ♂ flowers

Norway Maple *Acer platanoides* Up to 30m Resembling Sycamore but a smaller tree and more colourful in both spring and autumn. Trunk often short, with greyish, smooth or finely fissured bark. Branches sparse, twigs dull green tinged with red. Opposite leaves 10-15cm long, with five to seven slender-toothed lobes. Yellowish-green flowers appear before the leaves in erect clusters, males and females separate. Five sepals, five petals. Yellowish fruits 3.5-5cm, paired, the wings forming a wide angle or horizontal. *Flowering:* April. *Distribution:* Forest tree, native to much of Europe, but only in mountains in the south. Widely planted as a street or park tree, especially the cultivar cv. 'Crimson King' which has dark red foliage.

Acer obtusatum

Italian Maple *Acer opalus* 15-20m Small, broad-crowned tree, sometimes a shrub. Bark pink-tinged, forming oblong plates, peeling in young trees to leave orange patches. Twigs brown. Opposite leaves up to 10cm long, three-lobed, occasionally with two extra smaller basal lobes; lobes all narrowly pointed. Young leaves dark green above, hairy below, mature leaves hairy only on the veins. Pale yellow flowers hanging on thin stalks appear before leaves, in separate male and female clusters. Fruits about 2.5cm long, paired, the green and pink wings almost parallel. *Flowering:* April. *Distribution:* Mountain tree native to the western Mediterranean and southern Alps, from Spain to Germany and Italy; also planted in parks. Similar **A. obtusatum** has leaves up to 12cm long with five, occasionally three, broad, bluntly rounded lobes; underside and petiole remaining densely hairy. Native from Italy to Greece and Yugoslavia.

Field Maple

Field Maple *Acer campestre* Up to 25m Small tree, sometimes a large shrub, with twisted trunk and rounded crown. Twigs brown with fine hairs and often developing corky wings. Opposite leaves 4-12cm long, usually three-lobed, the outer lobes often further lobed, all with rounded teeth towards the tip. Young leaves pinkish, becoming dark green when mature, and turning reddish or yellow in autumn. Yellowish-green flowers have five sepals and five petals, appearing with the leaves, males and females together in erect clusters. Fruits 2-4cm long, paired, the green- or red-tinged wings spreading horizontally. *Flowering:* April to May. *Distribution:* Native and common in northern Europe, especially as a hedgerow tree on chalk soils.

Acer granatense

Balkan Maple *Acer hyrcanum* Up to 16m Usually a small tree with grey-brown bark splitting into squares. Crown rounded, branches erect or spreading. Opposite leaves up to 10cm long, with five, or occasionally three, lobes cut halfway to the base, the largest three parallel-sided, all blunt at the tip, with shallow teeth; petiole slender, pinkish or yellowish. Flowers few, yellowish, on thin stalks, appearing before the leaves, males and females in separate clusters. Fruits 1.5cm long, paired, the greenish-yellow wings more or less parallel. *Flowering:* April. *Distribution:* A woodland tree, native to the Balkans and the Caucasus. Two species are similar to Balkan Maple. **A. granatense**, endemic to southern Spain, Mallorca and North Africa, has leaves about 7cm long, the undersides and petioles almost totally covered in hairs. **A. stevenii**, endemic to the Crimea, has grey-green leaves with five narrow lobes, the leaves on the flowering shoot divided more than halfway to the base.

Norway Maple

Norway Maple

Italian Maple

Field Maple: autumn

Field Maple

Balkan Maple

Martini's Maple

Montpelier Maple *Acer monspessulanum* Up to 12m Small tree or shrub with domed crown and black or grey cracked bark. Twigs thin, brown. Opposite leaves up to 8cm long, with three oval, entire lobes; the lateral lobes form a wide angle with the middle lobe. Mature leaves leathery, dark green above, greyish-blue beneath. Yellowish-green flowers on long, thin stalks appear after the leaves, males and females in separate clusters; erect at first, drooping later; both sexes lack petals. Fruits 1-2cm long, paired, wings parallel, greenish at first, but developing a crimson tinge. *Flowering:* June. *Distribution:* Scattered throughout southern Europe, extending as far north as Germany. **Martini's Maple** (*A. martinii*) differs in having larger leaves, more heart-shaped at the base, with three to five toothed lobes. A very rare tree only found with certainty near Lyons in France.

Cretan Maple *Acer sempervirens* Up to 12m Low-crowned evergreen tree, or large shrub. Bark dark grey, with the occasional orange patch, fairly smooth. Branches twisted, twigs shiny brown. Opposite leaves 2-5cm long, either three-lobed, unevenly lobed or undivided, with entire margins. Flowers greenish, appearing with the leaves, males and females in separate, erect clusters. Fruits have green or red wings, almost parallel, or spreading at a narrow angle. *Flowering:* April. *Distribution:* Endemic to Crete and mainland Greece.

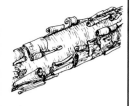

Paper-bark Maple: bark

Box-elder *Acer negundo* Up to 20m Fast-growing tree, with an uneven, irregularly domed crown. Short trunk often has swellings or bosses. Bark smooth and grey, becoming darker and developing shallow cracks with age. Twigs green, glabrous. Opposite leaves pinnate, 10-15cm long, with five to seven oval, pointed and toothed leaflets. Red male and greenish female flowers appear before the leaves on different trees. Both sexes lack petals. Fruits about 2cm long, paired, with the wings making a narrow angle. *Flowering:* March. *Distribution:* Native to eastern North America, but commonly planted as a street tree or ornamental and occasionally naturalised. The cultivar cv. 'Variegatum', with yellow and green variegated leaves, is the most commonly planted cultivar. **Paper-bark Maple** (*A. griseum*) is a very attractive and widely planted ornamental, native to China. It has cinnamon-coloured bark which peels off in thin papery layers exposing the reddish younger bark. The leaves have only three toothed leaflets.

Montpelier Maple

Cretan Maple

Box-elder

Box-elder

Horse-chestnut *Aesculus hippocastanum* Up to 35m Handsome, wide-spreading tree with a stout trunk. Bark brown-grey, cracking into plates. Twigs reddish-brown, in winter bearing large, very sticky buds up to 3.5cm long. Leaves opposite, the five to seven leaflets lacking petioles and spreading like fingers on a hand, each 10-25cm long, oval but widest above the middle, toothed and bright green. Flower-spikes up to 30cm long, erect, conical to pyramidal. Flowers about 2cm across with four to five recurved petals, the lower two largest, all frilly, white with a yellow or pink base; stamens usually six, long and curving downwards. Fruit up to 6cm across, with a thick, usually spiny husk containing one or more shiny brown seeds (conkers); these frequently germinate, but rarely mature. *Flowering:* April to May. *Distribution:* Native to mountain areas of the Balkan Peninsula, but planted throughout Europe for timber and shade and as an ornamental in parks and streets.

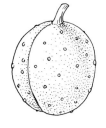

Red Horse-chestnut: fruit

Red Horse-chestnut *Aesculus x carnea* Up to 30m Closely resembling its parent Horse-chestnut, this tree differs in having pink or red flowers. Leaves resemble those of Horse-chestnut but have five darker green leaflets drooping as though from lack of water. Flowers also like Horse-chestnut but pink or red, in spikes up to 20cm long. Fruits more or less smooth, with few, if any, spines. *Flowering:* April to May. *Distribution:* A hybrid between Horse-chestnut and the North American **Red Buckeye** (*A. pavia*), commonly planted as an ornamental tree, and occasionally becoming naturalised.

Yellow Buckeye

Indian Horse-chestnut *Aesculus indica* Up to 20m Resembles Horse-chestnut but is a smaller, more delicate tree. Trunk stout, with smooth grey-green or pinkish tinged bark. Main branches almost erect, giving a narrow crown. Leaves like those of Horse-chestnut but with much narrower, petiolate leaflets. Flower-spikes 10-15cm long, erect, pyramidal. Flowers like Horse-chestnut, white tinged with pink or yellow, but petals not frilly; five to eight stamens. Fruit has a rough, but not spiny, thin husk containing two to three wrinkled, glossy brown seeds. *Flowering:* June. *Distribution:* Native to the Himalayas, often planted as a park, garden or street tree. Similar **Yellow Buckeye** (*A. flava*) is native to North America and also planted as an ornamental. It has non-sticky winter buds, broader leaflets with shorter petioles and reddish-brown down beneath, and yellow flowers.

Horse-chestnut

Horse-chestnut

Horse-chestnut

Red Horse-chestnut

Red Horse-chestnut

Indian Horse-chestnut

Balearic Box

Box *Buxus sempervirens* Up to 5m Usually a very dense evergreen tree or shrub. Young twigs green and four-angled, with persistent white hairs. Opposite leaves 1.5-3cm long, oval to oblong, notched and with entire, rolled-down margins, thick and leathery, dark and glossy above, pale green beneath with white hairs on the basal half. Tight axillary flower-clusters of 5mm diameter contain five to six male flowers surrounding a single female flower; all flowers lack petals. Blue-green, woody capsule about 7mm long and tipped with three spreading horns ripens brown before opening explosively to disperse seeds. *Flowering:* April. *Distribution:* Scattered through western Europe on chalky soils. Rare in the wild in some areas (including Britain), but often grown in gardens for hedges and topiary. Similar **Balearic Box** (*B. balearica*), endemic to the Balearics, Sardinia and a few places in southern Spain, is a glabrous tree with stouter, stiff twigs, paler, duller leaves 2.5-4cm long, flower-clusters 10mm in diameter and long, curved capsule horns.

Holly *Ilex aquifolium* 3-15m Evergreen tree with handsome, dark, glossy green but very prickly foliage. Usually a small, conical tree but often only a shrub. Tips of young branches curve upwards. Smooth, silver-grey bark eventually becomes finely fissured. Alternate leaves 5-12cm long, stiffly leathery, waxy, wavy and spiny on the margins, dark green and very shiny above, much paler beneath. White flowers about 6mm in diameter, four-petalled, in small axillary clusters, males and females on different trees, only the males fragrant. Trees growing in deep shade are often sterile. Berries 7-12mm long, bright scarlet. *Flowering:* May to August. *Distribution:* Native throughout western and southern Europe, common in scrub, hedgerows and as a shrub layer in woods. Often planted; cultivars with leaves variegated green and yellow are common.

Highclere Holly *Ilex* x *altaclarensis* Up to 20m Evergreen generally similar to Holly but the much smaller leaves not nearly so prickly. Domed, rather dense-crowned tree with spreading branches. Bark purplish-grey, twigs with purplish marks. Small, alternate leaves up to 9cm long, oval to oblong and flat, entire or with up to ten small, weak, forward-pointing spines on each side. Flowers up to 12mm long, the five petals white and sometimes tinged purple at the base; male and female flowers on different trees. Berry 12mm long, bright scarlet. *Flowering:* May. *Distribution:* A hybrid between Holly and Canary Holly, vigorous and pollution-resistant, often planted in towns and near the coast. Various cultivars are common. **Canary Holly** (*I. perado*) is very similar, especially in the leaves, but has pale pink flowers. Native to the Atlantic islands of Azores, Madeira and Canaries and planted in parks.

Canary Holly

Box

Box

Holly

Holly: ♂ flowers

Holly

Highclere Holly

Japanese Spindle-tree

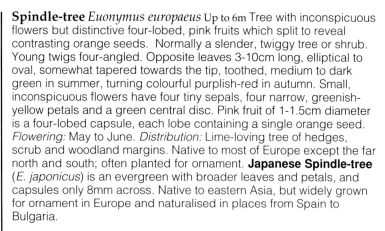

Spindle-tree *Euonymus europaeus* Up to 6m Tree with inconspicuous flowers but distinctive four-lobed, pink fruits which split to reveal contrasting orange seeds. Normally a slender, twiggy tree or shrub. Young twigs four-angled. Opposite leaves 3-10cm long, elliptical to oval, somewhat tapered towards the tip, toothed, medium to dark green in summer, turning colourful purplish-red in autumn. Small, inconspicuous flowers have four tiny sepals, four narrow, greenish-yellow petals and a green central disc. Pink fruit of 1-1.5cm diameter is a four-lobed capsule, each lobe containing a single orange seed. *Flowering:* May to June. *Distribution:* Lime-loving tree of hedges, scrub and woodland margins. Native to most of Europe except the far north and south; often planted for ornament. **Japanese Spindle-tree** (*E. japonicus*) is an evergreen with broader leaves and petals, and capsules only 8mm across. Native to eastern Asia, but widely grown for ornament in Europe and naturalised in places from Spain to Bulgaria.

Broad-leaved Spindle-tree *Euonymus latifolius* 2-6m Small tree generally similar to Spindle-tree, except for the flowers and capsules. Twigs four-angled but less distinctly so than in Spindle-tree. Opposite leaves up to 16cm long, oblong to elliptical or widest above the middle, with fine-toothed margins. Flowers have five broad, pink petals. Capsules 15-20mm wide, each of the four lobes narrowly winged on the angles. *Flowering:* May to June. *Distribution:* Common in woodland and scrub. Native to southern parts of central and eastern Europe north to Germany and west to southern France.

Zizyphus lotus

Common Jujube *Zizyphus jujuba* Up to 8m Small, spiny and very twiggy tree or straggling shrub. Young twigs green and markedly zigzagged; sterile twigs bear paired, spiny stipules, each pair with one long straight spine and one curved spine; flowering twigs are unarmed. Alternate leaves 2-5.5cm long, oblong and blunt, the margins with small gland-tipped teeth, shiny above, slightly hairy beneath. Dull or greenish-yellow flowers 3mm in diameter, five-petalled, in small, inconspicuous axillary clusters. Fleshy fruit 1.5-3cm long, ovoid, dark red to nearly black and sweet-tasting when ripe. *Flowering:* June to July. *Distribution:* Native to Asia, widely grown in southern Europe for the edible fruits and naturalised in much of the Mediterranean region. The shrubby **Z. lotus**, native to Spain, Sicily and Greece, is very similar but has grey twigs, minutely toothed leaves and deep yellow fruits.

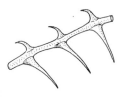

Christ's Thorn: spines

Christ's Thorn *Paliurus spina-christi* Up to 3m Formidably spiny small tree or shrub with numerous, clinging branches. Twigs flexible, zigzagging, all with pairs of needle-sharp spiny stipules, one hooked and one straight. Alternate leaves form two rows along the twig; they are 2-4cm long, oval and may be either entire or minutely toothed. Yellow, five-petalled flowers about 5mm across borne in loose axillary clusters. Woody fruits resemble broad-brimmed hats 2-3cm in diameter, the brim formed by a wavy, spreading wing. *Flowering:* July. *Distribution:* Native to hot, dry parts of the Mediterranean, especially the eastern end and the Balkan Peninsula, but absent from islands; sometimes used for farm hedges.

Spindle-tree

Spindle-tree: in fruit

Broad-leaved Spindle-tree

Broad-leaved Spindle-tree

Common Jujube

Christ's Thorn

Rhamnus persicifolius

Buckthorn *Rhamnus catharticus* 4-10m Spiny tree with opposite branches spreading at right angles and short, lateral twigs bearing leaves and flowers and ending in a spine. Scaling black bark reveals orange patches. Opposite leaves arranged in crowded pairs at 90 degrees to each other, 3-7cm long, oval to elliptical, pointed and finely toothed. Upper leaf-surface dull green, the lower pale green with two to four pairs of conspicuous lateral veins curving towards the leaf-tip. Fragrant greenish-white flowers 4mm long, solitary or in small clusters, males and females on different trees. Usually four narrow, pointed petals but some flowers have five. Berry-like fruits of 6-8mm diameter ripen black. *Flowering:* May to June. *Distribution:* Common on chalky soils, in hedges, scrub and deciduous woods. Native to all of Europe except the far south. Similar **R. persicifolius**, endemic to Sardinia, has narrow and more conspicuously toothed leaves, hairy beneath, and reddish fruits.

Alpine Buckthorn

Mediterranean Buckthorn *Rhamnus alaternus* Up to 5m Bushy evergreen tree or shrub of variable shape. Twigs and branches lack spines. Alternate, thick and leathery leaves 2-6cm long, lance-shaped or oval, sharp or blunt and entire or with small teeth towards the tip. Flowers with four or five yellow calyx-lobes but lacking petals, males and females on different trees in dense, hairy axillary clusters. Fruit berry-like but not fleshy, 4-6mm long, pear-shaped, ripening from reddish to black. *Flowering:* March to April. *Distribution:* Mediterranean species of evergreen scrub and stony soils. **Alpine Buckthorn** (*R. alpinus*), a lime-loving mountain species from southern and south-central Europe, is similar but has larger, deciduous leaves.

Frangula azorica

Alder-buckthorn *Frangula alnus* Up to 5m Small tree with leaves folding downwards on the twigs and turning shiny bright yellows and reds in autumn. Branches opposite, ascending at a sharp angle. Bark smooth. Twigs minutely hairy, green when young, later grey-brown. Mostly opposite, entire leaves 2-7cm long, widest above the middle with a short, abrupt tip and seven to nine pairs of lateral veins curving towards the wavy margins; young leaves covered with brownish hairs which soon fall. Greenish-white flowers 3mm across with five small petals and stout stalks form axillary clusters. Berry-like fruits of 6-10mm diameter ripen from green through yellow and red and finally to purplish-black. *Flowering:* May to June or even September. *Distribution:* Common in hedges, woods and bogs on damp acid soils in much of Europe, but absent from the far north and some parts of the Mediterranean. Evergreen **F. azorica** from the Azores and Madeira is larger, up to 10m tall; leaves are 10-18cm long with persistent hairs beneath.

Buckthorn

Buckthorn

Buckthorn

Mediterranean Buckthorn

Alder-buckthorn

Alder-buckthorn

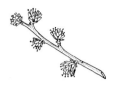

Sea-buckthorn:
♂ flowers

Silver-berry

Sea-buckthorn *Hippophae rhamnoides* Up to 11m Silvery tree; leaves and twigs especially covered with minute silvery or sometimes brownish scales. Sprawling shrub in exposed places but forms a densely branched tree in sheltered sites. Numerous suckers grow from the base of the trunk. Twigs thorny, black where the silvery scales have fallen. Alternate, narrow and rather drooping leaves, 1-6cm long and 0.3-1cm wide, silvery on both sides or dull grey-green above and silvery below; petiole very short. Greenish flowers 3mm in diameter, tubular with two sepals but no petals. They appear before the leaves in inconspicuous clusters, males and females on different trees. Oval, orange berries 6-8mm long. *Flowering:* March to April. *Distribution:* Native to much of Europe, mainly on coastal cliffs and sand dunes, but sometimes inland; intolerant of shade but planted as a sand-binder and ornamental and often naturalised in open sites.

Oleaster *Elaeagnus angustifolia* Up to 13m Resembling Sea-buckthorn but with an even more silvery appearance and only occasionally spiny. Silvery, shining young twigs become dark and smooth with age. Alternate, narrowly oblong or lance-shaped leaves 4-8cm long and 1-2.5cm wide with dense silver hairs beneath. Fragrant yellow flowers 8-10mm, tubular with four sepals but no petals, silvery outside, yellow within; solitary or in clusters of two to three, appearing with the young leaves. Fleshy oval berries 1-2cm long, also scattered with silver scales. *Flowering:* June. *Distribution:* Native to western Asia, grown in central and southern Europe for ornament and for the edible fruits; sometimes naturalised. The North American **Silver-berry** (*E. commutata*) is similar but has dry fruits and is also frequently planted and naturalised in Europe.

Hibiscus *Hibiscus rosa-sinensis* 1-3m, sometimes to 5m Small, spreading, evergreen tree or large shrub with striking flowers. Alternate leaves up to 15cm long, oval, toothed and glossy green. Flowers usually solitary in axils of upper leaves. Typically five petals, spreading, 5-12cm long and deep red with a darker patch towards the base. Numerous stamens form a distinctive, brush-like column; style long with five short branches bearing knob-like stigmas. Fruit a narrowly ovoid capsule seated in the persistent calyx. *Flowering:* More or less all year. *Distribution:* Unknown in the wild but cultivated as an ornamental throughout warmer parts of the world and widely planted in southern Europe.

Sea-buckthorn

Sea-buckthorn

Oleaster

Hibiscus

Tamarix canariensis

Tamarix dalmatica

Tamarix tetrandra

Tamarisk *Tamarix gallica* Up to 8m Diffuse evergreen with slender, feathery foliage. Much-branched, entirely glabrous tree or shrub. Bark dark purple or almost black. Alternate leaves tiny, only 1.5-2mm long, scale-like and clasping the shoot. Flowers tiny, crowded into long slender, clustered spikes 1.5-4.5cm long and 3-5mm wide. Each flower has a bract not extending beyond the middle of the calyx; five petals, 1.5-2mm long, pink or white, deciduous. Fruit a capsule releasing seeds tufted with hair. *Flowering:* Usually July to September. *Distribution:* Native to south-western Europe, usually near the coast but often cultivated and sometimes naturalised. Two similar species have reddish bark. **T. smyrnensis** has petals 2mm long with a raised keel on the back, and is native to the eastern Mediterranean and Aegean regions. **T. canariensis** is covered with short, hair-like papillae, has entire bracts equalling or exceeding the calyx and petals only 1.25-1.5mm long. Native to the western Mediterranean from Portugal to Sicily.

African Tamarisk *Tamarix africana* Up to 8m Generally similar to Tamarisk but with larger parts. Glabrous tree with black bark. Alternate leaves 1.5-4mm, scale-like and clasping the shoot, margins papery. Flowers crowded into solitary spikes 3-6cm long and 5-8mm wide. Each flower more or less stalkless with a bract usually exceeding the calyx; petals five, 2-3mm long, white or pink, persistent. Fruit like that of Tamarisk. *Flowering:* May. *Distribution:* Coastal tree of marshes and river-banks in south-western Europe from Portugal to southern Italy and Sicily. **T. dalmatica** has flower spikes 8-12mm wide, sepals with a raised keel on the back and four to five petals 2-5mm long. It grows in similar habitats, but in the eastern Mediterranean.

Small-flowered Tamarisk *Tamarix parviflora* Up to 6m Generally similar to Tamarisk but with flower-parts in fours. Small tree or shrub, glabrous or with a few hair-like papillae. Bark brown to purple. Alternate leaves 3-5mm long, scale-like and clasping the shoot, margins papery. Flowers in dense, solitary spikes 3-5cm long and 3-5mm wide. Each flower has an oblong and almost completely papery bract. Four, rarely five, petals up to 2mm long, white or pale pink and persistent. Fruit like that of Tamarisk. *Flowering:* May. *Distribution:* Mostly found in hedgerows and along rivers; native to the Balkan Peninsula and Aegean regions but cultivated for ornament in central and southern Europe and sometimes naturalised there. Very similar **T. tetrandra** has black bark, flower spikes 6-7mm wide, green bracts and deciduous petals 2.5-3mm long. Native to damp mountainous parts of the Balkan Peninsula.

Tamarisk

Tamarisk

African Tamarisk

Small-flowered Tamarisk

Small-leaved Lime:
fruit cluster

Small-leaved Lime *Tilia cordata* Up to 32m Shapely tree with dense crown of downwardly arching branches. Alternate leaves 3-9cm long, very broadly heart-shaped, finely toothed, dark shiny green above, paler with tufts of pale red-brown hairs in the vein-axils beneath. Flowers five-petalled, white and fragrant, in a pendulous cluster of 4-15 attached to a pale green, wing-like bract. Thin-shelled, globose nuts 6mm long, downy at first, becoming glabrous, usually ribbed. *Flowering:* July. *Distribution:* Native to limestone areas of Europe except the far north and south; often planted as a street tree.

Common Lime *Tilia* x *vulgaris* Up to 46m Tall tree with narrow crown and leaves often sticky with sap. Broad, alternate leaves 6-10cm long, base heart-shaped or cut straight across, dull green above, paler with tufts of white hairs in vein-axils beneath. Flowers five-petalled, yellow-white and fragrant, five to ten in a pendulous cluster attached to a yellowish-green, wing-like bract. Thick-shelled, ovoid to globose nuts, 8mm long, downy and weakly ribbed. *Flowering:* July. *Distribution:* Naturally occurring hybrid between Small-leaved and Large-leaved Limes; nowadays being replaced as a street tree by more fungal- and insect-resistant species.

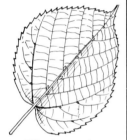

Tilia dasystyla

Caucasian Lime *Tilia* x *euchlora* Up to 20m Hybrid very similar to Common Lime with which it shares one parent. Differs from Common Lime in having leaves dark, shiny green above with reddish hairs in the vein-axils beneath, only three to seven yellow flowers per cluster and ellipsoid nuts tapering at both ends. *Flowering:* July. *Distribution:* Ornamental hybrid between Small-leaved Lime and *T. dasystyla* frequently grown in central Europe. **T. dasystyla** is a Crimean species with downy young twigs and leaves with yellowish hairs in the vein-axils beneath.

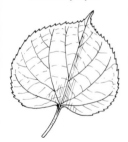

Tilia rubra

Large-leaved Lime *Tilia platyphyllos* Up to 40m Narrowly domed tree with a crown of ascending branches; it flowers before other limes. Alternate, heart-shaped leaves 6-9cm long, sharply toothed, hairy on both sides but especially beneath. Flowers five-petalled, yellowish and fragrant in a long-stalked, pendulous cluster of two to six, attached to a whitish, wing-like bract. Globose nuts 8-12mm long, hairy with three to five prominent ribs. *Flowering:* June. *Distribution:* Native to hills in central and southern Europe, planted as a street tree in other areas. Very similar **T. rubra** from south-eastern Europe has firmer, more glabrous leaves with teeth ending in hair-like points.

Silver Lime *Tilia tomentosa* Up to 30m Ascending branches give this compact tree a broadly domed crown. Young twigs downy white, becoming glabrous and green. Alternate leaves 8-10cm long, heart-shaped with asymmetric base and sharp-toothed margins, dark green above, densely silvery white with stellate hairs beneath. Flowers five-petalled, yellow or whitish, fragrant, six to ten in a pendulous cluster attached to a yellowish, wing-like bract. Ovoid nuts 6-12mm long, downy with five prominent ribs. *Flowering:* July to August. *Distribution:* Native from Hungary eastwards to Asia and often planted in Europe for its handsome foliage. **Weeping Silver Lime** (*T. petiolaris*) has weeping twigs; a common ornamental of unknown origin and perhaps merely an extreme form of Silver Lime.

Small-leaved Lime

Small-leaved Lime

Common Lime

Caucasian Lime

Large-leaved Lime

Silver Lime

Bungalay: fruit

Red Mahogany *Eucalyptus resinifer* Up to 40m Large, stately evergreen with a trunk up to 2m thick; bark very fibrous, rough and reddish, shedding in patches on the mature trunk. Juvenile leaves opposite, up to 6cm long and 2cm wide, lance-shaped or oval, with short petioles. Adult leaves alternate, 16cm long and 3cm wide, dark glossy green above. Flowers white, in clusters of five to ten, the stalks of the clusters up to 2cm long and flattened. Flower-buds up to 17mm long have an orange, conical or beak-like cap. Fruit 5-8mm long, hemispherical, stalked, with a small slightly domed disc at the apex, opening by four strongly projecting valves. *Flowering:* September to February. *Distribution:* Native to Australia (Queensland and New South Wales); in Europe grown as a timber tree on a variety of soils, particularly in sandy coastal areas in the Mediterranean region. Similar **Bungalay** (*E. botryoides*) is a smaller, denser tree which does not shed its bark, has hemispherical or conical bud-caps and barrel-shaped, stalkless fruits with a small disc and three to four triangular valves. It is used as a timber, shade or ornamental tree in Portugal, Sicily and Spain. *E.* x *trabutii* is an Algerian hybrid generally similar to Red Mahogany, but with more oval adult leaves, a shorter bud-cap and a fruit which is more tapered at the base. It is planted in southern Europe.

Swamp Mahogany: fruit

Swamp Mahogany *Eucalyptus robustus* Up to 30m Shady evergreen with tough, fibrous bark, dark in colour. Juvenile leaves opposite, up to 11cm long and 7cm wide, thick, lance-shaped or elliptical. Adult leaves alternate, up to 18cm long and 4cm wide, lance-shaped to oval, with pointed tips, shiny dark green above, dull green below. Flowers white, five to ten in clusters with a flat stalk 2-3cm long. Flower-buds have a beak-like cap. Stalked fruits up to 1.5cm long, cylindrical or urn-shaped with an oblique disc and deeply enclosed valves. *Flowering:* September to July. *Distribution:* Native to eastern Australia, planted as an ornamental or shade tree, and for wind-breaks in France, Italy, Portugal, Sardinia and Spain.

Tuart Gum: fruit

Tuart Gum *Eucalyptus gomphocephalus* Up to 40m Open evergreen with persistent, light grey, fibrous bark. Juvenile leaves opposite, about 6cm long and 4cm wide, oval but widest above the middle. Adult leaves alternate, up to 17cm long and 2cm wide, thick, narrowly lance-shaped and pointed, with a distinct petiole. Flowers three to seven in a cluster with a strap-shaped stalk. Stalkless flower-buds about 2.5cm long have a hemispherical or conical cap, broader than the calyx-tube. Fruits about 1.5cm long, bell-shaped with a disc that forms a rim around the strong, slightly projecting valves. *Flowering:* January to April. *Distribution:* Coastal tree native to Australia, resistant to drought and wind. It has been experimentally planted for afforestation of sand dunes, particularly in Italy, Sicily and Spain.

Red Mahogany

Swamp Mahogany

Swamp Mahogany

Tuart Gum

Tasmanian Blue Gum *Eucalyptus globulus* Up to 40m occasionally to 65m Large, fast-growing evergreen with grey-brown bark peeling away in long strips. Strongly coloured blue-green juvenile leaves opposite, up to 16cm long and 9cm wide, oval, and clasping the stem. Dark green adult leaves alternate and hanging, up to 30cm long and 4cm wide, narrowly oval or sickle-shaped, with a long slender tip. Flowers about 4cm across, white, almost stalkless, usually solitary or in clusters of two or three. Flower-buds up to 3cm long have a waxy, pale bluish, hemispherical cap. Woody fruit up to 2.5cm long, top-shaped and strongly ribbed, with a waxy white bloom. *Flowering:* September to December. *Distribution:* Native to Australia (Tasmania and Victoria). Planted on a very large scale in the Mediterranean region for timber, paper pulp and eucalyptus oil.

Maiden's Gum *Eucalyptus globulus* subsp. *maidenii* 15-45m Smaller and more open-crowned than Tasmanian Blue Gum, with smooth bluish-white bark that is shed annually. Juvenile leaves opposite, up to 16cm long and 12cm wide, ovate, often heart-shaped at the base, distinctly greyish. Adult leaves alternate, up to 20cm long and 2.5cm wide, narrowly lance- or sickle-shaped, dark shiny green, leathery. Flowers like those of Tasmanian Blue Gum but 1.5cm long in bud, with a beaked cap and borne in flat-stalked clusters 10-15cm long with three to seven or more flowers. Fruits usually on short stalks, 1cm long, bell-shaped or conical, with a waxy surface and a smooth, thick, disc partially fused to the projecting valves. *Flowering:* March to September. *Distribution:* Native to south-eastern Australia, successful on good or fairly heavy soils, and cultivated for timber in the Iberian Peninsula, Italy, Sicily and Sardinia. **Snow Gum** (*E. pauciflora* subsp. *niphophila*) is a small Australian mountain tree, rarely above 15m, with grey-green peeling bark and cup-shaped fruits about 12mm long on short stalks. It is planted as an ornamental in cooler areas such as Britain.

Snow Gum: fruit

Cider Gum *Eucalyptus gunnii* Up to 30m Generally similar to Tasmanian Blue Gum but smaller, the bark shedding to leave a smooth green-, pink- or white-tinged trunk but may persist in a greyish 'stocking' on the lower part of the trunk. Opposite, often circular juvenile leaves 3-4cm long clasp the stem. Alternate adult leaves up to 7cm long, grey-green. Flowers white, in clusters of three, the buds with shortly beaked caps. Fruit of about 1cm long has a small, depressed, blunt disc, and three to five narrowly projecting valves. *Flowering:* May to June. *Distribution:* Native to southern Australia and Tasmania, planted as an ornamental in the cooler parts of Europe.

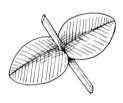

Cider Gum: juvenile leaves

Lemon-scented Spotted Gum *Eucalyptus citriodora* 25-40m Tall, slender evergreen with white or pinkish bark which is shed frequently. Juvenile leaves opposite, up to 15cm long and 6cm wide, elliptical, bristly. Adult leaves alternate, up to 25cm long and 4cm wide, narrowly lance-shaped and with a strong lemon scent. Flowers white, up to ten in each branched, flattened spike. Flower-buds 1.2cm long with a hemispherical cap. Fruit globose, narrow at the mouth, with a wide disc and three to four enclosed valves. *Flowering:* June to August. *Distribution:* Native to Australia (Queensland); cultivated as an ornamental in the Iberian Peninsula.

Lemon-scented Spotted Gum: fruit

Tasmanian Blue Gum

Tasmanian Blue Gum

Tasmanian Blue Gum

Maiden's Gum

Cider Gum

Lemon-scented Spotted Gum

Forest Red Gum:
fruit

Red Gum *Eucalyptus camaldulensis* Up to 40m Large, spreading, evergreen with a short, stout trunk and well-branched crown. White bark mottled pink and grey, shedding in plates. Juvenile leaves opposite, up to 9cm long and 4cm wide, oval, bluish-green. Adult leaves alternate, up to 25cm long and 2cm wide, narrowly oval, with a long, slender, drawn-out tip. Flowers white, in stalked clusters of five to ten. Flower-buds up to 1cm long with a brownish, conical or beak-like cap. Woody fruits 7-8mm long, hemispherical, opening by four inward-pointing teeth. *Flowering:* December to February. *Distribution:* Native to Australia, cultivated for timber in much of the Mediterranean region, especially Spain. Similar **Forest Red Gum** (*E. tereticornis*) has alternate juvenile leaves, pink or white flowers spindle-shaped in bud with a long cap, and ovoid fruits with prominently protruding valves. From eastern Australia, it is planted both for timber and ornament, particularly in Italy and the Iberian Peninsula. **Swamp Gum** (*E. rudis*) has grey, rough and persistent bark, grey-green juvenile leaves, cream to pale yellow flowers with conical bud-caps and fruits with prominently protruding valves. Widespread Australian tree grown for ornament and shade, also used to control erosion and waterlogging, particularly in Italy, Sardinia and Sicily.

Ribbon Gum *Eucalyptus viminalis* Up to 50m Large evergreen with a long, straight, unbranched trunk, the thin outer bark shredding and hanging in ribbons, revealing the white inner bark beneath. Juvenile leaves opposite, up to 10cm long and 3cm wide, the bases clasping the stem. Adult leaves alternate, up to 18cm long and 2cm wide, narrowly oval, with a long drawn-out tip. Stalkless flowers 1.5cm across, creamy white, in clusters of three. Flower-buds with scarlet, hemispherical or conical caps. Fruit almost spherical, opening by three to four valves. *Flowering:* December to June. *Distribution:* Native of southern and eastern Australia. Grown in Europe for shade, timber and as a cold-tolerant ornamental.

Ribbon Gum: fruit

Pomegranate *Punica granatum* Up to 8m Small tree with a slender trunk branching from near the ground and covered by pale brown, finely grooved bark. Crown irregular, with slender branches angled upwards and often spiny. Leaf-buds red. Opposite leaves 2-8cm long, oblong to narrowly oval but widest above the middle; petiole very short. Flowers solitary or paired at shoot-tips, five to seven petals distinctively crumpled before opening, five to seven hooded, leathery, red sepals joined into a long tube, which persists on the fruit. Stamens numerous, single stigma globular on a long style. Berry-like fruit 5-8cm long, globular, with a leathery skin, the numerous seeds embedded in purple or yellowish translucent pulp. *Flowering:* June to October. *Distribution:* Ancient introduction from western Asia into Europe, cultivated for its edible fruits and widely naturalised in the Mediterranean. The cultivar cv. 'Nanum' is sold as a pot plant.

Red Gum

Red Gum

Ribbon Gum

Ribbon Gum

Pomegranate

Pomegranate

Cornelian Cherry

Cornelian Cherry *Cornus mas* Up to 8m Small tree or shrub with dense clusters of bright yellow flowers appearing before the leaves. Crown open, with spreading branches and downswept twigs. Opposite leaves 4-10cm long, ovate to elliptical and pointed, yellowish-green and conspicuously veined. Flowers about 4mm across, four-petalled, bright yellow, appearing before the leaves in axillary clusters 2cm across. Fleshy berry 12-20mm long, oblong to ovoid, bright red and acid-tasting when ripe. *Flowering:* February to March. *Distribution:* Native to central and south-eastern Europe, in thickets and woods on all but acid soils; also cultivated for fruit and for ornament.

Chinese Persimmon

Date-plum *Diospyros lotus* Up to 14m Small tree with edible but rather insipid yellow fruits. Crown rounded, bark furrowed and cracked, grey or sometimes pinkish. Young twigs hairy. Alternate leaves 6-12cm long, elliptical to oblong with a rounded or wedge-shaped base and pointed tip, hairy when young but more or less glabrous when mature, margins wavy but entire, glossy green above, bluish-green below. Flowers urn-shaped, axillary, males and females on different trees; males 5mm long, in clusters of two to three, females 8-10mm long, solitary. Calyx with four short, fringed lobes hairy within, corolla reddish- or greenish-white with four recurved lobes. Fruit about 1.5cm in diameter, globose, ripening yellow or bluish-black and seated in the enlarged calyx. *Flowering:* July. *Distribution:* Native to Asia, cultivated throughout Europe, in the south as a fruit tree, in the north only as an ornamental. Similar **Common Persimmon** (*D. virginiana*) from North America has leaves ranging from 1-20cm long on the same twig, and flowers 1-1.5cm long. **Chinese Persimmon** (*D. kaki*) has much larger, yellow or orange fruits 3.5-7.5cm in diameter, becoming sweet when overripe.

Snowbell-tree

Storax *Styrax officinalis* 2-7m Tree with all parts more or less densely covered with white, stellate hairs. Small, rounded or flat-topped tree or shrub with smooth grey bark. Alternate leaves 3-7cm long, broadly oval to oblong with wedge-shaped base and blunt tip, green above, paler to whitish and more densely hairy beneath. Flowers about 2cm across, white, bell-shaped, with five deep lobes; in clusters of three to six hanging from leaf-axils or tips of twigs. Fruit ovoid, with dense grey hairs, tipped with the remains of the slender style and seated in the cup-like calyx. *Flowering:* April to May. *Distribution:* Woodland tree native to the Mediterranean from Italy eastwards; also naturalised in France. The gum, storax, is obtained by making cuts in the bark of the trunk and branches. Similar **Snowbell-tree** (*S. japonica*) flowers later, in June to July, and more profusely. Native to China and Japan and often grown for ornament in northern Europe.

Cornelian Cherry

Cornelian Cherry

Date-plum

Date-plum

Date-plum

Storax

Strawberry-tree *Arbutus unedo* Up to 12m Dense, rounded evergreen with fissured reddish bark flaking in strips from the short trunk. Young twigs red, with at least some glandular hairs. Alternate, glossy leaves 4-11cm long, oblong to lance-shaped, with sharp irregular teeth, those towards the leaf-tip tinged red; petiole about 6mm long, also red. Flowers 9mm long; calyx with rounded lobes, corolla urn-shaped, greenish- or pinkish-white; appearing in drooping clusters alongside the previous year's ripe fruits. Fruit 2cm in diameter, globose, warty and deep red when ripe. *Flowering:* October to November. *Distribution:* Native to the Mediterranean where it grows in evergreen scrub, and to mild parts of western Europe as far north as Ireland, where it occurs in young oakwoods.

Hybrid
Strawberry-tree:
flowers

Eastern Strawberry-tree *Arbutus andrachne* Up to 12m Evergreen tree resembling Strawberry-tree but differing in some characteristics of the bark, leaves and fruit, and in its flowering time. Bark smooth, rich orange-red, shed in papery sheets. Young twigs completely glabrous. Alternate leaves 3-6cm long, glossy green, usually entire; petiole 15-30mm long, green. Flowers like Strawberry-tree but the clusters erect, not drooping, and the calyx with narrow pointed lobes. Globose fruit 0.8-1.2cm in diameter, orange when ripe with a network of raised lines. *Flowering:* March to April. *Distribution:* Endemic to young evergreen woods and scrub in the Aegean region and the Crimea. **Hybrid Strawberry-tree** (*A.* x *andrachnoides*) is a vigorous hybrid between Strawberry- and Eastern Strawberry-tree, occurring where the parents grow together and sometimes also cultivated. It has the hairy twigs and red-tinged, toothed leaves of one parent and the bright bark of the other; may flower in autumn or spring.

Portugal Heath:
flower

Tree-heath *Erica arborea* Up to 7m Small evergreen tree or stout, dense shrub. Young twigs densely hairy, some hairs short and smooth, others long and spiky. Dark green leaves in whorls of four around the shoot, erect or spreading, 3-5mm long, very narrow with rolled-under margins concealing the underside. Flowers numerous in long, dense spikes, the corolla white and bell-shaped, the stout style tipped with a broad, knob-shaped white stigma. Fruit a small capsule. *Flowering:* March to May. *Distribution:* Native to the Mediterranean region and the Atlantic islands, in woods and scrub, sometimes the dominant tree. Similar **Portugal Heath** (*E. lusitanica*) reaches only 3.5m in height. It has only smooth hairs, light green leaves 5-7mm long, a pink-tinged corolla 4-5mm long, a slender style and a red stigma. Native to Iberia and southern France and naturalised in Britain.

Rhododendron: fruit

Rhododendron *Rhododendron ponticum* 2-5m, sometimes to 8m Small shrubby evergreen tree with spreading branches. Alternate leathery leaves 8-25cm long, elliptical to oblong, dark, shiny green above, paler beneath. Flowers in clusters of 8-15 on stalks 2-6mm long. Calyx very small, green. Corolla 4-6cm across, broadly bell-shaped and five-lobed, dull or violet-purple. Ten stamens. Fruit a dry capsule containing numerous small, flat seeds. *Flowering:* May to June. *Distribution:* Native to mountain woodlands on acid soils in southern parts of Portugal, Spain and the Balkans, but widely naturalised in north-western Europe from Belgium to Ireland.

Strawberry-tree

Strawberry-tree

Eastern Strawberry-tree

Tree-heath

Tree-heath

Rhododendron

Manna Ash: flower

Manna Ash *Fraxinus ornus* Up to 24m Showy clusters of creamy white flowers appear as this domed tree comes into full leaf. Bark smooth and grey. Winter buds grey or brown with a white bloom. Opposite, pinnate leaves up to 30cm long with five to nine leaflets each 3-10cm long, ovate, irregularly toothed, downy with white or brownish hairs on the veins beneath. Flowers in large clusters 15-20cm long, fragrant, with four narrow petals 5-6mm long. Slender, winged fruits 1.5-2.5cm long hang in dense clusters. *Flowering:* May. *Distribution:* Native to central and southern Europe, planted as a street tree and for the sweet, sticky, edible gum known as manna.

Common Ash: winter buds

Common Ash *Fraxinus excelsior* Up to 40m Large tree with tiny, inconspicuous flowers appearing before the leaves. Crown open and domed. Smooth grey bark eventually develops interwoven ridges. Twigs markedly flattened at the nodes. Prominent winter buds large, black and conical. Opposite, pinnate leaves 20-35cm long, with 7-13 leaflets each 5-12cm long, oblong-oval, pointed and toothed, with dense, white hairs along the midrib beneath. Flowers appear before the leaves in axillary clusters, males and females often on separate twigs. Both sexes purple, lacking sepals and petals. Winged fruits 2.5-5cm long form dense, hanging clusters. *Flowering:* April to May. *Distribution:* Native and common throughout Europe, also widely planted.

White Ash: fruit

Red Ash *Fraxinus pennsylvanica* Up to 25cm Resembling Common Ash but smaller, with furrowed, reddish-brown bark. Twigs stout and hairy. Winter buds brown. Opposite leaves pinnate, up to 22cm long with five to seven, rarely nine, leaflets each 8-15cm long and narrowly oval to oblong, pointed, finely and irregularly toothed, the blade often unequal at the base and continuing on to the short petiole; leaf-axis and undersides of leaflets have dense white hairs. Flowers in hairy axillary clusters appear before the leaves, red males and greenish females on different trees; females have four sepals, males none; both sexes lack petals. Winged fruits 3-6cm long. *Flowering:* April to May. *Distribution:* Native to eastern North America, planted and sometimes naturalised in central and south-eastern Europe. **Green Ash** (var. *subintegerrima*) is a glabrous variety of Red Ash with thick-textured leaves, also planted in Europe. **White Ash** (*F. americana*) has glabrous leaflets white beneath, the blades not continuing on to the petioles. Native to the same area as Red Ash and planted in Europe.

Fraxinus pallisiae

Narrow-leaved Ash *Fraxinus angustifolia* Up to 25m Somewhat resembling the larger Common Ash but with very narrow leaflets. Crown rather sparse with upwardly angled branches. Dark grey fissured bark becomes bubbly and warty. Winter buds coffee brown and hairy. Opposite, pinnate leaves 15-25cm long, with 5-13 leaflets each 3-9cm long, lance-shaped and long-pointed, toothed, glabrous or hairy only at the base beneath. Leaflets of older trees much narrower than those of younger trees. Flowers appear before leaves in axillary clusters; they are bisexual and lack sepals and petals. Winged fruits 2-4.5cm long hang in small clusters. *Flowering:* May. *Distribution:* Native to southern and south-eastern Europe, sometimes planted for ornament. Similar **F. pallisiae** from south-eastern Europe has densely hairy twigs, leaf-axes and petioles.

Manna Ash

Manna Ash

Common Ash

Common Ash

Red Ash

Narrow-leaved Ash

Olive *Olea europaea* Up to 15m Long-lived evergreen, old specimens with a broad crown and thick, gnarled and silvery trunk and main branches pitted with large cavities and holes. Opposite, leathery leaves 2-8cm long, lance-shaped, grey-green above with silver hairs beneath, and a very short petiole. Small, white, fragrant flowers four-petalled, in loose, many-flowered axillary spikes. Oily-fleshed ovoid fruit 1-3.5cm long, green in the first year, ripening black in the second; it contains a single large stone. *Flowering:* July to August. *Distribution:* Native to southern Europe; an important crop since ancient times. The cultivated tree (var. *europaea*) is grown throughout Mediterranean regions, forming shady groves, and is the source of olive oil. Wild trees (var. *sylvestris*) found in lightly wooded, rocky areas in southern Europe are smaller, bushy and spiny.

Phillyrea angustifolia

Phillyrea *Phillyrea latifolia* Up to 15m Small evergreen tree, sometimes a shrub, with a dense crown; branches of young trees erect, spreading in older trees. Bark smooth and grey. Slender twigs have dense short hairs. Opposite leaves of two kinds: those on young growth 2-7cm long, usually oval to heart-shaped, with toothed margins; those of mature growth 1-6cm long, lance-shaped to elliptical, entire or with short, fine teeth. Small flowers in short axillary clusters; calyx thin-textured, yellowish, with four triangular lobes; corolla greenish-white with four oblong lobes. Dry fruit 7-10mm in diameter, ovoid when young, globose and blue-black when ripe. *Flowering:* June. *Distribution:* Native throughout the Mediterranean region where it occurs in evergreen woodlands; planted for ornament in coastal areas. Similar **P. angustifolia** is shrubby, with all the leaves narrow and usually entire, a thick-textured brown calyx with rounded lobes, and fruits with a short slender point. Grows in similar habitats to Phillyrea but only in western and central parts of the Mediterranean.

Common Privet

Glossy Privet *Ligustrum lucidum* Up to 15m Dense evergreen with spreading branches and twigs flecked with white pores. Opposite leaves 8-12cm long, oval, long-pointed, thick and leathery, reddish when young, becoming dark green and very glossy above, paler and matt beneath. Loose, conical flower-heads 12-20cm long, axillary. Small flowers white, heavily scented, the tubular corolla with four spreading lobes. Berries about 1cm long, oval, black with a white bloom. *Flowering:* August to September or even later. *Distribution:* Native to China; widely used in southern Europe as a hedge, ornamental and street tree. Similar **Common Privet** (*L. vulgare*), a lime-loving, usually deciduous shrub native to woods and scrub in most of Europe, and the semi-evergreen **Oval-leaved Privet** (*L. ovalifolium*), from Japan, are both common as hedging plants in northern Europe.

Olive

Olive

Olive

Phillyrea

Glossy Privet

Glossy Privet

Hungarian Lilac

Orange-ball-tree:
flower head

Lilac *Syringa vulgaris* 3-7m Profusely flowering tree or dense shrub, suckering freely and often forming tall, twiggy thickets. Opposite, slightly leathery leaves of 4-8cm long, oval or heart-shaped and yellowish green. Showy, conical flower-heads 10-20cm long, borne in pairs at tip of twigs. Fragrant, rather fleshy flowers 8-12mm long, tubular with four spreading lobes, usually lilac, but may be white or cream in garden plants. Fruit an ovoid brown capsule about 1cm long. *Flowering:* May or June. *Distribution:* Native to rocky, scrub-covered hillsides in the Balkan Peninsula but widely cultivated for ornament and naturalised in many parts of Europe. Similar **Hungarian Lilac** (*S. josikaea*) is a rarer tree endemic to the Transylvanian and Carpathian Mountains and naturalised in Germany. It has narrower, elliptical leaves with wedge-shaped bases and solitary flower-heads.

Buddleia *Buddleia davidii* Up to 5m Often a robust shrub but frequently making a short-trunked small tree with straight or slightly arching branches. Twigs cylindrical or angled, hairy. Opposite leaves 10-25cm long, oval to lance-shaped, sharply toothed, glabrous or thinly hairy above, densely hairy beneath; petiole very short. Flowers crowded into dense, narrowly conical spikes at the tips of the twigs. Stalks of spikes, flower-stalks and calyces all densely covered with stellate hairs. Corolla with a narrow tube about 10mm long, with four spreading lobes 1-2mm long, lilac to deep violet, with an orange ring at the mouth of the tube. Fruit a capsule, persisting on the tree through winter. *Flowering:* June to October. *Distribution:* Native to China, commonly planted for ornament and widely naturalised on waste ground and sometimes in woods in much of western and central Europe. Several similar species are also planted as ornamentals and may be naturalised in places. **Orange-ball-tree** (*B. globosa*) from South America has globose heads of orange flowers. **B. alternifolia**, from China, has alternate leaves and flowers in stalkless, axillary clusters.

Shrub Tobacco *Nicotiana glauca* Up to 6m, rarely to 10m Usually a tall shrub but often making a slender, single-stemmed, thin-crowned tree resembling a sapling. Twigs green. Alternate leaves 5-25cm long, elliptical to oval, pale bluish-green. Flowers in loose clusters at tips of twigs. Calyx green, 10-15mm long, tubular with five short teeth; corolla yellow, 30-40mm long, tubular with five short lobes of 2-4mm. Fruit an ovoid capsule. *Flowering:* More or less all year. *Distribution:* Native to South America but cultivated for ornament in Europe and widely naturalised on waste ground, walls and roadsides throughout most of the Mediterranean region.

Lilac

Lilac

Buddleia

Shrub Tobacco

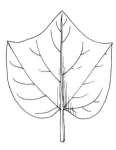

Yellow Catalpa

Indian Bean-tree *Catalpa bignonioides* Up to 20m Broadly domed tree with conspicuous, long, bean-like capsules persisting on the otherwise bare twigs in winter. Grey-brown bark smooth, eventually cracked and scaly. Leaves usually opposite, rarely in whorls of three, 10-25cm long, oval with a rounded or heart-shaped base and short, tapering tip, may be shallowly lobed; pale green or sometimes purple-tinged when young and densely hairy beneath. Flowers 5cm in diameter, with five frilled white petals spotted with yellow and purple and borne in loose, conical clusters 15-25cm long. Pendulous fruit capsules 15-40cm long and less than 1cm wide contain flat, papery seeds. *Flowering:* June to August. *Distribution:* Native to south-eastern North America and the commonest of several similar species grown as ornamentals and street trees in southern and western Europe. Two similar species are also planted for ornament. **Yellow Catalpa** (*C. ovata*), from China, has broader leaves with five short-pointed lobes, larger flower-heads and flowers 2.5cm long flushed with yellow and spotted with red. **Hybrid Catalpa** (*C. x erubescens*) is a hybrid between Indian Bean-tree and Yellow Catalpa with very large leaves up to 60cm long, unfolding purple.

Foxglove-tree

Foxglove-tree *Paulownia tomentosa* 12-26m Sparsely branched, spreading tree with huge leaves and large, tubular, purplish flowers. Stout, purplish twigs dotted with numerous lenticels. Opposite leaves 45cm long and 25cm wide, heart-shaped with a long, tapering tip, grey felted beneath, in young trees often with several shallow, tapering lobes: petioles 10-15cm long, rarely up to 45cm, densely hairy. Large, brown, hairy flower-buds formed in autumn, conspicuous on the twigs through winter. Flower-heads 20-30cm long, erect, appearing before the leaves. Violet flowers up to 6cm long, the corolla with a long tube coloured yellow within and ending in five spreading lobes. Fruit a glossy, sticky capsule 5cm long, ovoid with a tapering tip. *Flowering:* May. *Distribution:* Native to China, a striking ornamental tree common in gardens and sometimes planted as a street tree in southern Europe.

Jacaranda:
single pinna

Jacaranda *Jacaranda mimosifolia* Up to 50m, sometimes more Stately tree with feathery foliage, often flowering twice during each year. Semi-evergreen, shedding leaves in spring. Opposite leaves about 45cm long, twice-pinnate, each pinna with 14-24 pairs of elliptical to oblong, hairy leaflets. Loose, conical flower-clusters 20cm long are erect but the individual blue flowers are pendent. Corolla about 6cm long with a straight or slightly curved tube and five spreading lobes. Fruit a circular capsule 5cm in diameter, containing numerous winged seeds. *Flowering:* April to May and often again in autumn. *Distribution:* Native to Argentina, widely planted as an ornamental in warm, frost-free parts of Europe.

Indian Bean-tree

Indian Bean-tree

Foxglove-tree

Foxglove-tree

Jacaranda

Jacaranda

*Myoporum
tetrandrum*

Elder

Waterbush *Myoporum tenuifolium* Up to 8m Rounded evergreen tree with a short trunk, sometimes a shrub. Twigs pale green. Alternate leaves 4.5-10cm long, narrowly oval with a sharply tapered base, margins entire or with a few teeth, dark glossy green above and dotted with numerous pale, shiny glands. Fragrant flowers axillary, sometimes solitary but usually in clusters of five to nine, corolla 10-12mm across, bell-shaped with a short tube, five white, spreading lobes spotted with purple and curling white hairs on the inner surface. Fruit 7-9mm long, ovoid, slightly fleshy, ripening purplish-black. *Flowering:* April. *Distribution:* Native to Australia and New Caledonia, planted mainly for shelter in Iberia, the Balearics and the Atlantic islands and naturalised in places. **M. tetrandrum**,from Australia and Tasmania, is very similar but is usually a shrub with much smaller leaves widest above the middle and toothed towards the tip. It is planted for coastal shelter and is naturalised in Portugal.

Elder *Sambucus nigra* Up to 10m Small, bushy tree or shrub with headily fragrant flowers but foetid, unpleasant-smelling leaves. Main branches curve outwards but vigorous straight shoots often grow from the base of the short trunk. Grey or light brown bark is deeply grooved, thick and corky. Twigs have a white central pith. Opposite leaves pinnate with five to seven leaflets each 4.5-12cm long, ovate, sharply toothed, dull green above, sparse hairs beneath. Branched, flat-topped heads 10-24cm in diameter contain numerous small, white, five-petalled and fragrant flowers. The whole head nods when black berries of 6-8mm are fully ripe. *Flowering:* June to July. *Distribution:* Common in open woods, hedgerows and on waste ground where soil is disturbed and nitrogen rich. Native more or less throughout Europe.

Alpine Elder *Sambucus racemosa* Up to 4m Closely resembling Elder but smaller, the twigs with a reddish-brown central pith. Leaflets like those of Elder but glabrous when mature. Flower-heads ovoid and only 2.5-6cm long, with yellowish- or greenish-white flowers. Fruit scarlet. *Flowering:* April to May. *Distribution:* Mountain species native to continental Europe from the Baltic south to a line from the Pyrenees to Albania and Bulgaria.

Waterbush

Waterbush

Elder

Elder

Elder

Alpine Elder

Guelder-rose

Wayfaring-tree

Guelder-rose *Viburnum opulus* Up to 4m Small, spreading tree with hydrangea-like heads of large sterile flowers surrounding much smaller, fertile flowers. Twigs angled, greyish and hairy. Opposite leaves 3-8cm long, downy beneath with three or five spreading, irregularly toothed lobes. Flowers five-petalled, white in circular heads 4.5-10.5cm in diameter with sterile flowers 15-20mm long around the rim and fertile flowers only 4-7mm long in the centre. More or less globose fruits 8mm long, translucent red, often persisting on the tree well after leaves have fallen. *Flowering:* June to July. *Distribution:* Native to most of Europe, in moist wood margins, thickets and hedges. **Snowball-tree** (var.*roseum*) is a common garden ornamental, with globose flower-heads made up entirely of large, sterile flowers.

Wayfaring-tree *Viburnum lantana* Up to 6m Small, spreading tree or shrub found mainly on chalky soils. Twigs cylindrical, greyish with stellate hairs. Opposite leaves 4-14cm long, oval, shortly and finely toothed, rough, grey-green, with sparse stellate hairs, especially beneath. Flower-heads 6-10cm in diameter, branched and domed, many-flowered. Flowers 5-9mm across, five-petalled, white. Fruits 8mm long, oval, red at first, ripening suddenly but not simultaneously to black, so that each fruiting head contains a mixture of the two colours. *Flowering:* May to June. *Distribution:* Grows in hedgerows and on the fringes of woods, preferring chalky soils. Native to Europe as far north as Britain and Sweden.

Laurustinus *Viburnum tinus* Up to 7m Winter-flowering evergreen tree or shrub with dense crown and attractive pink and white flowers. Twigs weakly angled, glabrous or sparsely hairy. Opposite leaves 3-10cm long, narrowly to very broadly oval, entire, dark green and slightly glossy above, a few hairs beneath. Branched flower-clusters 4-9cm across. Flowers 5-9mm across, five-petalled, pale pink on the outside and white within. Fruits about 8mm, more or less globose, metallic blue. *Flowering:* February, but may continue to June. *Distribution:* Mainly found in woods and thickets on stony soils. Native to the Mediterranean region but frequently grown as an ornamental elsewhere.

Guelder-rose

Guelder-rose

Wayfaring-tree

Laurustinus

Cabbage-tree

Adam's Needle

Cabbage-tree *Cordyline australis* Up to 13m Palm-like evergreen with bare, forked trunks topped with dense tufts of narrow, sword-shaped leaves. Trunks fork after flowering and often sucker, forming clumps. Bark brown or greyish, cracked into a regular pattern of squares. Leaves 30-90cm long, hard and sharp-pointed, dark green or often tinged yellow, the youngest erect, the oldest hanging down and obscuring the trunk. Fragrant flowers about 1cm across, creamy white, in a huge, branched cluster 60-120cm long, growing from the centre of the crown. Six perianth-segments occur in two whorls of three. Berries 6mm in diameter, globose, usually bluish-white. *Flowering:* June or July. *Distribution:* Native to New Zealand, quite hardy and a popular ornamental and street tree in southern and western Europe, but only near coasts.

Spanish Bayonet *Yucca aloifolia* Up to 10m Resembles Cabbage-tree but more robust with a smooth, stout trunk and much-branched crown. Stiff bluish-green leaves form tufts at the tips of branches, 50-100cm long, sword-shaped with shortly toothed margins. White flowers 4-6cm long; perianth bell-shaped with six purple-tinged lobes. Edible fruit elongated, ripening purplish black. *Flowering:* April to May. *Distribution:* Native to southern North America and the West Indies, widely grown for ornament in southern Europe and occasionally escaping into the wild. **Adam's Needle** (*Y. gloriosa*), native to eastern North America and also planted for ornament, is very similar but has a much shorter, unbranched trunk with a single dense tuft of leaves.

Dragon-tree *Dracaena draco* Up to 6m, sometimes to 15m Extremely long-lived evergreen with a massive, fluted and buttressed trunk. Short, thick branches fork regularly and bear dense tufts of leaves at the tips, giving a broad, flattened or slightly domed, umbrella-like crown. Bark silvery. Tough leaves up to 50cm long, sword-shaped, bluish-green. Small flowers greenish-white, in large much-branched clusters emerging from the centres of the leaf-tufts. Six perianth-segments, fused towards the base. Berries about 1cm in diameter, globose, yellowish-orange when ripe. *Flowering:* August to September. *Distribution:* Endemic to the Canary Islands and Madeira but planted as an ornamental and street tree in the Mediterranean region.

Banana *Musa acuminata* Up to 3m Strictly a giant herb growing from a horizontal underground stem, but tree-like in appearance. Hollow 'stem' consists of elongated, closely sheathed leaf-bases and dies after fruiting. Crown formed of oar-shaped leaf-blades 120-200cm long which often become split and ragged with age. Complex inflorescence 100cm long grows up through the hollow 'stem' emerging from the crown and hanging downwards; it is protected by large, sheathing, purplish bracts which peel back to reveal the flowers. Male flowers borne towards the tip of the inflorescence, females in rings below. Fruits curve backwards as they ripen from green to yellow. The abortive seeds are contained in a thick, creamy white pulp. *Flowering:* March to September. *Distribution:* Native to tropical Asia. Many cultivars and clones are known, some of which are cultivated as a fruit crop on terraces and in small plantations in coastal parts of the Mediterranean region.

Cabbage-tree

Spanish Bayonet

Dragon-tree

Banana

European Fan
Palm: ♂ flower

European Fan Palm *Chamaerops humilis* Up to 2m, rarely to 6m Dwarf palm with stiff, fan-shaped leaves. Thick, fibre-covered trunks usually form clumps but are often completely absent in wild trees. Rather stiff, green, greyish or bluish leaves of 100cm diameter are deeply divided into numerous narrow, tapering segments, forked or notched at the tip; old leaf-bases persist as white or grey fibres on the trunk. Bright yellow male and greenish female flowers usually on different trees, in dense, branched clusters 35cm long emerging from protective sheathing bracts. Both sexes have perianth-segments in two whorls of three, the outer spreading. Fruits up to 4.5cm diameter, globose or oblong, yellow, orange or brown when ripe. *Flowering:* March to June. *Distribution:* The only common native palm in Europe, mainly found in sandy coastal regions in western Mediterranean regions.

Chinese Windmill Palm *Trachycarpus fortunei* Up to 14m Compact palm with a brown and shaggy trunk covered with the matted fibrous bases of dead leaves, at least on the upper part near the crown. Fan-shaped or circular leaves up to 100cm in diameter, divided almost to the base into stiff, narrow, pleated segments; long petioles fibrous at the base. Many-branched, conical flower-clusters 70-80cm long, sheathed with white or brown bracts, males and females on different trees; flowers fragrant, yellow, the inner three perianth-segments larger than the outer three. Three-lobed fruits about 2cm long, purplish-white. *Flowering:* March to June. *Distribution:* Native to China. Grown as an ornamental and roadside tree in the Mediterranean, but quite hardy and grown as far north as southern England.

Petticoat Palm *Washingtonia filifera* Up to 15m Fast-growing, hardy palm with a thick trunk slightly swollen at the base. Bark grey, ringed and slightly rough, but usually hidden by a dense skirt of dead leaves unless these are deliberately disturbed. Grey-green leaves 150-200cm long, divided at least to halfway into narrow, two-lobed and drooping segments joined by fine, white threads. Slender, branched flower-clusters 300-500cm long and arching down from the crown have sheathing, eventually papery bracts. Flowers numerous, white, the outer three perianth-segments fused into a bell-shaped tube, the inner three fused only at the base and soon falling. Fruit 6mm long, ovoid, brownish-black when ripe. *Flowering:* March to June. *Distribution:* Native to southern North America and Mexico, commonly planted for ornament in Mediterranean regions.

Petticoat Palm:
fruit

European Fan Palm

European Fan Palm: immature fruit

Chinese Windmill Palm

Petticoat Palm

Canary Island Date Palm *Phoenix canariensis* Up to 20m Stout palm
with a thick trunk up to 150cm in diameter and scarred from old leaf-
bases, and a dense crown of over 100 feathery leaves. Pinnate leaves
reach 5-6m with numerous, narrow and distinctly V-shaped leaflets
40-50cm long which radiate in all planes, those nearest the base of
the leaf viciously spiny. Broom-like flower-clusters numerous, each up
to 200cm long with a single sheathing, deciduous bract. Male and
female flowers on different trees, creamy yellow with six perianth-
segments, the outer three forming a cup. Inedible orange or purplish
fruits about 2cm long, hanging in massive clusters from the crown.
Flowering: March to May. *Distribution:* Native to the Canary Islands,
often planted for ornament in streets, parks and leisure areas in the
Mediterranean region and south-western Europe.

Date Palm: spiny
leaf base

Date Palm *Phoenix dactylifera* Up to 35m Resembles Canary Island
Date Palm but a taller and much more slender tree. It suckers freely at
the base but these are usually cut away in cultivated trees. Crown
thin, with only 20-40 grey-green leaves each up to 400cm long.
Leaflets 30-40cm long but otherwise like those of Canary Island Date
Palm, as are the flower clusters. Fruits larger, 2.5-7.5cm long, usually
orange when ripe, fleshy and sweet. *Flowering:* April to May.
Distribution: Planted on a small scale in southern Europe, especially in
southern Spain, for its fleshy, edible fruits.

*Phoenix
theophrasti:* fruit

Phoenix theophrasti Up to 10m Resembles Canary Island Date Palm
but a much smaller tree with far fewer leaves. Trunks slender and
usually several together. Leaves like those of Canary Island Date Palm
but the leaflets smaller, shorter and bluish-green except for the spiny
leaflets near the base which are yellowish. Male flowers produce
copious, foul-smelling pollen. Fruit about 1.5cm long, dry and fibrous,
ripening from yellowish-orange to blackish. *Flowering:* April.
Distribution: Endemic to Crete and parts of Anatolia where it grows in
sandy soils near the sea.

Chilean Wine Palm *Jubaea chilensis* Up to 30m Large slow-growing
palm with a very thick trunk up to 200cm in diameter and distinctive
lead-grey bark with wide, diamond-shaped leaf-scars. Leaves up to
400cm long, erect and arranged in nearly vertical rows; leaflets
numerous, split at the tips and arranged in two rows. Dense, erect
flower-clusters of about 150cm, protected by a woody, sheathing and
persistent bract. Flowers purplish, males and females in the same
cluster. Six perianth-segments, the outer three narrow in male flowers,
broad in females. Fruit 4-5cm in diameter, globose, pale yellow and
fleshy when ripe. *Flowering:* July to September. *Distribution:* Native
only to a small coastal area of Chile and now rare in the wild, often
planted as an ornamental and street tree in Mediterranean regions.
Two similar palms are also grown for ornament in southern Europe.
Sentry Palm (*Howeia forsterana*), from Lord Howe Island, is a slender
tree with a distinctly ringed trunk and drooping leaflets. **Queen Palm**
(*Arecastrum romanzoffianum*), from South America, has a swelling
near the middle of the trunk and leaflets spreading in all planes.

Canary Island Date Palm

Canary Island Date Palm

Date Palm

Phoenix theophrasti

Phoenix theophrasti: ♂ flowers

Chilean Wine Palm

Field Equipment

When observing or identifying plants it is always preferable to work from fresh or, better, living material. This applies especially to trees, since a complete specimen can hardly be brought home for further study! Tree identification is of necessity largely a field activity.

Various items of field equipment are helpful, but a few are essential. These are a hand-lens, ruler and notebook. A hand-lens or magnifying glass is used to examine very small features or minute details such as hairs or the structure of tiny flowers. It should give a magnification of at least x 10. This is sufficient for most purposes, although one of the more sophisticated models giving both x 10 and x 20 magnifications can be useful. The ruler is obviously used for measuring the various organs and the notebook for recording observations, with sketches of particular features where this is helpful. With these few items, a keen eye and some experience, you can identify the majority of trees.

Although the short list of equipment given above is perfectly adequate, two other items can be very helpful. Trees are generally tall structures and, with frustrating regularity, the only flowers, fruits or whatever organs are required to confirm the identity of a particular specimen are to be found near the top of the tree, well out of reach of the observer. A small pair of binoculars can neatly circumvent this problem and often repay the extra carriage involved. The second item is a camera. Even a simple automatic model will provide records of the shape of a tree and features of the bark which can be studied at leisure later.

A final item of equipment is a field guide! As already mentioned, it is difficult to bring a whole tree home and, however careful one's observations, it is very easy to find - too late - that the vital information has been overlooked. Far better to have the field guide to hand at the same time as the specimen.

Collecting

The casual collecting of specimens of trees, even for identification, should be discouraged, certainly in any quantity. Although it may be tempting to remove a small twig, the breaking off of large portions can cause considerable damage, especially if done clumsily. It is in any case usually unnecessary. A single leaf or flower is often sufficient to confirm identification, especially when allied to careful observations and notes. Various items can often be collected from the ground beneath a tree, particularly fruits. Care must be taken that these do indeed come from the tree in question and not from similar neighbouring trees which might be of another species.

Conservation

Forests still cover some 30 per cent of the land surface of the world. They survive for a variety of reasons – because they are not worth clearing, or will be cleared when resources are available, or have been cleared but allowed to revert to forest. All too few are deliberately maintained. As the role of forests in world ecology has become better appreciated, so the need and the pressure for their conservation have increased, never more so than in recent years. Nowadays tropical rainforests are seen as the prime example of areas in need of conservation, but the same principles apply to forests everywhere, including those of Europe.

Trees are ecologically important in several ways. They play an active role in soil conservation and erosion control, in the recycling of water, oxygen and carbon dioxide and as a renewable resource for timber, food, medicines and genetic material. They also have a role in recreation and, of course, provide a wide range of habitats for other wildlife. Why we need trees is self-evident, but we need to consider how best to use and conserve, and, if necessary, replace them.

A surprising number of ancient natural or semi-natural forests and woods survive in Europe today. For them the future looks relatively good. Increased agricultural efficiency has reduced pressure for farmland. Coupled with a change in public opinion towards the destruction of forests and trees in general this has meant increased protection for these ancient habitats. Even old woodsman skills such as coppicing are making a comeback and modern management is more sympathetic towards these sites. Of course not all is rosy. Ancient hedgerows which are themselves remnants of felled forests are still being destroyed and the use of modern machinery for cutting and maintenance inflicts considerable damage on the survivors. Pollution from acid rain and other sources is a potential cause for concern, although this has yet to be fully understood or assessed.

Afforestation, which has led to many areas being replanted with trees, is often less welcome than it should be. Much of twentieth century afforestation consists of alien monoculture, with large plantations containing a single foreign species of tree. In Britain the most planted tree is the North American Sitka Spruce, so often seen forming lowering doormats of plantations on the crests of distant hills or growing in place of the original mixed woods. Their dense, year-round shade and rot-resistant needles suppress ground plants and reduce the size and variety of habitats available to other wildlife. The Mediterranean equivalent is vast plantations of *Eucalyptus* which bring similar problems, with the additional drawback of greatly increased fire risk. Even campaigns encouraging us to plant new trees to replace losses - remember 'Plant a Tree in '73'? - need careful thinking. Simply planting any tree is not good enough. Alien species compete poorly with local, native trees and suffer more in natural disasters such as the hurricane of 1987.

Despite these problems, the situation is improving. Natural forests can grow and yield well without losing any of their ecological integrity. A multiple-use forest providing timber and sites for wildlife and recreation is more likely to survive than a single-use forest. A further advantage of using native, local trees is the conservation of a diversity of genetic resources, crucial for guarding against such disasters as Dutch elm disease. A number of organisations are now attempting to achieve these goals. The keys are thoughtful use, management and, above all, understanding.

Organisations

The following is a selection of organisations which promote the planting, conserving or understanding of trees. In Britain, county naturalists' trusts and nature conservation groups – the addresses of which can be obtained from local libraries – are also actively concerned with trees and woodlands within their individual areas.

Arboricultural Association
Brokerswood House, Brokerswood, Nr Westbury, Wilts BA13 4EH

Commonwealth Forestry Association
c/o Commonwealth Forestry Institute, South Parks Road, Oxford OX1 3RB

Council for the Protection of Rural England
4 Hobart Place, London SW1W 0HY

Countryside Commission
John Dower House, Crescent Place, Cheltenham, Glos GL50 3RA

International Union for the Conservation of Natural Resources (IUCN)
Avenue du Mont Blanc, CH – 1196, Gland, Switzerland

Men of the Trees
Turners Hill Road, Crawley Down, Crawley, W. Sussex RH10 4HL

National Trust
42 Queen Anne's Gate, London SW1H 9AS

Nature Conservancy Council
19-20 Belgrave Square, London SW1X 8PY

Royal Forestry Society
102 High Street, Tring, Herts HP23 4AH

Tree Council
35 Belgrave Square, London SW1X 8QN

Woodland Trust
Westgate, Grantham, Lincs NG31 6LL

Arboreta

There are numerous gardens and arboreta throughout Europe where collections of trees can be seen. They are owned and run by governments, universities, commercial companies and private individuals. The following are just a very small selection, all open to the public.

Austria
Alpengarten Franz Mayr - Melnhof, Frohnleiten

Belgium
Arboretum, Kalmthout
Aboretum Geographique, Overijse

Bulgaria
Hortus Botanicus Academiae Scietiarum Bulgaricae, Sofia

Czechoslovakia
Arboretum Borova hora VSLD, Zvolen
Slezské Museum - Arboretum, Steborice
"Arboretum Mlynany" - Institute of Dendrobiology of the Slovak Academy of Sciences, Slepcany, District Nitra

Denmark
The Forest Botanical Garden, Aarhus
Forstbotanisk Have, Charlottenlund

Eire
The John F. Kennedy Park, New Ross, County Wexford
National Botanical Gardens, Dublin

Finland
Arboretum Mustila, Elimäki

France
Arboretum de Maison Blanche, Marseilles
Arboretum et Alpinetum Vilmorin, Verrieres-le-Buisson
Muséum National d'Histoire Naturelle, Jardin des Plantes, Paris

Germany
Botanische Garten der Johannes Gutenberg-Universität Mainz, Mainz
Botanische Garten der Stadt Dortmund, Dortmund-Brünninghausen
Forstbotanischer Garten der Technischen Universität Dresden Sektion Forstwirtschaft, Tharandt
Bereich Botanik und Arboretum des Museums für Naturkunde der Humbolt-Universität zu Berlin, Berlin-Baumschulenweg

Hungary
Research Institute for Botany of the Hungarian Academy of Sciences, Vácrátót
Arboretum, Szarvas
Erdészeti és Fairpari Egyetem Botanikus Kertje, Sopron

Italy
Giardino Botanico Hanbury, Latte
Orto Botanico di Napoli, Naples

Netherlands
Arboretum "Poort-Bulten", DeLutte bij Oldenzaal
University Botanic Gardens, Utrecht (and the several annexes, especially the Von Gimborn Arboretum at Doorn)
Stichting Arboretum Trompenburg, Rotterdam

Norway
The Norwegian Arboretum, Store Milde, near Bergen
Ringve Botaniske Hage, Trondheim

Poland
Polish Academy of Sciences, Kórnik Arboretum of the Institute of Dendrology, Kórnik
Wyzsza Skola Rolnicza w Poznaniu, Arboretum Goluchów, Powiat Pleszew

Portugal
Department of Botany of the Faculty of Sciences and Technology of the University of Coimbra, Coimbra

Spain
Real Jardin Botánico, Madrid

Sweden
Göteborgs Botaniska Trädgard, Gothenburg
Arboretum Draffle, Alandsbro

Switzerland
Conservatoire et Jardin botaniques, Geneva
Jardin Alpin d'Aclimatation Floraire, Geneva

United Kingdom
Batsford Arboretum, Moreton-in-Marsh, Gloucestershire
Bicton Gardens, East Budleigh, Devon
Cambridge University Botanic Garden, Cambridge
Castlewellan, Newcastle, Co. Down, N. Ireland
Dawyck Arboretum, Stobo, Peebles, Scotland
Granada Arboretum, Nantwich, Cheshire
Hillier Arboretum, Ampfield, Hampshire
National Pinetum, Bedgebury, Kent
Tresco Abbey Gardens, Tresco, Isles of Scilly
Royal Botanic Garden, Edinburgh, Scotland
Royal Botanic Gardens, Kew, Richmond-upon-Thames, Surrey
Westonbirt Arboretum, Tetbury, Gloucestershire
Wisley Gardens, Woking, Surrey

USSR
Main Botanical Garden, Moscow
Botanical Garden and Schreder's Dendrarium of the Moscow Timiryazev Agricultural Academy, Moscow
Dendrological Park "Trostyanets" of the Central Republic Botanical Garden of the Ukrainian Academy of Sciences, Ichnya Region, Ukraine

Yugoslavia
Arboretum Volcji potok, Radomlje, Slovenia

BIBLIOGRAPHY

The books listed below are just a few of the many dealing with various aspects of trees. They will serve to guide you in extending your studies of and interest in trees.

Bean, W.J. *Trees and Shrubs Hardy in the British Isles* ed. 8. John Murray, London. 1970-1988

Bernatzky, A. *Developments in Agricultural and Managed-forest Ecology, 2. Tree Ecology and Preservation.* Elsevier, Amsterdam. 1978

Blombery, A. and Rodd, T. *Palms.* Angus and Robertson, London. 1982

Edlin, H.L. *The Natural History of Trees.* Weidenfeld and Nicolson, London. 1976

Edlin, H.L. *What Wood is That?.* Stobart and Son, London. 1985

Heywood, V.H. (Ed.) *Flowering Plant Families of the World.* Oxford University Press, Oxford. 1979

Hultén, E. and Fries, M. *Atlas of the North European Vascular Plants.* Koeltz, Königstein, West Germany. 1986

Krüssman, G. *Manual of Cultivated Broad-leaved Trees and Shrubs.* Batsford, London. 1984-1986

Krüssman, G. *Manual of Cultivated Conifers.* Timber Press, Portland, Oregon. 1985

Mabberly, D.J. *The Plant Book.* Cambridge University Press, Cambridge. 1987

Meikle, R.D. *Willows and Poplars of Great Britain and Ireland.* Botanical Society of the British Isles, London. 1984

Phillips, R. and Rix, M. *Shrubs.* Pan, London. 1989. (includes various species which form trees)

Rackham, O. *Trees and Woodland in the British Landscape* revised ed. Dent and Sons, London. 1990

Tompkins, S. *Forestry in Crisis. The Battle for the Hills.* Christopher Helm, London. 1989

Tutin et al, (Eds) *Flora Europaea.* Cambridge University Press, Cambridge. 1964-1980 (vol. I revised 1990)

Wilks, J.H. *Trees of the British Isles in History and Legend.* Anchor Press, Tiptree, Essex. 1972

INDEX

Common Names

Abelitzia 126
Acacia, False 174
Adam's Needle 230
Albizia, Plume 172
Alder, Common 106
    Green 106
    Grey 106
    Italian 106
    Smooth 106
Alder-buckthorn 200
Almond 160
Apple, Crab 142
    Cultivated 142
    Japanese Crab 142
    Paradise 142
    Purple Crab 142
    Siberian Crab 142
Apricot 160
    Briançon 160
Ash, Common 218
    Green 218
    Manna 218
    Narrow-leaved 218
    Red 218
    White 218
Aspen 98
    American 98
    Big-toothed 98
Avocado 134
Azarole 150

Balm-of-Gilead 100
Banana 230
Bay, Sweet 134
Bean-tree, Indian 224
Beech 112
    Oriental 112
    Roble 112
Birch, Downy 108
    Paper-bark 108
    Silver 108
Blackthorn 162
Blackwood 170
Box 196
    Balearic 196
Box-elder 192
Broom, Mount Etna 178
Buckeye, Red 194
    Yellow 194
Buckthorn 200
    Alpine 200
    Mediterranean 200
Buddleia 222
Bullace 162

Bungalay 208
Butter-nut 102

Cabbage-tree 230
Carob 176
Catalpa, Hybrid 224
    Yellow 224
Cedar, Atlantic 72
    Chinese 182
    Japanese Red 76
    -of-Lebanon 72
    Pencil 84
    Western Red 76
    White 76
Cherry, Autumn 166
    Bird 168
    Choke 168
    Cornelian 214
    Japanese 164
    Rum 168
    Saint Lucie 162
    Sargent's 164
    Sour 166
    Spring 166
    Tibetan 164
    Wild 166
    Yoshino 164
Chestnut, Sweet 112
Christ's Thorn 198
Citron 180
Cork-tree, Amur 178
Cotoneaster, Himalayan Tree 146
    Weeping 146
Cottonwood 100
Cypress, Hinoki 78
    Italian 80
    Lawson 78
    Leyland 78
    Mexican 80
    Monterey 80
    Nootka 78
    Sawara 78
    Smooth Arizona 80
    Rough-barked Arizona 80

Damson 162
Date-plum 214
Deodar 72
Douglas-fir 56
    Large-coned 56
Dragon-tree 230

Elder 226
    Alpine 226

Elm, Caucasian 126
    Dutch 124
    English 124
    European White 124
    Small-leaved 124
    Wych 124

Fig 128
Filbert 110
Fir, Algerian 46
    Alpine 48
    Caucasian 46
    Chinese 76
    Colorado White 48
    Common Silver 46
    Grand 48
    Grecian 46
    Nikko 48
    Noble 48
    Siberian 48
    Sicilian 46
    Spanish 46
Foxglove-tree 224

Golden-rain-tree 182
Grapefruit 180
Greengage 162
Guelder-rose 228
Gum, Cider 210
    Forest Red 212
    Lemon-scented Spotted 210
    Maiden's 210
    Red 212
    Ribbon 212
    Snow 210
    Swamp 212
    Tasmanian Blue 210
    Tuart 208

Hawthorn 148
    Five-seeded 152
    Hungarian 152
    Midland 148
    Oriental 148
Hazel 110
    Turkish 110
Heath, Portugal 216
Hemlock-spruce, Eastern 56
    Mountain 56
    Western 56
Hibiscus 202
Hickory, Bitternut 104
    Mockernut 104
    Pignut 104

Shagbark 104
Shellbark 104
Holly 196
Canary 196
Highclere 196
White 134
Hop-hornbeam 110
Eastern 110
Hop-tree 178
Hornbeam 110
Eastern 110
Horse-chestnut 194
Indian 194
Red 194

Jacaranda 224
Judas-tree 176
Jujube, Common 198
Juneberry 152
Juniper 82
Chinese 84
Grecian 84
Phoenician 82
Prickly 82
Spanish 84
Stinking 84
Syrian 82

Karo 134
Keaki 126

Laburnum 178
Scotch 178
Voss's 178
Larch, Dahurian 70
European 70
Hybrid 70
Japanese 70
Siberian 70
Laurel, Cherry 168
Portugal 168
Laurustinus 228
Lemon 180
Lilac 222
Hungarian 222
Persian 182
Lime, Caucasian 206
Common 206
Large-leaved 206
Silver 206
Small-leaved 206
Sweet 180
Weeping Silver 206

Locust, Clammy 174
Honey 176
Loquat 146

Maidenhair-tree 86
Magnolia, Evergreen 136
Mahogany, Red 208
Swamp 208
Maple, Balkan 190
Cretan 192
Field 190
Heldreich's 188
Italian 190
Lobel's 188
Martini's 192
Montpelier 192
Norway 190
Paper-bark 192
Red 188
Silver 188
Sugar 188
Tartar 188
Mastic-tree 186
Medlar 146
Mespil, Snowy 152
Monkey Puzzle 76
Morinda 50
Mulberry, Black 128
Paper 128
White 128

Nectarine 160
Nettle-tree, Caucasian 126
Southern 126
Nutmeg, California 86

Oak, Algerian 120
Cork 114
Downy 120
Evergreen 114
Hungarian 120
Kermes 114
Macedonian 116
Pedunculate 118
Pin 122
Portuguese 120
Pyrenean 120
Red 122
Round-leaved 114
Scarlet 122
Sessile 118
Turkey 116
Valonia 116
Oleaster 202

Olive 220
Orange, Bergamot 180
Osage 128
Seville 180
Sweet 180
Orange-ball-tree 222
Osier 94

Pagoda-tree 174
Palm, Chilean Wine 234
Chinese Windmill 232
Canary Island Date 234
Date 234
European Fan 232
Petticoat 232
Queen 234
Sentry 234
Peach 160
Pea-tree, Siberian 174
Pear, Almond-leaved 138
Austrian 138
Caucasian 138
Common 136
Plymouth 140
Sage-leaved 138
Snow 138
Wild 138
Willow-leaved 140
Pepper-tree 184
Brazilian 184
Persimmon, Chinese 214
Common 214
Phillyrea 220
Phytolacca 134
Pine, Aleppo 62
Arolla 66
Austrian 58
Bhutan 68
Bosnian 58
Bristle-cone 68
Canary Island 64
Corsican 58
Digger 66
Dwarf Mountain 60
Jack 62
Jeffrey's 66
Loblolly 64
Lodgepole 58
Macedonian 68
Maritime 60
Monterey 64
Mountain 60
Norfolk Island 76
Northern Pitch 64

Red 58
Scots 60
Shore 58
Stone 62
Western Yellow 66
Weymouth 66
Pistachio 186
Pittosporum 134
Plane, London 132
Oriental 132
Plum 162
Cherry 160
Pomegranate 212
Pomelo 180
Poplar, Black 100
Grey 98
Hybrid Black 100
Lombardy 100
Western Balsam 100
White 98
Privet, Common 220
Glossy 220
Oval-leaved 220

Quince 144

Rauli 112
Redwood, Coast 74
Dawn 74
Rhododendron 216
Rowan 154
Hupeh 154
Japanese 154
Sargent's 154
Vilmorin's 154
Rubber-tree, India 128

Sallow, Grey 94
Rusty 94
Sea-buckthorn 202
Service-tree, Bastard 156
True 154
Wild 158
She-oak, Drooping 134
Horsetail 134
Silver-berry 202
Siris, Pink 172
Snowball-tree 228
Snowbell-tree 214
Spanish Bayonet 230
Spindle-tree 198
Broad-leaved 198
Japanese 198
Spruce, Black 54

Blue 52
Brewer's Weeping 50
Colorado 52
Dragon 52
Engelmann 54
Norway 50
Oriental 50
Red 54
Serbian 54
Siberian 50
Sitka 52
Tiger-tail 54
White 54
Storax 214
Strawberry-tree 216
Eastern 216
Hybrid 216
Sumach, Common 184
Stag's-horn 184
Swamp-cypress 74
Sweet-gum 132
Oriental 132
Sycamore 188

Tamarisk 204
African 204
Small-flowered 204
Tangerine 180
Thorn, Broad-leaved Cockspur 150
Cockspur 150
Hybrid Cockspur 150
Tobacco, Shrub 222
Tree-heath 216
Tree-of-Heaven 182
Downy 182
Tulip-tree 136
Chinese 136
Turpentine-tree 186

Varnish-tree 184

Walnut 102
Black 102
Waterbush 226
Wattle, Black 172
Green 172
Golden 170
Silver 172
Swamp 170
Sydney Golden 170
Wayfaring-tree 228
Wellingtonia 74
Whitebeam 158

Austrian 156
Broad-leaved 156
Greek 158
Rock 158
Swedish 156
Willow, Almond 88
Bay 88
Crack 88
Cricket-bat 90
Dark-leaved 92
Goat 94
Golden 90
Golden Weeping 90
Purple 96
Violet 96
Weeping 90
White 90
Wingnut, Caucasian 104
Chinese 104
Wreath, Golden 170

Yew 86
Plum-fruited 86

244

INDEX

Scientific Names

Abies alba 46
  balsamea 48
  borisii-regis 46
  cephalonica 46
  concolor 48
  grandis 48
  homolepis 48
  x insignis 46
  lasiocarpa 48
  nebrodensis 46
  nordmanniana 46
  numidica 46
  pardei 46
  pinsapo 46
  procera 48
  sibirica 48
Acacia dealbata 172
  farnesiana 172
  karoo 172
  longifolia 170
  mearnsii 172
  melanoxylon 170
  pycnantha 170
  retinodes 170
  saligna 170
Acer campestre 190
  granatense 190
  griseum 192
  heldreichii 188
  hyrcanum 190
  lobelii 188
  martinii 192
  monspessulanum 192
  negundo 192
    cv. 'Variegatum' 192
  obtusatum 190
  opalus 190
  platanoides 190
    cv. 'Crimson King' 190
  pseudoplatanus 188
  rubrum 188
  saccharinum 188
  saccharophorum 188
  sempervirens 192
  stevenii 190
  tataricum 188
  trautvetteri 188
Aesculus flava 194
  hippocastanum 194
  indica 194
  x carnea 194
  pavia 194
Ailanthus altissima 182
  vilmoriniana 182
Albizia julibrissin 172
  lophantha 172
Alnus cordata 106
  glutinosa 106

  incana 106
  rugosa 106
  viridis 106
Amelanchier lamarckii 152
  ovalis 152
Araucaria araucana 76
  heterophylla 76
Arbutus andrachne 216
  x andrachnoides 216
  unedo 216
Arecastrum romanz-
  offianum 234

Betula papyrifera 108
  pendula 108
  pubescens 108
Broussonetia papyrifera 128
Buddleia alternifolia 222
  davidii 222
  globosa 222
Buxus balearica 196
  sempervirens 196

Caragana arborescens 174
Carpinus betulus 110
  orientalis 110
Carya cordiformis 104
  glabra 104
  laciniosa 104
  ovata 104
  tomentosa 104
Castanea sativa 112
Casuarina equisetifolia 134
  stricta 134
Catalpa bignonioides 224
  x erubescens 224
  ovata 224
Cedrela sinensis 182
Cedrus atlantica 72
  deodara 72
  libani 72
Celtis australis 126
  caucasica 126
  glabrata 126
  tournefortii 126
Ceratonia siliqua 176
Cercis siliquastrum 176
Chamaecyparis lawsoniana 78
  nootkatensis 78
  obtusa 78
  pisifera 78
Chamaerops humilis 232
Citrus aurantium 180
  bergamia 180
  grandis 180
  limetta 180
  limon 180
  medica 180

  paradisi 180
  reticulata 180
  sinensis 180
Cordyline australis 230
Cornus mas 214
Corylus avellana 110
  colurna 110
  maxima 110
Cotoneaster frigidus 146
  x watereri 146
Crataegus azarolus 150
  calycina 148
  crus-galli 150
  laciniata 148
  laevigata 148
  x lavallei 150
  monogyna 148
  nigra 152
  pentagyna 152
  x prunifolia 150
Cryptomeria japonica 76
Cunninghamia lanceolata 76
x Cupressocyparis leylandii 78
Cupressus arizonica 80
  glabra 80
  lusitanica 80
  macrocarpa 80
  sempervirens 80
    forma horizontalis 80
    forma sempervirens 80
Cydonia oblonga 144

Diospyros kaki 214
  lotus 214
  virginiana 214
Dracaena draco 230

Elaeagnus angustifolia 202
  commutata 202
Erica arborea 216
  lusitanica 216
Eriobotrya japonica 146
Eucalyptus botryoides 208
  camaldulensis 212
  citriodora 210
  globulus 210
    subsp. maidenii 210
  gomphocephalus 208
  gunnii 210
  pauciflora subsp. nipho-
    phila 210
  resinifer 208
  robustus 208
  rudis 212
  tereticornis 212
  x trabutii 208
  viminalis 212
Euonymus europaeus 198

japonicus 198
latifolius 198

Fagus orientalis 112
  sylvatica 112
Ficus carica 128
  elastica 128
Frangula alnus 200
  azorica 200
Fraxinus americana 218
  angustifolia 218
  excelsior 218
  ornus 218
  pallisiae 218
  pennsylvanica 218
    var. subintegerrima 218

Genista aetnensis 178
Ginkgo biloba 86
Gleditsia triacanthos 176

Hibiscus rosa-sinensis 202
Hippophae rhamnoides 202
Howeia forsterana 234

Ilex x altaclarensis 196
  aquifolium 196
  perado 196
Jacaranda mimosifolia 224
Jubaea chilensis 234
Juglans cinerea 102
  nigra 102
  regia 102
Juniperus chinensis 84
  communis 82
  drupacea 82
  excelsa 84
  foetidissima 84
  oxycedrus 82
  phoenicea 72
  thurifera 84
  virginiana 84

Koelreuteria paniculata 182

Laburnum alpinum 178
  anagyroides 178
  x watereri 178
Larix decidua 70
  x eurolepis 70
  gmelinii 70
  kaempferi 70
  russica 70
Laurus nobilis 130
Ligustrum lucidum 220
  ovalifolium 220
  vulgare 220
Liquidambar orientalis 132

styraciflua 132
Liriodendron chinense 136
  tulipifera 136

Maclura pomifera 128
Magnolia grandiflora 136
  x soulangiana 136
Malus baccata 142
  dasyphylla 142
  domestica 142
  florentina 144
  x floribunda 142
  pumila 142
  x purpurea 142
  sylvestris 142
  trilobata 144
Melia azederach 182
Mespilus germanica 146
Metasequoia glyptostroboides 64
Morus alba 128
  nigra 128
Musa acuminata 230
Myoporum tenuifolium 226
  tetrandrum 226

Nicotiana glauca 222
Nothofagus obliqua 112
  procera 112

Olea europaea 220
  var. europaea 220
  var. sylvestris 220
Ostrya carpinifolia 110
  virginiana 110

Paliurus spina-christi 198
Paulownia tomentosa 224
Persea americana 130
Phellodendron amurense 178
Phillyrea angustifolia 220
  latifolia 220
Phoenix canariensis 234
  dactylifera 234
  theophrasti 234
Phytolacca dioica 134
Picea abies subsp. abies 50
  subsp. obovata 50
  asperata 52
  breweriana 50
  engelmannii 54
  glauca 54
  mariana 54
  omorika 54
  orientalis 50
  polita 54
  pungens 52
    cv. 'Glauca' 52
  rubens 54

sitchensis 52
  smithiana 50
Pinus aristata 68
  banksiana 62
  canariensis 64
  cembra 66
  contorta 58
    var. latifolia 58
  halepensis 62
  heldreichii 58
  jeffreyi 66
  leucodermis 58
  mugo 60
  nigra subsp. laricio 58
    subsp. nigra 58
  peuce 68
  pinaster 60
  pinea 62
  ponderosa 66
  radiata 64
  resinosa 58
  rigida 64
  sabiniana 66
  strobus 66
  sylvestris 60
  taeda 64
  uncinata 60
  wallichiana 68
Pistacia atlantica 186
  lentiscus 186
  terebinthus 186
  vera 186
Pittosporum crassifolium 134
  tenuifolium 134
  tobira 134
  undulatum 134
Platanus x hispanica 132
  orientalis 132
Podocarpus andinus 86
Populus alba 98
  x canadensis 100
  candicans 100
  x canescens 98
  deltoides 100
  grandidentata 98
  nigra 100
    var. italica 100
  tremula 98
  tremuloides 98
  trichocarpa 100
Prunus armeniaca 160
  avium 166
  brigantina 160
  cerasifera 160
    var. pissardii 160
  cerasus 166
  domestica 162
    subsp. insititia 162

dulcis 160
laurocerasus 168
lusitanica 168
mahaleb 162
padus 168
persica 160
  cv. 'Nucipersica' 160
sargentii 164
serotina 168
serrula 164
serrulata 164
spinosa 162
subhirtella 166
  cv. 'Autumnalis' 166
virginiana 168
webbii 160
x *yedoensis* 164
Pseudotsuga macrocarpa 56
  menziesii 56
Ptelea trifoliata 178
Pterocarya fraxinifolia 104
  stenoptera 104
Punica granatum 212
  cv. 'Nanum' 212
Pyrus amygdaliformis 138
  austriaca 138
  bourgaeana 138
  caucasica 138
  communis 136
    var. *culta* 136
  cordata 140
  elaeagrifolia 140
  nivalis 138
  pyraster 138
  salicifolia 140
  salvifolia 138

Quercus brachyphylla 120
  canariensis 120
  cerris 116
  coccifera 114
  coccinea 122
  congesta 120
  crenata 116
  dalechampii 118
  faginea 120
  frainetto 120
  ilex 114
  ithaburensis subsp
    macrolepis 116
  mas 118
  palustris 122
  pedunculiflora 118
  petraea 118
  polycarpa 118
  pubescens 120
  pyrenaica 120
  robur 118

rotundifolia 114
rubra 122
suber 114
trojana 116
virgiliana 120

Rhamnus alaternus 200
  alpinus 200
  catharticus 200
  persicifolius 200
Rhododendron ponticum 216
Rhus coriaria 184
  typhina 184
  verniciflua 184
Robinia pseudacacia 174
  viscosa 174

Salix acutifolia 96
  alba var. *alba* 90
    var. *caerulea* 90
    var. *vitellina* 90
  appendiculata 92
  babylonica 90
  borealis 92
  caprea 94
  cinerea subsp. *cinerea* 94
    subsp. *oleifolia* 94
  daphnoides 96
  elaeagnos 96
  fragilis 88
  myrsinifolia 92
  pedicellata 92
  pentandra 88
  purpurea 96
  x *rubens* 88
  x *sepulcralis* 90
  x *smithiana* 92
  triandra 88
  viminalis 94
Sambucus nigra 226
  racemosa 226
Schinus molle 184
  terebinthifolia 184
Sequoia sempervirens 74
Sequoiadendron giganteum 74
Sophora japonica 174
Sorbus aria 158
  aucuparia 154
  austriaca 156
  commixta 154
  domestica 154
  graeca 158
  hupehensis 154
  hybrida 156
  intermedia 156
  latifolia 156
  meinichii 156
  mougeotii 156

rupicola 158
sargentiana 154
torminalis 158
umbellata 156
vilmorinii 154
Styrax officinalis 214
  japonica 214
Syringa vulgaris 222
  josikaea 222

Tamarix africana 204
  canariensis 204
  dalmatica 204
  gallica 204
  parviflora 204
  smyrnensis 204
  tetrandra 204
Taxodium distichum 74
Taxus baccata 86
Thuja occidentalis 76
  plicata 76
Tilia cordata 206
  dasystyla 206
  x *euchlora* 206
  petiolaris 206
  platyphyllos 206
  rubra 206
  tomentosa 206
  x *vulgaris* 206
Torreya californica 86
Trachycarpus fortunei 232
Tsuga canadensis 56
  heterophylla 56
  mertensiana 56

Ulmus canescens 124
  elliptica 124
  glabra 124
  x *hollandica* 124
  laevis 124
  minor 124
  procera 124

Viburnum lantana 228
  opulus 228
    var. *roseum* 228
  tinus 228

Washingtonia filifera 232

Yucca aloifolia 230
  gloriosa 230

Zelkova abelicea 126
  carpinifolia 126
  serrata 126
Zizyphus jujuba 198
  lotus 198